# BATTLING NELL

**SOUTHERN BIOGRAPHY SERIES**

Bertram Wyatt-Brown, *Series Editor*

# BATTLING NELL

## *The Life of Southern Journalist Cornelia Battle Lewis, 1893–1956*

ALEXANDER S. LEIDHOLDT

LOUISIANA STATE UNIVERSITY PRESS ⚜ BATON ROUGE

Published by Louisiana State University Press

Manufactured in the United States of America
FIRST PRINTING

DESIGNER: Amanda McDonald Scallan
TYPEFACE: Whitman, text; Bodoni, display
TYPESETTER: J. Jarrett Engineering, Inc.
PRINTER AND BINDER: Thomson-Shore, Inc.

LIBRARY OF CONGRESS CATALOGING-IN-PUBLICATION DATA

Leidholdt, Alexander.
Battling Nell : the life of southern journalist Cornelia Battle Lewis, 1893–1956 / Alexander S. Leidholdt.
p. cm. — (Southern biography series)
Includes bibliographical references and index.
ISBN 978-0-8071-3455-9 (cloth : alk. paper) 1. Lewis, Nell Battle, 1893–1956. 2. Women journalists—North Carolina—Biography. 3. Journalists—United States—Biography. I. Title.
PN4874.L425L45 2009
070.92—dc22
[B]

2009009711

The paper in this book meets the guidelines for permanence and durability of the Committee on Production Guidelines for Book Longevity of the Council on Library Resources. ♾

To Dorchen, who helped open my eyes

# CONTENTS

# ACKNOWLEDGMENTS

I am deeply indebted to the many librarians and archivists who assisted me in my research. At the University of North Carolina's Southern Historical Collection reference librarian Matthew Turi, university archivist Janis Holder, and the staff in the Manuscripts Department provided invaluable assistance. At the North Carolina Collection curator Robert Anthony, reference associate Harry McKown, and photographic archive assistant Keith Longiotti aided my research. Within the North Carolina State Archives state archivist Dick Lankford, archivist Larry Odzak, and nontextual materials archivist Kim Cumber provided vital help. At the University of Virginia's Albert and Shirley Small Special Collections Library director Mike Plunkett and reference coordinator Margaret Hrabe furnished important assistance. The staff at Duke University's William R. Perkins Library generously made its holdings available to me.

The excellent librarians and archivists at the schools and colleges Nell Battle Lewis attended patiently worked with me throughout many research trips. I am deeply grateful for the expertise provided me by Diana Williams, director of the Kenan Library at St. Mary's School; Tara Olivero, special collections librarian and college archivist at Goucher College; and Nanci Young, college archivist at Smith College.

At James Madison University, Ralph Alberico, dean of libraries and educational technologies; Mikki Butcher, interlibrary loan manager; and Kate Worley, reserves/periodicals coordinator, provided me with access to their collections, heroically managed to produce obscure material via interlibrary loan, and even purchased special lenses for the microfilm-reading machines to broaden my research.

I received funding for this project from the North Caroliniana Society, which awarded me an Archie K. Davis Fellowship. The Virginia Foundation for the Humanities generously furnished me with a residence fellowship to facilitate the writing of this book. I appreciate immensely the support the foundation's Rob Vaughan, Roberta Culbertson, Ann Spencer, and Carol Hendrix have provided me over a period of many years.

David Jeffrey—dean of James Madison University's College of Arts and Letters, a specialist in southern literature, and a former newspaper reporter—

endorsed my study and oversaw the provision to me of several grants and awards and an educational leave. Steve Anderson, director of the School of Media Arts and Design and a former journalist, took a strong interest in my work and allocated funding to defray my travel expenses. Colleagues Dolores Flamiano, John Gruver, and Dietrich Maune lent their expertise and support to my research and writing.

Two of Nell Battle Lewis's nieces, Martha Stanley and Lottie Woolen, generously consented to interviews and provided me with important information that strengthened my research.

I have long admired Louisiana State University Press, and I am gratified that director MaryKatherine Callaway and executive editor John Easterly elected to publish this book. Rand Dotson, senior editor for U.S. history and southern studies, supported my project early on and wisely guided it to completion. Bertram Wyatt-Brown, editor of the Southern Biography Series, made many useful suggestions and influenced my work through his prodigious and important scholarship. I count myself fortunate to have produced two books for the series under his guidance. Julian Pleasants, professor emeritus at the University of Florida's History Department, thoroughly reviewed my manuscript for the press and encouraged me to make revisions that decidedly strengthened its quality. Elizabeth Gratch, with meticulous attention to detail, copyedited the manuscript and made many important changes that vastly improved its quality.

Throughout my academic career I have been fortunate to have friends and mentors such as Maurice Berube, eminent scholar emeritus of Urban Services at Old Dominion University, and Robert Mason, a former editor of the *Norfolk Virginian-Pilot,* who introduced me to scholarship and the study of southern journalism and who unfailingly encouraged my efforts. Mr. Mason, who died in 2001, knew many of the key figures in this book intimately and aided my research. My father, Edwin Leidholdt, who died several years before this project was completed, continues to serve as my role model and is continually in my thoughts.

A number of remarkable women have helped shape my life and have contributed greatly to my ability to author this study, my first biography of a female southern journalist. My paternal grandmother, Anna Leidholdt, a German immigrant, courageously held her family together in poverty and throughout difficult circumstances. My maternal grandmother, Pearl Crowgey, a mathematics and Latin teacher, possessed a brilliant mind and boundless wisdom.

My sister, Dorchen, a nationally prominent feminist attorney and a leading international advocate working to prevent trafficking in women, has influenced my thinking and values from an early age. My mother, Louise Leidholdt, an outstanding editor and a native southerner with deep knowledge of the region and its traditions, has contributed significantly to my development as a writer. My wife, JoAnne Holman, who teaches with me in the School of Media Arts and Design and who specializes in public participation in telecommunications policy, accompanied me on numerous research trips and discussed with me many issues of interpretation pertaining to this study. I could not have completed this book without her love and support.

# INTRODUCTION

Cornelia "Nell" Battle Lewis inhabits a unique and notable niche in the annals of the southern press. She also claims a significant rung in the liberation and advancement of women in the American South and beyond. Her invasion of the fourth estate as North Carolina's first female columnist and one of a very few in the nation created a fissure in that bastion of masculinity that had theretofore accepted women as society editors only. Lewis's admission to the state's almost exclusively male bar gnawed further into southern chauvinism. Her widely publicized activism in both of these fields set examples and broadened the occupational choices and opportunities of women who would follow in ever-widening streams. In her advocacy for workers, women, children, prisoners, and the mentally ill, she protested inequities, exposed horrors, and worked for change.

Nell Lewis was born in 1893 in Raleigh, North Carolina, into the upper stratum of a Dixieland culture rigidly segmented by class, race, and gender. Her forebears had acquitted themselves nobly in both the Tar Heel State and neighboring Virginia—the men professionally and in the public sphere and the women as quintessential embodiments of the Southern Lady.

Reared mainly in the sternly Victorian charge of an overbearing stepmother alongside three older half brothers, Nell predictably would chafe under the conventions imposed on her sex. Lacking playmates as a result of her family's relocation during her infancy to a plantation just outside the state capital, she spent much of her time with books and superstitious farm and household help and developed an active imagination.

She attended public schools in Raleigh before entering socially prestigious St. Mary's, where she shone in letters with her poetry, essays, presidency of a debating society, and editorship of the yearbook and monthly magazine. After then completing a mysteriously unmentioned year of study at Goucher College, in Maryland, she took a baccalaureate degree and delivered the Class Day address at Smith College in Northampton, Massachusetts.

She applied and was accepted for World War I service with the YMCA in France, apparently motivated in part by a budding romance with fellow Tar Heel Lenoir Chambers, who was stationed there with the Allied Expeditionary

Forces. When she debarked in France, the war had ended, as would the romantic attachment that had blossomed while she worked there during the demobilization. The breakup would leave an enduring scar.

In mid-1920 the *Raleigh News and Observer* hired Lewis as a reporter / feature writer preparatory to her appointment as society editor. Shortly after assuming that responsibility the following year, she introduced in her space a column, "Incidentally," that would weigh in on nearly every current subject of importance in the region and the country. No passive reporter, Lewis imbued her writing with strong opinions and advocacy that became "must" reading for a range of citizenry, from the lowly to the state's high and mighty. Within approximately a decade "Incidentally" and Lewis herself drew accolades from leading journalistic lights as far afield as the *Baltimore Sun*'s H. L. Mencken and Gerald Johnson; Virginius Dabney of the *Richmond Times Dispatch;* and the nation's most celebrated political columnist, Heywood Broun of the *New York World.* Edwin Mims devoted nearly a chapter to Lewis in his publication of *The Advancing South* in 1926. W. J. Cash, in *The Mind of the South*–the culminant treatment of southern, history, culture, and psychology—praised Lewis. Defeated presidential candidate Al Smith informed her that he had framed one of her columns and planned to hang it in his library.

Lewis demonstrated conclusively the sincerity of her liberal prose with her championship of workers in 1929. In the wake of the disastrous communist-inspired labor uprising at the Loray Mill in Gastonia, North Carolina, she worked exhaustively on site, incurred vilification in person and in the press, and exposed herself to physical danger in the interest of justice for accused mill hands and their leaders. She confirmed the workers' grievances and pleaded that the conditions they were protesting be rectified. Two years later, in another high-profile case, she ferreted out atrocities at a showpiece reformatory for girls, at heavy cost to herself in friendships and support from feminists. For over a decade she earned widespread acclaim and vituperation as a leading patron of the downtrodden and voiceless.

In a column posted in 1932 during her hospitalization for a baffling illness, Lewis signaled an abrupt about-face from her longtime liberal perspective by siding with management against labor. She would recant her former activism and embrace her new persona with all the conviction and fire she had invested in the old. The 1954 *Brown v. Board of Education* decision would set aflame in Lewis the powerful racism intrinsic to her apartheid upbringing.

She interacted warmly with the illustrious Josephus Daniels as her editor and a family friend and came to detest his successor, his son Jonathan, whose politics she now flagrantly opposed. Massive resistance's foremost propagandist, James J. Kilpatrick, editor of the *Richmond News Leader,* expressed to Lewis his amazement that Jonathan had not fired her "before breakfast." Her old friend Frank Porter Graham suffered her abuse in silence in a calamitous sequence of events.

Lewis's biography scrutinizes not only a remarkable life but also the fermentation aboil in the South as industrialization and racial integration began to tear at the region's conservative fabric. Her journey brings to life the sometimes violent struggle between the aristocracy into which she was born and the labor it oppressed to maintain a traditional social order. Her story examines resistance by the academic, business, and government establishments to modernization and scientific thinking in higher education; anti-Semitism in admission policies nationally; and communist infiltration into universities and workplaces.

Lewis's narrative exhumes a shameful episode in North Carolina's history—a virulently racist and dishonest election that sullied the reputation of a leading liberal and debunked the myth of North Carolina as a progressive state. The story tells of the exploitation of racial prejudice for political gain and the misapplication of media power to infuse hysteria into a gullible public. It also tells about the family conflicts, money worries, and experimentation with a nontraditional religion and the supernatural that punctuated Lewis's private life. Long bouts of melancholy interrupted her work and affected her outlook and relationships.

The reader is invited to accompany a feisty, ground-breaking woman journalist through a turbulent and historic era in the post-Reconstruction Jim Crow South and to speculate about what accounted for her extraordinary transformation.

# 1 A GILDED CAGE

Cornelia "Nell" Battle Lewis's birth on 28 May 1893 in Raleigh, North Carolina, occurred at a crossroads in the state's history. With the Cotton Mill Campaign and industrialization running full tilt, the myth of the New South subsumed that of the Lost Cause as the state and region's dominant ideology. The factory and the city, southern intellectuals and businessmen alike glowingly proclaimed, had replaced the plantation as the nucleus of their society. The human toll of this exchange remained virtually unexamined.[1]

An ascendant elite, the New White Man—skeptical of Confederate hagiolatry, pragmatic, efficient, and often with humble roots and a common touch—had come to town and supplanted the leaders of the previous generation, the Bourbons and Brigadiers. While professing its allegiance to democratic principles, this cadre worshiped at the altar of the Democratic Party, whose hegemony an edgy interracial fusion between the state's Republicans and a vigorous agrarian Populist Party increasingly imperiled. For a short-lived moment economic issues seemed to matter more to many poor farmers than a rigid devotion to white supremacy. The New White Man ruthlessly prepared to wrest back power by "hollering Nigger" and evoking the specter of black men as defilers of Pure Southern Womanhood. The disenfranchisement that occurred at the decade's end would usher in the nadir of Jim Crow and enable the Democratic Party to eradicate much of the progress many blacks had forged.[2]

Tar Heel women, building on their work in missionary societies, entered

1. Daniel Joseph Singal, *The War Within: Victorian to Modernist Thought in the South, 1919–1945* (Chapel Hill: University of North Carolina Press, 1982), 11–33.

2. Glenda Elizabeth Gilmore, *Gender and Jim Crow: Women and the Politics of White Supremacy in North Carolina, 1896–1920* (Chapel Hill: University of North Carolina Press, 1996), 63–89; C. Vann Woodward, *A History of the South*, ed. Wendell Holmes Stephenson and E. Merton Coulter, vol. 9: *Origins of the New South, 1877–1913* (Baton Rouge: Louisiana State University Press and the Littlefield Fund for Southern History, University of Texas, 1951), 276–77; William S. Powell, *North Carolina through Four Centuries* (Chapel Hill: University of North Carolina Press, 1989), 427–31; Anastatia Sims, *The Power of Femininity in the New South: Women's Organizations and Politics in North Carolina, 1880–1930* (Columbia: University of South Carolina Press, 1997), 34–40; Jeffrey J. Crow, Paul D. Escott, and Flora J. Hatley, *A History of African Americans in North Carolina* (Raleigh: North Carolina Division of Archives and History, 1992), 95–118.

the public arena in the 1880s and 1890s to exercise their moral authority in support of temperance. Stepping down from their assigned pedestal, many white women encountered for the first time the poor, the diseased, and the tumult of politics as the Woman's Christian Temperance Union (WCTU) fought to mitigate the conditions that fostered alcohol abuse and to dry up the state's counties and towns. Their "work probably changed their lives a great deal more than [it] changed the lives of the recipients of their beneficence," southern scholar Glenda Elizabeth Gilmore writes. Black women, too, with an eye toward racial uplift and interracial cooperation, participated in the struggle for temperance. Despite the tension that existed between these two groups, their common goals gave rise to an ephemeral sisterhood. The Democratic Party's machinations at the century's close would end that, but "organized women," as they called themselves, would play an increasingly prominent role through women's clubs, the suffrage movement, the YWCA, and public service.[3]

Nell, like other southerners born in her era, grew up surrounded by the stories of an older generation marked indelibly by the devastation wrought by the Civil War and by its Reconstruction experiences. Primitive medical care and the disease that flourished in her backward region also affected her deeply and impressed upon her the fragility of human life.

Nell's mother, Mary Gordon Lewis, came from an Albemarle County, Virginia, family with a long and distinguished history in both the Commonwealth and its southern neighbor. Her father, George Loyall Gordon, a planter in Louisa County, Virginia, had practiced law and edited a newspaper after completing his education at the University of Virginia in 1850. He enlisted in the Edgecombe Guards in North Carolina, after that state's belated secession from the Union. Serving as his company's adjutant, he died in the summer of 1862, during the last of the Seven Days battles, Malvern Hill.[4]

3. Anne Firor Scott, *The Southern Lady: From Pedestal to Politics, 1830–1930* (Charlottesville: University Press of Virginia, 1970), 135–63; Jacquelyn Dowd Hall and Anne Firor Scott, "Women in the South," in *Interpreting Southern History: Historiographical Essays in Honor of Sanford W. Higginbotham*, ed. John B. Boles and Evelyn Thomas Nolen (Baton Rouge: Louisiana State University Press, 1987), 488–92; Gilmore, *Gender and Jim Crow*, 46–47, 58–59; Sims, *Power of Femininity*, 3–53; Margaret Supplee Smith and Emily Herring Wilson, *North Carolina Women: Making History* (Chapel Hill: University of North Carolina Press, 1999), 187–91; Elna C. Green, *Southern Strategies: Southern Women and the Woman Suffrage Question* (Chapel Hill: University of North Carolina Press, 1997), 19–26.

4. Armistead C. Gordon, *Gordons in Virginia, with Notes on Gordons of Scotland and Ireland* (Hackensack, N.J.: William M. Clemens, 1918), 70–71, 148; Special Staff of Writers, *History of Virginia*, vol. 4: *Virginia Biography* (New York: American Historical Society, 1924), 3; Clement A. Evans, *Con-*

Nell's maternal grandmother, Mrs. George Loyall Gordon (née Mary Long Daniel), the daughter of a North Carolina Supreme Court justice, was a member of the inaugural class—"the original thirteen"—that in 1842 enrolled in St. Mary's, a prestigious Episcopalian "School for Young Ladies" in Raleigh. During the war Mrs. Gordon fled with her young children from her home in embattled Virginia to a North Carolina cotton plantation.[5]

Mary Gordon Lewis, the youngest of five children, was born only two months after Confederate batteries opened fire on Fort Sumter. Her father's death the following year and the loss of both of her sisters, one in infancy and the other in childhood, must have staggered the surviving members of her family. Mary received her education at the celebrated Edgehill School for Girls in Albemarle County, "where every stimulus was given to her native talent for poetry, music and painting; and the pursuit of art was a never ceasing pleasure to her." Perhaps she met her future husband at Raleigh's elegant and socially prominent Christ Episcopal Church, where she taught Sunday school and Dr. Richard Lewis held the position of senior warden. She married him in 1890 and died—apparently of typhoid fever—only two years after giving birth to Nell. A devout and retiring woman, before her marriage Mary had contemplated entering a convent. She was ill throughout Nell's infancy, and Dr. Lewis later predicted that when Nell became the age of her mother—particularly when his younger daughter underwent menopause—she, too, would be "hit . . . very hard."[6]

---

*federate Military History* (Atlanta: Confederate Publishing Co., 1899), 5:72–75; Janet B. Hewett, ed., *North Carolina Confederate Soldiers: 1861–1865, Unit Roster* (Wilmington, N.C.: Broadfoot Publishing Co., 1999), 3:1058; Powell, *North Carolina through Four Centuries*, 344–48, 356; *Students of the University of Virginia: A Semi-Centennial Catalogue with Brief Biographical Sketches* (Baltimore: Charles Harvey & Co., 1878), 69; *Catalogue of the University of Virginia Session of 1848–1849* (Richmond: H. K. Ellyson, 1849), 9; J. Kelly Turner and Jno. L. Bridgers Jr., *History of Edgecombe County, North Carolina* (Raleigh: Edwards & Broughton, 1920), 218–19.

5. Special Staff of Writers, *Virginia Biography*, 3; Martha Stoops, *The Heritage: Education of Women at St. Mary's College, Raleigh, North Carolina, 1842–1982* (Raleigh: The College, 1984), 1, 4; "Nell Battle Lewis, 1911," Nell Battle Lewis Papers, Saint Mary's School Archives.

6. William S. Powell, ed., *Dictionary of North Carolina Biography* (Chapel Hill: University of North Carolina Press, 1991), 4:63; *Raleigh News and Observer* (hereafter cited as *N&O*), 3 September 1895, 7 August 1926, 7 February 1937; Joseph B. Cheshire, "Dr. Richard H. Lewis: An Intimate Sketch by a Life-Long Friend," *Carolina Churchman* (October 1926): 3–4; David Perkins, ed., *The News & Observer's Raleigh: A Living History of North Carolina's Capital* (Winston-Salem: John F. Blair, 1994), 34–35; unknown author to Peg, 27 June 1932, Ivey Foreman Lewis (hereafter cited as IFL) to Kemp Plummer Lewis (hereafter cited as KPL), 19 March 1932, both in Kemp Plummer Lewis Papers (hereafter

Nell was named for Dr. Lewis's deceased first wife, Cornelia "Nellie" Battle Lewis, the oldest daughter of University of North Carolina president and historian Kemp Plummer Battle. In her nine years of marriage Cornelia had given birth to four children: Richard "Dick" Henry Jr., Martha "Pattie" Battle, Kemp Plummer, and Ivey Foreman. More than a decade separated Nell from her youngest half brother.[7]

The *Raleigh State Chronicle*'s eulogy for Nell's namesake recalled her many commendable ladylike qualities, including her "perfect tranquil, self-forgetting grace and [the] calm sweetness of her expression and character." Despite the fact that the devoted young mother "did not talk much [and] shrank from prominence, or anything that in the least looked like 'taking the lead,'" her death affected those around her "like the extinguishing of . . . sunlight."[8]

Dr. Lewis was born on a plantation in Pitt County, North Carolina, in 1850. Despite his family's affluence, he had experienced much adversity during his formative years. His father died when Dr. Lewis was a young child, and a tubercular hip crippled him. For the remainder of his life he would walk aided by crutches and cane.[9] An alumnus of the universities of North Carolina and Virginia, he received his medical training at the latter institution, the University of Maryland, and London's Royal Ophthalmic Hospital. He quickly established a successful practice as a specialist in Savannah and chaired the department of diseases of the eye and ear at the medical college there. After his marriage to Cornelia Battle, he relocated to Raleigh in 1877 and joined in a partnership with his brother-in-law, Kemp Plummer Battle Jr., whose training and expertise matched Lewis's in many respects.[10]

His long-standing chairmanship of the North Carolina Medical Society's Legislative Committee augmented his close connections to government officials and the newly formed State Board of Health, and he quickly became an

cited as KPL Papers), Southern Historical Collection, Wilson Library, University of North Carolina at Chapel Hill; Victoria L. Mitchell, "Nell Battle Lewis: From 'South-Saving' Reformer to Southern Reactionary" (honors essay, University of North Carolina, 1985), 8; Gordon, *Gordons in Virginia*, 71–72; *Charlottesville Daily Progress*, 31 August 1950.

7. Powell, *Dictionary of North Carolina Biography*, 4:63.

8. *Raleigh State Chronicle*, 19? October 1886.

9. IFL to Nell Battle Lewis (hereafter cited as NBL), 31 March 1954, author; *N&O*, 7 August 1926, 15 September 1935, 8 August 1937.

10. IFL to NBL, 31 March 1954, author; W. S. Rankin, "Richard Henry Lewis: 1850–1926," Nell Battle Lewis Papers, North Carolina State Archives (hereafter cited as NBL Papers).

invaluable consultant in public health matters. For the next seventeen years he would direct the agency and build support for its pioneering policies by patiently educating the state's citizenry and officials regarding the need for his crucial work.[11]

Working out of his private medical office part-time, unsalaried, he began the regular inspection of public water supplies and established the foundation of a State Laboratory of Hygiene. Under his leadership North Carolina adopted a vital statistics law (the first in the South) and became a regional forerunner in its efforts to eradicate hookworm infection and to acknowledge pellagra as a critical health concern. Dr. Lewis helped enact legislation to protect children from epidemic diseases. He obtained diphtheria antitoxin for the state at a greatly reduced cost and successfully lobbied for a Sanatorium for the Treatment of Tuberculosis. Finally, he secured from the General Assembly the provision for a full-time health officer and resigned his position to allow for the appointment of a successor who would devote his undiminished attention to the job.[12]

Functioning also as one of the nation's leading public health experts, Dr. Lewis earned an international reputation for his work. In 1905 his peers elected him president of the Conference of the State and Provincial Boards of Health of North America and two years later appointed him president of the American Public Health Association.[13] His commitment to public service further extended to education, the University of North Carolina preeminently. For thirty-five years he served the institution as a trustee and frequently as a member of its powerful executive committee.[14]

Dr. Lewis's public-spiritedness extended to blacks. For twenty-eight years he held an appointment as a professor of diseases of the eye and ear at Shaw University's Leonard Medical School, which trained black physicians and

11. W. S. Rankin, "Richard Henry Lewis: 1850–1926," NBL Papers; J. Howell Way, "Richard Henry Lewis, M.D., LL.D., F.A.P.H.A. (Hon.): An Appreciation," *Southern Medicine and Surgery* 88, no. 12 (December 1926): 783.

12. Cheshire, "Dr. Richard H. Lewis," 3–4; W. S. Rankin, "Richard Henry Lewis: 1850–1926," NBL Papers; Way, "Richard Henry Lewis," 783–84; *N&O*, 8 August 1937.

13. W. S. Rankin, "Richard Henry Lewis: 1850–1926," NBL Papers; Way, "Richard Henry Lewis," 784; *N&O*, 8 August 1937.

14. W. S. Rankin, "Richard Henry Lewis: 1850–1926," NBL Papers; *N&O*, 8 August 1937; John Shelton Reed and Dale Volberg Reed, *1001 Things Everyone Should Know about the South* (New York: Doubleday, 1996), 249; *Chapel Hill Weekly*, 18 March 1964; Powell, *Dictionary of North Carolina Biography*, 4:60; *Who's Who in the South* (Washington, D.C.: Mayflower Publishing Co., 1927), 443.

whose hospital provided free care for indigent members of their race. He also served for over thirty years as a trustee and member of the executive committee of Saint Augustine's Normal School and Collegiate Institute.[15]

For over two decades St. Mary's School also received Dr. Lewis's guidance as a trustee and executive committeeman. While he enthusiastically endorsed the Christian education and ladylike atmosphere at St. Mary's, whose curriculum included two years of collegiate coursework, he did not approve of "college-bred women." He also deplored coeducation at the University of North Carolina and sought to limit the dormitory space it allocated for female students.[16]

Around the time of Nell's birth the Raleigh physician underwent a spiritual awakening and became a staunch Episcopalian. From that point on, religion played a much more prominent role for him and the Lewis household. Unquestionably with Mary's assent and perhaps at her behest, he required his family to pray and read the Bible together each morning and evening.[17]

Although for a southerner of his era—a North Carolinian in particular—Dr. Lewis had received an exceptionally advanced education and a highly unusual exposure to urban and cosmopolitan culture through his prolonged residence in Baltimore, then a major American city many times the size of Raleigh, and his study in London, the mores of his time and native region shaped his worldview to a great extent. Like most southern men, Lewis harbored traditional expectations for women and sought to preserve the legacy of the Southern Lady.[18]

Dr. Lewis almost certainly manifested a similarly circumscribed comprehension of blacks' potential. The scientific racism of noted French surgeon Paul Broca and the widely read popularizations of his work, such as Madison Grant's *The Races of Europe: A Sociological Study* and William Z. Ripley's *The*

15. Way, "Richard Henry Lewis," 784; Edward H. Beardsley, *A History of Neglect: Health Care for Blacks and Mill Workers in the Twentieth-Century South* (Knoxville: University of Tennessee Press, 1987), 12–13; *N&O*, 27 September 1942; Perkins, *News & Observer's Raleigh*, 83–86.

16. Stoops, *Heritage*, 134–39, 152, 175, 242, 443; Katherine Batts Salley, ed., *Life at Saint Mary's* (Chapel Hill: University of North Carolina Press, 1942), 100–104; *N&O*, 8 August 1937, 14 July 1940, 1 January 1950; Cheshire, "Dr. Richard H. Lewis," 3–4; Mitchell, "Nell Battle Lewis," 16.

17. Cheshire, "Dr. Richard H. Lewis," 3–4; *N&O*, 4 November 1923, 8 August 1937; Mitchell, "Nell Battle Lewis," 15.

18. Marjorie Spruill Wheeler, *New Women of the New South: The Leaders of the Woman Suffrage Movement in the Southern States* (New York: Oxford University Press, 1993), 5–13; Stoops, *Heritage*, 231.

*Passing of the Great Race*, held sway throughout Dr. Lewis's career and provided a theoretical rationale for white supremacy. The illiterate blacks he knew as hands and servants on his farm and as menials in Raleigh probably confirmed for him his belief in the race's inferiority.[19]

"We didn't particularly enjoy most of our childhood," Nell Lewis, employing pronouns royally, would later write. Her mother's illness and death cast a pall over the Lewis household during Nell's earliest years. A black servant, Margaret Selby, a former slave whom she addressed as "Mammy," helped raise the child and softened her loss. Selby's death several years later also affected Nell deeply. As a young girl at Cloverdale she once met her mammy's spirit in the form of a "miniature ghost" and felt "comforted" by the encounter.[20]

In 1897, after Nell turned four, Dr. Lewis married Annie Blackwell Foreman. Outwardly, she personified the consummate southern matron, busying herself managing the servants in the Lewis home and calling on neighbors. Annie, "a most passionate Confederate," reveled in the grandeur of the Lost Cause and recounted for Nell her stepmother's exciting experiences as a child and teenager in eastern North Carolina during the war and her subsequent fierce defiance of the Union troops who had occupied her hometown. Annie had delighted in playing and singing Confederate songs as loudly and vehemently as possible to pique the Yankees and hoped they would make her a martyr by locking her up in the local jail. These stories left an enduring imprint on Nell, who in her childhood became a "very ardent little Confederate."[21]

Annie strictly attempted to instill piousness and obedience in her young stepdaughter. A relative visiting Cloverdale soon after Annie's marriage to Dr. Lewis believed that Annie was achieving these goals and failed to discern in Nell any sign of the unhappiness she later recalled. "They have prayers night and morning, and everything is so orderly, no discord, no unpleasantness—only harmony," the kinswoman reported. "The home life is truly beautiful, a typical Christian home, and all are so bright and happy. Little Nellie is a remarkably intelligent and interesting child of five, her ready and cheerful obe-

19. Charles Reagan Wilson and William Ferris, eds., *Encyclopedia of Southern Culture* (Chapel Hill: University of North Carolina Press, 1989), 1358–60; William Ripley, *The Races of Europe: A Sociological Study* (New York: D. Appleton, 1910); Madison Grant, *The Passing of the Great Race* (New York: Charles Scribner's Sons, 1916); J. Douglas Smith, *Managing White Supremacy: Race, Politics, and Citizenship in Jim Crow Virginia* (Chapel Hill: University of North Carolina Press, 2002), 81–82.

20. *N&O*, 4 November 1921, 9 March 1924, 24 June 1956.

21. Mitchell, "Nell Battle Lewis," 12–13; *N&O*, 31 October 1917, 4 November 1921, 26 November 1939, 10 June 1951, 23 August 1953, 12 May 1957; unknown author to Peg, 27 June 1932, KPL Papers.

dience is a lovely trait in her character and she is the pet of the home—but by no means spoiled."[22]

Inwardly, however, Nell resented much of her upbringing and in small ways resisted endeavors to instill in her the qualities that historian Anne Firor Scott, in *The Southern Lady*, calls the "ideals of perfection and submission." Nell attended Sunday school and services at Christ Church "more or less sullen and inwardly protesting," peeved all the more by having to put on a "clean, prissy dress and . . . shoes and stockings."[23] Her father and stepmother restricted her reading on the Sabbath to "100 per cent sanctified literature," such as the innocuous-sounding *A Wreath from the Woods of Carolina* by Mary Ann Mason, the wife of an earlier Christ Church rector. Nell likely enjoyed the book's colored illustrations of the region's wildflowers, but the parables through which the author intended to inculcate deference to elders and Christian conduct horrified its young reader. A representative story told of a girl who disobeyed her mother's edict not to touch a trumpet blossom with dew on it. (The plant's leaves and flowers are poisonous if ingested.) The child died in excruciating agony, which seemed to Nell a fate excessively out of proportion to the transgression of displaying natural curiosity. It seems, however, that Mason and other founts of Nell's religious indoctrination at least partially achieved their intended effect. During a total eclipse of the sun that coincided fantastically with her seventh birthday, she grew convinced that she soon would stand before a vengeful Jehovah, who would "straightway consign [her] to eternal torment" for a lie she had told regarding the origin of a corn silk cigarette hole in her clothing.[24]

As an adult, Nell described Annie and the Lewis home in a withering portrayal that powerfully contradicted her relation's idyllic description:

> My step-mother, who . . . completely dominated the "Cloverdale" household for twenty years, was a domineering, selfish, narrow-minded woman of violent temper and limited intelligence. She was passionately attached to the place which represented to her financial security and comfort which she had not known during the fifty years of her life be-

22. Pennie Norcom to Mary Hood, 1 December 1898, NBL Papers; Mitchell, "Nell Battle Lewis," 12.

23. Scott, *Southern Lady*, 7; *N&O*, 4 November 1923, 3 January 1926, 15 September 1935.

24. *N&O*, 7 September 1924, 6 March 1927; Mary Ann Bryan Mason, *A Wreath from the Woods of Carolina* (New York: General Protestant Episcopal Sunday School Union and Church Book Society, 1859).

> fore she married my father. She kept the house filled with her own relatives and for a number of years her psychopathic son by a former marriage, the center of her emotional interest, and his long-suffering wife [who] lived there with her and my father. She was determined to outlive my father and often spoke of the disposition of personal property after his death.[25]

Despite Nell's dislike of her stepmother and the often-stultifying role religion played in the Lewis household, growing up on a farm provided countless delights and many opportunities to escape close adult supervision and exert independence. Cloverdale's enormous barn and its straw-filled loft furnished a perfect place to play hide-and-seek. The mules, which supplied the estate's motive force, and the horses used to pull the Lewises' carriage and buggy exhibited engaging personalities.[26]

A stream that flowed in the woods behind the house afforded endless prospects for adventures. Barefoot, garbed in the checked apron that young children often wore in that era, and accompanied by Ivey or another brother who was home from Chapel Hill, Nell waded into the cool water when the weather turned hot. Ivey aspired to become a biologist and searched for specimens for his classes, but he took the time to fashion from bark and paper toy boats that his adoring half sister reveled in sailing. The shady and mossy banks of a little pool seemed to Nell, who fantasized frequently about sprites and other kindred spirits, the ideal vicinage for a fairy colony.[27]

The rhythms of country life enveloped her. The yearly butchering of hogs, the farm's most thrilling time, filled her with morbid excitement, despite the fact that she could never bring herself to watch the slaughter. Nell also looked forward to corn shucking. Black shuckers continued their work well past her bedtime, forcing her to miss a portion of the festivities, to her great dismay. Threshing time completed the trinity of Cloverdale's most eagerly anticipated events. Hands harnessed Cloverdale's steam engine to a clattering machine that wondrously separated oats from straw. Laborers from the surrounding area came to help and stayed all day. Young Nell and her fox terriers closely "supervised" the doings. She evinced a precocious interest in journalism by

25. "'Cloverdale' as a Haunted House," 24 February 1945? NBL Papers.

26. *N&O*, 5 December 1926, 15 September 1935.

27. *N&O*, 9 March 1924.

observing all of these happenings and many others and devoting part of a day each week to reporting on them by laboriously printing in pencil a farm newspaper, which she dubbed "The Pioneer."[28]

According to a childhood friend, Nell developed into a tomboy and played mostly with her much older half brothers and their male friends, who sometimes attempted to evade her. As an adult, she almost never referenced her half sister, Pattie, fourteen years Nell's senior, who died in her twenties, shortly after marrying, reportedly from hyperemesis gravidarum, a rare disorder characterized by severe nausea and vomiting during pregnancy. Pattie, like both Nell's namesake and her mother, seems to have assumed for the young girl the form of an unworldly archetype, pious and distant, whose early death underscored for Nell and the Lewis men the frailty of her sex. Mary Lewis's death notice in the *Raleigh News and Observer* exemplifies the qualities these three women shared:

> Far beyond all ideal artistic accomplishments were her spiritual attainments. She was gifted with a rare personal magnetism, and turned many sad hearts toward the light of God's love by her words and ministry. Hers was an inward fellowship with the saints and "to covet earnestly the best gifts" was her prayer answered in its fullness. . . . "Let me do all the good I can; I will not pass this way but once," was the undertone to which her innermost soul vibrated. To animate and cheer the sorrowful, to solace the afflicted, to give warmth and comfort the desolate, and to guide the feet of little children into happy ways was her blessed mission. She was absorbed in a life of obedience to God and "Christian Endeavor" was her watchword.

The deceased Lewis women undoubtedly developed into even more iconic representations of the Southern Lady through the romanticized portrayals of them in stories told and retold by Nell's father and brothers.[29]

28. *N&O*, 15 September 1935.

29. Linda Lou Green "Nell Battle Lewis: Crusading Columnist, 1921–1938 (master's thesis, East Carolina University, 1969), 3; Darden Asbury Pyron, "Nell Battle Lewis (1893–1956) and the 'New Southern Woman,'" in *Perspectives on the American South*, ed. James C. Cobb and Charles R. Wilson (New York: Gordon and Breach Science Publishers, 1985), 3:65, 83; *N&O*, 3 September 1895; "Hyperemesis Gravidarum" (cited 30 July 2007), www.rarediseases.org/.

Dr. Lewis chose to enroll Nell in Raleigh's Murphey School rather than a private academy, which some of her friends attended. He instructed his younger daughter "to burgeon out" and interact democratically with children from different backgrounds and economic groups. She enjoyed her time at the Murphey School immensely.[30] She entered Raleigh High School around 1905, studied there for several years, and grew to like the city even more as a result of the freedom afforded her by a new bicycle, which she would park after classes at Dr. Lewis's medical office. Her father would take her home at the day's end in his buggy drawn by a willful horse named Supple Sam.[31]

In 1907 Nell enrolled at St. Mary's School as a freshman, a member of the class of 1911. Three and a half decades later she would coauthor a history of the school, which the University of North Carolina Press then published. In a chapter entitled "From 'Floradora' to 'Tipperary': 1900–1915," Lewis, often with pungent wit, depicted her alma mater from the time of a popular turn-of-the-century comic operetta whose lyrics were all the rage at St. Mary's (*Men:* "Tell me, pretty maiden, are there any more at home like you?" *Girls:* "There are a few, kind sir, but simple girls and proper, too") to early World War I—an epoch evoked by the rollicking British marching anthem.[32]

"Specializing in the education of daughters of the Southern Quality," Lewis wrote of the period:

> Saint Mary's was permeated by the conventional atmosphere surrounding the southern woman of the best class, in which she was regarded as primarily the charming, modest, religious home-maker. This was excellent for the development of character, but otherwise in education it left something to be desired. It was a viewpoint, long prevalent in the South, which had produced in this region a breed of women who probably were unsurpassed in charm, grace, personal purity, and moral rectitude by those of any society in the world, but who in the advance of women in education, economic independence, and political interest lagged behind most of their sisters in the rest of the United States.
>
> . . . From afar rumors had reached them of certain unsexed females who wanted the ballot and of still others who had attended those in-

30. James L. Leloudis, *Schooling the New South: Pedagogy, Self, and Society in North Carolina, 1880–1920* (Chapel Hill: University of North Carolina Press, 1996), 143–45; *N&O*, 15 September 1935.

31. *N&O*, 15 September 1935.

32. Salley, *Life at Saint Mary's*, 100–142; *St. Mary's Muse* (Raleigh: St. Mary's School, 1908), 33.

> stitutions of higher learning which aped the colleges for men, such as those established by Matthew Vassar on the Hudson River and by Sophia Smith in the valley of the Connecticut; but like their mothers, fathers, and brothers, most Saint Mary's girls of that period regarded these peculiar females with pitying scorn and something of horror as displeasing and pathetic anomalies of the gentler sex.[33]

Nell's arrival at the school coincided with the inauguration of a new rector, the Reverend George William Lay, who sought to challenge this ethos by transfusing the institution with more academic rigor. Despite Lay's birth in Alabama, he had received considerable exposure to the North through his education at St. Paul's, a boys' Episcopal School in Concord, New Hampshire; degrees earned from Yale and the prestigious General Theological Seminary in New York City; and nearly a decade's experience as a master at St. Paul's. Nell would come to admire Lay greatly, despite the fact that he frequently meted out to her strict but impartial discipline.[34]

The decorous portals through which Nell passed at St. Mary's cosmeticked some decidedly inelegant features of the school. The dining room windows, like those of the rest of the institution, had no screens, and little black boys with fans shooed flies away from the tables. Cattle occasionally sauntered across the grounds, and the odors of the stables and sties in the back of the campus could sometimes be detected far away. Lay looked askance at these blemishes and set to work.[35]

The pompadour hairdo, boosted by the "rat," reached the height of its popularity during Nell's freshman year. (Pictures of her in the school's 1908 yearbook, the *Muse*, reveal that her own expansive hairstyle—coiled at the nape of her neck and parted in the middle—in no way rivaled many of her classmates' intimidating coiffures, inspired undoubtedly by the illustrations of Charles Dana Gibson.) Openwork stockings occasionally peeked out from under the fashionable slender sheath skirts and caused elders to cluck disapprovingly. "Say it ain't so, Mable!" entered the girls' argot and provided an arch and presumably endlessly repeated retort.[36]

Social life at St. Mary's revolved almost entirely around its many clubs and

33. Salley, *Life at Saint Mary's*, 100–101.
34. Stoops, *Heritage*, 170–73; *N&O*, 21 August 1932.
35. Salley, *Life at Saint Mary's*, 124; *N&O*, 5 June 1932.
36. Salley, *Life at Saint Mary's*, 126; *St. Mary's Muse* (1908), 40, 49.

other organizations. Nell pledged and was accepted into one of the four sororities, Gamma Beta Sigma, whose membership, she later wrote, consisted of "Old North Carolina Quality of the more conservative sort." These sisterhoods "skimmed the social cream of the school" and "flourished to the more or less smug satisfaction of their members and for the heartaches and occasional tears of some of those who were excluded."[37]

She joined Epsilon Alpha Pi (EAP, named for Edgar Allan Poe), one of two literary societies, whose annual debates provoked an exuberance and rivalry so intense that dear friends belonging to different clubs "might be estranged in stony silence for days." The previous year the two groups had squared off over the proposition "Resolved: That the higher education of women makes happier homes." EAP still smarted over the humiliation that Sigma Lambda (honoring Georgia poet Sidney Lanier), arguing the negative, had triumphed.[38]

Nell enjoyed sports, and despite her lack of imposing height—she stood at approximately five feet four inches—played on one of the Olympian Athletic Association's basketball teams. Wearing middy blouses and full skirts, the cagers usually vied on an outdoor dirt court, and final scores often did not exceed single digits. Interested also in art, Nell participated in the Sketch Club. She must have come to know Nell Wilson, the youngest daughter of future president Woodrow Wilson, who also belonged to these two organizations.[39]

As her academic career progressed, Nell became an increasingly prominent student, albeit one whose behavior did not always rise to St. Mary's genteel standards and sometimes exasperated its administration. She once climbed to the top of Smedes Hall's high peaked roof to verify that workmen had placed its Cross straight up. "I wasn't very good," she conceded later in life.[40]

Although she continued to play sports and led the Athletic Association during her sophomore year, Nell's principal contribution to the school lay in letters and journalism. Her upbringing in an exceptionally literate household apparently nourished an innate aptitude; she became president of EAP and editor-in-chief of both the annual *Muse* and the monthly magazine of the same name.[41]

37. Salley, *Life at Saint Mary's*, 106; *St. Mary's Muse* (1908), 49, 51.

38. Salley, *Life at Saint Mary's*, 105, 109, 121; *St .Mary's Muse* (1908), 40–41.

39. *St. Mary's Muse* (1908), 66–67, 74–75; NBL passport, KPL Papers.

40. "Nell Battle Lewis," *Saint Mary's School Bulletin* 28, no. 2A (March 1939): 6–7; *Belles of St. Mary's*, 26 January 1940.

41. *St. Mary's Muse* (Raleigh: St. Mary's School, 1909), 60; *St. Mary's Muse* (Raleigh: St. Mary's School, 1911), n.p.

The monthly *Muse* consisted of editorials (presumably written or superintended by its editor), school news, features, and samples of the students' literary efforts. The magazine had received accolades in *College Magazine*, which appraised the *Muse* as "the pick of the flock" of a sampling of publications at women's schools. Nell earned a reputation for willfulness during her student years, but a lead editorial entitled "St. Mary's Spirit" appearing in the first edition of the publication that she directed bore no trace of the "Battling" Nell to come. "Let us take care that we do not lose . . . that characteristic which has distinguished the St. Mary's girl from the beginning," it lectured readers. "Let us always remember the qualities for which St. Mary's has been representative—culture, refinement, and above all, the highest type of Southern womanhood."[42]

Most of Nell's many contributions to the *Muse* did not adopt this sort of chiding tone. She displayed considerable talent in writing poetry, particularly clever verse such as "Battle Cry," which poked fun at the vanity of St. Mary's students.

> We'll pass straight by dear Cally's,
> His luscious fruits we'll spurn,
> And if he speaks of "Loves Delight,"
> The shoulder cold we'll turn.
>
> Not the joys of chicken salad,
> Not the last "Best Seller's" fame,
> Not the charms of Brantley's sherry
> Can our worthy ardor tame.
>
> Not the most delicious package
> Of the sweets that Royster hath
> Can serve to turn our feet aside
> From duty's rugged path.
>
> And we'll pass the tempting "Fashion"
> Without e'en a fleeting look,
> For we're on our way to Tyree's
> To have our pictures took."[43]

42. Stoops, *Heritage*, 194; "New Officers," *St. Mary's Muse* 15, no. 2 (October 1910): 56; "St. Mary's Spirit," *St. Mary's Muse* 15, no. 3 (November 1910): 120.

43. "The Battle Cry," *St. Mary's Muse* 15, no. 5 (December 1910–January 1911): 155–56.

In her sophomore year there appeared on campus a new instructor, who would lead Nell to ponder possibilities she had not yet considered and who appealed to her independent spirit. Georgina Kellogg lived in New York City and had graduated from Smith College four years earlier. For a prolonged period she had studied languages in Europe, and the administration at St. Mary's had hired her to teach French. Poised and beautiful, Kellogg displayed an inner direction that must have raised the eyebrows of many at the ecclesiastical institution. The liberal education Kellogg had received at the northern college, Lewis later wrote, left her so "untrammeled . . . that during divine services in the [St. Mary's] Chapel on the holy Sabbath day she sat serenely in the grove and openly sewed—sewed on Sunday!—and the Almighty didn't strike her down!" Kellogg's "refreshing independence . . . and her unconventional behavior put quite a new light upon the higher education of women in at least one youthful mind. If Smith could turn them out like that, why, then it might be a college well worth attending." For reasons unknown the young linguist's tenure at the school would not last long; the monthly *Muse* at the start of Nell's senior year explained abruptly, "Miss Kellogg will give up teaching."[44]

In her junior year Nell and a partner debated a Sigma Lambda duo. The monthly *Muse* termed it "the most exciting and the most looked-forward-to event of the school year." Throughout the preceding week the societies' colors had festooned the campus. EAP argued the negative in the query, "Resolved: That life imprisonment with a restricted power of pardon on the part of the executive should be substituted for capital punishment." Nell and her teammate gave their arch foe its comeuppance. (The previous year Sigma Lambda had easily persuaded the judges that extending suffrage to women would not "improve the condition of society" and the year before that had established the fatuousness of assumption that Jefferson Davis's contribution to the Confederacy surmounted Robert E. Lee's.) All of the debaters had prepared well, the *Muse* conceded; however, "Nell Lewis not only had a good paper, but delivered it in such a way that those who heard her will never forget it." Looking back on the experience in her historical treatment of her alma mater, she remarked on the irony that she would one day atone for her "youthful blood-lust" by crusading in her newspaper column against the death penalty.[45]

44. "Notes of the Faculty—The Old and the New," *St. Mary's Muse* 13, no. 1 (June–July 1908): 25–30; "With the Faculty—The Teachers Old and New," *St. Mary's Muse* 15, no. 1 (September 1910): 3; *St. Mary's Muse* (Raleigh: St. Mary's School, 1910), 23; Salley, *Life at Saint Mary's*, 130.

45. "April 30—The Annual Debate," *St. Mary's Muse* 14, no. 8 (May 1910): 183–84; Salley, *Life at Saint Mary's*, 131, 133; *St. Mary's Muse* (1910), 78–79.

"Mr." N. B. Lewis led "with great success" the opening german in the fall of her senior year, the *Muse* announced. "The old girls for the most part went as the 'suitors' and each took one of the season's 'debutantes.'" Dances such as this one enabled the girls to practice social graces for affairs held at the University of North Carolina and other men's schools. The St. Mary's germans during this era featured "all of the etiquette of a formal ball—programs, gold pins as favors, even a stag line," wrote Martha Stoops in her excellent history of the institution. Beaux wore white shirtwaists, stiff standing collars, black bow ties, and long black skirts. The *Muse* reported that "all of the ladies were very becomingly dressed and the many colors harmonized beautifully." The overabundance of stags ensured that every belle had a grand "rush" and left no "wallflowers."[46]

Regarding Nell's sexuality, one should reach no inferences based on the conspicuously fluid gender role played by Nell and the other upperclassmen at the St. Mary's german—a custom that made the formal affair possible at the all-girl school. She relished attending soirees at Chapel Hill, where she danced the night away with male partners and in the morning traveled with die-hard revelers by horse and buggy to an overlook on the edge of campus to see the sun rise. In 1980, many years after Lewis's death, Elizabeth Lay Green, one of the rector's daughters (and the wife of Pulitzer Prize–winning playwright Paul Green), whose life in theater doubtlessly acquainted her with men and women of varying sexual orientations, reflected on her friend, whom she and her husband had known closely. In an era in which Green could discuss homosexuality candidly, she described her classmate at the girl's school as "masculine" but not physically attracted to the other students.[47]

Nell seems to have regarded the religiosity at St. Mary's ambivalently. Girls attended chapel every morning and evening during school days and a Sunday lesson, morning service, meditation hour, and evening service every Lord's day. She vowed that after her education she would never again attend church. But in chapel, as she resentfully listened to the "incomparable psalter," she recalled a decade after her graduation, "almost against our will, its beauty sang itself into our mind so that we can never forget it." (Not all of the religious teachings at St. Mary's centered on sacred doctrine. Lay, who regarded his chaplaincy as a principal responsibility, preached to each new class a sermon

46. Stoops, *Heritage*, 146; "The German," *St. Mary's Muse* 15, no. 2 (October 1910): 56; Salley, *Life at Saint Mary's*, 107.

47. Pyron, "Nell Battle Lewis," 65; *N&O*, 1 January 1950.

entitled "The Duty of Being Good Looking.") Perhaps under pressure from school authorities, she joined the Altar Guild in her senior year.[48]

At Nell's commencement ceremony in 1911, Bishop Joseph B. Cheshire exhorted the graduates to "be of service and make others happy." The "heathen saying" carpe diem contained much wisdom, he declared. The collegiate class consisted of only six members, and Nell delivered neither the valedictory nor the salutatory. Despite her undistinguished academic record, her classmates selected her as "most versatile" student, and she displayed her talent for letters by reading one of her compositions, "The Poetry of Kipling," which had earned top honors. "Miss Lewis has high literary ability," the *Muse* remarked. "The English used was choice, the language graphic, the entire essay was one of real merit." The audience applauded her loudly and bestowed upon her many bouquets of flowers.[49]

Dr. Edwin Mims, a notable University of North Carolina faculty member and social and literary critic, delivered an insightful address entitled "Types of Southern Women." Women's emancipation, he said, despite its manifestation "in many extreme forms . . . and certain eccentricities and extremes," had brought about numerous needed reforms. Many female colleges and universities now equaled those for men in terms of quality. Women graduates and members of the club movement had brought about changes that resulted in expanded opportunities for their sex in a range of professions and volunteer activities that did not militate against "the true interests of the home." He informed his audience that "the test of a college like [St. Mary's] may be found particularly in the contributions its graduates make to the communities. You should go back to your homes and attempt to make conditions of farm life satisfactory; to help along in any other legitimate way schools and churches and other organizations. You will do this without losing any of the womanly qualities that have been the particular characteristics of Southern women."[50]

Mims's remarks would one day form the basis of "The Revolt Against Chivalry," a chapter in *The Advancing South: Stories of Progress and Reaction*, which nearly won a Pulitzer Prize and secured for him a national reputation as the foremost publicist for the social and artistic improvements taking place in the New South. Then a professor at Vanderbilt University, he would recognize

48. "The Routine," *St. Mary's Muse* 16, no. 3 (November 1911): 79–80; *N&O*, 4 November 1923, 15 September 1935; Stoops, *Heritage*, 33, 201–2, 209.

49. "The Graduation Exercises and Address," *St. Mary's Muse* 16, no. 1 (June 1911): 11, 16–23.

50. "Graduation Exercises and Address," 11–13.

Nell conspicuously in his book—positioning her as one of the South's most significant and influential journalists—and appraise "Incidentally" as unsurpassed by other columns throughout the country in literary quality and liberal social and intellectual commentary.[51]

As the St. Mary's faculty and administration and Nell applauded their distinguished guest's commencement address that May morning, however, neither these dignitaries nor she would have predicted that she would ever, despite her obvious potential, earn such lofty praise. Reflecting on that day from a vantage point twenty years distant, she would write that she had learned virtually nothing from her studies at St. Mary's except for developing a lasting regard for the beautiful English in the *Book of Common Prayer.* She passed finally through the school's portals, she believed, "to the heart-felt and undisguised relief of those in authority there. For while in school I had left undone those things I ought to have done and had done those things I ought not to have done and the consensus of opinion was that there was no health in me, and that the riddance was a good one."[52]

51. Michael O'Brien, *Rethinking the South: Essays in Intellectual History* (Athens: University of Georgia Press, 1993), 131–56; Edwin Mims, *The Advancing South: Stories of Progress and Reaction* (Garden City, N.Y.: Doubleday, Page & Co., 1926), 239–50.

52. *N&O*, 5 June 1932.

# 2 BEYOND THE PALE

For a student who had not displayed a sustained interest in academics during her tenure at St. Mary's, Nell Lewis seemed to choose unaccountably to attend the most rigorous woman's college in the South, Baltimore's newly named Goucher College. At St. Mary's she had played the role of what Goucher's student magazine, the *Kalends*, referred to as the "all-round girl," a "breezy, athletic girl, brandishing a tennis racket in one hand and a contribution for [the] *Donnybrook* [the school yearbook] in the other, greeting everyone with a hail-fellow-well-met air, rushing from the Glee Club to dramatics rehearsal, from dramatics to tennis, from tennis to a committee meeting." The college's leadership, while not dismissing extracurricular activities entirely, decidedly preferred scholarship and deference to the tenets of the Methodist Episcopal Church.[1]

The juncture following her graduation from St. Mary's, in which Nell almost certainly resided at Cloverdale (perhaps entreating her father to reconsider his opposition to "college-bred women"), and including her freshman year at Goucher during the 1912–13 session remains among the most poorly documented periods of a life that would contain several puzzling hiatuses. During the year she lived at home, she came to know the new English teacher and athletic and debate coach at Raleigh High School, young Frank Porter Graham, the future president of the University of North Carolina. One wonders whether Graham, who had begun during his brief stint as a schoolteacher to question the excesses of capitalism and regarded himself as having a "socialistic bent," ever discussed with Nell his views on social and economic questions. With the single exception of her acquaintance with Graham, neither her sizable collection of personal papers, which include various biographical statements, nor the abundant references to her formative experiences in "Incidentally" mention this period. The numerous interviews she provided journalists and students chronicling her life, in which she discussed many aspects of her

1. "The Grind and the All-Round Girl," *Goucher Kalends* 24, no. 2 (December 1912): 60–62; "Ideals," *Bulletin of Goucher College*, 2d ser., 5, no. 1 (January 1911): 15.

education in great detail, also omit any reference to attending Goucher, her first prolonged absence from home.[2]

Nell's decision to advance her education in Baltimore may have resulted in part from the dearth of opportunities for genuine collegiate study for women in her native region. Of the nearly 150 southern woman's "colleges," only 4—Goucher, Agnes Scott, Randolph-Macon, and Sophie Newcomb—had earned the recognition of the Association of Colleges of the Southern States, and among the top tier Goucher alone had received a Class I ranking by the Bureau of Education. This placed the institution alongside the elite northern woman's colleges and the top half-dozen men's universities in the South, including the University of North Carolina, which had only recently achieved this status.[3]

The college's location may also have influenced her selection. Baltimore existed as a southern outpost in a northern land. Dr. Lewis knew the city well from his own student days and probably felt more comfortable with his younger daughter attending school in a familiar landscape and ensconced in a cultural climate that she would not find alien.[4] Additionally, Goucher's binding ties to the Methodist Episcopal Church would have pleased both Dr. Lewis and Bishop Cheshire. Nell's father may have been ambivalent about the Reverend Dr. John Goucher's ambition for the college to foster "the most perfect development of the mental nature of woman," but the Raleigh physician would have lauded the prominent cofounder, benefactor, and former president's intent to instill in the institution's graduates "deep, gentle, tolerant Christianity, undemonstrative generosity and ministry, graciousness and sincerity of approach, modesty and self-effacement, [and] quiet dignity."[5]

"Baltimore is a most charming and interesting city," wrote one of Nell's classmates in the *Kalends*, "and college girls with such surroundings as we have at Goucher, close at hand, have an unusual opportunity for personal acquaintance with matters of historical, commercial and aesthetic interest to the

2. *N&O*, 17 August 1947, 1 January 1950; Warren Ashby, *Frank Porter Graham: A Southern Liberal* (Winston-Salem: John F. Blair, 1980), 32–34.

3. Anna Heubeck Knipp and Thaddeus P. Thomas, *The History of Goucher College* (Baltimore: Goucher College, 1938), 209; Elizabeth Avery Colton, "Standards of Southern Colleges for Women," *School Review* 20, no. 7 (September 1912): 465.

4. Marion E. Warren and Mame Warren, *Baltimore—When She Was What She Used to Be, 1850–1930* (Baltimore: Johns Hopkins University Press, 1983), 3, 8–9.

5. Knipp and Thomas, *History of Goucher College*, 120–22, 130.

city which ought to form part of the 'broadening' influence of our life here." The natural curiosity Goucher's students displayed in the picturesque city in which they resided notwithstanding, the college's administration sequestered them in closely monitored residence houses and unsparingly attempted to shield its charges from exposure to the Monumental City's many nefarious temptations.[6]

Nell thus probably did not directly encounter the harbor city's sordidness or many of its colorful rapscallions, who were so lovingly chronicled by Henry L. Mencken. Mencken was at that time fomenting discord with his editorials and column, the "Freelance," which appeared daily in the newly established *Evening Sun*. Nell's residence in Baltimore undoubtedly exposed her to Mencken, likely for the first time.[7] Nevertheless, the appearance and temperament of "Bawlamer," as natives pronounced it, would have astonished her. Her first impressions of the city might have resembled those of expatriated Tar Heel newspaperman, essayist, and author Gerald W. Johnson, when he initially encountered his new home. "The amazed newcomer to the city," he recalled, "is almost persuaded that she has studied ugliness, practiced it long and toilsomely, made a philosophy of ugliness and raised it to a fine art, so that in the end it has become a work of genius more fascinating than spic-and-span tidiness could ever be."[8]

The college, when Nell arrived there, served nearly four hundred students, most of them from Maryland but many from the surrounding Middle Atlantic region. Goucher's Baltimore location furnished it with a decidedly southern flavor, wrote the authors of an institutional history, replete with "graciousness and charm in all of the social life of the students, and a southern cordiality and good fellowship in its management and in the student spirit."[9] Indeed, considering the large number of young women from north of the Mason-Dixon Line who attended the institution, the Southern Club exerted a disproportionate influence. It carefully screened potential members and tapped only Dixieland

6. "Baltimore," *Goucher Kalends* 24, no. 5 (March 1913): 151–54.

7. H. L. Mencken, *Happy Days, 1880–1892* (New York: Alfred A. Knopf, 1940); H. L. Mencken, *Newspaper Days, 1899–1906* (New York: Alfred A. Knopf, 1941); H. L. Mencken, *Heathen Days, 1890–1936* (New York: Alfred A. Knopf, 1943); Fred Hobson, *Mencken: A Life* (Baltimore: Johns Hopkins University Press, 1994), 95–96.

8. Warren and Warren, *Baltimore*, 57; Vincent Fitzpatrick, *Gerald W. Johnson: From Southern Liberal to National Conscience* (Baton Rouge: Louisiana State University Press, 2002), 81–82.

9. "The Classification of Students," *Bulletin of Goucher College*, 3d ser., 1, no. 1 (October 1913): 89; Knipp and Thomas, *History of Goucher College*, 539–40.

natives perfervidly devoted to the Lost Cause. One jamboree sponsored by the group had reportedly featured a paroxysm of loyalty in which the participants rent Old Glory and stomped on it. Among other activities the club sponsored the Southern Prom, perhaps the year's most anticipated social event. Held in Goucher Hall, the affair featured southern music and prominently displayed rebel flags. An article in the 1914 *Kalends* bemoaned only one aspect of the festive occasion: "They won't let you dance."[10]

Rules of this kind sometimes exceeded even those of St. Mary's in terms of their austerity. The religious and social strictures of the late Victorian Age, intensified by the powerful influence of the Methodist Church, which had marked student life so indelibly in the years immediately following the college's founding in 1885, continued in only slightly abated form. By 1912, however, a few chinks in its rigid code of behavior had begun to appear.

Goucher had interdicted dancing, not only at school functions such as the Southern Prom but also "elsewhere at public receptions or on similar occasions when [students] may be allowed to accept invitations." By the time Nell arrived on campus, the administration had begun to grant some exceptions to this ban, but men would not attend dances at Goucher for another two decades. The college had recently softened its inviolable proscription against students' attending plays and operas off campus, but prospective theatergoers had to provide written permission from their parents, obtain approval from either the president or the dean of students, and be accompanied by at least two classmates. Rules in the student handbook still prohibited card playing and allowed freshmen, sophomores, and juniors to receive gentlemen callers in hall parlors until ten o'clock on Friday evenings only. And only recently had a student petition enabled male faculty members and the fathers of senior thespians to join women in the audiences for the carefully vetted and scrupulously correct plays the students performed.[11]

Nell entered Goucher less prepared for its challenging academics than some students in her freshman class, a number of whom had transferred there from other colleges. Either regarding her education at St. Mary's dubiously or lacking familiarity with the school's academic standards, the Goucher admin-

10. Knipp and Thomas, *History of Goucher College*, 530–31; Lilian Welsh, *Reminiscences of Thirty Years in Baltimore* (Baltimore: Norman, Remington Co., 1925), 149.

11. Knipp and Thomas, *History of Goucher College*, 440, 445–46, 459–60; "Social Notes," *Goucher Kalends* 24, no. 2 (December 1912): 72; *Students' Handbook: Goucher College, 1913–1914* (Baltimore: Waverly Press, 1913), 19, 20–21, 30.

istration elected not to admit her by certificate and required her to take a series of examinations. The October 1912 *Bulletin of Goucher College* indicated that she, like a quarter of the entering students, had failed to meet all of the admission requirements, which mandated fifteen units in English, algebra, geometry, Latin, and other specified subjects. Probably due to the coursework she would have to make up to obtain "reg." (regular) status, her transcript identified her as a "spec." (special) student.[12]

Despite her precarious academic standing, Nell apparently made an immediate and positive impression on her schoolmates. In September they elected her president of the freshman class. Many of the entering students from Maryland and elsewhere knew one another as a result of having attended the same high schools. That they selected Goucher's lone North Carolinian as the principal officer of their class bespeaks the power of her personality. Many years later one of her classmates recalled Nell's "friendliness, her vivacity, her straightforwardness, and her readiness to stand up for her beliefs" at the college.[13]

Like their peers at other woman's schools and colleges, many of Goucher's students, often unselfconsciously, developed highly sentimental relationships with each other, and "crushes" of varying kinds permeated campus culture. An editorial in the January 1913 *Kalends* reflected the burgeoning concern among medical authorities, educators, and parents regarding these abstruse and sometimes worrisome ties. Its author divided these affinities into three categories: "sane, affectionate, loyal friendship[s]," natural one-sided "admirations" of younger students for their older classmates, and "abnormal and perhaps injurious . . . cases."[14]

12. "Students," *Bulletin of Goucher College,* 2d ser., 6, no. 4 (October 1912): 5–47; "Entrance Inquiries and Applications," *Bulletin of Goucher College,* 2d ser., 6, no. 2 (March 1912): 18–31; NBL transcript, Goucher College; Knipp and Thomas, *History of Goucher College,* 403.

13. "Students," 5–47; "Class Notes," *Goucher Kalends* 24, no. 1 (November 1912): 33–34; *Donnybrook Fair* (Baltimore: Norman T. A. Munder, 1914), 82; "Nell Battle Lewis," *Goucher Alumnae Quarterly,* 35, no. 2 (winter 1957): 32.

14. Barbara Miller Solomon, *In the Company of Educated Women: A History of Women and Higher Education in America* (New Haven: Yale University Press, 1985), 98–100; Ronald Story, ed., *Five Colleges: Five Histories* (Amherst, Mass.: Five Colleges and Historic Deerfield, 1992), 90–91; Rona M. Wilk, "'What's a Crush?' A Study of Crushes and Romantic Friendships at Barnard College, 1900–1920," *Organization of American Historians Magazine of History* 18, no. 4 (July 2004): 20–22; "'Cases' and Friendships," *Goucher Kalends* 24, no. 3 (January 1913): 102–5.

Readers could help bring these unsettling infatuations to an end by ridiculing the sweethearts. "Teasing, however cruel it may seem, often gets at the root of an evil of this sort, as all the subtle suggestion and wise advice in the world could never do." This could help halt "the lack of restraint which has brought this abnormal relationship to its present pass." (The post–World War I popularization of Freudian and other psychiatric ideas regarding women's sexuality would spur greater scrutiny of crushes and diminish or force underground many intimacies between female students.)[15]

A freshman such as Nell frequently either developed an unreciprocated crush on a junior or senior or failed to pay absolute deference to the older student's lofty status. Such transgressions often resulted in the infliction of a "squelch" or in extreme circumstances a "d. s." (dead squelch) to teach the culprit her proper place. The 1912 *Donnybrook Fair* contained an arch "college primer" that discussed the use of this correction:

> Who is this Sweet Young Thing?
> Oh, this is an Innocent Freshman.
> Where is she Going?
> She is going to be Squelched.
> How Strange! why does she Do It?
> Because she does Not Know any Better.
> Will she Feel Bad?
> At first she will Look Around to see Who was
> Looking, but after awhile she will Not Care.
> Is it not Cruel to Taunt this Trusting Soul?
> No, for Some Day she will be a Sophomore and
> Must be Shown How.[16]

Hazing in a mild form also helped initiate freshmen into Goucher's social hierarchy. Soon after Nell arrived on campus, the sophomores "entertained" the new students at a "hazing party," the *Kalends* wrote. Nell's class had to perform in a play, and some members, singled out capriciously by their superiors,

15. "'Cases' and Friendships," 103; Wilk, "What's a Crush?'" 22.

16. *Donnybrook Fair* (Baltimore: Norman T. A. Munder, 1912), 162; "Slang of College Girls—The 'Crush,' 'Dead Squelch,' and Other Terms Expressive of College Life," "Articles about Smith 1873–," Smith College Archives, 1893, n.p.

delivered impromptu speeches on two of the day's most polemic issues: the "race question and woman's suffrage."[17]

Nell may have displayed her budding feminist consciousness and characteristic willingness to assert herself by participating along with Goucher faculty and students in a suffrage parade in the nation's capitol on 3 March 1913 that upstaged President Woodrow Wilson's inauguration the following day. "Scarcely a score of persons noticed his automobile as it whizzed through the silent streets, and only a few applauded him as he reached his hotel," reported the *New York Times* on the president-elect's arrival. In an "astonishing demonstration" five thousand suffragists of all ages, races, and social classes, borrowing tactics from their militant British sisters, marched down Pennsylvania Avenue as a half-million onlookers unrestrained by police surged toward the protestors. Drunken men climbed on floats and bellowed insults, and one law officer informed the dignified spouse of a congressman, "If my wife were where you are, I'd break her head." The tumult so unnerved young Helen Keller, who later became known for her work on behalf of the blind, that she could not address the rally.[18]

Although the trustees had refused to grant a holiday to allow the college's many proponents of suffrage (who included the institution's male acting president but not its namesake) to attend the demonstration, students cut class to march en masse alongside the female professoriate. Clad in caps and gowns, they mustered behind a conspicuous banner labeled GOUCHER. The eloquence of the event's speakers and the bravery displayed by the protestors in confronting hooliganism and bigotry impressed many people across the nation, recalled Lilian Welsh, the college physician and a prominent faculty member. Undoubtedly, the protest influenced Goucher's students—even those who did not march—mightily. The widespread support for suffrage on campus may have had the greatest impact on the smattering of students from homes south of the border state by inculcating in them beliefs that ran counter to the mores of their region. One collegian from South Carolina explained to Welsh, an ardent supporter of women's rights, "It is bad enough for me to have come to col-

17. "Social Notes," *Goucher Kalends* 24, no. 1 (November 1912): 32.

18. *New York Times* (hereafter cited as *NYT*), 4 March 1913; Nancy F. Cott, ed., *No Small Courage: A History of Women in the United States* (New York: Oxford University Press, 2000), 396–97; Sara M. Evans, *Born for Liberty: A History of Women in America* (New York: Free Press, 1989), 166; Sheila Rowbotham, *A Century of Women: The History of Women in Britain and the United States* (New York: Penguin, 1997), 41.

lege; if I went home and said I was a suffragist I should be looked upon as an outcast."[19]

Several possible explanations exist to account for Nell's leaving Goucher. Academics certainly figured prominently. The fall *Bulletin* stated that she had enrolled in a challenging series of courses in Latin, French literature, chemistry, English composition and literature, and solid geometry. Her June transcript, which made no mention of Latin, reported a failure in geometry, a "conditioned" in chemistry, and credit for only her English and French courses.[20]

Nell did not lack for intelligence; perhaps extracurricular activities distracted her from schoolwork, St. Mary's had prepared her inadequately, or the stress of being away from home and adapting to a new environment figured in her lackluster achievement. She may have suffered from a mental or physical illness. She may have chafed and grown demoralized in the college's repressive environment and wished to study elsewhere. Also, during her year there Goucher teetered on the edge of insolvency, and it appeared to even the school's most optimistic advocates that it would soon close its doors. In the unlikely event that the administration would have allowed Nell to return, Dr. Lewis may have decided to cut his losses and reassess his daughter's options, including terminating her formal education or enrolling her at an institution that was on firmer footing.[21]

Whatever the reason or reasons for Nell's disastrous debut in higher education, she found her failure embarrassing and would henceforth relegate it to oblivion. After having previously overcome her father's opposition to her going to college, she surely knew as she traveled back to Cloverdale that summer that her plans for her future would evoke much debate.

When Nell stepped off the train in Northampton, Massachusetts, in mid-September 1913 to begin her studies at Smith College, she must have felt as if she had arrived in a foreign land. She could hardly have missed the statues of Union soldiers and sailors flanking the entrance to Main Street's Memorial Hall, an immaculate example of General Grant architecture. A tiny handful of southerners attended Smith, which with nearly seventeen hundred students had grown to become the world's largest woman's college. She may have felt

19. Welsh, *Reminiscences of Thirty Years in Baltimore*, 106–7, 111–13, 150, 156–57.

20. NBL transcript, Goucher College; Knipp and Thomas, *History of Goucher College*, 430.

21. Knipp and Thomas, *History of Goucher College*, 195–208; Joan S. Abelson, "The First 100 Years: Goucher College 1885–1995," *Goucher Quarterly* 62, no. 4 (summer 1984): 10–11.

isolated at first. Certainly, her accent and use of the word *ma'am* attracted attention; "R's and G's were sounded all around me," she later recalled. Nearly all of her peers came from northern states, and at least some of them regarded her native region as benighted. During her first year a classmate unfamiliar with Nell's background solicited funds from her for the "degenerate and illiterate North Carolinians."[22]

Unquestionably, Nell, who like many of her classmates commuted about campus and Northampton on bicycle, experienced more autonomy than she had at any point thus far in her life. Nonsectarian Smith engendered great social freedom for its time and from its founding had enforced but one sacrosanct rule: lights out at ten o'clock. The *Students' Hand-Book* enunciated only the expectation that students would attend church in town on Sundays and campus chapel during weekday mornings. With the restrictions of St. Mary's and Goucher lifted, Nell breathed a sigh of relief and began to enjoy herself enormously. Reflecting on her years in Northampton, she later wrote, "When women shall be as free and joyous in the world at large as, in general, they are in college, then we shall be at least partially civilized."[23]

President Marion LeRoy Burton and Dean Ada Louise Comstock had embarked on an energetic campaign to modernize the college's organization and to democratize student life. Burton opened up admissions by accepting students from high schools that had not offered a classical secondary education. He increased salaries, encouraged faculty revision of the curriculum, and expanded the campus. Comstock began to lay groundwork for the construction of dormitories that would militate against the hierarchical all-round girl culture and the social elitism promoted by Northampton's many off-campus "invitation houses," which often enabled students to group themselves according to class. The Plymouth apartment house, adjacent to campus, provided an over-the-top case in point. It contained marble-covered salons, a gymnasium and pool, and a dining room replete with a stage. This lavishness stuck in the dean's craw. "Of all the disguises which the human spirit assumes," she wrote,

22. L. Clark Seelye, *The Early History of Smith College, 1871–1910* (Boston: Houghton Mifflin, 1923), 149; *Smith College Weekly*, 15 November 1916; *Smith College Class Book, 1914* (College Archives, Smith College), 195; *N&O*, 30 October 1932.

23. Story, *Five Colleges: Five Histories*, 88; Seelye, *Early History of Smith College*, 214–16; Smith College Association for Christian Work, *Students' Hand-Book of Smith College, 1916–1917* (Smith College, 1916), 11, 37–38; *N&O*, 23 March 1924, 10 March 1935.

"none is so complete as that embodied in circumstances of living." Nell may have encountered or perhaps even guiltily engaged in some of this snobbishness; later in life she wrote approvingly of the administration's efforts to eliminate the exclusionary policies of the residences.[24]

Nell may have secured admission to Smith by omitting mention of her failure in Baltimore. At any rate her study there would remain unreferenced on her Smith transcript. She must have arrived on campus determined to buckle down and apply herself more fully to her studies. This attitude was probably emphatically reinforced by Dr. Lewis, whom she must have lobbied long and hard for permission to attend the northern college. From the outset she comported herself well in the classroom. Her deplorable year at Goucher had strengthened her scholastic foundation (and almost certainly loomed large in her decision to avoid mathematics entirely over the next four years). In an era not characterized by grade inflation, she regularly earned As and Bs and graduated a member of Phi Beta Kappa, which included twenty new Smith inductees out of a senior class of well over three hundred students. A decade after her arrival in Northampton, however, Nell dismissed her academic achievement there by maintaining that she had not studied enough to "give [her] mind any sort of real discipline." "The courses we liked were a pleasure," she recalled; "the ones we didn't, we attended to as best we could the week before examination."[25]

Nell also brushed aside the idea that the politics that had prevailed at the college influenced her strongly. She insisted that conflict alone could stimulate intellectual awakening and that her carefree years at Smith had immersed her in little strife. Still, it appears unlikely that she could have gone entirely unaffected by the progressive pulse that filtered through the campus. Indeed, her family believed that the northern institution shaped her thinking powerfully. She returned to Raleigh "filled with liberal ideas," a niece later recalled. Nell's transformation prompted her half brothers to limit their daughters' enrollment to the conventional campuses of St. Mary's and Virginia's Sweet Briar College.[26]

Northern colleges such as Smith introduced southern students to new ways

24. Story, *Five Colleges: Five Histories*, 88–89, 95–99; *N&O*, 3 March 1946.

25. NBL transcript, Smith College; *Smith College Class Book* (Buffalo: Hausauer-Jones, 1917), 17–83, 93; *N&O*, 16 March 1924.

26. *N&O*, 16 March 1924; Lottie Woolen, telephone interview by author, 8 May 1992.

of thinking about racial issues, sometimes in an overt fashion. Black students had begun attending Smith around 1900, and Nell likely came in contact with them. One southern alumna, who graduated a few years after Nell and later played a role in reopening desegregated Central High School in Little Rock, Arkansas, credited the college with broadening her racial views: "At Smith there was no one else from this part of the country and for the first time I knew New Englanders and northerners and a few far westerners. I think it was rubbing shoulders with these girls that opened the world to me." She also received her initial exposure to integrated education by studying alongside a black classmate, whose intelligence and work ethic impressed her.[27]

Black leaders and black cultural groups visited Smith routinely. Booker T. Washington spoke there on his work at Tuskegee Normal and Industrial Institute and the mission of its graduates to uplift their race and convince southern whites of the importance of educating black children. "I am proud to belong to a race with the privilege of having such great difficulties to overcome," the great accommodationist educator and social reformer told the students. Washington also underscored the injustice of southern school funding, which in one area devoted fifty-six cents per capita to black public school students per year, compared to twenty-two dollars for whites.[28]

Singers and representatives from Hampton Normal and Agricultural Institute traveled to Smith to solicit donations and build sympathy for their school, whose curriculum consisted of farming and fourteen trades. "Lantern pictures of negro life" illustrated the vital need for this sort of training, and one speaker optimistically concluded that the southern states had begun to realize the importance of educating blacks. What the members of this "cheerful race" ask, the *Smith College Weekly* reported, "is the chance to be decent and self-respecting." Hampton Institute's renowned singers achieved a following at Smith and returned time and again.[29]

Washington's successor as principal at Tuskegee Institute, Robert R. Moton, a newly commissioned army major charged with increasing the morale of black troops, spoke at a Sunday vesper service at Smith. Moton proposed

27. Nanci Young, interview by author, 17 July 2003; Jacqueline Van Voris, *College: A Smith Mosaic* (Westfield, Mass.: Smith College, 1975), 49–50; Lynne Olson, *Freedom's Daughters: The Unsung Heroines of the Civil Rights Movement from 1830 to 1970* (New York: Scribner, 2001), 99.

28. *Smith College Weekly*, 14 January 1914.

29. *Smith College Weekly*, 10 February 1915, 19 January 1916, 10 January 1917.

that "no other situation which this country has to face is more perplexing and embarrassing than the necessity of race adjustment." The teachings of Christ, he told the congregation, "should make us willing to overcome superstition, prejudice and sin."[30]

The moderate tone of these spokespersons and activities notwithstanding, one should not underestimate the impact of such events on southerners like Nell. A decade earlier the innocuous claim by John Spencer Bassett, a professor at Trinity College (now Duke University), in the fledgling *South Atlantic Quarterly* that "Washington is a great and good man, a Christian statesman, and take him all in all the greatest man, save General Lee, born in the South in a hundred years; but he is not a typical negro," had nearly precipitated the ruin of the little institution. Convulsed by a witch hunt orchestrated by the Lewises' close family friend Josephus Daniels, North Carolina's press tore into the college and Bassett, a native North Carolinian, with such a frenzied rage that in 1906, after making a show of not having been scared out of town, he accepted a position in Smith's history department. (For the remainder of his life he refused to forgive Daniels, whom he referred to as "a wicked and narrow man." Although Nell did not study under Bassett, she almost certainly knew the story of the notorious "Bassett Affair." No documentation has surfaced regarding whether she ever spoke with the professor, whom she must have encountered on campus periodically.)[31]

The *Weekly* habitually highlighted and promoted the activities of settlement and social workers and the many career opportunities for graduates in these professions. It also encouraged students to volunteer their services to the numerous benevolent agencies and organizations in the surrounding area.[32] Smith sponsored a College Settlements Association, which alumnae had played a prominent role in founding twenty-five years earlier, and its

30. *Smith College Weekly*, 17 January 1917; Herbert Aptheker, ed., *A Documentary History of the Negro People in the United States*, vol. 3: *From the N.A.A.C.P. to the New Deal* (New York: Citadel Press, 1973), 296–97; Robert Russa Moton, *Finding a Way Out: An Autobiography* (College Park, Md.: McGrath, 1969), 234–65.

31. NBL transcript, Smith College; John Spencer Bassett, "Stirring Up the Fires of Racial Antipathy," *South Atlantic Quarterly* 2, no. 4 (1903): 304; *N&O*, 1 November 1903; Earl W. Porter, *Trinity and Duke, 1892–1924: Foundations of Duke University* (Durham: Duke University Press, 1964), 96–139, 155–58; Mims, *Advancing South*, 241–43; O'Brien, *Rethinking the South*, 245–46.

32. *Smith College Weekly*, 22 October 1913, 6 May, 11 November, and 9 December 1914, 24 May 1916, 17 January 1917.

chapter had grown to become one of the largest at a woman's college. Among its many activities it brought to the campus speakers ranging from an advocate for mountain schools for poor whites to Jane Addams, who discussed her work at Chicago's Hull House to an auditorium packed with Smith students and faculty. The association also recruited students to work at settlement houses throughout the country during their Christmas, spring, and summer vacations.[33]

A chapter of the National Consumers League, which sought to exert financial pressure on employers exploiting women and child workers, further raised the students' social consciousness. One presenter sponsored by the league endorsed the enforcement of the Federal Child Labor Law. "Stereopticon slides showing children at work in the cotton mills of the South, in the coal fields of Pennsylvania and in the beet fields of Colorado emphasized the fact that no portion of the country is free from child labor," the *Weekly* reported. "The results of it were shown in the pictures of undersized and undernourished children. . . . Child labor is becoming a thing of the past and we must continue the banishment of this menace."[34]

The word *feminism*, used to communicate its new egalitarian and political meaning, began to appear in college publications. Dr. Lyman Abbott, a major religious leader and magazine editor and a moderate proponent of the social gospel, censured capitalism and sanctioned feminism during a Sunday vesper service at Smith. "The law of industry in the state is primarily one of self-interest," he preached; "each individual is concerned exclusively with the effort to reap the best possible results from his labor. But it is through the feminist movement that the nobler family idea of working for the common welfare can be made to supersede this selfish law. The government has begun to realize this ideal in its rulings in regard to railroads, corporations, and trade unions."[35]

Harry W. Laidler, a founder of the Intercollegiate Socialist Society and the editor of its magazine, addressed the college in December 1916. The socialist author maintained that the excesses of private monopoly had led to a "wave in favor of communistic control." Far from being a utopian dream, socialism would result in "a larger democracy, . . . liberty and the happiness of man."

33. *Smith College Weekly*, 18 February 1914, 3 March and 26 May 1915.

34. Kathryn Cullen-DuPont, *The Encyclopedia of Women's History in America* (New York: Da Capo, 1998), 42–43; *Smith College Weekly*, 25 April 1917.

35. Evans, *Born for Liberty*, 167; *Smith College Weekly*, 9 December 1914.

Laidler's "clear and convincing lecture . . . was greatly appreciated by a large audience," remarked the *Weekly*.[36]

Suffrage provided abundant grist for dialogue at Smith, and early in Lewis's freshman year students inaugurated a Suffrage Discussion Club. A few months later, however, the club's founders bemoaned the fact that they had failed to provoke any debate on the topic. No one attending the meetings had voiced opposition to extending the ballot to women. "If we want to take a broad minded view of the Feminist Question we must hear both sides presented, each by its own advocates," a correspondent to the *Weekly*'s public opinion department wrote.[37]

Speakers such as Margaret Hatfield, a Smith alumna, spoke at club functions and provided articulate and persuasive arguments in favor of suffrage. She dismissed the contention that women's voting would swell the electorate with uninformed and undeserving participants. Hatfield cited statistics revealing that more girls than boys graduated from high school and that men provided 94 percent of penitentiary inmates. Alumnae sweepingly favored the franchise; one open meeting featured four graduates, all of whom expressed "the need for the ballot which they themselves have felt in their personal experience."[38]

World War I, looming in the distant background initially but metastasizing with terrifying speed, began to intrude on the sheltered lives of Smith's students in 1914, during Lewis's sophomore year. It would cast a growing shadow on the campus as the extent of the carnage and misery emerged. "Work for the relief of the war-sufferers! Knit a muffler! Sew a sheet! Roll a bandage!" a lead editorial in the *Weekly* exhorted in early November. "The war shows no sign of coming to an end in the immediate future." The paper's "World News" column increasingly carried ominous reports from Belgium as well as more exotic lands such as Russia, Turkey, Albania, and Poland, demonstrating that the conflict had become a global war.[39]

Students responded by forming a War Relief Committee to purchase raw materials and coordinate the production of clothing and supplies requested by the Red Cross. All around campus signs appeared, reading:

36. *Smith College Weekly*, 13 December 1916; Mari Jo Buhle, Paul Buhle, and Dan Georgakas, eds., *Encyclopedia of the American Left* (New York: Oxford University Press, 1998), 427–28.

37. *Smith College Weekly*, 8 October 1913, 18 February 1914.

38. *Smith College Weekly*, 18 February 1914, 16 February 1916.

39. *Smith College Weekly*, 4 November 1914.

Come into the Reading Room—any time will do—
If you don't know how to knit, we will teach you to.
Knit a muffler or some hose
So the soldiers won't be froze.[40]

Gray mufflers replaced the colorful sweaters the students previously had knit, and the residence houses reduced the extravagance of their receptions to purchase supplies for Belgian refugees. The committee's chair would soon announce shipment of 718 bandages, 176 bundles of absorbent pads, 760 towels, 20 dozen sheets, 109 pillow cases, 3 night shirts, 10 flannel petticoats, 1 abdominal band, 2 pairs of wristlets, and 97 mufflers to New York for transport overseas. More consignments soon followed this one.[41]

Efforts to aid the war victims, however, sometimes produced moral quandaries. If the junior class chose to forgo its grand ball, the newspaper asked, would each member really confer the five to twenty-five dollars she would have spent on her attire and related expenses to the relief fund? Might some students simply pocket the money? Thankfully, the Debating Union helped parse the dilemma. The affirmative side, arguing the issue of "Resolved: That the junior class should give up its Prom and donate the proceeds to the Red Cross Society," won out.[42]

The sinking in the spring of 1915 of the RMS *Lusitania* by a U-boat off the coast of southern Ireland ended any illusion that the United States would remain unaffected by the conflict. A single torpedo detonated the contraband munitions secreted aboard the ship, and it sank to the bottom in just eighteen minutes. One hundred and twenty-eight Americans, mostly women and children, died—among them several prominent socialites. Their countrymen shook with rage, and as they directed their wrath at Germany, sentiment for neutrality waned. Smith's students waited angrily and impatiently for the Foreign Ministry in Berlin to respond to President Wilson's protest letter and attended closely to the *Weekly*'s digests of the crisis.[43]

Lewis set *The Transient*, a play she based on the events in Europe, in this period. It advanced a decidedly unheroic view of the war's impact. A working-

40. *Smith College Class Book* (Buffalo: Hausauer-Jones, 1915), 166–67.

41. *Smith College Weekly*, 2 and 9 December 1914

42. *Smith College Weekly*, 2 and 9 December 1914.

43. Gary Mead, *The Doughboys: America and the First World War* (New York: Overlook Press, 2000), 25–37; S.L.A. Marshall, *World War I* (Boston: Houghton Mifflin, 1964), 166–67.

class British draftee early in the conflict returns unexpectedly to his family cottage in Devonshire. He surprises his fiancée and widowed mother, who are quarreling over the mother's admonishment of her son for registering for conscription belatedly. The young man nervously informs the pair that authorities have granted him sick leave, but the mother soon learns from a party of soldiers that he has deserted and that troops have surrounded her home. She strikes a bargain with the sergeant in charge of the patrol to surrender her son the following morning in order to provide the young lovers with an evening in which they can, heedless of what the future holds, plan their lives together and escape from England. Judges at Smith awarded Nell a prize for the play's creativity.[44]

At home in August, preparing to return to Smith to begin her junior year, Lewis penned a poem entitled "Tomorrow" that expressed the enthusiasm with which she anticipated her future:

> Tomorrow is a shadowy thing,
> But, oh, its lure for me!
> What joys unguessed its dawn may bring!
> Tomorrow is a shadowy thing:
> With hope of it my heart's a-wing:
> It's fair and fresh and free!
> Tomorrow is a shadowy thing,
> But, oh, its lure for me![45]

Back in Northampton the next month, she authored another short poem, "Distance," which seemingly implicated a Carolina summer romance in her youthful ardor.

> A little, floating-feather moon,
> Caught in the net-work of a tree:
> How many miles it shines upon
> Between my love and me!
> But he, too, sees this thin new moon
> Tonight, and wishes it might be

44. Nell Battle Lewis, *The Transient*, Class of 1917 Records, Smith College Archives.

45. Nell Battle Lewis, "Tomorrow," August 1915, Nell Battle Lewis Papers, Saint Mary's School Archives.

I were with him,—how short the way
Between my love and me![46]

The *Weekly* as well as the *Smith College Class Book* and *Smith College Monthly*, which published the students' literary efforts, and the local newspaper, the *Daily Hampshire Gazette*, provide abundant evidence of Lewis's all-round girl status as an upperclassman. She served as an editor of the *Monthly*, and her contributions appeared frequently in the magazine. She set many of her poems and short stories in the South and featured numerous black menial characters speaking Negro dialect. Minstrel song writers—Stephen Foster, for one—and authors such as Mark Twain, Joel Chandler Harris, Thomas Nelson Page, and Thomas Dixon had frequently employed black vernacular and made the genre popular.[47]

Lewis further cemented her standing as an all-round girl at Smith by participating busily in a gamut of associations and activities. Phi Kappa Psi, an honor society, elected her a member for her academic and artistic achievements. She joined the Philosophical and Biological societies. And she belonged to the Blue Pencil Club, whose members sought "to find, encourage, and improve literary talent by friendly criticism," and the Novel Club, which existed to encourage its affiliates "a) to write a good novel and b) to have a good time." As she had at St. Mary's, Lewis continued to display her athletic talents, playing on the basketball and hockey teams.[48]

Lewis served as "chairman" of a political rally early in her senior year. The national movement for women's suffrage was gaining power, and that fall students gathered in Smith's Greene Hall to cast votes in a mock presidential election. Lewis provided opening and closing remarks and introduced students representing the various candidates: Woodrow Wilson, Charles Evans Hughes, and Allan L. Benson, the nominees of the Democratic, Republican,

46. Nell Battle Lewis, "Distance," September 1915, Nell Battle Lewis Papers, Saint Mary's School Archives.

47. Nell Battle Lewis, "Banjo Love Song," *Smith College Monthly* 22, no. 6 (March 1915): 343; "Black Devil's Rock," *Smith College Monthly* 22, no. 7 (April 1915): 366–71; "Translation of the 11th Ode of the 1st Book of Horace," *Smith College Monthly* 22, no. 7 (April 1915): 387–88; "Coin of the Realm," *Smith College Monthly* 23, no. 1 (October 1915): 13–18; "When Gabriel Blows," *Smith College Monthly* 24, no. 6 (April 1917): 299–301.

48. *Smith College Class Book*, 1917, 97–99, 113, 118, 140, 143; "Guide to Clubs at Smith College, A–Z" (Smith College Archives, n.d.), n.p.

and Socialist parties, respectively. "This meeting of patriots," she began, "will please come to order."

> In looking over this collection of potential votes so many of which are as yet unrecognized by those barbarous states, over which, to quote a member of the faculty, the light of civilization has not yet dawned, I say, when I face this intelligent and enlightened audience, I experience the most profound regret that only the accident of sex prevents us from making our influence directly felt throughout the country at this approaching stirring time—I regret, I say, that as a result of this accident, Miss Jones from New York, be she ever so intelligent, cannot help to tip the scales for Hughes, nor Miss Brown from Alabama, no matter what state of enlightenment she finds herself in, cannot put another vote in for Wilson.

Despite women's inability to participate in the national election, Lewis viewed the rally she directed with great optimism. "This meeting tonight may be regarded as a triumph and glory for those who wave the yellow flag and follow in the ranks so ably headed by Mrs. Carrie Chapman Catt," she declared, referring to the emblem of the National American Woman Suffrage Association and its president. "This is an extraordinarily significant moment in American history, for here for the first time since the Pilgrims left their staterooms in the Mayflower and set their feet upon the welcome rock and ordered their crowds in the general direction of Plymouth, the women of every state in this union vote in a presidential election." Hughes, a Supreme Court associate justice and the former progressive governor of New York, bested Wilson by over a hundred votes in Smith's contest.[49]

Students competed hotly for the various dramatic roles in Smith's energetically produced plays, and Lewis's casting and performance in Shakespeare's *Twelfth Night* as the wise and ironical fool Feste earned her the admiration of her classmates during her final semester at the college. The *Springfield* (Mass.) *Daily Republican* provided an elaborate and complimentary review of the play and devoted special attention to Lewis's portrayal. The critic termed her performance of Feste's comic songs "delightful" and said she "did exceptionally

49. *Northampton* (Mass.) *Daily Hampshire Gazette*, n.d.

fine work." The newspaper printed a promotional picture of Lewis in costume. As toastmistress for the senior class supper, she, along with other players, reprised scenes from the play.[50]

President Wilson's declaration of war on Germany two months earlier tempered the exuberance at Lewis's graduation that June. Following President Burton's welcome, she delivered to the assembly an address entitled "A Wise Provincialism." In it she acknowledged that many might regard a speech on localism discordant with the wartime emphasis on unity and national loyalty. She did not feel that way; love for community deepened her commitment to her country. Smith served as a melting pot for its students, who hailed from diverse corners of the United States, but Lewis believed that "the man whose affection for his country has no local root is a man whose patriotism is but a poor abstraction."[51]

All regions, she said, possessed value and character. She told several amusing stories about North Carolina to illustrate both its backwardness and its charm, and she appraised the strengths and weaknesses of Tar Heels. "Down home I see a people in many ways behind the times," she continued, "but a century ahead in love: a simple, kindly folk who are as eager now in their desire to aid America in making the world safe for Americans as are their fellow citizens from other points of the national compass." She finished her remarks by celebrating her own heritage with a verse from Rudyard Kipling's "To the City of Bombay." "As a provincial," she said, "let me say, of my province, and thus of the United Provinces":

> So thank God my birth
>     Fell not in isles aside,
> Waste headlands of the earth,
>     Or warring tribes untried
> But that she lent me worth
>     And gave me right to pride.

Although her speech seemed at many points highly personal, the audience received it well. "War prompted the high words of youth . . . this morning," the *Republican*'s reporter wrote. "From Josephus Daniels's own town, Ra-

50. *Smith College Class Book*, 1917, 180, 184; *Springfield* (Mass.) *Daily Republican*, 15 January 1917.

51. *Springfield* (Mass.) *Daily Republican?* 19 June 1917? *Northampton* (Mass.) *Daily Hampshire Gazette*, 19 June 1917.

leigh, N.C., came Miss Nell Battle Lewis to speak on 'Our wise provincialism.' [Woodrow Wilson had appointed Daniels secretary of the navy four years earlier.] She did it cleverly, brilliantly even for a class-day orator. Yet beneath all the surface sparkle of humor and the pleasant course of anecdote ran the somber burden of her thought: That one loves one's country most and serves it best by loving North Carolina and New York, and Tombstone, Ariz., like the family hearth." Smith had spurred Nell's intellectual development, provided her with a plethora of opportunities to hone her writing and speaking skills, and introduced her to political and social doctrine she would not have encountered back home, but it had not diminished the loyalty and sentimental regard with which she viewed her native region.[52]

President Burton's commencement speech, "The Meaning of America," left no question regarding the liberalizing influence he had sought over the previous four years to impart to the young women assembled before him. "Individualism for decades has manifested itself in an excessive personal ambition, in a narrow ambition, in a desire to achieve what men call success regardless of the consequences to others and to the standards of our public life," he declared. "And not only has there been this rampant individualism, but there has as a consequence been a failure to develop a corresponding high social-mindedness. . . . We have permitted the exploitation of the foreign worker, we have tolerated industrial slavery. We have recognized openly public political corruption."

Burton informed Lewis and her classmates that the world war had placed upon them an obligation "to help make real to the world the promise of American democracy. . . . Like every growing, virile organism, America has her defects and her limitations. This democracy has suffered from grievous ills. At the present moment conditions prevail which no true American can contemplate with composure. Lend your energies to the speedy correction of our social disorders, of our political evils and of our industrial wrongs."[53]

Few documents in Lewis's papers treat the period immediately following her graduation from Smith College. Fortunately, a number of allusions to her during this interval reside in the papers of Lenoir Chambers, with whom she engaged in a romance. Chambers, a twenty-six-year-old graduate of the Univer-

52. Joseph L. Morrison, *Josephus Daniels: The Small-d Democrat* (Chapel Hill: University of North Carolina Press, 1966), 48; *Springfield* (Mass.) *Daily Republican?* 19 June 1917?

53. *Northampton* (Mass.) *Daily Hampshire Gazette*, 19 June 1917.

sity of North Carolina and a scion of a socially prominent Charlotte family, had attended Columbia University's School of Journalism during the 1916–17 academic year. He may have been the love interest to whom Lewis referred in "Distance." Certainly, social events at Chapel Hill provided numerous opportunities for the two young people to become acquainted with one another that summer.[54]

Columbia and New York City, as Smith and Northampton had done for Lewis, significantly broadened Chambers's perspective. The journalism program attracted a particularly creative and militant student body. Its members lionized Max Eastman—editor of the soon-to-be-banned periodical *The Masses*—and John Reed, who propounded their radical views there, and the young journalists formed the core of the university's strident Anti-Militarism League. No record of Chambers's impressions of his study at Columbia has come to light, but a young intellectual of his caliber would have critically weighed the heady politics he encountered against the conservative values of his Carolina homeland. Lewis's and Chamber's experiences living and studying in the metropolitan North would have provided a natural subject for conversation as the two grew closer.[55]

In July 1918, after having attended officers' training school in Tennessee, Chambers, who had earned a commission as a first lieutenant in the army, returned to New York City with his unit, for transport overseas. Lewis traveled from Raleigh to join his sister in seeing him off. While there, they discussed Lewis's plans to join him overseas. "I hardly know what to say except that she is the only person in the world I would have wanted here outside of my own family," Chambers wrote to his mother, informing her of his budding romance. "There is no formal engagement, of course. About the only definite thing we do know is that there is nothing definite now—may never be. But she came up from Raleigh to see me and I am glad she did." Should his mother encounter Nell, he instructed, she should simply treat the young woman as one of his friends. He believed that little chance existed for such a meeting, however, "because she will probably go to France soon with the YMCA." Cham-

54. Alexander S. Leidholdt, *Standing before the Shouting Mob: Lenoir Chambers and Virginia's Massive Resistance to Public-School Integration* (Tuscaloosa: University of Alabama Press, 1997), 11–12.

55. Leidholdt, *Standing before the Shouting Mob*, 12–13; *NYT*, 15 December 1916, 14 February, 30 March, and 3 April 1917; Richard Terrill Baker, *A History of the Graduate School of Journalism, Columbia University* (New York: Columbia University Press, 1954), 83–85.

bers and his entourage rushed about the city "spending money like water," kitting him out. Lewis purchased a money belt for him at Wanamaker's.[56]

For over a year Lewis apparently lived in New York City. She later informed an interviewer that she did not return from the North to live in North Carolina until the end of the war. In Gotham she studied art and commercial advertising, and a bank employed her to do mechanical drawing and perhaps stenography.[57]

The very month she bade Chambers farewell, the YMCA, backed by General John J. Pershing, began to recruit women, to the vehement objection of critics. Many argued that women could not withstand the physical rigors they would encounter in a war zone and would simply get underfoot. Others supported sending working-class women overseas as cooks and maids but insisted that "ladies would only embarrass the men, deprive them of freedom, and be themselves disgusted with contact with common soldiers."[58]

Regardless of these protests, the YMCA plowed ahead. Women's initial function consisted solely of freeing men who would have staffed canteens and cafeterias to assume military duties. Soon, however, authorities enlarged the association's purview widely to include organizing and maintaining leave areas, operating post exchanges, furnishing educational activities, and providing an array of social and religious services for soldiers and sailors. Women recruits found themselves involved in all of these duties, and their titles evolved formally from "canteen workers" to the YMCA's traditional appellation of "secretary," a gender-neutral designation. In day-to-day circumstances many people simply referred to the female staff as "Y girls."[59]

Lewis undoubtedly encountered frustrations aplenty as she lobbied the Y

56. Lenoir Chambers to Grace Chambers, 4 July 1918, Lenoir Chambers Papers (hereafter cited as LC Papers), Southern Historical Collection, Wilson Library, University of North Carolina at Chapel Hill.

57. "Alumnae Notes," *Smith Alumnae Quarterly* 9, no. 4 (July 1918): 391; Kate Covington, "Interviewing Nell Battle Lewis," *Meredith College Acorn* 27, no. 4 (May 1936): 16–17.

58. Lettie Gavin, *American Women in World War I: They Also Served* (Niwot: University Press of Colorado, 1997), 130.

59. Frederick Harris, ed., *Service with Fighting Men: An Account of the Work of the American Young Men's Christian Associations in the World War* (New York: Association Press, 1922), 2:57, 61; Richard C. Lancaster, *Serving the U.S. Armed Forces, 1861–1986: The Story of the YMCA's Ministry to Military Personnel for 125 Years* (Schaumburg, Ill.: Armed Services YMCA of the USA, 1986), 54–80; Katherine Shortall, *A "Y" Girl in France, Letters of Katherine Shortall* (Boston: Gorham Press, 1918).

to send her overseas. All candidates seeking posts in Europe endured a thorough investigation by the War Personnel Board and a separate screening by the Military Intelligence Bureau. This process created for the applicants a tremendous bottleneck that remained unbroken until the armistice. Lewis may have stayed in New York, where the association maintained its national headquarters, in order to monitor the status of her application closely.[60]

In September, having surmounted these bureaucratic obstacles, Lewis traveled to the Y's southeast district headquarters in Atlanta for a formal interview, which she passed with flying colors. She clearly possessed in large measures the qualities the organization sought—physical strength, common sense, sociability, and character. Her mastery of French must have further fortified her application. And, too, she must have exuded patriotism and a desire to serve her country. She later informed an interviewer that the slogan "a war to end war" had inspired her greatly during this period. "We were all so particularly impressed with her personality and qualifications that we decided as soon as we saw her that we needed her for overseas services," an administrator wrote to Dr. Lewis. "I . . . only wish that we had the opportunity of sending overseas more women in whom we can place the same confidence as we have in Miss Lewis."[61]

A fortnight after the 11 November 1918 armistice, Lewis finally sailed for France. She had missed the war, but the military desperately required her help. The American brass determined that troops—regardless of their tenure and combat experience—would repatriate as divisions, not individuals. Not enough ships existed to support a rapid withdrawal, and General Pershing and his staff confronted the daunting prospect of commanding an army of nearly four million civilian soldiers with deteriorating discipline and too much time and pay on their hands.[62]

Venereal disease posed a threat to the men's health but not nearly as dire a peril as the influenza epidemic that the most recently arrived members of the Allied Expeditionary Force (AEF) had brought from America. The medical corps reported ten thousand new cases sweeping through the ranks each week. French price-gouging and patronizing, harsh living conditions, and food and mail service that did not improve with the peace diminished morale even further. "My present ambition is to get out of the army at the earliest possible

60. Lancaster, *Serving the U.S. Armed Forces*, 53–54, 76.

61. B. M. Boykin to Richard H. Lewis, 17 September 1918, KPL Papers.

62. Mead, *Doughboys*, 397; Marshall, *World War I*, 457.

moment," one disgruntled doughboy wrote to his aunt that November. "It is an awful thing to be in. The war isn't so bad, but the army—O my!" The resumption of hard field training resulted in much grousing but had its intended effect.[63]

Pershing sent an urgent appeal to the Y during this "trying" and "important" period to render all the help it could in keeping officers and men "wholesomely and enjoyably occupied during periods not needed for other military duties and as a means of keeping them in a state which breeds contentment." The association reined in its many programs and refocused its efforts on a single mission: entertaining the troops.[64]

After debarking in Liverpool, Lewis wired Chambers, who had commanded a company briefly in trench combat but whose Sixth Division had largely been spared heavy fighting. He now found himself distressingly recast as his division's recreation officer. His new duties included organizing a football team and horse show and booking and transporting entertainment acts throughout his jurisdiction. A short while later Lewis traveled across the English Channel and landed in Le Havre.[65]

"Nell Lewis is in France," Chambers wrote to his mother that December. "I had a wire . . . from Paris and to-day I hear that she has been assigned to Nice and is leaving immediately." He would have preferred her attachment to his division but expressed satisfaction with her posting in the cultured Riviera port city only a stone's throw from Monte Carlo. "Whenever I get a leave . . . I am going straight to Nice," he declared.[66]

The Y had organized leave centers throughout the country, many in posh resorts, casinos, and spas. In these often luxurious circumstances, where soldiers sometimes found themselves billeted in suites previously occupied by European royalty, the association endeavored to ensure that the Yanks' "moral well-being was safeguarded by keeping them occupied in interesting activities, including American-type recreation," and at arm's length from the wine and cognac shops and the enticing delights that flourished in "gay Paree." "This is

63. Mead, *Doughboys*, 396, 402–5; S.L.A. Marshall, *World War I* (Boston: Houghton Mifflin, 1964), 457–58; *A Red Triangle Girl in France* (New York: George Doran, 1918), 21; Shortall, "Y" *Girl in France*, 55–57.

64. Lancaster, *Serving the U.S. Armed Forces*, 81–82.

65. Leidholdt, *Standing before the Shouting Mob*, 13–14; Nell Battle Lewis, "On Returning," June 1919, Nell Battle Lewis Papers, Saint Mary's School Archives.

66. Lenoir Chambers to Grace Chambers, 15 and 25 December 1918, LC Papers.

no place for our nice boys," one secretary wrote home from Paris. "Every one says so." Ten leave centers existed by the time Lewis disembarked.[67]

In late December 1919 she arrived in Nice, where she helped operate a canteen installed in a sumptuous hotel's elegant bar. Her daytime duties, which she later described as "graciously adding the home-touch to the war," probably included staffing an information booth, library, and writing area; serving untold sandwiches and cups of hot chocolate; and selling candy, cigarettes, and stationery. She also served as the assistant editor of an American newspaper, which the association probably distributed to the Sammies. In Nice she quickly discovered that the Y did not limit its concern to protecting the virtue of America's manhood. Her supervisor, a Mrs. Williams, zealously fended off any threats to the maidenhood of her female charges. Posting a listing prominently on the canteen's bulletin board, she laid down the "Nice Leave Area Rules":

> GIRLS must wear uniform as prescribed in the regulations.
> THEY must not lunch or dine with a man without permission.
> THEY must not go to the following restaurants:—Savoy, Ernest's, Maxim's or the Belle Mouniere.
> THEY must not smoke or drink in public.
> THEY must not dance anywhere except at the Casino or Officer's club.
> THEY must have a chaperone if looking on at hotel dances.[68]

From their initial involvement in the war women secretaries had displayed fortitude and, in some situations, outright heroism. Two died in combat, thirteen earned the Croix de Guerre, and many others received citations for bravery. After the cessation of hostilities, however, Nell Lewis and her peers exhibited physical courage not on the battlefield but on the dance floor. No one should underestimate their ordeal.[69]

"The conception of dancing as a social enjoyment of the idle must be put aside when this feature of the women's activity in the AEF is considered," one

67. Lancaster, *Serving the U.S. Armed Forces*, 67; Gavin, *American Women in World War I*, 135–36; Shortall, *"Y" Girl in France*, 61.

68. Gavin, *American Women in World War I*, 155; "Nice Leave Area Rules" [1919?], NBL scrapbook, 1918–19, KPL Papers; Marian Baldwin, *Canteening Overseas, 1917–1919* (New York: Macmillan, 1920), 66–67, 71; "Alumnae Notes," *Smith Alumnae Quarterly* 10, no. 4 (July 1919): 378; *N&O*, 5 May 1935.

69. Gavin, *American Women in World War I*, 147; Harris, *Service with Fighting Men*, 58.

account of the YMCA's World War I service discloses. "To the men it was the favorite recreation, but their incessant demands put a severe strain on their partners." Indeed, Brigadier General Johnson Hagood, who commanded the Service of Supply, upon observing the rigors the secretaries and other women engaged in supporting the army now faced, fired off a telegram to Y headquarters stressing the vital need for "several hundred young women workers of pleasing personality." At one dance he had witnessed twenty-one YMCA and Red Cross workers and telephone operators mobbed by fifteen hundred doughboys. "These women you have on the job are overworked and do not have even an opportunity to eat their meals," he admonished the association's leadership. "Of course we have to let the boys cut in on the dances," one secretary wrote home. "[We] average about fifty partners to each dance, of which there are some twenty of an evening. The men all wear hob-nailed shoes and you should see my bruised ankles!"[70] Confronted by overwhelming manpower, the Y improvised new tactics. It concentrated its forces and employed mobility. Mechanized "flying squadrons" of women secretaries and their chaperones converged on ballrooms in coordinated assaults to grapple with the military men.[71]

In retrospect Lewis adjudged neither this aspect of her duty nor her posting along the Mediterranean Sea as the least bit disagreeable. A decade later, in an editorial concerning a memorial in the nation's capital honoring women's world war service, she urged affixing to it a large plaque commemorating the YMCA "heroines who fought the terrible battle of the French Riviera; who night after night went to bed foot-sore and weary from having danced all afternoon and evening; who, from motives of the purest patriotism, gamboled over the beautiful countryside, pleasantly partaking of the beverages for which that region is famous; who, to make the world safe for democracy, met more young men in three months than, ordinarily, they'd have met in three life-times; and who, [in] an inspiring sacrifice for God and country, had a perfectly elegant time."[72]

At her Y counter Sammies—many of whom had seen combat at Château-Thierry, Soissons, Saint-Mihiel, and the Argonne Forest—crowded about her, flaunting "beaucoup souvenirs" and pictures of their stateside sweethearts. They delighted in gabbing with Lewis and her fellow workers and complained

70. Harris, *Service with Fighting Men,* 62; Baldwin, *Canteening Overseas,* 187–88.

71. Harris, *Service with Fighting Men,* 62–63.

72. *N&O,* 11 March 1928.

bitterly about the "Frog girls" (Frenchwomen). Men tarried and buttonholed her, asking about the armistice celebrations back home, as she passed out packages of cigarettes and the line in front of her grew even longer. The country she represented to the men seemed wonderful to her.[73]

Lewis did not exaggerate the overabundance of soldiers expressing romantic interest in her. Although not a *belle dame*, she had wit and vivacity that attracted a deluge of suitors. The mathematics of her setting additionally enhanced her appeal. Indeed, from the moment she set foot in France, she found herself surrounded by admirers, many of them impulsive and effusive. "It's been a long, long time since I've met a girl that so thoroughly captivates me," one love-besotted doughboy wrote to her. "I'm perfectly wild about your eyes—and that merry little laugh. Nobody but that somebody from Raleigh NC could do it." An infatuated sergeant five years younger than she begged forgiveness for having written two times in as many days. "I promise not to do it again," he vowed, pulling himself together, "but I couldn't help it. I wanted so much to be able to speak with you and hear your voice that I had to get it out of my system." He begged for a picture of her and confessed that he "felt weak and caved in" when he thought he might never see her again.[74]

She did not succumb to this flattery and remained true to Chambers, who took leave in Nice in March, writing to his mother, "I am with her every second she is not on duty and if you want to know the truth, we don't do anything but plan the future—not neglecting however to enjoy the present." The two had their pictures taken along an ancient ledge. Chambers cuts a dashing figure, thrusting his hands in his enormous greatcoat's pockets, his overseas cap atilt on his head, and sporting the thin mustache he had grown as a company commander. In her Y cape Lewis—penning a note or verse or perhaps sketching—cocks her head and looks back over her shoulder into the camera, smiling. Both seem very happy. He promised to send copies of the photographs home and reassured his mother about his romance: "It's all very fine, Mums, and I have a great deal to tell you. I am a lucky young man if there ever was one."[75]

73. Nell Battle Lewis, "Behind a 'Y' Counter," March 1919, Nell Battle Lewis Papers, Saint Mary's School Archives; Gavin, *American Women in World War I*, 155.

74. Hugh C. Calhoun to Nell Lewis, 5 January 1919, Edward B. Gordon to Nell Lewis, 1919? KPL Papers.

75. Lenoir Chambers to Grace Chambers, 19 March 1919, LC Papers; NBL scrapbook, 1918–19, KPL Papers.

Their increasingly serious romance did little to dampen Lewis's allure for the Sammies flooding her recreation center. "I was in love with you (and I'm more so now even though you are engaged)," one corporal wrote to her. "Somehow I knew that Lieut Chambers was your fiancé. If I ever see him I shall tell him that he is the luckiest man in the world." In an admittedly "nervy" overture the soldier beseeched the object of his affection for a rendezvous after they returned home. "I had great hopes of seeing you in the States but I suppose you won't let me come to see you. You'll be too busy with the 'wedding probably in early 1920.' Can't I possibly see you before your marriage? Say 'yes' and make me happy."[76]

In "?" a poem written that month in Nice, Lewis contemplated what the future would bring for her and Chambers:

> I wonder what they hold for us,
> Those years ahead we talk about;
> And if a length of common days
> Shall see fires, leaping now, die out;
> And shall I ever find you old,
> And will Time put our dreams to rout.[77]

By late April a wedding seemed very much in the offing for the young lovers. "Both of us want the date fixed with some degree of accuracy so that at the very least it will be a mark to shoot at, and both of us want it to be soon," Chambers wrote to his father. "That's flat—there's no talk there." Dr. Lewis had sent his younger daughter money to purchase items for her trousseau.

Chambers solicited advice from his father. He had just begun to embark on his career as a journalist when the war broke out. He deeply desired to return to Charlotte to work for the *Observer* or the *News*, and he knew he would have to start at the bottom. Was he foolish in contemplating marriage with such an uncertain future? "If I were well enough fixed, I'd marry her just as soon as we got home," he said.

> I've talked a lot about that to Nell. She wants to work herself—after marriage, I mean. "Why not?" she says. "I'm a good stenographer and I can earn enough money anywhere to support myself. Why not work?"

76. Harry Gilrie to NBL, 6 March 1919, KPL Papers.

77. Nell Battle Lewis, "?" March 1919, Nell Battle Lewis Papers, Saint Mary's School Archives.

> And she would do it. She wants to. Of course, people would talk a lot and it might be sometimes embarrassing for me and in one sense a bit humiliating. But that doesn't worry her. What people think about her has never influenced her life to any appreciable extent. "It's the twentieth century," she says, "and why not, why not?" The general idea being to bring nearer the day. "Of course it will be a struggle," she says, "but don't you know you are robbing me if you don't let me share the struggle with you?"[78]

In *Southern Liberal Journalists and the Issue of Race* historian John Kneebone discusses the important role European service during World War I played in expanding the horizons of young southern journalists. Along with Lewis and Chambers, who would one day earn a Pulitzer Prize for distinguished editorial writing for his racial advocacy, a generation of future liberal editors, many of the region's best and brightest, including Gerald Johnson, Louis Jaffé, and Julian Harris, received Continental exposure to ideas and values that they contrasted perforce to those of their region. "At the beginning of their careers," writes Kneebone, "they had gained an awareness of alternatives to the southern way of life."[79]

Almost certainly Europe augmented Lewis's awareness of the capabilities of blacks and other nonwhite racial groups. In the many memoirs of white YMCA secretaries' overseas experiences, exposure to other races receives frequent treatment. Encountering a group of Indian soldiers, one secretary from the American North "found a respect in me growing . . . for these weird black boys" and remarked on the "friendly relationship—the human bond—between these husky Indian lads and their Anglo-Saxon officers." She observed a regiment of "our broadly smiling colored boys" and thought they looked out of place in the French countryside. Renowned orchestra conductor James Europe—"arrayed in shoulder straps and the silver bars of a First Lieutenant!"—marched his "screaming but . . . marvelous band" of "twenty-eight darkies" to her leave center's train station to meet incoming American troops, and the French townspeople went wild over the musicians. Other white secretaries' racial interactions ranged from one young woman's refus

78. Lenoir Chambers to Lenoir Chambers Sr., 24 April 1919, LC Papers.

79. John T. Kneebone, *Southern Liberal Journalists and the Issue of Race, 1920–1944* (Chapel Hill: University of North Carolina Press, 1985), 18–19; Alexander S. Leidholdt, *Editor for Justice: The Life of Louis I. Jaffé* (Baton Rouge: Louisiana University Press, 2002), 80–108; 253–54; Fitzpatrick, *Gerald W. Johnson*, 33–39.

ing to heed the warning of a white southern officer and going alone into a barracks housing black soldiers to lend them her guitar, to another secretary's obdurate enforcement of a canteen policy prohibiting the sale of cigarettes to Indochinese war workers. Even this latter and less-than-heartening incident inserted the secretary into a situation she would never have encountered at home and at the very least made her aware of the Y's discriminatory policies.[80]

France opened Chambers's eyes. He called it "the most civilized and cared-for country" he had ever seen. While in Nice visiting Lewis—perhaps in some instances accompanied by her—he noticed that blacks there enjoyed freedoms unimaginable in the Jim Crow South. "In my hotel lives an American Negro prize-fighter, a fine-looking figure of a man, very well dressed," he related in a letter home. "He eats . . . where I eat sometimes, and he talks very pleasurably and intimately with the French." The multinational and multiracial nature of the Allied troops also impressed him: "Great numbers of them. Every nationality, race, color, and variety of uniform."[81]

Regardless of the liberalizing impact of these sorts of experiences on young southerners such as Lewis and Chambers, traditional racial attitudes prevailed among Americans serving overseas during the Great War. Within the American military bigotry flourished among white soldiers and their officers, a disproportionate percentage of whom claimed Dixie as their birthplace and remained militantly racist. Of the many organizations that sponsored American women's involvement in the war—the American Red Cross, the Army Nurse Corps, the U.S. Army's Signal Corps and Quartermaster Branch, the Salvation Army, and the Quakers—only the YMCA retained a black overseas staff, albeit one that was segregated and woefully under-resourced. Black combat troops, many of whom had surmounted nearly insuperable obstacles to place their lives on the line and prove their mettle, earned accolades from the French soldiers with whom they served but found their courage, intelligence, and morality undermined by a vicious whispering campaign systematized by the AEF's leadership. The overwhelming majority of black recruits found themselves consigned to the Service of Supply, where they performed essential but frequently demeaning work under the direction of white officers. The same pattern held true for the United States Navy, whose secretary, Josephus Daniels, despite his claim that the war would establish a "new

80. Baldwin, *Canteening Overseas*, 36–37, 69, 132; *Red Triangle Girl in France*, 124–25; Shortall, *"Y" Girl in France*, 71–72.

81. Lenoir Chamber to Grace Chambers, 19 July 1918, 19 March 1919, LC Papers.

spirit of universal equality and brotherhood," relegated blacks to assignments as mess attendants, cooks, stewards, and firemen and thus officially rebutted the policy that had existed within the service until the Spanish-American War of not segregating seamen.[82]

Lewis's overseas service exerted other liberalizing effects on her. Working for the YMCA amid and often under the leadership of other capable and energetic women confirmed her ardently held belief in the rich potential of her sex. Her duty, in addition to introducing her to a French culture that featured a comparatively benign posture toward its nonwhite residents, exposed her to American troops with a startlingly diverse array of ethnic and national backgrounds—Polish, Jewish, Italian, Greek, Serbian, Irish, German, and many others. In these ways her European experience broadened her outlook and instilled in her an antipathy toward the intolerance and chauvinism that characterized her native region.[83]

Finally, like so many of the American soldiers who had placed themselves in harm's way in France, she soon grew disillusioned with the jingoism and naïveté that she believed had fueled her nation's entry into the putative war to end war and that had resulted in the deaths of fifty thousand of her countrymen for no advantage she could discern. Her ironic account of her sacrifice in the "terrible battle of the Riviera" to the contrary, the eerie demography she confronted in her host nation, effected by a death rate approaching one in five among *poilus,* and the faces she encountered of the untold *mutilés de la guerre,* their lives inalterably diminished, moved her greatly. Like many of her cohort of liberal journalists, she developed a loathing for what she termed the "patriotic ballyhoo" and the "baloneyous flag-waving" that masked the "horrible, sickening, insane, tragic, devastating, catastrophic, [and] barbarous" nature of warfare.[84]

Having completed a five-month tour in Nice, Lewis—apparently at this

82. Gerald Astor, *The Right to Fight: A History of African Americans in the Military* (Cambridge: Da Capo, 1998), 108–44; Mead, *Doughboys,* 78–79; S.L.A. Marshall, *World War I* (Boston: Houghton Mifflin, 1964), 458–59; Moton, *Finding a Way Out,* 234–65; John Whiteclay Chambers II, ed., *The Oxford Companion to American Military History* (New York: Oxford University Press, 1999), 8; Aptheker, *Documentary History of the Negro People,* 3:212.

83. Mead, *Doughboys,* 74–75.

84. John Keegan, *The First World War* (New York: Alfred A. Knopf, 1999), 423; Kneebone, *Southern Liberal Journalists,* 19; Alex Leidholdt, "Virginius Dabney and Lenoir Chambers: Two Southern Newspaper Editors Face Virginia's Massive Resistance to Public School Integration," *American Journalism* 15, no. 4 (fall 1998): 39; *N&O,* 19 November 1939.

time—traveled to Versailles, where secretaries received their assignment orders. She and other recruits attended briefings in the Hotel Pompadour, which long ago Louis XV had built to accommodate his famous mistress, the Marquise de Pompadour. Lewis relished the incongruity of the Y's convening the "painfully moral . . . gatherings" in which she participated in a site that had once hosted such wickedness. One of the rooms contained a portrait of the monarch's paramour; Lewis could imagine the marquise's lip curling scornfully as she looked down on the prim and industrious women assembled before her.[85]

As the Allies congregated in the storied city for the peace conference and negotiators configured the Treaty of Versailles, she observed a troop of French cavalry in soiled gray-blue uniforms file by slowly and ghostlike in the cold rain. The mournful scene, situated in a setting so rich in history, underscored for her war's folly and the ephemeral nature of life. "Always in my mind they will seem part of the mob of a great and tragic play passing from the stage," she later wrote.[86]

When Lewis's European stint drew near its close and she was awaiting transport home, she worked for several weeks operating a soda fountain in Paris. In July 1919 she boarded the USS *Huron*, an interned German passenger liner, and sailed for Newport News, Virginia. In love and in the prime of life, she enthusiastically anticipated her future. Seeing Virginia's coast emerge on the horizon, she expressed her emotion in a sestet she entitled "From a West Bound Transport":

> Up from the water's edge I see it rise:
> America,—under the summer skies!
> The Promised Land, for which my longing cries!
> My journeyings at end; my wanderings past,—
> God loves the shores on which my oars are cast!
> Let Life fling wide its doors: I am home at last![87]

85. *N&O*, 13 July 1924.

86. *N&O*, 13 July 1924.

87. "Alumnae Notes," July 1919, 378; Nell Battle Lewis, "From a West Bound Transport," July 1919, Nell Battle Lewis Papers, Saint Mary's School Archives.

# 3 A MIND OF HER OWN

Within less than a half-year despondency replaced the optimism with which Lewis had viewed her future upon returning from France. Her love affair with Chambers ended unexpectedly, painfully, and humiliatingly. Neither the Chambers nor the Lewis papers tell the cause of the romance's ending, but two of Lewis's nieces, Lottie Woolen and Martha Stanley—both daughters of Kemp Lewis—recalled discussions they had with Nell Lewis and perhaps other relatives regarding the breakup.

Dr. Lewis reportedly figured prominently in the matter. Nell confided to Stanley that the girl's birth in late December 1919 occurred on the same day that Dr. Lewis "ruined" her aunt's romance. "Her father had decided she had a mental illness," Stanley remembered, and he conveyed his diagnosis to Chambers. Nell's mother, Mary, had ostensibly suffered a "mental breakdown," and Dr. Lewis believed his daughter had inherited his second wife's instability. He apparently concluded that Nell would impart her alleged illness to her offspring or that she lacked the capacity to raise children or perhaps both. The currency of eugenic thought at the time, with its emphasis on selective breeding, may have colored the distinguished physician's deliberations and possibly have shaped the views of other members of Nell's immediate family. Stanley's recollections provide no clue about why Dr. Lewis, who "ruled the roost," would have funded his daughter's purchase of items for a trousseau and soon thereafter have asserted his strong opposition to her marriage.[1] Identifying Chambers by name, Lewis also recounted her disappointment to Woolen, who regarded him as the great love of her aunt's life and surmised that the hurtful breakup had influenced Lewis's attitude toward subsequent intimate relationship with men.[2]

Lewis authored two poems earlier in 1919—one in August and the other in September—that may have alluded to a growing distance between her and Chambers. "And They So Easily Might Have" referenced great romantic heroes such as Leander, Menelaus, and Romeo and humorously imagined them opt-

1. Woolen, interview, 8 May 1992; Leidholdt, *Standing before the Shouting Mob*, 16.

2. Martha Stanley, telephone interview by author, 8 May 1992.

ing not to follow their hearts and letting reason prevail. This caution would have curtailed much heartache and mayhem, the poem concluded:

> But then,—Leander, he got drowned,
> And Romeo had a poisonous thirst,
> And Meny's was a trying siege,—
> *Perhaps* it's better,—"Safety First!"[3]

"Possession," written the following month, featured an entirely different and highly personal tone. The graceful Petrarchan sonnet, in which Lewis declares the perpetuity of her love and somberly considers the possibility of its dismissal, may reflect her introspection at the time:

> You can never go from me: this I know;
> Though all the leagues of space should come between;
> Or, separation thousand-fold more keen,
> Your heart no longer fare where mine might go.
> You shall stay with me always,—I should keep
> So many gifts no dearth could take away,
> So many little gifts of yesterday
> Lying within my heart. Though I should weep
> To lose the living comfort of your hands,
> To know my dearest hopes were all still-born,
> You could not leave me utterly forlorn,
> Nor ever break the memory-woven bands:
> For such possession of you thought should bring,
> Life were less vital than remembering.[4]

Both poems were written several months before the affair ended. If these texts furnish insight into the state of the relationship, they suggest that Chambers had developed reservations about his impending marriage well before breaking up with Lewis.

Although Lewis had informed at least one of her many eager suitors in

3. Nell Battle Lewis, "And They So Easily Might Have," August 1919, Nell Battle Lewis Papers, Saint Mary's School Archives.

4. Nell Battle Lewis, "Possession," September 1919, Nell Battle Lewis Papers, Saint Mary's School Archives.

France of her "engagement" to Chambers, whether the involvement had actually progressed to that point remains uncertain. She may have created an impression of betrothal simply to allay unwanted attention. Chambers's courtly manners and respect for tradition seemingly would have dictated that he abide by contemporary southern social protocol for members of his class and formally petition Dr. Lewis for his daughter's hand in marriage. Perhaps the two principals' overseas war service, the waning influence of parents in the region over their unwed daughters' lives, and the increasing willingness of some young southern women such as Lewis to assert their autonomy precluded or obviated such niceties, but no mention of Lewis's engagement appears in the *Smith Alumnae Quarterly*, which reported on her work in New York and her YMCA service and which meticulously recorded the impending weddings of the college's students and graduates.[5]

Chambers's thoughts and actions regarding the rupture figure entirely as the subject of speculation. Conceivably, Dr. Lewis, one of the foremost medical authorities in the region and an imposing personality, persuaded his daughter's beau of her mental illness. But it seems unlikely that the twenty-eight-year-old Chambers, who had received an unusually advanced education for a southerner, lived in both the cosmopolitan North and France, and served as a company commander in combat, would have accepted Dr. Lewis's diagnosis so uncritically. Chambers's innate courtesy might have dictated that he hear the elder man out, but the returning war veteran would have reached his own conclusions in such a serious matter. His lonely stand many years later as the editor of one of the few white newspapers in the South to support the Supreme Court's mandate racially integrating the region's public schools would attest to his resolute nature and inclination to think for himself.[6]

The chronology surrounding the relationship's unraveling indicates that despite developments that appeared to augur well for the couple's matrimony, Chambers's and Dr. Lewis's enthusiasm for the marriage began to wane shortly after the lovers' stateside return. Chambers almost immediately obtained a position as director of publications at the University of North Carolina and an academic posting there as an assistant professor of journalism. His employment, while not highly remunerative, removed his only expressed reservation

5. Leidholdt, *Standing before the Shouting Mob*, 41–54; Peter Taylor, *The Old Forest and Other Stories* (New York: Picador Press, 1996), 45–46; Smith and Wilson, *North Carolina Women: Making History*, 237; Scott, *Southern Lady*, 212–31; "Alumnae Notes," July 1919, 378.

6. Leidholdt, "Virginius Dabney and Lenoir Chambers," 35–68.

regarding his marriage. Dr. Lewis's strong affection for the university ensured that he would have viewed his future son-in-law's appointment there favorably. The couple's residence in Chapel Hill, which both regarded fondly, would have placed them within a liberal social circle that would generally have endorsed Lewis's desire to seek employment and located her near her family.[7]

Lewis's half brothers must have played some role in the imbroglio. Despite their respect for their father, surely they would have interceded if they believed he had misrepresented Nell's mental condition to Chambers. Did Dick, Kemp, and Ivey have concerns similar to Dr. Lewis's at this time? They may have expressed such views to Chambers. Well into their impressive careers and with detailed knowledge of Nell and her mother, the three brothers could have provided influential testimony.

In the end, however, Chambers almost certainly would have required convincing firsthand evidence of Lewis's instability before ending their romance. He must have observed behavior that concerned him. Her modern ideas troubled her father and may have bothered her brothers—possibly they could have judged her unwillingness to play the Southern Lady as confirming the presence of a disorder—but Chambers found her independence and spirited nature engaging. These attributes, so uncharacteristic of young women in his native region, had attracted him to Lewis, not repelled him. He would not have seen her budding feminism as a manifestation of a disturbed mind.

The meager evidence surrounding the episode allows for only guarded interpretation, but possibly Nell's family—most significantly her father, who had long harbored misgivings regarding his daughter's stability—and Chambers witnessed actions after her return to Raleigh that they perceived as aberrant. The denouement may have occurred after Chambers talked privately with Dr. Lewis while visiting Cloverdale during the Christmas holidays. This scenario conforms closely to Woolen's account and appears consistent with the character and reasoning of the various participants. Contemporary attitudes that regarded mental illness as disgraceful and as a subject discussed reluctantly if at all may have prevented a thorough airing of Lewis's real or imagined problems. Interestingly, Chambers and Lewis retained sporadic and apparently friendly contact for a number of years.[8]

7. Leidholdt, *Standing before the Shouting Mob*, 18; Louis R. Wilson, *The University of North Carolina, 1900–1930: The Making of a Modern University* (Chapel Hill: University of North Carolina Press, 1957), 421.

8. Ruth Draper to Lenoir Chambers, 13 May 1926, Elisabeth Burgess, Norfolk, Va.

When her love affair ended, Lewis sought solace in Christ Church, which she had since childhood regarded ambivalently. She had done so, she later wrote in a personal journal that she kept briefly, because she felt dejected and "was consciously wrong, inferior and unhappy." In "Where I Stand," which appeared in "Incidentally" in January 1926, Lewis recalled her "desperate need, . . . perplexity, and . . . distress" six years earlier.[9]

She found little comfort, however, in the church services she and her family had attended for many years. She quickly grew bewildered by what she perceived as a body of dogmatic theology inextricably linked to the Episcopal Church and to organized Christianity's paternalism, which she believed silenced women. She sought advice from several church members, perhaps including Bishop Cheshire, but none of their answers satisfied her. In her father's study she happened upon one of her mother's books, entitled *The Very Words of Jesus.* As she read, she grew convinced that institutional Christianity no longer represented the meaning of Jesus' teachings. In her journal she recalled, "The Church was . . . for me then the veil of the temple, one which seemed to hide God from me when I wanted with all my heart to find Him." She believed that the militarism displayed by much of organized religion in its support for the recent global conflict had refuted the Gospel: "In failing to denounce the World War . . . the Christian Church was plainly and shamefully false to Jesus Christ."[10]

Lewis considered the notion of basing spiritual belief on Jesus' divinity absurd. "What on earth did it matter to me how Jesus was born, since He lived as He did?" she later declared in a speech to the Raleigh Religious Forum. "Of what significance was it to me whether His bodily resurrection was a fact or a legend when his life had demonstrated the immortality of love?" Many years afterward she wrote in "Incidentally" that during this earlier period she had judged Dr. Lewis's devotion to Christ as tremendously naive: "One might ad-

9. Lewis did not identify the quotation's source, *The Varieties of Religious Experience* by William James, who is regarded by many as the father of modern American psychology. His book, which focused on the psychology of religion, considered individual spiritual experiences as the core of religious life and concluded that some dimensions of consciousness lay beyond the realm of everyday experience. Mitchell, "Nell Battle Lewis," 33; William James, *The Varieties of Religious Experience* (New York: Longmans, Green and Co., 1935), 189; Howard M. Feinstein, *Becoming William James* (Ithaca, N.Y.: Cornell University Press, 1984), 206–7, 214, 241–50; Jacques Barzun, *A Stroll with William James* (New York: Harper & Row, 1983), 14–18; *N&O,* 3 January 1926.

10. Mitchell, "Nell Battle Lewis," 33–34; *N&O,* 23 November 1925; Max Eastman, "The Religion of Patriotism," *Masses* 9, no. 9 (July 1917): 8–12.

mire Jesus, I then thought; one might even consent to worship Him; but how could one possibly 'love' Someone whose earthly career had ended almost two thousand years ago!" Probably early in 1920, Lewis severed her long and conflicted ties to Christ Church. No member of her family had ever even contemplated such a break. Her highly visible estrangement from her father's congregation undoubtedly disturbed and embarrassed the prominent churchman, a consequence that perhaps she consciously or unconsciously desired.[11]

Nell continued to distress Dr. Lewis, whose age and deteriorating health occasionally prevented him from working. His hip had grown more painful and sometimes produced excruciating spasms. Annie Blackwell Lewis had died several years earlier, and the family expected Nell to play a primary role in managing Cloverdale and ministering to her father's needs. One of Annie's relatives, Annie Payne, and others of their kin attempted to insinuate themselves into the household, with an eye toward eventual inheritance. Nell and her brothers regarded these forays dubiously, and Nell bitterly resented Payne, with whom she had had many unpleasant interactions. This unhappy situation compelled Nell to reside at home, although undoubtedly she would have preferred living by herself in Raleigh. The relationship between father and daughter grew increasingly strained, and the two frequently quarreled.[12]

The tension would soon escalate. One day in the summer of 1920, while riding her horse past the *News and Observer* office, Nell impulsively dismounted, entered the building, and asked for a job. Editor R. W. Haywood "seemed a little startled when he saw [my] riding-breeches and boots," she recalled many years later. After she left, he asked managing editor Frank Smethurst incredulously, "Does she always wear 'em?"[13]

Publisher Josephus Daniels soon thereafter announced his appointment of "Miss Nell Battle Lewis, a gifted young woman who has embraced the profession of journalism." He informed his readers that they lived in a "woman's age" and then proceeded to express his enthusiastic support for women's entry into the public sphere. "Woman is to lose nothing of her grace and charm

11. Mitchell, "Nell Battle Lewis," 33–34; Green, "Nell Battle Lewis: Crusading Columnist," 6; *N&O*, 23 November 1925, 3 January 1926, 8 August 1937.

12. "'Cloverdale' as a Haunted House," 24 February 1945? NBL Papers; *N&O*, 31 October 1917; Richard Henry Lewis (hereafter cited as RHL) to KPL, 5 November 1920; Richard Henry Lewis Jr. (hereafter cited as RHL Jr.) to KPL, 6 November 1920; IFL to KPL, 3 December 1920, all in KPL Papers.

13. *N&O*, 15 September 1935, 13 July 1948; Covington, "Interviewing Nell Battle Lewis," 16.

because she is to become an equal partner in governmental housekeeping," he wrote. Daniels believed that "the acquisition of Miss Lewis as an editorial writer would enable [the *News and Observer*] to lead along new paths of progress" and to become "a true exponent and evangel of the New Day."[14]

Lewis began work in July, likely serving as the *News and Observer*'s only female staff reporter. Her sex and unabashed feminism undoubtedly provided her with an entrée into North Carolina's burgeoning suffrage community, headquartered in Raleigh's Yarborough Hotel and galvanized over the glorious possibility that the state that summer would become the thirty-sixth to ratify the Nineteenth Amendment and thus secure women's right to vote. (The cub reporter undoubtedly knew many of the key figures in the North Carolina Equal Suffrage League headed by Gertrude Weil. The diminutive Weil, the forty-year-old daughter of a prominent Jewish family in Goldsboro, had graduated from Smith College—the first North Carolinian to do so—and served as the most prominent leader among the state's organized women. Weil recalled that Lewis, before assuming her position with the newspaper, had joined the organization and would "hang around" its headquarters, enthusiastically waiting to run errands.) The heady times notwithstanding, the league comported itself with dignity and restraint. Lewis later sardonically observed, "It may be that a few parades, some heckling, a smashed window or two and a little arson here and there would have made more impression."[15]

Although suffrage opponents concocted many outlandish arguments against the amendment—such as the claim that it would "masculinize" women, "feminize "men," and lead to "organized female nagging forever!"—states' rights and white supremacy provided the antisuffragists with their most powerful themes, according to historian Anastatia Sims. Federal meddling with the region's restrictive voting laws would not only enable black women to vote but would also reopen the polls to black men. "We plead in the Name of Virginia Dare, that North Carolina Remain White," one broadside beseeched its readers.[16]

Lewis relished her many "amusing experiences" covering the Southern

14. *N&O*, July? 1920.

15. Powell, *Dictionary of North Carolina Biography*, 6:153–54; Sims, *Power of Femininity*, 183; Linda Williams Sellars, "South Saver: Nell Battle Lewis in the 1920s" (master's thesis, University of North Carolina, 1984), 15; Green, "Nell Battle Lewis: Crusading Columnist," 25; Smith and Wilson, *North Carolina Women*, 259; *N&O*, 25 July 1920, 10 May 1925.

16. Sims, *Power of Femininity*, 177–78.

Women's Rejection League. She evidently made little effort to conceal her derisive attitude toward the organization at its headquarters in the Hotel Raleigh. During a visit there, she later recalled, "One of the anti-suffrage leaders [apparently a friend and St. Mary's alumna], knowing that I had betrayed the faith of my fathers by wanting to vote, looked at me sadly, sighed deeply, and said, 'Anyway, you were BORN a lady!' My subsequent complete degeneration, however, was clear."[17]

Lewis's initial reporting efforts must have immediately impressed Smethurst, because on 13 August she found herself reporting news and making history in the House of Representatives press box in the state capitol. "New Figure Appears at House Press Table" and "Woman Reporter Behaves Better than Old Timers," a *News and Observer* head and subhead read. Lewis's attendance at Governor Thomas W. Bickett's speech to the legislature, in which he tepidly endorsed the equal suffrage amendment on the grounds of its "inevitable" passage, raised eyebrows during a sweltering special session of the General Assembly. No woman had occupied a seat in the box since the building's construction eighty-two years earlier. "The woman—dapper young lady, to be a little less conventional, with the thought of this New Freedom—was Miss Nell Battle Lewis, a full-fledged member of the staff of the *News and Observer*," the story read. "When it was all over, she walked out of the hall with notes and pencil in her skirt pocket, and, just like any other human being, came to the office and put her impressions down in the shape of food for a battery of hungry linotypes."[18]

Despite the inclusion of suffrage planks in the platforms of North Carolina's Democratic and Republican parties, President Wilson's lobbying efforts, and the forceful support of Josephus Daniels and his peers at virtually all the state's newspapers, many Tar Heel solons tried desperately to torpedo the initiative. Four days after Bickett's speech, the Senate, after rancorous debate, narrowly voted to postpone considering the amendment. The dejection of suffrage forces, however, turned to jubilation the very next day, when "woman suffrage" became the law of the land.[19]

"On August 18, 1920, it was quite a sensation to be a young southern woman

17. Sims, *Power of Femininity*, 177, 183; *N&O*, 10 May 1925; Stoops, *Heritage*, 229.

18. *N&O*, 14 August 1920, 10 May 1925; Sellars, "South Saver," 15.

19. Smith and Wilson, *North Carolina Women: Making History*, 218; Sims, *Power of Femininity*, 176–77, 184–85; Albert Coates, *By Her Own Bootstraps: A Saga of Women in North Carolina* (n.p., 1975), 148–49; *N&O*, 15 August 1920, 10 May 1925.

just slapped in the face by her State," Lewis remembered. "To come out of a session of the North Carolina legislature, an assembly by which only yesterday one had been made to realize acutely in how small esteem women are held in this State, to walk down Fayetteville Street in the heat of that terrible August and to hear at the post office corner a newsboy's cry that was like a song, "Tennessee's ratified." Something went over me like a cool shower. I thought of the Old Southern Gentlemen in North Carolina who had so chivalrously protected me from the ballot. They made me laugh out loud!"[20]

The time commitment, night work, and travel demanded by Nell Lewis's new job worried and sometimes angered her brothers and father. "I have been thinking a great deal about the situation at Cloverdale, and I think it is very unsatisfactory," Kemp Lewis, who managed Erwin Mills in Durham, North Carolina, wrote to his father in September. "I think that Nell's method of living is not only improper, but highly dangerous. I think it is extremely risky for her to come home late at night, and I would not be surprised any time to hear some distressing news in connection with same." Kemp also voiced concern that she had chosen a bedroom upstairs, far from her father's in the isolated estate, and that her duties at the paper prevented her from providing him with companionship.[21]

Although Nell made an effort to pacify her family by moving into a room closer to Dr. Lewis's a few days later, the situation at Cloverdale stayed tense. In early November, when she had traveled overnight to report on a meeting of the state Federation of Women's Clubs in nearby Henderson, Kemp received a letter from his father implicating his daughter in the discord and alleging her instability. "Nell is the main trouble," he confided. "She is as you also [know] very abnormal and eccentric." The elder Lewis cautioned his middle son not to confront his sister but to interact with her "with as much clarity and patience . . . as possible and avoid an outbreak." Offering advice would only worsen matters because "Nell resents any suggestions from outside and frequently from me, and I want to preserve the peace as far as possible."[22]

That same day Dick Lewis, who managed a cotton mill in Oxford, North Carolina, met with Nell in Henderson as he traveled to Cloverdale to assess its condition. She expressed concern for their father's health and her willingness to quit her job in order to devote full attention to overseeing the house-

20. *N&O,* 10 May 1925.

21. KPL to RHL, 13 September 1920, KPL Papers.

22. RHL to KPL, 5 November 1920, KPL Papers.

hold. Dick disclosed to Kemp, however, his opinion that "her talk to me is entirely out of line with her actions, and no reliance can be put in it." When Dick arrived at the farm he found a "deplorable" state of affairs. Moreover, he learned from Dr. Lewis that Nell avoided and neglected him and practiced a disconcerting level of independence. "She pays no attention to Father," the oldest Lewis son wrote, "except when absolutely necessary, is now refusing to accept any money from him, won't take her allowance, won't let him have her car fixed, or do anything at all for her." Only a "disordered mental state" could explain her disposition toward the head of their family. Dick felt "very sorry [for his sister], for she is not responsible for her actions."[23]

Kemp responded to the letter two days later. He suggested hiring a male nurse. The medical background of the employee would allow him to care for the infirm Dr. Lewis and enable the attendant to withstand Nell's "behavior and probable abuse." "She is evidently insane," he continued, "and the mental attitude of the man would have to be that she is sick and must be endured." The missive also contained an ambiguous sentence that may have referred to a time in the past when Nell had been institutionalized for mental illness: "I personally do not think [she] will be out of the asylum but just a little while."[24]

After Dr. Lewis received an invitation from Kemp to reside with his family, the elderly physician conveyed his deep gratitude but emphasized that he hoped to live in his own house as long as circumstances would permit. He had resolved, however, that if Nell continued "to be as ugly as she has been for quite a while," he would "not submit to it any longer." He would provide his daughter with a "liberal allowance," break up his household, and move in with one of his sons. "The question of Nell is a most difficult one," he agreed. "She is my daughter—unfortunately of a very abnormal character and I can't run her off."[25]

In late November Ivey weighed in on the dilemma. In a letter to Kemp the distinguished University of Virginia biologist characterized his half sister as "insane." Ivey's wife, Margie, had recently visited Dr. Lewis and believed her father-in-law would die within the year as a result of "Nell's bad behavior." Ivey deplored the declining state of affairs at Cloverdale: "I can't imagine how they are getting on at night, with nobody to put on the fuel and keep the fire going." He felt that the three brothers should tell Nell "to behave or get out" and

23. RHL Jr. to KPL, 6 November 1920, KPL Papers.

24. KPL to RHL, 8 November 1920, KPL Papers.

25. RHL to KPL, 12 November 1920, KPL Papers.

expressed his frustration that their father prohibited any discussion with Nell that might lead to a confrontation.[26]

Did Lewis suffer from mental illness? She may have believed so; during this period she purchased and "devoured" many books on psychoanalysis. Her conduct and emotional state perhaps suggested manic depression, possibly bipolar II disorder. The feelings of inadequacy, confusion, and sadness she experienced in the aftermath of her failed romance, if prolonged, might have signaled the onset of clinical depression. Psychosocial stressors such as a failed love affair often trigger episodes of this sort. Her subsequent behavior, including the spontaneity and exuberance she displayed in examining the role religion played in her life, applying for a reporting job at the *News and Observer*, and carrying out her journalistic responsibilities—in conjunction with her purported argumentativeness, refusal to accept her father's assistance, and unwillingness to discuss Cloverdale's deteriorating conditions—possibly indicated hypomania, a muted form of manic disorder. Among people suffering from bipolar II disorder the overwhelming majority experience hypomania immediately preceding or following a major depression. The euphoria associated with bipolar II does not significantly diminish one's functioning.[27]

People with manic depression—estimated today at about two million Americans—may make rash decisions, but they also frequently exhibit exhilaration, passion, and heightened confidence and productivity, characteristics often associated with creativity. According to one psychological authority, artists display rates of bipolar disorder by a magnitude of ten to forty times that of the general population. Painter Vincent Van Gogh, poet Sylvia Plath, and writer Virginia Woolf suffered from various forms of this illness. Manic depression usually begins in the late teens or early twenties and disproportionately affects people in higher-than-average socioeconomic groups and with advanced educations.[28]

Bipolar II disorder constitutes a relatively new diagnosis, but clinicians and researchers began to develop a modern understanding of what they termed "manic-depressive psychoses" in the waning years of the nineteenth century. Dr. Lewis, as a result of his professional reading, public health leadership, and close friendship with his medical partner, Kemp Plummer Battle, who had

26. IFL to KPL, 28 November 1920, KPL Papers.

27. *N&O*, 29 May 1927; Dianne Hales and Robert E. Hales, *Caring for the Mind: The Comprehensive Guide to Mental Health* (New York: Bantam Books, 1995), 96–115.

28. Hales and Hales, *Caring for the Mind*, 96–115.

served an internship at Blackwell's Island Insane Asylum in New York, probably exercised a basic grasp of the symptoms and etiology of the disease, which contemporary specialists then with considerable accuracy "supposed to be hereditary taint." Dr. Lewis may earlier have observed signs of the illness in his daughter, as perhaps he had in her mother. This may further explain his intervention in Nell's relationship with Chambers.[29]

Although Lewis's family genuinely and uniformly believed that she suffered from mental illness, an alternative interpretation of the fragmentary evidence regarding her psychology and actions during this period could easily construe the distress she experienced over the ending of her love affair as normal and her subsequent behavior as natural in light of her nontraditional views regarding women's capabilities and roles. Her collegiate education, residence in New York City, and overseas experience had buttressed her innate independence, strengthened her confidence, and inevitably set her in conflict with her conservative family. The initiative and agency she displayed in obtaining her job and succeeding at it and her willingness to assert herself could represent strength of character and soundness of mind. And the disregard and occasional anger she directed at her father could understandably have resulted from his prejudicial stereotyping of women, meddling in her romance, and what she regarded as antiquated religious beliefs that had long stifled her freedom. The expectation of her family that she should subordinate her intelligence and talent and compliantly assume the roles of caretaker and dutiful daughter could have provoked wholly warranted outbursts by Lewis.

An interplay of these two possibilities could also account for Lewis's behavior. The chauvinism she encountered in her interaction with her family and throughout her native region may have exacerbated her purported instability. Certainly, the mores and doctrine that circumscribed women's roles in her homeland impelled her to contest with growing vitality the injustice she encountered and would provide her with plenty of grist as she began her journalistic career.

In interviews and biographical materials Lewis described her early duties at the *News and Observer* as general news reporting, feature and editorial writing, and—after she had accrued about a year's experience—editing the society

29. Hales and Hales, *Caring for the Mind*, 99–101; William A. White, *The Outlines of Psychiatry* (Washington, D.C.: Nervous and Mental Disease Publishing Co., 1932), 147.

page. For unknown reasons she neglected to mention that one of her initial responsibilities included writing and illustrating a children's page, "A Corner for Kiddies," which required great energy and creativity and depicted many of the often incongruous influences that resided within her. The inaugural edition appeared in the Sunday paper on 18 July 1920. On company letterhead Lewis printed an open letter written in verse to the "Kids Who Take the N. & O.," in which she cleverly introduced her page.[30]

She could not resist politicizing even her premiere edition. The fledgling journalist abruptly introduced the subject of Woodrow Wilson, who was then convalescing from a severe stroke and devoting virtually all of his diminished mental abilities and political influence toward making the 1920 presidential election a referendum on the Treaty of Versailles, which included his proposal for the League of Nations Covenant. Lewis dubbed him "The Greatest Man in the World." He deserved this title, she declared, because "he doesn't want there ever to be another war, when people's fathers and brothers and uncles and cousins get killed, and so he has thought of a Way to End War if people will only agree to it." In addition to showcasing her pacifist leanings, this "Corner" also displayed a progressive bent. Children learned of an outdoor camp and an adjacent hospital that philanthropists sponsored to provide sick urban "tots" and their "tired mothers" with fresh air and medical care.[31]

On this page, however, as on many that would follow, a paean to all things Tar Heel claimed the predominant role. A section entitled "Your Own State" sang the praises of her birthplace: "You all know . . . that North Carolina is the best State in the whole union. If you don't, ask anybody—in the State—and see if he, she or it doesn't tell you so. Everybody really thinks so, but those folks who aren't lucky enough to live in North Carolina just don't like to admit it."[32]

Despite her modernism, she espoused chauvinism and glorified the Lost Cause, especially extolling the courage displayed in their youth by "those fine old gentlemen in gray uniforms who live out at [Raleigh's] Soldiers Home." "I want to tell you something right now, that you must never forget," she catechized her youthful readers in "Tar Heels." "There never was another army in the whole world that fought more bravely than the Confederate Army, and the North Carolinians were just about the bravest of all the Confederate soldiers:

30. *N&O*, 18 July 1920.
31. *N&O*, 18 July 1920.
32. *N&O*, 18 July 1920.

they just wouldn't run away, no matter how many Yankee soldiers they had to fight with."[33]

"A Corner for Kiddies" abruptly departed from the paper after October. It returned in January 1921 and appeared erratically and in an abbreviated form until the summer of 1921, when it disappeared entirely. Lewis's waning enthusiasm for the page may have stemmed from the lack of feedback she received from readers. Perhaps she grew to believe that "Corner" had failed to attract a sizable audience.[34]

Working at the paper during this time "was like having your hand on the pulse of the State," Lewis remembered many years later. "The more you learned about North Carolina, the more interesting it became." For the young reporter women's increasing participation in public life became the most intriguing story. In her initial bylined articles she focused on her own experience casting a ballot in the November 1920 election and shared her perceptions about other women voting. She reported on the members of her sex pursuing higher education at Greensboro's North Carolina College for Women and at the University of North Carolina. And she profiled women leaders such as Harriet Morehead Berry, who headed the state's good roads movement.[35]

After completing about a year's service with the *News and Observer*, Lewis assumed responsibility for the society page. She loathed every moment of her six-month stint as "sassiety editress," as she sometimes referred to her new title. Her duties included writing about teas, weddings, and women's meetings. She also maintained a social calendar and compiled on a daily basis a daunting array of information, including the identities of North Carolina residents staying at the capital city's four major hotels and persons traveling to and from Raleigh. Some of these details came from correspondence, personal interviews at the paper, and the telephone calls she fielded for an hour each afternoon and evening, but she also journeyed to hotel desks and attempted to decipher their guest registers (misspelled cognomens undoubtedly prompted complaints from indignant readers), and she "worked the trains" at Union Station, collecting the names and particulars of passengers coming and going.[36]

Lewis wrote a feature article in June 1921 entitled "On the Limitless Scope

33. *N&O*, 10 October 1920.

34. Sellars, "South Saver," 23; see, e.g., *N&O*, 25 July, 1, 8, and 15 August, and 3 October 1920.

35. *N&O*, 15 September 1935; Sellars, "South Saver," 21.

36. *N&O*, 4 and 11 May 1924, 4 September 1932; Sellars, "South Saver," 25.

of a Real Society Page," in which she revealed the monotonous nature of much of what she covered. She bemoaned the fact that regardless of a woman journalist's ambitions and talents, she invariably found herself assigned to the society page: "She may demur, protest, balk, renig, rave, and even flatly refuse, but I assure you that if she stays on the paper, she will inevitably end by recounting the doings 'In The Social Realm.'" Male colleagues strongly believe that "it is HER PLACE, and there's an end of it. It belongs to her sex as indivisibly as her skirt. She wears one, then she writes the other."[37]

Acclaimed writer and witty social observer Florence King, who served a tour of duty in the *News and Observer*'s Woman's Department in the 1960s, devoted a chapter of *Southern Ladies and Gentlemen* to chronicling her many travails at the paper, interacting with "debs," "honorees," brides, and their often vexatious mothers. Undoubtedly, Lewis's work on the society page faced the same intense and sometimes tearful scrutiny from the "southern gynecocracy" as King's underwent four decades later.[38]

On 7 September 1921 there appeared on the society page several hundred words under a small boxhead that read "'Incidentally' By N.B.L." This addition, Lewis later observed, "was really incidental to my main job of editing the society page, a job that came nearer to putting me in my grave from sheer boredom than anything else I ever did. To save myself from such untimely extinction, I began to write every day a few paragraphs for my own diversion." The Miles-Elmore wedding announcement perhaps drove Lewis to distraction that day. "Then came the bride on the arm of her father," Lewis wrote, "never looking more beautiful than in her wedding gown of blue duveltyn, trimmed with squirrel, hat and [gloves] to match."[39]

The opening sentence in the inaugural "Incidentally" reinforced a hurtful racial stereotype that would not have pleased the capital city's blacks: "If a 'furrener' had reached Raleigh for the first time yesterday about noon, and had formed a conception of the South from picture post-cards showing Negroes sticking grinning teeth into crimson watermelons, he would have had that conception immediately confirmed." Lewis went on to describe how "a dusky belle" and two dusky male companions sitting on Nash Square's lawn had made short work of their meal. "Peace, perfect peace shone from three dark countenances, and radiated with the heat that blistered the Square. White

37. *N&O*, June? 1921; Sellars, "South Saver," 23–24.

38. Florence King, *Southern Ladies and Gentlemen* (New York: St. Martin's Press, 1975), 107–26.

39. *N&O*, 7 September 1921, 13 June 1948.

teeth gleamed at intervals over the succulent fruit. Contented laughter broke forth frequently, and the red meat of the melon disappeared rapidly."[40]

For the next several months "Incidentally," at first under Lewis's initials but soon beneath her full name, appeared as a peripheral item in single column form on the society page. Although in her early commentaries she did not hesitate to satirize pretense, skewer social evils and backwardness, and celebrate women's accomplishments, she also expressed her deep love for the simplicity of her native state and the folkways of the traditional South. Often intensely personal, "Incidentally" revealed much about its author's upbringing and thinking and the sometimes conflicting influences that resided within her.[41]

Later that September Lewis lampooned the metastasizing Ku Klux Klan, which had recently resurrected itself with the aid of practitioners of the modern sciences of public relations and advertising. The organization's beguiling fraternity, nativism, and rituals had already induced a hundred thousand members of a nation of joiners to surrender ten-dollar initiation fees. In a few short years five million "one hundred percent Americans" would pledge allegiance to the hooded empire. In "Kweer Kustomers" she employed doggerel to lampoon the Kluxers' weird alliterative idiom:

Kourageous Ku Klux Knights Konfer
On English words, and, Kareless
  flout 'em;
And Konduct of that Kind doth
  Kause
The Kritic to write verse about 'em.

Continuing in this vein, Lewis mocked the society's hostility to criticism, its secrecy, and its racial violence and declared her hope that a powerful series of investigative reports by the *New York World* would "put a Kwick, Komplete Kwietus" to the Klan. Clever parodies on the society page, however, had next to no impact in stifling the growth of the order. In the next few years it would spread quickly and quietly throughout the state. Raleigh and the surrounding area became a center of Klan activity, and many prominent citizens joined the organization. A popular newly elected Superior Court judge, Henry A. Grady,

40. *N&O*, 7 September 1921.
41. *N&O*, 4 September 1932.

emerged as North Carolina's Grand Dragon and the likely heir apparent to Imperial Wizard William J. Simmons.[42]

Lewis may have deplored the bigotry that lay behind the Klan, but in an early column she expressed paternalistic ambivalence regarding the South's evolving racial relations. "The years are cementing the friendship between the races among liberal minded persons of both," she wrote, "but the newer days necessarily produce a different type of negro, as they produce a different type of white." She nostalgically recalled the deference and loyalty an elderly black servant, born into slavery, had displayed toward the Lewises many years ago. And she expressed pride in the fact that a "mammy" had nursed her and her three brothers during their childhoods. She believed black leaders in the present era should strive to build on the good relations an earlier generation of blacks had developed with whites.[43]

That winter Lewis applauded the inclusion of nine North Carolina women in a recently released edition of *Who's Who in America.* The publication included notable figures such as Sallie Southall Cotten, a founder of the state's club movement, which had helped train a cadre of remarkable women leaders; Jane Simpson McKimmon, a home economist who had established an impressive network of women ministering to families' nutritional and health needs; and Lucy Henderson Owen Robertson, the first woman president of the Greensboro Female College. Lewis expressed her hope that another luminary would soon be added to this "glittering constellation": Kate Burr Johnson, the recently appointed state commissioner of public welfare, who had previously headed the North Carolina Federation of Women's Clubs and directed the state's Division of Child Welfare. Lewis and Johnson had established a warm friendship, and the columnist had begun to direct her attention increasingly toward the State Board of Charities and Public Welfare's pioneering work in caring for what one official publication later termed the "unfortunate elements of the State's population."[44]

42. *N&O,* 24 September 1921; David M. Chalmers, *Hooded Americanism: The First Century of the Ku Klux Klan, 1865–1965* (Garden City, N.Y.: Doubleday & Co., 1965), 32, 92–97; Nancy MacLean, *Behind the Mask of Chivalry: The Making of the Second Ku Klux Klan* (New York: Oxford University Press, 1994), 5; *New York World,* 5 and 19 September 1921; Jeffrey Alan Van Dyke, "Bedsheets and Broadsheets: Covering the Ku Klux Klan in North Carolina" (master's thesis, University of North Carolina, 1986), 28–31.

43. *N&O,* 4 November 1921.

44. Smith and Wilson, *North Carolina Women: Making History,* 180, 201–4, 221, 250–53, 335; A. R. Newsome, comp., *North Carolina Manual, 1929* (Raleigh: North Carolina Historical Commis-

Angry over the General Assembly's refusal to ratify the Nineteenth Amendment and determined to capitalize on their new political power, suffragists, led by Gertrude Weil, in 1920 remodeled the Equal Suffrage League of North Carolina into the North Carolina League of Women Voters. The new association had two primary goals: to educate women on political issues and to implement social reforms that would result in the development of girls' reformatories, improvements in the conditions of prisoners, and protections for women and child workers. A year earlier, to coordinate the progressive activities and lobbying efforts of the state's principal women's organizations, Weil's compatriots—most notably Cornelia Petty Jerman, who had received exposure to the American North during her study at the New England Conservatory of Music and whom Josephus Daniels dubbed "The State's First Woman"—had created the Legislative Council of North Carolina Women.[45]

Although Johnson's appointment in 1921 as the board's first female commissioner marked an important early accomplishment for members of her sex in the post-suffrage era (no other woman had risen to such a high administrative position in North Carolina or had held a similar title throughout the United States), the contretemps surrounding her installment confirmed that men's attitudes would not change easily. In an attempt to circumvent widespread political head choppings, the state's solons had nervously promised to designate Johnson as commissioner. "They were scared to death of what women with the vote might do," she told historian Anne Firor Scott many years later. Despite their bargain, the governor and the assembly appointed and confirmed Johnson only reluctantly. One representative condescendingly remarked, "Well, we might as well put her in; she's pretty and won't give us any trouble." Scott observed that this "forecast was inaccurate"; the new commissioner "soon stood high on the legislature's list of troublemakers."[46]

The legislature had provided the board with an extensive purview: to inspect and report on penal and charitable institutions, study social problems

---

sion, 1929), 152–60; *N&O*, 31 January 1922; A. Laurance Aydlett, "The North Carolina State Board of Public Welfare," *North Carolina Historical Review* 24, no. 1 (January 1947): 20.

45. Smith and Wilson, *North Carolina Women: Making History*, 218–19, 260; Sims, *Power of Femininity*, 51; *N&O*, 24 May 1925.

46. Scott, *Southern Lady*, 207, 263; Anne Firor Scott, "After Suffrage: Southern Women in the Twenties," *Journal of Southern History* 30, no. 1 (February 1964): 304–5; Powell, *Dictionary of North Carolina Biography*, 3:295–96; Smith and Wilson, *North Carolina Women: Making History*, 335; Aydlett, "North Carolina State Board of Public Welfare," 20–25; *N&O*, 17 May 1925.

and recommend related legislation, advance the welfare of dependent and neglected children, license child-caring institutions, oversee the treatment of the mentally ill, and—very significantly—appoint and supervise county boards of charities and public welfare and approve by certificate the election of county welfare superintendents, who acted as the state board's local representatives.[47]

Lewis found herself drawn to assist her friend with her challenging assignment and in 1922 accepted a position as the board's publicity director. (She also performed similar duties at about this time for a range of women's organizations, including the League of Women Voters, the Federation of Women's Clubs, and the Legislative Council.) For the next two years she served in this capacity while continuing her employment at the *News and Observer*. Working alongside Johnson, Lewis recalled, "was to have part in an experiment in feminism new in North Carolina, a radical experiment, most old-timers thought." Headquartered in the board's offices atop a drugstore near the Capitol, Lewis attempted to educate North Carolinians about her organization's activities and accomplishments and fielded requests for information. She often found it easy to have the reports she authored reprinted in newspapers around the state. Johnson rarely shrank from controversy, and "not infrequently she was front page stuff."[48]

Soon after assuming her position with the board, Lewis had expressed in "Incidentally" the ambivalence she felt about serving in organizations staffed solely by female personnel. In "Working with Women" she constructed a discussion between two imaginary figures regarding the merits of sex segregation. According to the exchange, in women's organizations the Southern Lady vanished, and men's chivalry did not distract from the tasks at hand: "No unmerited halo of mid-Victorian manufacture is placed upon your blushing brow, nor does any fellow worker vainly attempt to make you feel that your presence in a place of business is suffered only because of some large humanitarianism and unparalleled forbearance with the unfortunate. Sex consciousness goes briskly by the boards, and you have the privilege of forgetting completely at times that you are a woman; and of enjoying instead the sneaking

47. Aydlett, "North Carolina State Board of Public Welfare," 18–19; Newsome, *North Carolina Manual, 1929*, 152–53; Samuel Huntington Hobbs Jr., *North Carolina: Economic and Social* (Chapel Hill: University of North Carolina Press, 1930), 296–306.

48. *N&O*, 4 September 1932, 15 September 1935; Green, "Nell Battle Lewis: Crusading Columnist," 25–26.

suspicion that in spite of hairpins, you are pretty nearly a human being."[49] But in a column just a few days later Lewis, writing in her own voice as one of a tiny handful of female journalists working in the region's hyper-masculine newsrooms, undercut her earlier ascertainment: "This thing of working with women,—well, I dunno!"[50]

Historian Darden Asbury Pyron maintained that Lewis's conflicted feelings reflected contemporary divisions, including those among feminists, regarding whether women and men differed fundamentally or merely culturally in superficial ways. Pyron observed that during the first half of the 1920s Lewis ruminated about whether separatism might pose a partial answer to women's social and political problems. She vacillated frequently on the topic during this period.[51]

Lewis's musing over the strengths and weaknesses of sex segregation in facilitating women's advancement had no effect on her work with the board. She passionately fulfilled her new duties. The board faced difficult obstacles in convincing the state's citizens and politicians to support the expansion of resources necessary for its progressive undertaking. Many new welfare workers required hiring and training, and voters viewed any expansion of government infrastructure or increase in state powers suspiciously.[52]

By the middle of 1922 forty-six of North Carolina's one hundred counties had full-time welfare superintendents; part-time staff or school superintendents served as welfare heads in the remaining localities. Although this administrative system represented an improvement over what had previously existed, Lewis wrote in an article in the *Journal of Social Forces* that Johnson believed state resources and facilities remained "sadly" deficient, particularly in regard to children's welfare. The commissioner advocated "adequate child-caring institutions, whole-time superintendents of public welfare in every county, efficient juvenile court and probation service and the support of intelligent public opinion behind the child welfare program."[53]

The following year the legislature—at Johnson's behest—enacted a moth-

49. *N&O*, 22 November 1922.

50. *N&O*, 26 November 1922.

51. Pyron, "Nell Battle Lewis," 71–72.

52. Aydlett, "North Carolina State Board of Public Welfare," 20–22.

53. Aydlett, "North Carolina State Board of Public Welfare," 22; Nell Battle Lewis, "North Carolina Conference for Social Service," *Journal of Social Forces* 1, no. 3 (1 March 1923): 267.

er's aid law that called for state matching of county contributions to enable women deprived of their husbands' support to raise their children in their own homes. During roughly the same period the board worked with the General Assembly to provide for the treatment of tubercular prisoners at the state sanitarium and to establish reform schools for delinquent white and black boys. Johnson and her allies further recommended construction of a farm colony for women inmates, elimination of flogging and the confinement of prisoners to dark cells, increased regulatory power for the board's oversight of county jails, employment of matrons to supervise women's wards, and the abolition of the convict lease system. The state soon adopted many of these reforms.[54]

Not all of Johnson's efforts met with success. In 1923 North Carolina's League of Women Voters, Federation of Women's Clubs, and Young Women's Christian Association had debated asking the U.S. Department of Labor to conduct a survey examining the conditions under which the state's more than 150,000 women industrial workers discharged their duties. No systematic study had yet explored their welfare. Deciding, however, that powerful Tar Heel industrialists would upend such an endeavor by berating it as an intrusion on sacrosanct states' rights, the women requested that the state Child Welfare Commission manage the investigation. Not surprisingly, this agency administered the only two already-existing laws pertaining to women industrial workers: one requiring seats for female employees and the other mandating separate toilets for sexes and races.[55]

Johnson served as the ex officio chair of the commission, which also included two male directors, the superintendent of public instruction and the secretary of the state board of health. Another man, executive secretary E. Frank Carter, oversaw the body's day-to-day activities. The survey's proponents regarded Carter dubiously. He had for many years worked in the textile industry, and the mill owners had figured prominently in his appointment to his present position. Lewis termed him a "creature of the manufacturers." The

54. Aydlett, "North Carolina State Board of Public Welfare," 22–24; Newsome, *North Carolina Manual, 1929*, 155; Lewis, "North Carolina Conference for Social Service," 266; "Summary of Kate Burr Johnson's Accomplishments as Commissioner of State Board of Charities and Public Welfare," 1924? Kate Ancrum Burr Johnson Papers, Joyner Library, East Carolina University.

55. NBL, "Bucking the North Carolina Mill Owners," 1926? NBL, "Summary of the Efforts of the Organized Women of N.C. to Secure a Survey of Women in Industry in That State," 1927? both in NBL Papers; Newsome, *North Carolina Manual, 1929*, 160.

state's organized women believed he lacked the education and experience to oversee the study.[56]

Despite the fact that the commission publicly endorsed the need for the survey, it failed to follow through, claiming it lacked funds. Carter matter-of-factly clipped a paragraph from his biennial report, pasted it to a blank sheet of paper, and announced to the women that he had provided them with all the information they requested. Johnson seethed. The inflamed relations between her and the superintendent of public instruction and the secretary of the state board of health, who shared Carter's esteem for unregulated capitalism, became increasingly contentious as the two men repeatedly impeded investigation of the working conditions in the state's factories and mills.[57]

In July 1926 Johnson—having refused to allow Carter to supervise the survey of women industrial workers, which undoubtedly would have resulted in a whitewash of the manufacturers, and frustrated by her exclusion from the many meetings between the superintendent of public instruction, the secretary of the state board of health, and Governor Angus W. McLean—resigned her chairmanship of the Child Welfare Commission. In a letter appearing in the *News and Observer*'s "People's Forum," Lewis rebuked the governor for implying that Johnson had abdicated her position out of "caprice." Had the commissioner "acted otherwise, she would have been derelict in her plain duty which I have never known her to be." Given the state's refusal to carry out a legitimate examination, the columnist now advanced the controversial recommendation that the Women's Bureau of the Federal Department of Labor conduct the inquiry. This proposal undoubtedly set the teeth of North Carolina's mill owners on edge. Lewis presciently warned the manufacturers that the "retribution for [their recalcitrance] is not necessarily swift, but it is always sure. We shall pay for this eventually, we may be certain. And we shall be fortunate if in time we do not pay for it with industrial disorders that will rock the foundations of this State."[58]

56. NBL, "Bucking the North Carolina Mill Owners," 1926? NBL, "Summary of the Efforts of the Organized Women of N.C. to Secure a Survey of Women in Industry in That State," 1927? both in NBL Papers; *N&O*, 20 July 1926, 23 January 1927.

57. NBL, "Bucking the North Carolina Mill Owners," 1926? NBL, "Summary of the Efforts of the Organized Women of N.C. to Secure a Survey of Women in Industry in That State," 1927? both in NBL Papers.

58. *N&O*, 20 July 1926.

Lewis clipped "The People's Forum" from the newspaper and forwarded it to McLean, whose impressive background in the private sector had included founding three textile mills. Embarrassed by the publicity surrounding his principled public servant's resignation, the governor emphasized in a letter to Lewis his support for Johnson: "Among us, we must manage in some way to let the State of North Carolina know that absolutely the only thing that the politicians have against Mrs. Johnson is that she has consistently refused to allow her decisions to be influenced by political considerations."[59]

In spite of Johnson's failure to implement the survey, her accomplishments began to earn North Carolina a national reputation for its innovative welfare system. Lewis viewed the example set by the commissioner's resoluteness and independence as her greatest contribution. "The Commissioner of Public Welfare has steadily and consistently refused to let politics take precedence over the best interests of the unfortunate people she is elected to serve," Lewis wrote, shortly after resigning her publicity position in 1924. "This refusal has made many bitter enemies for her among the politicians and many staunch friends among liberal and disinterested people in the State." The columnist also applauded Johnson's demonstration that members of her sex could serve effectively as high government officials and the fact that women now occupied over one-third of the essential county superintendent of welfare positions in the state.[60]

In an "Incidentally" written in May 1923, entitled "The Personality Repertoire," Lewis told how her work with the board had forced her to add yet another identity to the many roles she played to please various audiences. She still lived at Cloverdale with Dr. Lewis and thus often adopted the persona of "Your Father's Daughter," which she subtitled "The Perfect Lady." She found this characterization very challenging. It required a deep reverence for the state and its history and university. "One must play it with decorum and considerable restraint. No rough stuff here! In this, naturalness would be simply fatal to a successful performance. It would leave the audience absolutely cold,—if not worse." This personality must deliver the few lines she normally spoke in a refined and well-modulated voice. Her part grew much larger, however, if she referred to "Apostolic Succession and the Thirty-Nine Articles of

59. Angus W. McLean to NBL, 22 July 1926, Kate Ancrum Burr Johnson Papers; Powell, *North Carolina through Four Centuries*, 474–45.

60. *N&O*, 17 May 1925, 1 June 1930; Powell, *Dictionary of North Carolina Biography*, 3:296.

Religion." Lewis confided that "in the role of 'Your Father's Daughter,' we have never evoked any noticeably hearty round of applause." Although the tensions at Cloverdale appear to have lessened somewhat, Nell's and Dr. Lewis's conflicting viewpoints continued to provide a source of mutual frustration.

She played three "Sister" roles, one of them—for Ivey—much more successfully than the others, she reported. This particular sibling part required much speaking and "considerable furbishing of the mental apparatus to do it justice, because there isn't a stupid line in it." Her dialogue ranged from discussion of the political columns of the *New York World*'s Heywood Broun to her brother's area of scholarly expertise, Mendelian theory and eugenics. Much of her acting consisted of "straight-comedy," and she noted that her performance of this character for its discriminating audience improved with the passage of time.

When Lewis visited her maternal relations in Virginia, she adopted the persona of "Your Mother's Daughter." She had never, she wrote, portrayed this "stimulating" personality—"a poet and a wit together with something of a religieuse"—to her and her onlookers' complete satisfaction. The role required a good deal of private rehearsal, and she found that gazing at the University of Virginia's rotunda in the moonlight helped her get into character. Although her mother had died during Lewis's infancy, she enigmatically felt that this personality, despite its deep devotion to tradition, came to her "more naturally than any of the others." Lewis's iconoclasm to the contrary, Mary's specter continued to loom large in her daughter's life.

"The Writer of Incidentally" found herself at a loss for words when she encountered her readers, and to them she often muttered banalities about the weather. "We haven't much respect for the audience which expects this role, since we are always conscious of its lack of real critical ability."

She found her most recent characterization—"The Publicity Agent," which acted in a "sociological problem-play entitled, 'What's Wrong with the World,'"—a particularly challenging role. "It [is] extremely difficult," she wrote, "to assume the socially-minded facial expression necessary to get this role across." She also found her lines hard to learn; they required exhaustive memorization of the day's leading social science treatises. She not only had to master these complex ideas but also had to "deliver them across the footlights with spontaneity and warmth." Lewis viewed her personality repertoire as a social necessity, and she attempted to perform each of the roles with as much panache as her limited dramatic background permitted. Nevertheless, she confided that she felt most like her real self while waiting without makeup in the wings between acts.[61]

In a contemporaneous "Incidentally" the columnist engaged in further psychoanalysis and explored her true identity more closely. She had recently discovered "Our Real Self," and the initial meeting astonished her. The blunt and unsentimental "stranger" repudiated the Southern Lady and dismissed many of the articles of faith and platitudes that outwardly ordered Lewis's existence and, by extension, the lives of other women throughout the region. Her "new acquaintance" charged that the South's romantic nature vanished upon close inspection, and she challenged the superiority of the Democratic Party. She brushed aside male supremacy by archly inquiring, "Have you ever worked with men?" H. G. Wells's writings even led the self to doubt that "God . . . is in His heaven and all's right with the world." A little nervously, Lewis had asked the stranger what she thought about the present moral code, but the columnist had blushed and changed the subject when her "uninhibited . . . Primitive Ego" began to respond. People hid their real selves behind barriers of "traditions and conventions and other group ideas . . . where only the psychoanalysts get a look-in through a knot-hole in the fence." Boosters and preachers frightened selves and kept them repressed. Lewis's own family and relatives played such a role. As the two parted, her self had cautioned that although she might materialize in highly select company, she had no intention of ever joining the writer of "Incidentally" in the "gallery of the Legislature." Despite the whimsical tone of the editorial, it provided a piercing deconstruction of Ladydom.[62]

Lewis did not confine her personality collection to her alter egos; "Incidentally" frequently featured correspondence from a bevy of characters she contrived, such as the nattering belles "Miss Pollyanna," "Miss Kamelia," and "Miss Kutie" and the scold "Mrs. U. P. Lift."[63]

In her column on her personality repertoire, Lewis had expressed her intention to play her publicity agent part for "several seasons," but her state employment soon ended abruptly. Questions arose about whether *News and Observer* readers might regard the opinions she expressed in "Incidentally" as reflecting the board's official positions. She had passionately thrown herself into her duties with the organization; naturally, issues pertaining to it ap-

61. *N&O*, 6 May 1923.

62. *N&O*, 4 March 1923.

63. Pyron, "Nell Battle Lewis," 85.

peared in her column. Lewis pulled few punches in her newspaper work, and Johnson may have grown concerned that her publicity director would alienate important constituencies.[64]

Lewis later disclosed that "it came to a choice of writing 'Incidentally' without restraint, as it had been written up to that time, and severing my connection with the Board; or trimming the column to the Board's measure and remaining a member of its staff." She chose to remain true to her column. Her mentor's ultimatum notwithstanding, the two remained close friends, and Lewis continued in "Incidentally" to champion the commissioner energetically.[65]

The decision to resign her publicity director's position shows that despite her personal and professional ties to progressive women leaders and their organizations, Lewis viewed herself first and foremost as a columnist—albeit one acutely sensitive to women's issues—and that she valued her editorial autonomy highly. Johnson's concern over the possible impact of "Incidentally" on public perceptions of the board confirms that only three years after the column's humble inception it had grown to attract considerable attention within the capital city. Indeed, Lewis had by this point fully found her voice, and "Incidentally"—which management had relocated to the paper's literary page two years earlier, when it had expanded Lewis's duties to include book reviewing—had matured to assume the proportions and style it would retain for the remainder of its long life. It had in fact begun to earn for its author a reputation that extended far beyond Raleigh.[66]

64. *N&O*, 4 September 1932.
65. *N&O*, 4 September 1932.
66. *N&O*, 15 April 1922.

# 4 A KNIFE IN THE BACK

Lewis had assumed her role. The many injustices and disadvantages she confronted, as well as her passionate need to interpret and reconcile the conflicting forces within her, provided the columnist with abundant material for "Incidentally," feature articles, and reportage and with publication in a widening range of literary and national magazines. By the decade's midpoint—a mere five years after her modest beginnings as the author of "A Corner for Kiddies"—she would unquestionably have achieved stature as one of the South's most prominent liberal intellectuals and social critics, arguably the most significant woman journalist in the region. As she first began to speak out, she understandably looked over her shoulder to gauge the reactions her sometimes quirky and often iconoclastic and controversial columns provoked in her employer. Although Josephus Daniels afforded her great editorial autonomy, she nevertheless initially engaged in some minor self-censorship when she feared she had transgressed his limits.

In the summer of 1922 Lewis discussed in "Our Private Morgue" how "bloody with murder are our otherwise spotless paws" after dispatching a number of the interesting "evil children of our brain." She had laid to rest the "late-lamented Mrs. U. P. Lift" and several other ill-fated characters as well as numerous pages of sarcastic verse. She and a few close friends, for their amusement, would occasionally steal into the morgue to "commune with the degenerate departed." Her belief that she could not expect her employer to countenance some of the more unconventional aspects of her column had evoked this matricide. "And, as you may have noted," she wrote with tongue in cheek, "discretion is our middle name." Lewis had no intention of disinterring her private stash for her general readers. "We aim to hold our job!" she explained. The next year Lewis suggested that sometimes the "black hat" of Daniels, whom she affectionately dubbed "The Old Codger," loomed over her.[1]

Soon, however, as a result of her growing experience and confidence—and perhaps as a consequence of the celebrity she had earned—Lewis expressed

1. *N&O*, 2 July 1922, 11 November 1923.

nonchalance regarding the frequently divergent positions that "Incidentally" and the *News and Observer*'s editorial page espoused. "There is, of course, and has always been a definite distinction between [these] opinions," she observed. "That distinction is that the editorial page represents the policy of *The News and Observer* with which I am in no way connected, and this column represents the personal opinions of N. B. Lewis." A highly professional newspaper "always leaves a columnist free even when his views are at variance with the paper's editorial policy."[2]

Later in life Lewis expressed great gratitude for the freedom Daniels provided her. "I have written scores and scores of things of which he did not approve, but never once has he called me down." She admitted, however, that she had reined in her attack on Prohibition out of deference to her employer's intense support for the Eighteenth Amendment. In retrospect she regretted "trimming" her column in even this single respect. Lewis would continue throughout her career to insist that she alone dictate the direction of "Incidentally."[3]

Early in her tenure as the writer of "Incidentally," Lewis introduced a theme that would provide the column throughout its long life with its abiding signature: herself. Her exploration of this topic ranged from discussions of her external appearance to allusions to her most private feelings. In the spring of 1924 she discussed her modern and liberating new coiffure. Having her tresses cut short made her realize a woman could "sit in parliaments without end, but until her hair is bobbed, she will never know how sweet is freedom." Despite the fact that the "more romantic sex" might prefer empty-headed women, many had fine minds, and having experienced the liberation of short hair and skirts of a more moderate length, those women would refuse to suffer the repression forced on them by traditional fashion. This apostasy would have a profoundly subversive effect on her homeland. "I know this is an awful blow to Southern Chivalry," she conceded. "With an exposed ear to the ground I think I hear the foundations of The Home, the bulwark of civilization, the shrine of our pure and beautiful Southern womanhood, the shelter of tender and innocent childhood cracking ominously."[4]

The strong connections Lewis had forged with the state's organized women

2. *N&O*, 22 March 1925.

3. *N&O*, 4 September 1932; NBL to IFL, 1949? NBL Papers.

4. *N&O*, 20 April and 11 May 1924.

and her own powerful feminist politics ensured that throughout the decade she would continue to champion fiercely the agenda of the Legislative Council of North Carolina Women and its constituent associations. The council's activism gained wide public attention in 1925, when the organization proposed a particularly ambitious series of bills and measures, including adoption of the Australian ballot and a children's eight-hour labor law; construction of a separate women's prison; state administration and funding of a reformatory for black girls, operated by the North Carolina Federation of Colored Women's Clubs; and advance publication of marriage notices to reduce the number of hasty unions.[5]

Early that year Lewis argued forcibly in "Incidentally" for secret voting, which she perceived as the council's most crucial recommendation. She had observed during elections "eager gentlemen . . . hanging around the polls . . . 'helping' the more docile women to mark their ballots." At her own polling place she had noticed one such character, who had earned an unsavory reputation. He had attempted to approach Lewis, when a companion of hers intercepted him and warned him of his imminent peril. The columnist regretted her friend's intervention. "I should have liked to receive his amiable suggestions as to how I should vote, in return for which he would have received a large gratuitous portion of my mind. I love these eager, helpful boys—they are so gallant and so ingenuous."[6]

Although she also strongly urged adoption of the state children's labor law, she made clear that, regardless of her liberalism, she harbored the same distrust that white southerners almost universally displayed toward the federal government and that she had little patience for starry-eyed crusaders. North Carolina had recently rejected a federal child labor amendment, but she wrote that it still hung "like a Damoclean sword over the heads of the so-called sovereign states." The amendment's passage would make Washington the "superparent" of everyone less than eighteen years of age. "What is this?" she asked. "Russia?" Many children, unfortunately, had to work to help support their families. She advised the "squawking sentimentalists that go about shedding tears about 'exploited childhood'" to bear this in mind. Virtually all other liberal southern journalists shared Lewis's allegiance to states' rights and would

5. *N&O*, 24 May 1925.

6. *N&O*, 4 January 1925.

continue to do so for many years. Her vigorous objection to the federal amendment seems mild compared to the reactions of southern senators, one of whom denounced the measure as "part of a hellish scheme laid in foreign countries to destroy our government." Another senator claimed it would "destroy a civilization based on the Bible."[7]

If Lewis's suspicion of the federal government placed her in accord with the prevailing thought in her native region, her support for the black girls' reformatory demonstrated her readiness to interrogate sacred southern dogma and raise hackles. She felt certain the measure would face much opposition. "It will surprise me," she wrote, "if we are not told by the chivalric that Negro women have a standard of morals lower than that of the white and that, hence, such an institution is absurd. Most of that sort of talk is nothing but conventional Southern blah, as flimsy and obvious a defense mechanism for miscegenation as any moron could think up in an idle hour." The inevitable demagogy, however, would serve a useful purpose. She intended to "prick an attentive ear" and name names in her column.

The energetic lobbying of Lewis and organized women came to naught. None of their program passed during the 1925 General Assembly. The legislature came close to enacting the Australian ballot, but the child labor law received just a single vote in committee. Lewis commented acidly, "It was probably very presumptuous of the women to think that any manufacturer should be inconvenienced for the sake of children. The gross and blatant materialism of the defeat of that bill sickens me."[8]

Lewis's newly assumed procedure of capitalizing *Negro* in her column placed her at odds with nearly all of the region's white newspapers (including her own), which wounded racial pride by spelling the word with a lowercase *n*. Journalism historians David Sloan and Laird B. Anderson credit the *Atlanta Constitution* in 1938, under Ralph McGill's editorship, as "perhaps" the first southern newspaper to adopt the practice of capitalizing the word. Gunnar

7. *N&O*, 4 January 1925; Leidholdt, *Editor for Justice*, 152; Kneebone, *Southern Liberal Journalists*, 148–49; George Brown Tindall, *A History of the South*, vol. 10: *The Emergence of the New South, 1913–1945*, ed. Wendell Holmes Stephenson and E. Merton Coulter (Baton Rouge: Louisiana State University Press and the Littlefield Fund for Southern History, University of Texas, 1967), 322; William A. Link, *The Paradox of Southern Progressivism, 1880–1930* (Chapel Hill: University of North Carolina Press, 1992), 304–11.

8. Mims, *Advancing South*, 244–45.

Myrdal, in his landmark study *An American Dilemma*, observed in 1944 that many of the region's white newspapers obstinately continued to print the noun without a capital letter.[9]

The racial progressivism displayed by Lewis of course stopped far short of advocating an end to separation between blacks and whites. No white southern journalist would do so for another generation, until *Brown v. Board of Education* furnished a handful of courageous liberal newspaper editors with an imprimatur to challenge segregation. Even then, these editors would rarely attack the inequities of Jim Crow; they simply urged compliance with the Supreme Court's unanimous decision, the law of the land. Lewis's solution to the race problem in her early journalistic career consisted principally of a blend of leadership, moral guidance, and resources, which members of her race would paternalistically furnish, coupled with black uplift and self-help.[10]

By contemporary standards in the white southern press, however, Lewis espoused a particularly advanced racial view. In "Negro Education Reaches High Point in This State," an article in a November 1926 edition of the *Raleigh News and Observer*, Lewis disputed the lore repeated endlessly by white southerners that their upbringing among blacks resulted in a deep understanding and harmony between the two groups, a myth to which she had subscribed and which she had broadcast in "Incidentally" until only recently. "Few white people in North Carolina will admit that they do not know the Negro, yet probably less than a score in the State really do," she declared. "The average Southerner knows the Negro almost entirely in a servile capacity, a capacity in which the average Southerner believes the Negro to belong." In reality whites comprehended "virtually nothing of the deeper currents of Negro life, of the intellectual trends among the more intelligent members of the race, of the achievements and aims of the Negro in the arts, education, business and the professions. The Negro is a neighbor with whom the white southerner comes in daily contact but whose inner life he does not penetrate. Behind a wall of old prejudices, fears and suspicions the Negro lives his real life." Lewis suggested that her white readers had no idea whether the educated blacks

9. Wm. David Sloan and Laird B. Anderson, *Pulitzer Prize Editorials: America's Best Editorial Writing, 1917–1993*, 2d ed. (Ames: Iowa State University Press, 1994), 144; Gunnar Myrdal, *An American Dilemma: The Negro Problem and Modern Democracy* (London: Transaction Publishers, 1966), 2:661.

10. John Egerton, *Speak Now against the Day: The Generation before the Civil Rights Movement in the South* (New York: Alfred A. Knopf, 1994), 460–67, 616.

they knew followed the "bitter, inflammatory [W.E.B.] Du Bois, the visionary [Marcus] Garvey or the sane, conservative [Robert Russa] Moton."[11]

To improve communion between the two races, Lewis recommended Tuskegee Institute's recent publication of the *Negro Year Book*, which provided an extensive treatment of black progress and interracial cooperation as well as a discussion of racial discrimination and violence. She found the book's statistical information regarding disparities in state funding for black and white education enlightening. Only the Deep South states exceeded North Carolina's discriminatory ratios. It had invested an average of $52.08 in public school property for each white student, compared to only $12.90 per black pupil. Moreover, a typical white schoolchild received an allocation of $25.31; his or her black counterpart obtained an allocation of just $7.52. She applauded the leadership and financial contributions the state's blacks had furnished, which had figured prominently in the decision by the Julius Rosenwald Fund's administrators to support black education in North Carolina more extensively than in any of its southern peers.[12]

The Raleigh columnist augmented reasoned analyses such as this discussion of racial inequities with provocative probings of Jim Crow's nether regions. In a review she wrote in New York in 1924 of the popular musical *The Chocolate Dandies,* which featured an all-black cast, Lewis made sport of the rubes back in Carolina. By touting the play's "pretty chorus" of "high-stepping mulatto gals," she undoubtedly inflamed—and titillated—the many apostles of racial integrity packing the klaverns in Raleigh and the surrounding area. She confessed, however, that the racially mixed chorus girls had left her with a strange and uneasy feeling. Analyzing her "quite primitive bristling," she postulated that her reaction stemmed from "the point of view of the Southern white woman in regard to miscegenation and of the connection of 'Southern chivalry' with the Negro woman, a connection of course elaborately disguised."[13]

Throughout the early 1920s Lewis continued her assault on the Ku Klux Klan, deriding it as forcefully as any journalist in the territory. Her highly personal column enabled her to ridicule the order with a rhetorical exuber-

11. *N&O,* 30 November 1926; Sarah Patton Boyle, *The Desegregated Heart: A Virginian's Stand in a Time of Transition* (New York: William Morrow, 1962), 10–42.

12. *N&O,* 30 November 1926.

13. *N&O,* 2 November 1924.

ance unsuitable for southern liberal newspaper editors, who generally constructed their anti-Klan editorials in a more conventional and staid fashion. Unconstrained by the chivalry that prevented her male colleagues from deconstructing and assailing Ladydom, she laid bare the construct and taunted its women subscribers, many of whom lent their support to the hooded order. During the July 1924 Democratic National Convention she praised the North Carolina delegates who favored denouncing the secret society. A Georgia representative, who had bolted from his delegation and flayed the Klan, received a kiss from one woman. Lewis deplored the fact that she had not attended the gathering: "If I . . . could have reached him, I am happy to announce, he would have been kissed by two. I can't answer for the other, but one kiss, at least, would have been resounding and fervent."[14]

The following week she employed a frequent contributor to "Incidentally" to lampoon the organization. She had previously concocted Miss Pollyanna, a defender of southern tradition, who violently disputed all the columnist's modernisms. Lewis had just learned from Pollyanna that she now affiliated herself with the Klan's women's auxiliary. The "chief Kutie of the Kamelia" expressed the belief that "Jews are Jews, niggers are niggers and Catholics are Catholics, and it is the imperative and patriotic duty of the pure white 100 per cent American Protestant to assert his unquestioned racial and religious superiority over them individually and collectively." Miss Pollyanna informed Lewis in vague terms of the country's critical condition and warned that "this is no time to be talking about tolerance or liberty." Lewis concluded by telling her readers that her correspondent "has the Christian patriot's clear, unprejudiced eye. Michael and his angels—or their moral equivalent—are at present wearing convenient hoods and helping valiantly to deadlock national political conventions and beating up the 'immoral' [at] night and doing a little branding with red-hot irons here and there for the glory of a white Protestant God and the honor of a 100 per cent American Flag. And that's the whole thing in a Knut-shell, says Miss Pollyanna—she being, I take it, the Knut."[15]

Lewis continued to apply her knack for verse to taunting the hooded empire. Early that fall "My Hero" appeared in "Incidentally." The speaker of the rhyme batted her eyes at the protector of Pure Southern Womanhood and avowed her admiration for its morality, as exemplified by its affiliates' efforts

14. *N&O*, 6 July 1924.

15. *N&O*, 13 July 1924.

to uncover sin by spying on their neighbors. She also lauded the order's bravery, as in its masked lynching of defenseless blacks.[16]

Lewis's jeering proved too much for the local klaverns. She received a series of anonymous letters announcing that the Klan secretly monitored her activities and that it had groomed a replacement for her. "Now you can rap the K. K. K. all you want," "A KNIGHT" warned her. "We got a K. K. K. chief of police and we will have a daughter Kamelia on your job soon. Learn to let the invisible empire alone." This correspondence perked Lewis up. "I am encouraged," she informed her readers. "I must be getting effective." She eagerly looked forward to meeting her successor, "who will write 'Incidentally' and make this column safe for the pure white Protestant. I have a sort of Jewish-nigger-Catholic hunch that daughters Kamelia are my meat."[17]

Lewis displayed courage in ridiculing the hooded order, but it appears unlikely that her stand provoked repercussions more menacing than the missives she received. Raleigh's Klan had in fact played an important role in electing the city's chief of police, but it contained a number of leading citizens who were not predisposed to lawlessness, and the state's Grand Dragon, Judge Henry A. Grady, attempted mightily to restrain his followers. Without question her advocacy enjoyed the protection and thorough support of Josephus Daniels, who had voted twice at the rancorous Democratic National Convention to denounce the Klan as un-American.[18]

Although Lewis scoffed at the Klan, she, like nearly all white southerners, sanctioned racial purity and subscribed to the scientific racism it tapped. Nevertheless, she informed her readers that demagogues appropriating and twisting the new science of eugenics might easily exploit America's racial anxieties. Her viewpoint likely generated numerous contentious discussions between her and her youngest brother, Ivey.

The Old Dominion in the 1920s furnished a national exemplar for leadership to ensure the purity of the white race. Indeed, one of the commonwealth's most active proponents of racial integrity during this time touted Virginia for having the "most effective anti-miscegenation laws in existence." Ivey Lewis and a cadre of other notable University of Virginia faculty—many hired at his

16. *N&O*, 14 September 1924.

17. *N&O*, 24 August and 30 November 1924.

18. Kenneth T. Jackson, *The Ku Klux Klan in the City, 1915–1930* (Chicago: Ivan R. Dee, 1992), 81; Morrison, *Josephus Daniels*, 152; Chalmers, *Hooded Americanism*, 94–95; *N&O*, 21 December 1926, 22 February 1927.

behest—helped furnish their state with the scientific warrant for its assiduous eugenics activism. His impressive credentials, which included a doctorate from Johns Hopkins University, postgraduate study in Germany and Italy, and service as the first chief executive of the Virginia Academy of Science, vested him with formidable scientific authority. Many academics within Virginia and North Carolina had long speculated that his accomplishments and reputation would one day earn him the presidency of one of the two states' universities.[19]

In the mid-1920s, while generally eschewing the limelight, Ivey worked closely and energetically with the founders of Virginia's Anglo-Saxon Clubs: internationally acclaimed concert pianist, composer, and ethnomusicologist John Powell and Major Earnest Sevier Cox, an author and explorer who had toured "the belt of black around the world" to study what he perceived as race problems. The Anglo-Saxon Clubs espoused goals nearly identical to those of the Klan, while eschewing its violence and secrecy, and sought (without success) to export chapters to other states, including North Carolina. The clubs never attracted a mass following, but Powell and Cox functioned as effective lobbyists and left their legacy on Virginia's racial policies for another four decades.[20]

In April 1924 Ivey Lewis, sponsored by the University Post of Anglo-Saxon Clubs, delivered at Madison Hall a talk entitled "What Biology Says to the Man of Today." The *New York Times* reported that he told the students at Mr. Jefferson's University that all good citizens should make it their duty to support immigration restrictions and work to maintain the purity of the white race. Citing statistics, the professor convincingly demonstrated that the birthrate among the "intelligent members" of the commonwealth had decreased alarmingly, while the percentage of the population belonging to the "lower groups" had increased. The singular lesson learned from the study of biology in the

19. *Richmond Times-Dispatch*, 22 July 1923, 17? March 1964; *N&O*, 18 March 1964; *College Topics*, 1 May 1923; Wilson, *University of North Carolina*, 312; NBL to Frank Porter Graham (hereafter cited as FPG), 30 September 1931, Frank Porter Graham Papers (hereafter cited as FPG Papers), Southern Historical Collection, Wilson Library, University of North Carolina at Chapel Hill.

20. Gregory Michael Dorr, "Assuring America's Place in the Sun: Ivey Foreman Lewis and the Teaching of Eugenics at the University of Virginia, 1915–1953," *Journal of Southern History* 66, no. 2 (May 2000): 265, 281; Smith, *Managing White Supremacy*, 76–79, 85; Leidholdt, *Editor for Justice*, 164–66; Pocahontas Wight Edmunds, *Virginians Out Front* (Richmond: Whittet & Shepperson, 1972), 345; Earnest Sevier Cox, *White America* (Richmond: White America Society, 1923), 402; "Anglo-Saxon Clubs of America," [1923?], John Powell Papers, Manuscripts Division, Special Collections Department, University of Virginia Library.

twentieth century, he propounded, "is that the idea of environment molding something out of nothing is sheer nonsense. What goes into the hereditary mill is what comes out of it." He dismissed the notion of "the great American melting pot, into which one can put the refuse of three continents and draw out good, sound American citizens."[21]

Armed with the severe new Racial Integrity Act and existing laws forbidding intermarriage between whites and blacks, Virginia's authorities would surveil an untold number of its citizens, persecute hundreds of mixed-race residents, and irrevocably disarrange their lives. A panoply of additional legislation and local ordinances already mandated racial separation on public conveyances and segregation in residential neighborhoods, and a 1926 Public Assemblages Act would separate blacks and whites in public areas. Virginia's white leaders often boasted that a superior racial climate in the state elevated it above its Deep South brethren, but in reality the commonwealth adopted a highly repressive system of apartheid.[22]

Although Nell Lewis apparently accepted the underlying premises of her learned brother's racial beliefs, she discerned danger in their misappropriation, especially by organizations that lacked the educated and refined membership of the Old Dominion's Anglo-Saxon Clubs. A month after Ivey's University of Virginia address, she acknowledged in "Incidentally" her credence "that eugenics in which race purity is fundamental is one of the most important things in the world." She admired the English, strongly condoned immigration restrictions, and expressed satisfaction that so few aliens resided in North Carolina.[23]

"BUT," she cautioned," it seems to me that there is lots of dynamite in all this talk of Nordic supremacy. It is becoming the sort of thing that sows the seeds of war. Witness the way the Ku Klux Klan, of course one of the greatest social menaces at present, has taken up the refrain." The "Kluckers" knew nothing about eugenics and the laws of heredity, she said, and could not describe Nordic characteristics or explain their desirability. "This business . . . seems to me to be fast degenerating into a pretty rank Chauvinism that is as dangerous as it is ridiculous." She believed getting "lots more people worked

21. *NYT*, 6 April 1924; *College Topics*, 4 April 1924.

22. Smith, *Managing White Supremacy*, 76; Leidholdt, *Editor for Justice*, 203–6; *Acts and Joint Resolutions of the General Assembly of the State of Virginia* (Richmond: Division of Purchase and Printing, 1926), 945–46.

23. *N&O*, 11 May 1924.

up about Nordic superiority and then mak[ing] them talk about it all the time at the top of their lungs" might easily result in the start of a new war.[24]

Lewis had issued a prescient warning. Despite John Powell's Virginia niceties, his rhetoric bore an eerie resemblance to that of another artist, Adolf Hitler, then hacking away at *Mein Kampf* in a Bavarian prison. "The impossibility of an immediate final solution of the negro problem necessitates legislation which will insure us a breathing space pending the final solution," the prominent University of Virginia graduate declared.[25]

In 1927, in a section of "Incidentally" entitled "Books Outgrown," Lewis demonstrated her further alienation from the racial integrity movement. She disparaged an illustrious text in the order's canon, Madison Grant's 1916 book *The Passing of the Great Race.* She had placed that "glorification of the Nords" in her "intellectual discard." At one point in her life "it had made me all puffed up with pride. My vanity was flattered by being like Mr. Grant, one of [his] superior Anglo-Saxons." She no longer believed, however, in "chosen people."[26]

This position undoubtedly frustrated Nell's youngest brother. Grant, like the professor, had strongly endorsed the Old Dominion's Racial Integrity Act. Adoption of the legislation "would be living up to Virginia's great traditions," the famous author had written to Powell in 1924 in a letter prepared to lobby the General Assembly. Moreover, *The Passing of the Great Race* occupied a prominent place on Nell's brother's reading list for his biology class. Twenty years after his sister's dismissal of the book in her widely read column, Ivey Lewis, then dean of the College of Arts and Sciences at the University of Virginia, deplored the "sap-headed thinking" displayed by "sociologists, especially the Jewish ones," who "deride and laugh to scorn such books as Madison Grant's 'Passing of the Great Race.'" Ivey's deep skepticism of nonbiological solutions to social problems, such as the remedies fervently endorsed by his sister and her mentor, Kate Burr Johnson, must have generated spirited debate between the two siblings.[27]

In a coauthored article appearing in Howard Odum's outspoken *Journal of Social Forces* during its inaugural year, 1923, Nell and Johnson celebrated the many progressive individuals, organizations, and institutions working to

24. *N&O*, 11 May 1924.

25. *Richmond News Leader*, 5 June 1923.

26. *N&O*, 29 May 1927; Grant, *Passing of the Great Race;* Ripley, *Races of Europe.*

27. Dorr, "Assuring America's Place in the Sun," 273; Madison Grant to John Powell, 1 February 1924, John Powell Papers.

remedy the Tar Heel State's social ills. The Board of Charities and Public Welfare, of course, received conspicuous treatment. The authors also lauded the University of North Carolina's activism and outreach, which brought expertise "'to the folks,' thus broadening their social outlook and aiding them in the solution of their problems." Odum's recently established School of Public Welfare received special praise. The Federation of Women's Clubs, the Library Commission, and the many organizations represented by the North Carolina Legislative Council of Women had also played a vital role in advocating the "continued and increasing social betterment of the people of a state which has already made bold and phenomenal progress towards that end."[28]

Lewis's discussions of pacifism in "Incidentally" during this period further provoked southern traditionalists and the many members of the region's multitudinous patriotic societies. She renounced entirely her own war service and embraced a fierce nonviolence. "Nobody is going to beat a drum and wave a flag at me and get me all worked up for slaughter again," she proclaimed in 1924. "I am getting into training every day now to be the most belligerent sort of pacifist when the next war comes." She vowed she would go to jail to protest American involvement in a future military conflict and when incarcerated she would "certainly be disappointed if I am not branded as a 'Red.'" Her repugnance toward militarism and Americanism offended numerous readers. One National Guard lieutenant colonel, dismayed by her editorials containing "affronts to the flag," expressed surprise to "learn that the author, Miss Nell Battle Lewis, is a descendant of a distinguished North Carolina family who, herself, saw service in France." He had imagined that "birth, education and experience [would] lead to clearer thought."[29]

Boosterism and pretentiousness provided Lewis with additional fodder during the first years of "Incidentally." She regarded her native state fondly, especially its residents' simplicity, grace, quiet intelligence, and sense of humor. But in her view Babbittry and affectation undermined North Carolina's essential character and diminished its unique charm. She repelled any attempt to downplay its singularity and to compare its development to states in other regions, the Midwest in particular. She especially denounced the vociferous self-promotion she observed in the Tar Heel State. "North Carolina's posses-

28. Dorr, "Assuring America's Place in the Sun," 271–72; Kate Burr Johnson and Nell Battle Lewis, "A Decade of Social Progress in North Carolina," *Journal of Social Forces* 1, no. 4 (1 May 1923): 267.

29. *N&O*, 4 May and 24 September 1924, 3 December 1926.

sion of the largest hosiery mill in the world, the highest mountain east of the Rockies, third place in the production of peanuts, a climate reported to be superior to any on this sphere and so on ad nauseam has absolutely no influence in making me like to live here."[30]

Lewis's claim that "boosters are not the State of North Carolina but merely its comic mask" and her wickedly satirical piece "A Tar Heel Booster's Mother Goose" pushed Patriotic Pollyanna to her limits. She put her arch foe on notice that after reading these skewerings, "every drop of pure Nordic blood in my veins boils to a degree Fahrenheit where I feel myself impelled to write you that I consider you an enemy of Anglo-Saxon civilization." She had begun to wonder if the journalist "may not be clandestinely pro-German. The war, as I understand it, is over, and the hosts of righteousness have prevailed in making this a better world, but that term, 'Pro-German' still carries in my mind a significance which, I think, pretty well covers your case." Pollyanna asked Lewis her place of birth and her whereabouts during World War I. The patriotess thoughtfully enclosed a stamped, self-addressed envelope to expedite the journalist's reply. The letter ended on an indignant note: "I may add, my dear misguided young lady, that in spite of your many sallies, North Carolina, in all probability, will remain what it was intended to be, the Wisconsin of the South; and I, for one, shall be glad and proud to continue to advertise, at any time, at any place and in any company, its superlative achievements."[31]

Lewis guffawed when she received a request regarding her background from the pompous compilers of a social register, advertised as the state's "most exclusive publication." The mailing informed her that "North Carolina is one of the States whose very cow-paths are named with names to conjure; whose pioneers have left such imperishable historical instances coupled with the names, that one feels as if one treads on holy ground in North Carolina." She noted with a "blush of mortification that the appeal appears to be made primarily to women, as implying a weak mindedness on the part of that sex which is scarcely flattering." The register, Lewis volunteered, should disregard the existing Tar Heel seal and include a coat of arms consisting of a "Guernsey heifer couchant on a field verte quartered with a ten-dollar gold piece rampant on a field d'argent together with some such motto as 'Animus similis bovi' or 'Rien si non elite.'" The compilers had asked her to complete their form "as may best

30. Sellars, "South Saver," 29; *N&O*, 6 April 1924.

31. *N&O*, 27 January and 24 February 1924.

fit the applicant," and she intended to list her name as "Yolande Lucille De Trop" and her maiden name as "Yolande Lucille Frisque." She requested that the latter cognomen receive its French pronunciation, "'Friskay,' even though my ultramarine blood is ninety-nine and forty-four one-hundredths percent pure Anglo-Saxon." She also resolved to identify her organizational affiliations to include the "N. Y. Society for the Suppression of Vice," "Ladies' Auxiliary of the Ku Klux Klan," "United Federated Consolidated and Amalgamated Association of Legitimate Off-Spring of the Princess Pocahontas," and "Loyal Daughters of Army Cooks in the War with Mexico."[32]

A vital aspect of Lewis's advocacy throughout the 1920s consisted of exhorting the region's writers to jettison the romantic portrayals of the Old South that had characterized Thomas Nelson Page's novels and to embrace a social realism that trenchantly appraised the authors' present-day homeland. Through the interspersion of individual book and play reviews within "Incidentally" and the frequent literary criticism featured in her column in sections she entitled "The Four Inch Shelf" and "Book Reviews in Brief," Lewis gave sustenance to a young generation of creative book writers, dramatists, and essayists. Her patronage broke fresh ground; most southern newspapers attended poorly, if at all, to modern cultural developments. She also regularly contributed to and may intermittently have edited the *Raleigh News and Observer's* book page, which earned a reputation as one of the South's best.[33]

Although she esteemed prolific Richmond novelists Ellen Glasgow and James Branch Cabell, she also admired Julia Peterkin, whose marriage to a plantation manager imbued her with a sensitivity toward South Carolina's Gullah blacks, and the Palmetto State's DuBose Heyward, whose novel *Porgy* and his collaboration on its subsequent dramatizations would earn him lasting fame. With great regularity Lewis extolled the virtues of journalist Gerald Johnson, the associate editor of the *Greensboro Daily News* and University of North Carolina journalism professor then acquiring a well-deserved reputation as the South's foremost essayist, and she commended Julia and Julian Harris, who wielded the little *Columbus* (Ga.) *Enquirer-Sun* to battle the Klan in its heartland and would in 1925 win a Pulitzer Prize for that newspaper.[34]

32. *N&O*, 13 May 1923.

33. W. T. Couch, ed., *Culture in the South* (Chapel Hill: University of North Carolina Press, 1934), 161; Mims, *Advancing South*, 242; Fred C. Hobson, *Serpent in Eden: H. L. Mencken and the South* (Chapel Hill: University of North Carolina Press, 1974), 64; *N&O*, 15 April 1922, 11 July 1926.

34. "Miss Lewis Speaks at Library Luncheon: Raleigh Author and Columnist Traces Current

Lewis devoted her most enthusiastic energies, however, to nurturing the artistic seedlings closest to home: Frederick H. Koch, who directed the Carolina Playmakers, and his University of North Carolina student and later colleague, playwright Paul Green, whose work *In Abraham's Bosom* would receive a Pulitzer Prize in 1927. "Proff" Koch, who helped pioneer the genre of folk drama, organized the Playmakers, which performed productions written by its students.[35] In a *News and Observer* front-page feature article in the spring of 1924, Lewis described their creations as the "most interesting and the most significant artistic effort in this State." She depicted in great detail the process through which the organization crafted, refined, and produced its plays. In his dramaturgy class Koch tapped his students' personal experience regarding the North Carolina towns they grew up in and the people they knew there. "The plays are strictly home-made," Lewis wrote, "and one might venture to say, a made-in-Carolina product superior even to the output of the largest hosiery mill in the world. . . . The basis of the Playmakers' efforts is the correct assumption that the folk of North Carolina are dramatic: that is, that they possess in their common life, in their legends, their superstitions, and their history [a] rich self; no one should be able to interpret it so sincerely." She lobbied the university's administration to follow through with its promise to renovate the elegant Smith Building, which had served diverse purposes—one of them the stabling of General William Tecumseh Sherman's horses—into a theater.[36]

That same year, however, Lewis gently chided the thespians when they sought to interpret the state's past: "We have already paid our sentimental respects to the hoop-skirt (though what we should do with one Heaven alone knows). But the 1924 model calico wrapper of the mill hand in her hours of ease (?) frankly interests us more. The Revolutionary patriot is a brave figure,

---

Realism in Southern Writings," *N&O?* n.d. (clipping from NBL Papers); *N&O*, 21 October 1928; Gregory C. Lisby, "Julian Harris and the *Columbus Enquirer-Sun:* The Consequences of Winning the Pulitzer Prize," *Journalism Monographs*, no. 105 (April 1988): 4–8; Charles Pekor Jr., "An Adventure in Georgia," *American Mercury* 8, no. 32 (August 1926): 410; Pyron, "Nell Battle Lewis," 68–69; Robert Bain, Joseph M. Flora, and Louis D. Rubin, eds., *Southern Writers: A Biographical Dictionary* (Baton Rouge: Louisiana State University Press, 1979), 57–60, 180–83, 223–25, 247–49, 348–49.

35. "Miss Lewis Speaks at Library Luncheon: Raleigh Author and Columnist Traces Current Realism in Southern Writings," *N&O?* n.d. (clipping from NBL Papers); Pyron, "Nell Battle Lewis," 68–69; William D. Snider, *Light on the Hill: A History of the University of North Carolina at Chapel Hill* (Chapel Hill: University of North Carolina Press, 1992), 181.

36. *N&O*, 30 March 1924; Snider, *Light on the Hill*, 181.

but so is the ambitious boy struggling nowadays to free himself from the monotony of isolated farm life. As one in the audience we say to the Playmakers that it is easier for us to feel with the mill worker and the country boy because their lives touch our own more nearly than do those of the ante-bellum gallant and the Revolutionary patriot." She then proceeded to convey her manifesto for the region's artistic development: "Give us the masters and slaves of the present, the religious bigotry and scheming politics and pitiful ignorance and intellectual inertia and crude materialism which bind some of us so tightly now before you reproduce the plantation owner and his black bondsmen of the '50's. . . . We have had enough of flim-flam and fol-de-rol in letters in the South. We have been surfeited with pretty inanities and with inanities not even pretty, while Life itself with all its pity and terror, its stark ugliness, its honest laughter, its real courage, its actual beauty, has swirled around us untranscribed."[37]

Lewis's iconoclastic attacks on patriotic and nativist societies and on southern boosterism and business culture, and especially her literary advocacy, brought her to the attention of the nation's most notorious social and cultural provocateur, Henry Louis Mencken. From his perch in Baltimore, where he shared command of the influential *Sunpapers,* he directed his gaze with great interest southward, laying claim to the region as his "special territory." He saw in Lewis and like-minded southern intellectuals and artists the fruits of his contumelious earlier instigation.[38]

The "Sage of Baltimore" had for numerous years trained his weaponry on southern *Kultur.* In 1917, in a *New York Evening Mail* article entitled "The Sahara of the Bozart," a play on the French words *beaux arts,* he had fired his first salvo. Three years later he had expanded his diatribe in even more explosive form and included it in *Prejudices: Second Series.* Southerners, by and large, however remained blithely unaware of the barrage until "The South Begins to Mutter," a more restrained and constructive composition published in *Public Opinion* magazine, burst through the magnolia curtain. The essay's distribution coincided with the inauguration of Lewis's column. A legion of southern newspaper editors, who staunchly defended Dixie's status quo, belatedly mustered and hotly fired back at Mencken.[39]

In the expanded "Sahara," which Lewis had appreciatively read, its author

37. *N&O,* 24 February 1924.

38. H. L. Mencken, *Thirty-Five Years of Newspaper Work,* ed. Fred Hobson, Vincent Fitzpatrick, and Bradford Jacobs (Baltimore: Johns Hopkins University Press, 1994), 151.

39. Hobson, *Mencken,* 213; Hobson, *Serpent in Eden,* 24, 27, 193.

contended that the South, the birthplace of many of the country's previously preeminent statesmen and thinkers, had grown as arid and desolate as the world's greatest desert and now gave him the "creeps." With his signature deviltry he parodied the region and its inhabitants: "In all that gargantuan paradise of the fourth-rate there is not a single picture gallery worth going into, or a single orchestra capable of playing the nine symphonies of Beethoven, or a single opera house, or a single theater devoted to decent plays, or a single public monument that is worth looking at, or a single workshop devoted to the making of beautiful things." Excepting only James Branch Cabell, Mencken could not discern a "single Southern prose writer who can actually write. . . . When you come to critics, musical composers, painters, sculptors, architects and the like, you will have to give it up, for there is not even a bad one between the Potomac mud-flats and the Gulf. Nor a historian. Nor a philosopher. Nor a theologian. Nor a scientist. In all these fields the South is an awe-inspiring blank—a brother to Portugal, Serbia and Albania."[40]

The Sage wrote in his memoirs that "Sahara" had "made a dreadful pother in the South, and brought me a great deal of violent denunciation [much of it due, undoubtedly, to its assertion that many of the region's whites secreted black lineage and that mulattos displayed a marked superiority over the territory's whites artistically and intellectually], but all [of] the more enlightened Southerners had to admit its truth." Indeed, they did. He soon found himself thrust into the role of spiritual leader of a southern cultural renaissance. Mencken intimate Gerald Johnson, then an editorial writer at the *Greensboro Daily News,* recalled the cataclysmic force of the Sage's polemic and his subsequent astonishment when he found himself serving as counselor and mentor to a generation of young southern writers, artists, scholars, and journalists.[41]

In addition to Lewis, Mencken and the *Baltimore Evening Sun,* edited by Hamilton Owens, invigorated and promoted a Who's Who of liberal southern newspaper editors and journalists, including Johnson; the Harrises; and future Pulitzer Prize winners Grover C. Hall of the *Montgomery Advertiser,* Louis I. Jaffé of the *Norfolk Virginian-Pilot,* Virginius Dabney of the *Richmond Times-Dispatch,* and Charlotte editorial writer W. J. Cash, who would publish the

40. H. L. Mencken, *A Mencken Chrestomathy* (New York: Vintage Books, 1982), 184–86; *N&O,* 7 December 1924.

41. Mencken, *Thirty-Five Years of Newspaper Work,* 151; Mencken, *Mencken Chrestomathy,* 190–93; Gerald W. Johnson, foreword to *Serpent in Eden: H. L. Mencken and the South,* by Fred C. Hobson (Chapel Hill: University of North Carolina Press, 1974).

classic *Mind of the South* in 1941. Prominent college faculty, including University of North Carolina professors Paul Green, Addison Hibbard, who taught in the English department and also authored the widely distributed newspaper column "Literary Lantern," and Howard Odum, the South's foremost sociologist, received inspiration and support from the Sage. Many others—among them Julia Peterkin; Emily Clark, who helped edit the fledgling but influential *Reviewer*, a Richmond literary magazine that provided a venue for young southern writers; and Goucher College professor and short-story writer Sara Haardt—received his guidance and sponsorship.[42]

Although Lewis acknowledged Mencken's influence on her, she nevertheless appraised him critically and maturely. She informed her readers that despite the Sage's "gross exaggeration" and "marked boorishness," he had accurately portrayed the dismal condition of the arts south of the Mason-Dixon Line. "Impassioned condemnation of him leaves us absolutely cold," Lewis wrote in "Incidentally" in the summer of 1923. No one should regard him as an enemy of Dixie. She pointed out that Mencken revered the antebellum South and deeply desired the region to regain the cultural supremacy it had once enjoyed. (Subsequent scholars such as Cash would reveal the flaws in Mencken's belief that gentry akin to the Virginia gentlemen of the eighteenth century had predominated in the nineteenth-century South.) "Mr. Mencken, whatever else he may be, is a heady stimulant. To change the metaphor, he is, too, a powerful cathartic—an effective purgative for intellectual inertia and dry-rot complacency and asinine self-glorification and pathetic 'artistic' claptrap. And God knows we need one!"[43]

She echoed Mencken's incrimination and played to her audience's romantic and aggrandized view of its history: "My countrymen—as the local orators say—if you can find in peanut production, in hosiery manufacture, in boosters' clubs, in revival meetings, in moving picture shows, in community sings, something which is for you as appealing and as satisfying as is the thought of that picturesque, cultivated, leisurely, distinguished regime of the ante-bellum plantations, then it is not to you that Mr. Mencken speaks." She called not for

42. Hobson, *Serpent in Eden*, 58; Leidholdt, *Editor for Justice*, 141–42; Mencken, *Thirty-Five Years of Newspaper Work*, 117–18; Marion Elizabeth Rodgers, ed., *Mencken and Sara: A Life in Letters, The Private Correspondence of H. L. Mencken and Sara Haardt* (New York: McGraw-Hill, 1987), 35–50; Couch, *Culture in the South*, 188–89.

43. Hobson, *Serpent in Eden*, 18; W. J. Cash, *The Mind of the South* (New York: Alfred A. Knopf, 1941), 91–99; *N&O*, 8 July 1923.

"a return of that earlier culture but for another rooted in your own present which shall approximate [the previous society's] excellence and charm."[44]

In the October 1923 edition of the critically acclaimed *Smart Set*, which Mencken coedited with drama critic George Nathan, he lauded Lewis's role in advancing the renaissance he had provoked. Mencken expressed his approbation of the columnist's championship for southern letters. Her "criticism, perhaps, would attract little notice in the North, but in the South it is revolutionary, for, in essence, it is a repudiation of all the formulae that have hampered the fine arts in the South since the Civil War and a plea for the setting up of standards wholly devoid of sectional and patriotic touchiness. Miss Lewis argues that Southern poets should be judged henceforth as poets, and not as Southerners. It is as strange a doctrine to Southern ears as the doctrine that ladies are mammals."[45]

Lewis undoubtedly basked in the momentary celebrity that the Sage's endorsement had provided. But she took issue with his claim in the article that the *Greensboro News*—whose editorial page Earle Godbey and Gerald Johnson directed and where Lenoir Chambers now served as city editor—had provided a role model for her and had motivated her to adopt her iconoclastic stands. In an annotation on the *Smart Set* article, "Under the Southern Moon," which she clipped and sent to an unknown recipient, she wrote: "I don't think I was influenced by the *Greensboro News*,—do you? But I was influenced by the Sahara of the Bozart."[46]

Although Lewis may never have met Mencken, they enjoyed a connectedness. The prominent critic consumed southern newspapers voraciously, and his own column appeared near "Incidentally" in the Sunday *News and Observer*. Lewis published in the renowned *American Mercury*, which Mencken had founded in 1924, and the two corresponded. Additionally, both journalists involved themselves closely in the production of the *Reviewer*.[47]

At Mencken's urging, Clark and the other Richmond editors of the budding magazine agreed in 1924 to transfer it from Richmond to Chapel Hill. Mencken feared that if it remained headquartered in Virginia's conserva-

44. *N&O*, 8 July 1923.

45. H. L. Mencken, "Under the Southern Moon," *Smart Set*, no. 72 (October 1923): 62.

46. Mencken, "Under the Southern Moon," 62; Fitzpatrick, *Gerald W. Johnson*, 40–55; Leidholdt, *Standing before the Shouting Mob*, 18.

47. Hobson, *Serpent in Eden*, 101–2; *N&O*, 7 February 1926; Nell Battle Lewis, "North Carolina," *American Mercury* 8, no. 29 (May 1926): 36–43.

tive capital, writers such as Thomas Nelson Page would exert their authority over it and it would lose its role in helping foment the southern literary renaissance. Clark selected Green as editor, and Lewis, Gerald Johnson, and Addison Hibbard agreed to serve as directors. Under its new leadership the *Reviewer* featured an even greater number of southern writers, nearly all of whom explored their subjects with great realism, and the journal's quality grew stronger. Continuing a critical series suggested by Mencken on southern cities, Lewis authored an article wryly examining Raleigh. One frequent contributor observed that after its move to North Carolina, the magazine focused on "eradicating Southern prejudices and some phenomena of Southern politics" almost to the same degree as the highly controversial *Journal of Social Forces*. Despite the gallant efforts of its new administrators, the *Reviewer* survived only one year in its new home and then merged with another magazine. Its policy of paying small sums to authors, combined with a loss of financial sponsorship and limited readership, had left the little magazine deeply in debt.[48]

Throughout the 1920s and into the 1930s prominent figures promoting the southern cultural revival—in addition to Mencken—acknowledged Lewis's significance. Heywood Broun directed attention to the Raleigh journalist in his *New York World* column, "It Seems to Me." Julian Harris, writing in the *Baltimore Evening Sun*, which fomented and intently chronicled southern progressivism, underscored her membership in a tiny regional faction of key liberals working to "shake off the throttling grip of the Lilliputs, rid ourselves of our intellectual lethargy, purge our spirit of all corroding prejudices and take up again a leadership we should never have lost." In *Liberalism in the South* young Virginius Dabney lauded her "keenly discriminating mind" and emphasized the extension of her influence well beyond North Carolina. W. T. Couch, who directed the University of North Carolina Press and had begun to earn for it recognition as one of the nation's leading academic publishing houses, specified her importance in *Culture in the South*. W. J. Cash, struggling throughout the 1930s to give birth to the *Mind of the South*, placed Lewis in that book among the vanguard of regional progressive leaders.[49]

48. Hobson, *Serpent in Eden*, 36–48; Couch, *Culture in the South*, 177–79; *NYT*, 15 August 1926; Nell Battle Lewis, "Raleigh, Capital of a Neighborhood," *Reviewer* 5, no. 3 (July 1925): 63–70; Wilson, *University of North Carolina*, 492.

49. *New York World*, n.d., NBL Papers; *Baltimore Evening Sun*, 25 August 1925; Virginius Dabney, *Liberalism in the South* (Chapel Hill: University of North Carolina Press, 1932), 407; Couch, *Culture in*

But the most significant confirmation of Lewis's arrival as a major exponent of the South's cultural renaissance occurred with Edwin Mims's publication of *The Advancing South: Stories of Progress and Reaction* in 1926. Mims, who then headed Vanderbilt University's English department, intended for his book to serve as a refutation of Menckenism. The professor, a native southerner, who had for many years promoted cultural advancement in his region, had blanched when the Sage's criticism made Dixie a laughingstock to many northern intellectuals. Mencken's tirade discounted entirely the improvements Mims believed were flourishing there well before the publication of "The Sahara of the Bozart." He intended for the *Advancing South* to make clear that he and like-minded contemporaries had planted the seeds of progressivism for the postwar generation of southern liberals. His book became a remarkable popular success and nearly earned its author a Pulitzer Prize.[50]

Mims devoted a major portion of his chapter entitled "Revolt against Chivalry" to Lewis, whom he touted as the model new southern woman. He traced her impressive ancestry, education, and journalistic advocacy and her service with the Board of Charities and Public Welfare. He praised "Incidentally" and her "brilliant and unbridled mind." Other columnists had acquired more fame than she, he claimed, but "none that surpass her in delicate literary allusions, the free play of the mind about a variety of happenings and ideas, and withal a certain poise of mind and serenity of wisdom." Mims had earned an earlier reputation as one of the region's foremost literary critics, and his commendation of Lewis's erudition confirmed the Raleigh columnist's standing as a leading light in southern letters.[51]

Mims described the struggle Lewis had faced in speaking out against the traditions of her homeland. She felt powerful connections to the old order and abhorred much about the superficial culture that had supplanted it. She had written that she felt as though she "stuck a knife in a friend's back" when she criticized the traditions of the Old South, but she refused to let sentimentality and chauvinism circumscribe her intellectual honesty or soften her conclusions.[52]

---

*the South*, 161; Snider, *Light on the Hill*, 180; Cash, *Mind of the South*, 339; Bruce Clayton, *W. J. Cash, A Life* (Baton Rouge: Louisiana State University Press, 1991), 92–162.

50. Mims, *Advancing South;* O'Brien, *Rethinking the South*, 147.

51. Mims, *Advancing South*, 241–43; O'Brien, *Rethinking the South*, 134.

52. Mims, *Advancing South*, 241.

No issue more inflamed North Carolina and Lewis at the decade's midpoint than the attempt by fundamentalists to ban the teaching of Darwinian theory. The Jazz Age and the wrenching social changes it wrought furnished moral reformers throughout the country with a hodgepodge of hobgoblins to demonize and triggered a powerful backlash against modernism. In much of the South—the Tar Heel State, conspicuously—a legion of the religious fundamentalist majority, egged on by clergy, ecclesiastical leaders, and traveling evangelists, excoriated the teaching of evolution. They deemed it as transgressive a wickedness as fornication and inebriation. The theory, they claimed, had spawned diverse horrors such as Bolshevism, German militarism, materialism, and the disintegration of the family and white supremacy. Drawing foremost on Baptist preachers and laity, mostly from the Piedmont and western counties, and Presbyterians, whose elders had for many years fervently enforced orthodoxy within their fold, antievolutionists sought to banish the "godlessness" at Baptist-affiliated Wake Forest College and the state's public schools and institutions of higher education.[53]

Lewis, her peers in North Carolina's liberal press—most notably the *Greensboro Daily News* and William O. Saunders's small but dauntless and vociferous *Elizabeth City Independent*—and the handful of academics refusing to shrink from combat often found themselves drowned out and outgunned by the saviors of old-time religion. This latter assemblage could count on the sympathy and sometimes direct support from the state's numerous patriotic organizations such as the Ku Klux Klan, United Daughters of the Confederacy, American Legion, and Daughters of the American Revolution. Additionally, many powerful "business progressives," including Governor Cameron Morrison, who held office throughout much of the imbroglio, viewed Darwinian theory with open hostility and expressed absolutely no concern regarding the threat its banning posed to academic freedom. In the seminal study of the conflict historian Willard Gatewood observed that in North Carolina during this time "political and theological orthodoxy often emerged as Siamese twins: politicians proclaimed [the state] 'an old-fashioned Christian Commonwealth,' and clergymen boasted that their loyalty to Democracy was second only to their allegiance to the Christian faith."[54]

According to Lewis, Thomas Theodore Martin, the "Blue Mountain evan-

53. Willard B. Gatewood, *Preachers, Pedagogues & Politicians: The Evolution Controversy in North Carolina, 1920–1927* (Chapel Hill: University of North Carolina Press, 1966), 3–93.

54. Gatewood, *Preachers, Pedagogues & Politicians*, 21–28.

gelist," who had acquired his appellation from the remote Mississippi town in which he had once resided and who earned notoriety as the author of *Hell and the High Schools*, fired the controversy's opening salvo in 1920 by attacking in church publications and pamphlets Wake Forest's venerated president, William Louis Poteat. The prominent educator, public intellectual, and Baptist leader, who championed academic freedom despite his deep religious faith, had for many years stated his belief in evolution and had made no effort to conceal his teaching of the theory in his biology course. Despite Poteat's considerable rhetorical abilities, his skill in church politics, and the spirited defense conducted by Wake Forest students and alumni, he soon became the focal point of the antievolutionists' early attack.[55]

The distinguished scholar's simple and eloquent professions of faith temporarily forestalled his critics' efforts to remove him from his post, but Bible conferences held in the state by national fundamentalist organizations and rabble-rousing freelance evangelists soon reignited and expanded the controversy. These firebrands included such notable figures as Baxter "Cyclone Mack" McLendon, a former barber, whose gyrations in the pulpit often left him dripping with sweat, and Mordecai F. Ham, a sensational spellbinder, who noisily condemned not only the teaching of evolution but also welfare work and Jews. Billy Sunday toured the state and damned the theory, as did William Jennings Bryan, whose popular column appeared in his close friend Josephus Daniels's *News and Observer*.[56]

Lewis viewed the showing of the film *Creation* at Raleigh movie houses in the summer of 1922 as another factor contributing to the renewal of hostilities. In "Incidentally" she appraised *Creation* as "propaganda" and "immediately smelled a rat in the thing." The columnist informed her readers that a religious organization—backed by a northern multimillionaire who had donated twenty million dollars to fund an attack on the teaching of evolution—had produced the film. Its portrayal of the formation of the world according to Genesis fascinated her: "Man's creation was represented as perfectly spontaneous, even so far as the breech-clouts. The same with Eve, who, however, appeared to have been created with more clothes." Moreover, the movie's flora and fauna matched their present forms exactly.[57]

55. Suzanne Cameron Linder, *William Louis Poteat: Prophet of Progress* (Chapel Hill: University of North Carolina Press, 1966), 108–9; Gatewood, *Preachers, Pedagogues & Politicians*, 30–31.

56. Gatewood, *Preachers, Pedagogues & Politicians*, 39–58, 98–101; Morrison, *Josephus Daniels*, 153.

57. *N&O*, 17 August 1922.

"In this connection," Lewis wrote, "it is interesting to note that eleven professors of biology in more or less prominent colleges and universities in this country are reported already to have lost their positions because they will not foreswear belief in the doctrine of evolution—the successful beginnings of a latter-day inquisition." She predicted that the money supplied by the wealthy northern patron would also support attempts to enact state laws proscribing the theory's teaching and to pack the boards of colleges and universities with fundamentalist trustees.[58] The battle over evolution would continue, she informed her readers, but "it is a source of great satisfaction to many people in this State besides liberal-minded Baptists that in North Carolina the first round of this medieval fight against freedom of thought went in the case of Dr. W. L. Poteat of Wake Forest to the Christian scientists (not the Christian Scientists) instead of to the intellectual descendants of the persecutors of Galileo."[59]

The following summer the columnist tore into Ham—whose revivals chief executive Morrison attended and relished—and other "gospel oraytors." Lewis also frequented the services conducted by these traveling evangelists but regarded their assemblages belligerently. She labeled the preachers "pulpit promoters," who confused God's will with their own prejudices: "In the Babel of a stricken world, their dissonant and barbaric harangues contribute woefully to a confusion in which it is difficult enough, at best, to hear that guiding Voice."[60]

The evangelical preachers reciprocated the orthodox Presbyterian governor's esteem, and their admiration of him grew even stronger after he used his influence in early 1924 to have two biology textbooks that referred to evolution stricken from the state's public school curriculum. "One of these books teaches that man is descended from a monkey," he announced, "and the other that he is a cousin to the monkey. I don't believe either one." Lewis ridiculed Morrison's intervention by calling it "that executive decree extraordinaire by which science was put in its place in North Carolina." She found it difficult, however, to stay angry with the chief executive for very long. Despite his hostility to the teaching of evolution, he fought lynching, worked to improve racial relations, and embarked on an ambitious program to improve the state's roads and systems of public schools, higher education, and social services. The

58. *N&O*, 17 August 1922.

59. *N&O*, 17 August 1922.

60. *N&O*, 5 August 1923; Green, "Nell Battle Lewis," 69; Gatewood, *Preachers, Pedagogues & Politicians*, 106–7.

personable and colorful governor, a Tar Heel through and through, charmed and amused Lewis by thundering in the midst of his speeches, "Ya-a-a-s, my countrymen."[61]

The inauguration of Morrison's successor, Angus W. McLean, in January 1925 coincided with the introduction of an antievolution bill into the House Committee on Education by Representative David Scott Poole, a Presbyterian stalwart and the editor of the *Hoke County Journal*. Antievolutionists had succeeded in proscribing the theory's teaching in Oklahoma and Florida, and the national movement now concentrated its efforts on Tennessee and North Carolina. Should the organization prevail in these states, fundamentalist leaders believed they could persuade the federal government to adopt a national antievolution law. The proposed legislation, which Lewis dubbed the "Phoole bill," resolved that "it is the sense of the General Assembly . . . that it is injurious to the welfare of the people of the State of North Carolina for any official or teacher [supported by state funds] to teach or permit to be taught as a fact either Darwinism or any other evolutionary hypothesis that links man in blood relationship with any lower form of life."[62]

Lewis maintained that the bill simply mandated the "accuracy of teachers." She believed that no qualified educator "with or without legislative enactment" characterized a hypothesis as fact. The standard of competency the Poole Bill would decree should also apply to its sponsor. "A law making it a misdemeanor, or preferably, a hanging crime for anyone to introduce in the General Assembly a bill about a subject upon which he is not thoroughly informed would be excellent," she submitted. "Undoubtedly, it would cut down legislation considerably."[63]

Lewis refused to cede religion to the antievolutionists. Like Poteat, she asserted that the doctrine of evolution "glorifies and magnifies the infinite intelligence of God as no dogma of spontaneous creation could ever do." She asked her readers "why a God who through countless natural variations and adaptations during hundreds of thousands of years could make man from a bit of protoplasm in the prehistoric seas is any less worthy of reverence than a God who could make man out of the dust and woman out of a rib. Anyway,

61. *N&O*, 3 February 1924, 29 April 1928; Gatewood, *Preachers, Pedagogues & Politicians*, 106–7; Powell, *North Carolina through Four Centuries*, 470–73.

62. Gatewood, *Preachers, Pedagogues & Politicians*, 125–26, 233; Tindall, *Emergence of the New South*, 204; *N&O*, 18 January 1925, 23 January 1927.

63. *N&O*, 18 January 1925.

what has that to do with religion? Just how does that affect the Sermon on the Mount?"[64]

Warned by informants in the Assembly that the bill had acquired considerable legislative support and that the forces opposing it lacked organization, University of North Carolina president Harry W. Chase took charge. "You have fought our battles long enough," he told Poteat, "and now we are going to do some fighting ourselves." After instructing his faculty to stay put in Chapel Hill, Chase addressed the committee as the onlookers packing the Hall of the House of Representatives cheered. The bill would not only prohibit the teaching of evolution, he remonstrated, but would also abridge the First Amendment rights of teachers and faculty while leaving those of ministers untouched. When several professors the next morning asked him what effect his controversial speech might have on their institution's state funding, he responded, "If this university doesn't stand for anything but appropriations, I, for one, don't care to be connected with it." The moment of truth roused Daniels, a university trustee, from his lethargy, and he ended his tepid support of the antievolutionists. Bryan spent an afternoon with the editor in his study, trying to persuade him to change his mind, but the Great Commoner sulked away from the meeting, six months before his epic encounter with Clarence Darrow in Dayton, Tennessee.[65]

The two days of debate and parliamentary maneuvers devoted to the bill included such high points as the ridiculing of the resolution by state representative Samuel J. Ervin Jr. (the chairman-to-be of the congressional Watergate hearings), who claimed that it "serves no good purpose except to absolve monkeys of their responsibility for the human race." Lewis heaped scorn on the proceedings in "Capitol Theatre" by referring to them as another performance of a hoary and tiresome drama: "We now have a return engagement of Bigotry and Ignorance, The Great Barn-Stormers, in the World-Famous Morality Play Entitled, 'Thou Shalt Not Think!'" In mid-February, to the columnist's great satisfaction, the university's alumni in the General Assembly, bolstered by their Wake Forest peers, dispatched the resolution by a vote of sixty-seven to forty-six.[66]

64. *N&O*, 18 January 1925.

65. Gatewood, *Preachers, Pedagogues & Politicians*, 100–101, 129–33, 135; Gerald W. Johnson, *South-Watching: Selected Essays by Gerald W. Johnson*, ed. Fred Hobson (Chapel Hill: University of North Carolina Press, 1983), 177.

66. Gatewood, *Preachers, Pedagogues & Politicians*, 141–46; *N&O*, 15 February 1925.

In a coda the following month Lewis sighed and conceded that "Incidentally" belonged among the heathen members of the fourth estate, whom the *Hoke County Journal* had recently denounced. She confessed to her readers in a couplet, "Though it endangers my moral success / I'm rather strong for the infidel press." Perhaps alluding to the disparate positions "Incidentally" and the *News and Observer's* editorial page had adopted throughout the tumult, she remarked, "No newspaper is really complete without one infidel." She obliquely paid homage to Daniels by quoting from Heywood Broun's column "It Seems to Me." Many powerful figures surrounded themselves with sycophants, the popular *New York World* columnist had observed. "But there are others more shrewd . . . and it is their desire to keep company with turbulent skeptics who are invariably eager to challenge and argue against the expressed opinion of the King."[67]

Lewis's admiration for Chase's intrepid stand for free speech, as demonstrated by his willingness to place his university in harm's way in the evolution controversy, waned somewhat in December 1925, when he did not forcefully object to the refusal by the North Carolina Cotton Manufacturers Association to allow the Institute for Research in Social Science to survey the state's industrial conditions. David Clark, editor of the *Southern Textile Bulletin,* who had long decried "bolshevism in the colleges," warned the university it would pay a price if it pressed the issue. He informed a *News and Observer* reporter that the manufacturers could easily direct the legislature to cut the institution's appropriations. In Lewis's column and in "The University of North Carolina Gets Its Orders," an article she authored for the *Nation,* she charged that the institution "was spineless and timid" when the situation called for a courageous stand. "It is all very fine . . . to defy the anti-evolutionists who, compared with the mill owners, are not especially influential." It gave her "a sharp and shooting pain . . . to see the University lie down with sickening meekness and let the mill owners walk over it rough-shod."[68]

Lewis sometimes supplemented her journalistic defense for freedom of thought with direct advocacy. In late 1925, for example, she outraged many fundamentalists by accepting an invitation to speak at the controversial Raleigh Religious Forum. A liberal-minded sociologist at the North Carolina State

67. *N&O,* 22 March 1925; Perry J. Ashley, ed., *Dictionary of Literary Biography,* vol. 29: *American Newspaper Journalists, 1926–1950* (Detroit: Gale Research Co., 1984), 40–49.

68. *N&O,* 27 December 1925, 7 February 1926; Nell Battle Lewis, "The University of North Carolina Gets Its Orders," *Nation,* 3 February 1926, 114–15.

College for Agriculture and Engineering had previously organized the annual symposium to discuss contemporary issues of spirituality, and the conflict between fundamentalism and science provided a timely topic for the meeting. The columnist discussed her crisis of faith, which had led her to leave Christ Church and embrace a highly personal relationship with her Lord. Although many members of the audience appreciated her remarks, creationist ministers and publications upbraided the event. Lewis indignantly denounced the "violent outbursts" and "bitter diatribe[s]" directed at her and the other speakers. "I am not responsible to the clergy," she declared. "I am not responsible to the Church. I am only responsible to my own God, honestly, steadfastly sought and partially found, and to the integrity of the mind He gave me with which to seek him.[69]

The defeat in the 1925 General Assembly wounded the antievolutionists but did not end their agitation. Their Pyrrhic victory in the Scopes "Monkey Trial" galvanized creationists. Additionally, Bryan's death a few days after the curtain came down on the Dayton histrionics furnished the movement with a martyr. Outside forces redoubled their efforts in North Carolina, and native fundamentalists in 1926 formed a Committee of One Hundred in an attempt to bring their influence to bear in every Tar Heel county during the upcoming Democratic primaries. Convinced that many of her readers knew little about Darwinian theory, Lewis devoted a number of editions of "Incidentally" to "the ABC of Evolution Contest." Winners of the twenty-question quizzes received copies of Hendrik Van Loon's *Tolerance*, a history of the rise of religious understanding.[70]

The committee's internal squabbling and the extremist positions it espoused, however, alienated many voters, and antievolutionists fared poorly in the election. Nevertheless, Representative Poole introduced in the 1927 General Assembly a new bill that outlawed the teaching not only of evolution but of any theory that conflicted with creationism. The measure also mandated stiff penalties for educators violating the law. Lewis had long since grown weary of the controversy and believed it "uncivilized" to devote any more attention to the issue, but she girded herself and bore into the antievolutionists again. She believed the new bill resulted from a deep insecurity on the part of church leaders and criticized the legislation for its "dangerous," "absurd," "pathetic,"

69. Gatewood, *Preachers, Pedagogues & Politicians*, 158; *N&O*, 3 January 1926.

70. Gatewood, *Preachers, Pedagogues & Politicians*, 161–64, 186–89; *N&O*, 7 February 1926.

and "annoying" qualities. She also authored "Where Will You Be, Boys?" a poem exhorting Chase's peers at the state's principal public colleges and the state superintendent of public instruction, whose "unfortunate maladies" had prevented them from appearing before the General Assembly in 1925, to join the University of North Carolina's president in addressing the 1927 legislature to argue against the new Poole Bill. Her creation's final stanza read:

Will you speak out in meeting when next Thursday rolls around,
Or will you be in hiding with your ears glued to the ground,
And silent, as the spineless were in Tennessee?
Where will you be, Boys, where will you be?[71]

In the end the educators' presence proved unnecessary; the House Committee on Education overwhelmingly rejected the bill. This outcome emphasized to all but the most implacable creationists that the state's elected officials would not countenance the proscription of academic freedom, despite the fact that the majority of North Carolinians interpreted the Bible literally. Although some observers predicted yet another antievolution onslaught, a new menace to fundamentalists—more distant but even more ominous than Darwinian theory—had emerged in the form of a "wet," cigar-chomping, brown derby–wearing Roman Catholic pol from the "Sidewalks of New York" and the Fulton Fish Market.[72]

Lewis predicted in early 1926 that the presidential campaign of New York Governor Alfred "Al" Smith, the Democratic Party's heir presumptive for the 1928 election, would ignite "fireworks" in the South. The political contest would result in the columnist's pressing the flesh for Smith and setting off some of her own pyrotechnics. She had grown skeptical of her ability to influence public policy through her journalistic advocacy and activism in women's organizations, which Darden Asbury Pyron writes had traditionally "relied on the methods of the Lady—indirection, lobbying, the appeal to the heart and sentiment, and flattery of male lawmakers." She now believed that "reforms usually come when experienced, practical, hard-boiled people get the controlling politicians in a corner" and threaten "to soak [them] good and proper."[73]

71. Gatewood, *Preachers, Pedagogues & Politicians*, 221–22; *N&O*, 23 January and 6 February 1927.

72. Gatewood, *Preachers, Pedagogues & Politicians*, 227; Powell, *North Carolina through Four Centuries*, 466.

73. Pyron, "Nell Battle Lewis," 73; *N&O*, 5 August 1928.

As Lewis reflected on the efficacy of her activism, her father's death in August 1926 affected her deeply, triggering additional self-examination and altering her circumstances. Although she had continued to live with Dr. Lewis at Cloverdale, relations between the two appear to have grown less confrontational. A decade later she recalled that during this period her father had patiently listened to her liberal views and kept his own more conservative opinions to himself. The hiring of a cook, maid, and chauffeur improved the farm's chaotic living conditions that had so upset her brothers after her return from Europe. Bishop Cheshire, who had baptized her and known her mother intimately, conducted the funeral services for his lifelong friend at Christ Church. Nell likely sat alongside her brothers in the pew that her father had occupied for forty years. The occasion undoubtedly brought to the surface the many conflicted feelings she had for Dr. Lewis and Christ Church.[74]

Nell apparently would inherit from her father's estate savings, stock certificates, and property worth approximately fifty thousand dollars—enough money, if carefully managed, to provide her with financial security for the remainder of her life. To dispose of the farm, the four Lewis children formed a corporation named "Cloverdale, Inc." Kemp—distracted by his duties at Erwin Mills and his election as vice president of the Cotton Manufacturers Association and without experienced legal guidance—guided Cloverdale into a partnership with other investors and the Atlantic Coast Realty Company, which would subdivide the expansive domain and oversee the development of a residential community. The Lewises surrendered their land in return for preferred stock in the enterprise.[75]

Dr. Lewis's having designated his three sons as executors of his estate may explain why Nell went along with Kemp's venture despite the fact that she regarded it dubiously. In May 1927 an executive of Atlantic Coast Realty Company, seeking to alleviate Nell's anxieties, conveyed to Kemp the Virginia-based company's "full confidence" that barring an "abnormal depression in the real estate market," the investors would receive handsome profits from the sale of the land. By the fall of 1928 realtors had in fact sold over a dozen lots, but a slow real estate market required that the purchasers receive long-term financing.[76]

74. *N&O*, 15 September 1935, 8 November 1936.

75. "Dr. Lewis Leaves $250,000 Estate," *N&O*, [August 1926]; J. W. Ferrell to KPL, 13 May 1927, both in NBL Papers.

76. J. W. Ferrell to KPL, 13 May 1927, KPL to NBL, 24 September 1928, NBL to IFL, 11 July 1930, all in NBL Papers.

Lewis used a considerable portion of her inheritance to build a house across the street from St. Mary's College and to prepare to enter the masculine arenas of the courtroom and perhaps even the legislature. In 1926 she began reading for the law under a North Carolina assistant attorney general, Walter D. Siler. The following summer she took leave from writing her column and resided in New York, where she enrolled in several law courses at Columbia University. Her brief matriculation at Columbia undoubtedly exposed her to the rancorous debate raging between members of the law school faculty about whether women merited admission as official candidates for the bachelor of laws degree. In the fall of 1927 the faculty voted to admit tentatively two female students—one a Smith College alumna, whose study at that institution overlapped with Lewis's.[77]

Being in New York afforded Lewis an opportunity to learn more about—perhaps to witness directly—the fruits of Governor Smith's administration, which included many influential female members, such as his close advisor Belle Moskowitz and administrative assistant Frances Perkins, who later served as President Franklin D. Roosevelt's secretary of labor. The many progressive stances of the "Fighting Governor" impressed Lewis greatly. She considered the Empire State's social legislation the most advanced in the country. With notable success Smith had sponsored an extensive series of laws and measures designed to curb the exploitation of women and child laborers, limit their working hours, and secure minimum wages for them. He had implemented a Child Welfare Act that provided pensions to widows with children and had convened a commission that spearheaded changes in laws to protect minors further. He had battled against powerful corporate interests to make gas and electric power affordable for his fellow citizens and to prevent profiteering in the sale of food. Beyond a doubt Lewis weighed these attainments against the rudimentary results she, Johnson, and their liberal allies had achieved in the Tar Heel State.[78]

Her high regard for the governor and enthusiasm for the triumph of democracy that the election of someone of his humble origins and non-Protestant re-

77. Sellars, "South Saver," 16; Mitchell, "Nell Battle Lewis," 57; "Nell Battle Lewis, 1911," Nell Battle Lewis Papers, Saint Mary's School Archives; Julius Goebel Jr., *A History of the School of Law, Columbia University* (New York: Columbia University Press, 1955), 290–91.

78. Mathew Josephson and Hannah Josephson, *Al Smith: Hero of the Cities, A Political Portrait Drawing on the Papers of Frances Perkins* (Boston: Houghton Mifflin, 1969), 197, 342, 352; *N&O*, 7 October 1928.

ligion signified clouded her judgment. She confidently predicted his victory and at first saw no possibility of a fissure in the Solid South. In reality Smith faced difficult odds. His opponent, Herbert Hoover, could point to the prosperous economy associated with Republican president Calvin Coolidge. And Smith's success depended not just on winning the Northeast and the cities but on building a coalition that also included portions of the West and, most significantly, the states below the Mason-Dixon Line, a sizable faction of whose voters' allegiance to the Democratic Party the New Yorker's candidacy strained to the breaking point.[79]

As a concession to southern Democrats, the party held its convention in Houston that June, and its platform skirted the contentious issue of Prohibition. But these actions did nothing to curb a contemptible anti-Smith propaganda campaign, orchestrated in the crucial southern battleground by the Klan and clerical politicians such as Methodist Bishop James Cannon. Soon the enormity of the religious, regional, ethnic, and class prejudice Smith and his wife, Catherine "Katie," would have to surmount became apparent.[80]

As the Democrats prepared for their Texas convention, Lewis threw her own hat in the ring by releasing a single-sentence statement declaring her intent to run for a seat in the General Assembly. "County Has First Woman Candidate" and "Well Known Writer and Club Woman Formally Enters June Democratic Primary," read a *News and Observer* headline and subheading. The paper printed a picture of the columnist sporting a modern bobbed hairdo and announced she would vie for one of Wake County's three seats in the 1929 House of Representatives. The article listed her credentials, which included her impressive history of service and leadership in women's organizations.[81]

Like Smith, Lewis faced an uphill struggle. Her brother Dick regretted her decision to run for office, believing that she stood little chance of winning and that her candidacy would only compound her considerable unpopularity with the state's business and political establishment. Kemp had mixed feelings about his sister's political ambitions. Although he did not want to see her disillusioned by defeat, he believed that many of the stands she would take in the legislature regarding the textile industry would embarrass him. He confided

79. Josephson and Josephson, *Al Smith*, 376–77; *N&O*, 17 January 1926, 13 July 1928.

80. Edmund A. Moore, *A Catholic Runs for President: The Campaign of 1928* (New York: Ronald Press Co., 1956), 169; Josephson and Josephson, *Al Smith*, 367, 381; Virginius Dabney, *Dry Messiah: The Life of Bishop Canon* (New York: Alfred A. Knopf, 1949), 173–89.

81. *N&O*, 12 February 1928.

in Ivey that he had "always felt that it would be a very pleasant thing to have her take her criticisms about some other industry than the one that supports her two brothers." Judging "discretion [as] the better part of valor," however, he did not share his opinion with her.[82]

Lewis indeed faced many obstacles, but she nearly proved Dick wrong. Strictly—and perhaps naively—abiding by a state $160 primary campaign expenditure limit, she nevertheless received more votes than half of the twelve candidates and entered a runoff. The *News and Observer* remarked on the "considerable interest" her showing had evoked. Motivated no doubt by her fierce sponsorship of an industrial survey, manufacturers met secretly to contrive her defeat. Other opposition came from fundamentalists, who regarded her unorthodox religious beliefs as evidence of her atheism and initiated a whispering campaign against her. And many voters regarded women as poorly suited to hold political office; only three female representatives had ever served in the General Assembly. In the midst of all of this opposition Lewis refused to rein in her column. "Oh, that mine enemy had writ a book!" she exclaimed, as she reflected several years later on the paper trail she had left. "My opponents had it on me irrevocably, in black and white." Despite the efforts of Kate Burr Johnson and the county's organized women, in the runoff Lewis could not overcome the sentiment against her in the rural areas of the county and the mill town of Wake Forest.[83]

Her defeat must have disappointed her, but she displayed her characteristic pluck and panache and could take comfort in her respectable showing—she had received more votes in Raleigh than the other candidates—and in having broken a little more ground for women. Taking no time to lick her wounds, she threw herself into the battle royal engulfing Al Smith. During her own campaign she had honed her speechmaking abilities, and in the rush up to the presidential election, she traveled "from stump to stump," barnstorming North Carolina to deliver nineteen passionate speeches—including at least one broadcast via radio—on behalf of her "hero." In "Incidentally" she refuted the scurrilous attacks on Smith and blazoned his dynamic record as governor.[84]

82. Green, "Nell Battle Lewis: Crusading Columnist," 33; KPL to IFL, 14 June 1928, KPL to NBL, 14 June 1928, both in KPL Papers.

83. *N&O*, 3 and 30 June and 1 July 1928, 4 September 1932; Esther Lowell, "A Columnist with a Purpose," *Woman's Journal*, March 1929, 24–25; "Nell Battle Lewis, 1911," Nell Battle Lewis Papers, Saint Mary's School Archives; Kate Burr Johnson to J. M. Templeton, 11 June 1928, NBL Papers.

84. *N&O*, 1 July, 14 October, and 11 November 1928.

Her friend Frank Porter Graham, now an ebullient young history professor at the University of North Carolina who shared Lewis's progressive vision for their state, expressed in a letter the regret of the institution's faculty for her loss in the election and his admiration of her stand for Smith. Graham had achieved a growing reputation through his liberality, tireless promotion of the university, and articulate defense of Chase when the university came under attack by the antievolutionists. "We are all terribly sorry you are not going to be in the legislature," he wrote, "but I know you put up a good fight and had a lot of fun. I only wish the fun were going to continue in the General Assembly." He congratulated her for her persuasive speeches for Smith and closed his letter by bidding "strength to your arm, point to your pen, and reach to your voice."[85]

Few if any Tar Heels campaigned more fervently for Smith than did Lewis. In "Incidentally" she reminded her readers of native Catholics who had brought honor to North Carolina such as Judge William Gaston, a state Supreme Court associate justice, whose civic service and brilliant legal mind had spurred a grateful General Assembly a century earlier to end a ban on his coreligionists' holding public office. Lewis expressed her belief that some of Smith's opponents would like to see such a proscription reinstated at a national level. Not even her veterancy of the fierce evolution engagements prepared her for the extent of the prejudice directed at Smith by fundamentalists. The *North Carolina Christian Advocate* included an article entitled "A Bit of Roman-Catholic History," which dredged up ancient fiendish abuses committed or condoned by the Church such as the Inquisition and the torture of heretics by Catholic British monarchs. This record of persecution made "every drop of Protestant blood [within the *Advocate*'s editor] run hot." Lewis added to this fragmentary chronicle the Catholic Church's preservation of civilization and Christianity during the Dark Ages and its innumerable works of compassion and charity. She admonished the South's Protestants who were fanning the flames of religious bigotry not to forget that they and Catholics worshiped the same Lord.[86]

Lewis's unrelenting partisanship and her rebuke angered many Smith adversaries. One woman from Rocky Mount charged in a letter to the editor that

85. FPG to NBL, 8 October 1928, FPG Papers; Snider, *Light on the Hill*, 203–5; Ashby, *Frank Porter Graham*, 59–70.

86. *N&O*, 15 April and 2 and 30 September 1928; Powell, *North Carolina through Four Centuries*, 272–80.

the columnist had "gone too far in her accusations, for if we were what she accuses, then we are unfit to be American citizens, unfit for citizenship in any country." The correspondent alleged that despite Lewis's espousal of tolerance, she exhibited little of the quality for anyone who disagreed with her. The missive concluded with an advertisement for a wardrobe accessory that the overzealous Raleigh journalist should acquire to demonstrate her ardor for her hero—"Wanted: a feminine 'modification' of the little 'brown derby' to grace the head of Miss Nell Battle Lewis." Another letter writer believed that Lewis's misrepresentation of Hoover's supporters made it clear that the election provided voters with the opportunity to choose "Right against Wrong."[87]

Criticism such as this did not moderate Lewis's attacks on Smith's foes. She snickered when some members of North Carolina's political establishment feigned horror over Smith's Tammany Hall connections. Senator Furnifold M. Simmons had overseen a machine that had monolithically controlled Tar Heel politics since the turn of the century. The New York governor's campaign, she pointed out in "Incidentally," "had breathed the breath of life" into the Democratic Party in Dixie by forcing leaders such as Simmons—then leading a "bolt" to the party of Lincoln within the state—to show their true colors.[88]

The columnist marveled at the objections raised over Smith's open support for moderating the Prohibition amendment to permit states the option of determining whether their residents could legally consume light wine and beer. Perhaps, she speculated, "we have become so accustomed to politicians who drink wet and vote dry that consistency in this respect is naturally shocking to our sensibilities." Lewis broadened her charge of hypocrisy and indicted the electorate at large by quoting Will Rogers's wisecrack that "the people of this country will vote dry as long as they can stagger to the polls."[89]

Much of the opposition to Smith in North Carolina, Lewis believed, stemmed from a poorly examined source: the owners of the three private corporations—the Duke family, in particular—that controlled the state's generation of electricity. The New York governor's vanquishment of a rapacious electrical energy combine and his support for public ownership of water resources must have made the owners of the Duke Power, Carolina Power & Light, and Tallassee Power companies anxious. Among the states east of the

87. *N&O*, 8 and 20 October 1928.

88. V. O. Key Jr., *Southern Politics in State and Nation* (Knoxville: University of Tennessee Press, 1984), 212–13; *N&O*, 17 January and 13 July 1928.

89. *N&O*, 15 April and 13 July 1928; Josephson and Josephson, *Al Smith*, 376–77.

Mississippi River, the U.S. Geological Survey ranked North Carolina second only to New York in hydroelectric potential.[90]

A month before the election—in "Pity the Non-Partisan!"—Lewis expressed contempt for the state's newspapers' refusal to enter the fray. If the Tar Heel press genuinely desired to demonstrate its nonalignment, she suggested it could do so in a host of ways. "There are so many things that one can be joyfully independent of: for instance, the Simmons leadership that has bossed the State for years, the provincialism that is suspicious of other sections, the evangelical domination of local thought, the snobbery that wants a queen in the White House and thinks a brown derby is vulgar."[91]

On 11 October Lewis accompanied a party of North Carolina delegates to the Virginia border to join Governor Smith aboard his campaign train and escort him into the state. Crowds of spectators—supporters and opponents—filled the stations as the entourage proceeded to the capital. She arrived in Raleigh besotted by Smith's charisma—his "It" quality, she had earlier termed this aspect of his personality. "As a popular hero the rather small, red-faced man with the big nose and the broad grin fulfilled all my expectations," she revealed in an "Incidentally" lead editorial entitled "Genius": "As he sat on a table in the conference car of his special train, telling a joke on himself, I thought: 'What a wonderful thing you represent: that subtle potency with which Heaven endowed you, by which your fellow men are curiously moved to response to what you say and do.'"[92]

In the end, of course, the columnist lost her fight—heroically but humiliatingly. Hoover triumphed in a landslide and swept the electoral college overwhelmingly. Despite her certainty of voting outcomes in the Solid South, North Carolina, Virginia, Tennessee, Florida, and Texas bolted the Democratic Party. Only the Deep South, whose whites felt even more menaced by large percentages of blacks than by the specter of a papist president, stayed loyal to Jim Crow's historic party. Adding to her mortification, out of the five renegades only Florida exceeded her own state's percentage of votes cast for Hoover.[93]

90. *N&O*, 30 September 1928; Hobbs, *North Carolina*, 21–28.

91. *N&O*, 7 October 1928.

92. *N&O*, 13 July and 14 October 1928; "East Lawn Bulletin," 14 October 1928, Ivey Foreman Lewis Papers (hereafter cited as IFL Papers), Special Collections, University of Virginia Library.

93. Reed and Reed, *1001 Things Everyone Should Know about the South*, 119; Key, *Southern Politics in State and Nation*, 318–22.

The Sunday following the election, she devoted most of "Incidentally" to an "An Open Letter to Governor Smith." She informed the Democratic candidate that religious prejudice had figured most prominently in his rout: "All other opposition to you was inconsiderable beside that. This election has proved conclusively that the United States is a Protestant plutocracy, not a democracy—indeed, that it is worlds removed from the democracy conceived by Thomas Jefferson."[94] "You were defeated," she continued, "not because you were unfitted for the Presidency, since by both ability and experience you are eminently qualified for that office; not because you are Wet, not because you were supported by Tammany Hall, although these last two factors contributed; but, be it said to the everlasting shame of this country, in a campaign of the most infamous slander, you were beaten because you worship God in a way displeasing to the dominant sectarian group." She informed her readers that the prejudice Smith had faced violated not just the precepts of American democracy but, more important, all of the principles of Jesus Christ.

"Battling Nell" had earned a well-deserved reputation for not pulling her punches, but the roundhouse she threw at the Tar Heel Democrats who had deserted Smith must have surprised even her inveterate readers. "North Carolina is disgraced," she declared. Much of its thinking "is controlled by the evangelical clergy, many of whose members are ignorant and bigoted." If she could campaign again for Smith, she wrote, she would double the number of speeches she had given. She would do this not just because she considered him a great man, although she did, but with the hope that she could persuade her beloved state to redeem itself by voting for the governor and thus confirm her hopeful wish that tolerance and justice prevailed within its borders.

In the little space that remained in her column, she proposed a new doxology—"Glory to the Protestant god in the highest; in the United States intolerance and ill-will toward Roman-Catholics!"—and accused Virginia of being an even worse traitor than North Carolina because the commonwealth had betrayed its legacy as a cradle of democracy. A postscript she appended exemplified the combativeness that had earned Lewis her moniker: "Well, boys and girls, it certainly was a SWELL fight, and I wouldn't have missed it for a chair of gold and diamonds on the fence!"[95]

Her fierce advocacy—especially her oratorial abilities—impressed future

94. *N&O*, 11 November 1928.

95. *N&O*, 11 November 1928.

Smith biographer Frank Porter Graham. He asked her to join a steering committee of the Citizen's Library Movement. He had formed the organization, the earliest such body in the United States, with the ambitious goal of providing library services to every North Carolina county. He especially desired her participation in a speakers' bureau that would promote the movement. The professor planned to kick off his campaign in Charlotte. Lewis returned Graham's missive after scrawling an emphatic single-sentence response atop the invitation: "I won't make any more speeches to these G-d Protestants, but I'll be glad to serve on the committee."[96]

She undoubtedly expected a period of comparative quiescence after the donnybrook in which she had just participated, but she almost immediately found herself swept up into an even more violent struggle, one that would form her life's crucible. A month to the day after Smith posted his letter to Lewis, a motorcycle bearing Fred Beal singing "Solidarity" crossed the city limits of Charlotte, North Carolina.[97]

96. Snider, *Light on the Hill*, 205; John Ehle, *Dr. Frank: Life with Frank Porter Graham* (Chapel Hill, N.C.: Franklin Street Books, 1993), 36; FPG to NBL, 3 November 1928, FPG Papers.

97. Fred E. Beal, *Proletarian Journey: New England, Gastonia, Moscow* (New York: Hillman-Curl, 1937), 109–10.

# 5 BARBAROUS GASTON

Almost immediately after its founding in September 1928, the communist-controlled National Textile Workers Union (NTWU), which termed itself "a fighting organization controlled by the workers," had audaciously begun to reconnoiter Gastonia, a textile town twenty miles west of Charlotte. "North Carolina is the key to the South, Gaston county is the key to North Carolina and the Loray mill is the key to Gaston county," one organizer explained. The fortress-like five-story brick Loray factory represented a target of dizzying significance for the incipient union: the largest mill in the heart of the southern textile industry. Fred Beal, the stout redheaded southern district organizer of the newly formed workers' union, had arrived in Charlotte on New Year's Day 1929.[1]

Born in Massachusetts in 1896 into a religious family, Beal had grown up there and gone to work in a Lawrence textile mill at age fourteen as a bobbin boy. In 1912 he had participated in the Lawrence textile strike led by the Industrial Workers of the World (IWW). Drafted into the army during World War I, he had gone AWOL and picketed in uniform in another walkout in Lawrence in 1919. Three years later he had joined the One Big Union and the Socialist Party and participated in still another labor dispute in his hometown. He had helped lead the Dover, New Hampshire, and New Bedford, Massachusetts, strikes in 1925 and 1928. He had protested the executions of Nicola Sacco and Bartolomeo Vanzetti and joined the Communist Party, despite his religious beliefs and concerns regarding its methods. Notwithstanding his unprepossessing appearance and speaking style, his commitment to nonviolence—which set him apart from hot-blooded southern men—and his possible homosexuality, he would earn the respect and affection of the Loray strikers for his honesty and unassuming nature. The Communist Party remained distrustful of Beal because of his suspicion of leaders and his dislike of ideology.[2]

1. Irving Bernstein, *The Lean Years: A History of the American Laborer, 1920–1933* (Boston: Houghton Mifflin, 1960), 20–21; Albert Weisbord to Forrest Bailey, 26 December 1928, American Civil Liberties Union Papers (hereafter cited as ACLU Papers), University of Minnesota, Minneapolis; Beal, *Proletarian Journey*, 109–10; Fred Erwin Beal to editor of the *Gastonia Gazette*, 13 April 1929, *Gastonia Gazette* Correspondence, Southern Historical Collection, Wilson Library, University of North Carolina at Chapel Hill; *N&O*, 5 May 1929.

2. Beal, *Proletarian Journey*, 17–106; "Who Are the Gastonia Prisoners?" *Labor Defender*, Sep-

Loray furnished Beal with a highly individualized workforce unschooled in collective bargaining and labor militancy but simmering with anger. Until his arrival workers could express their discontent only by quitting, traditionally the sole means of protest in the industrial South. The long hours, short pay, and poor conditions at the mill, endemic in southern textile work and exacerbated by the severe postwar downturn in the industry's fortunes, rankled. Operatives also begrudged management's distant nature, a consequence of both the factory's size and its relentless emphasis on productivity. The various euphemisms used to describe work at the mill—"stretch out," "doubling up," "efficiency methods," "extended labor system," "rationalization," and "payroll economies"—shared a common meaning: fewer employees performing more work at reduced wages.

Although the fifty-five-hour shifts and low pay at Loray did not differ significantly from conditions at other mills in the Carolina Piedmont, dynamics within Loray set it apart from other textile communities, intensified the anomie among its operatives, and created a volatile environment. Workers referred to Loray as "the jail" because a fence surrounded it, and the highly visible mill police force locked them in during their shifts. The rambling nature of the village discouraged cohesion and communication among residents, and management had grouped families antagonistic to one another closely together. Moreover, the factory reportedly had the highest rate of turnover within Gaston County and earned a reputation for hiring "drifters." The mill's agents recruited actively in Georgia and South Carolina, where textile factories paid even more poorly than North Carolina's. Some laborers came straight from the hills and mountains and lacked any industrial experience, indeed had never worked for "cash money."[3]

Rhode Island–based Manville-Jenckes had pioneered the stretch-out system in the South at Loray in 1927, intending to compel its employees to work with the same degree of productiveness as northern operatives but for longer

---

tember 1929, 171; *Daily Worker* (hereafter cited as *DW*), 27 July 1929; Fred E. Beal, "I Was a Communist Martyr," *American Mercury* 42, no. 165 (September 1937): 33; *Charlotte Observer* (hereafter cited as *CO*), 15 October 1929; *N&O*, 14 July 1935; Mary Heaton Vorse, "Gastonia," *Harper's*, November 1929, 702–3; John A. Salmond, *Gastonia 1929: The Story of the Loray Mill Strike* (Chapel Hill: University of North Carolina Press, 1995), 18, 170; Vera Buch Weisbord, *A Radical Life* (Bloomington: Indiana University Press, 1977), 174, 206, 215; Robin Hood, "The Loray Mill Strike" (master's thesis, University of North Carolina, 1932), 113–14.

3. Weisbord, *Radical Life*, 184; Hood, "Loray Mill Strike," 14, 18, 26; Liston Pope, *Millhands & Preachers: A Study of Gastonia* (New Haven: Yale University Press, 1942), 222–28.

hours and less money. The company appointed Gordon Johnstone, a shrewd and overbearing businessman, as resident agent and ordered him to cut $500,000 a year in costs. Johnstone cut the factory's labor force from thirty-five to twenty-two hundred, implemented two 10 percent pay cuts, and increased production. Hank clocks measured pace and output. Women and children replaced men, and skilled foremen received walking papers. Large numbers of previously full-time employees, women especially, found themselves reduced to doing piecework and received no pay when machinery malfunctioned.[4]

In 1928 Loray workers expressed their dissatisfaction in a series of protests that foreshadowed the major labor unrest the following year. In early March the mill's weavers walked out. Johnstone had increased the number of looms they ran while cutting their wages in half. "All we are asking is simple justice," one operative told the *Gastonia Gazette*. Management increased its police force and broke the spontaneous strike by transferring other employees to the weave room. Later that year raucous employees staged a mock funeral procession down Gastonia's main street. Borne in a casket by pallbearers, an effigy of the unpopular resident agent periodically sprang to life, sat up, and shouted: "How many men are carrying this thing?" "Eight," members of the cavalcade bellowed back. "Lay off two; six can do the work," the effigy ordered.[5]

Nervous that a more serious labor disturbance might soon erupt, Manville-Jenckes expeditiously replaced its controversial resident agent with John A. Baugh, who adopted a more conciliatory attitude toward his workers and augmented the village's system of welfare work. These reforms did little, however, to improve meaningfully the conditions the work force labored under, and they came too late. Johnstone's policies and personality had engendered anger and distrust that would not be so easily assuaged.[6]

On the afternoon of 1 April, standing in back of the hastily secured wooden

4. *N&O*, 5 May 1929; William J. Dunne, *Gastonia: Citadel of the Class Struggle in the New South* (New York: Workers Library Publishers, 1929), 19–20; *DW*, 25 April 1929; Bernstein, *Lean Years*, 20–21; Pope, *Millhands & Preachers*, 229–30; Salmond, *Gastonia 1929*, 14; Brent D. Glass, *The Textile Industry in North Carolina: A History* (Raleigh: North Carolina Department of Cultural Resources, 1992), 69; Hood, "Loray Mill Strike," 24–30; Benjamin Ulysses Ratchford, "Toward Preliminary Social Analysis: II. Economic Aspects of the Gastonia Situation," *Social Forces* 8, no. 3 (March 1930): 360; I. A. Newby, *Plain Folk in the New South: Social Change and Cultural Persistence, 1880–1915* (Baton Rouge: Louisiana State University Press, 1989), 199.

5. Pope, *Millhands & Preachers*, 233–34; Vera Buch Weisbord, "Gastonia, 1929: Strike at the Loray Mill," *Southern Culture* 1, nos. 3–4 (winter 1974): 193.

6. Hood, "Loray Mill Strike," 31; Pope, *Millhands & Preachers*, 236.

shack in Loray Village that served as a union headquarters, Beal distributed copies of *Solidarity* to sympathetic workers. Then he spoke for an hour with such emotion that his mouth filled with blood. He called for a vote, and the members of the crowd—many whooping and some raising both hands—unanimously decided to walk out. They formed a picket line in front of the mill, but the enthusiasm of many strikers almost immediately waned as they noticed foremen jotting down names to compile a blacklist. Beal attempted to steady the nerves of the protesters by leading them in song. Inside the mill unionists and foremen loyal to the company furiously pressed their views on the undecided. "It was a feary time," one employee later recalled. At the 6:00 p.m. shift change nearly all eleven hundred workers joined the strike, and only a hundred or so night workers entered the mill to replace them. Tempers ran hot, but at no time did the situation descend into violence or lawlessness. Even the *Gastonia Daily Gazette*, which would soon earn a well-deserved reputation for incendiary reporting and editorializing, conceded that "there had been practically no disturbance among the agitated employe[e]s."[7]

Mayor Wiley T. Rankin consulted with the sheriff and Chief of Police Orville F. Aderholt and telephoned Governor Oliver Max Gardner. "The situation is beyond our control," Rankin informed the state's chief executive, "and we are asking you to send troops here to take charge of the situation." Gardner authorized calling out the local National Guard company and four others from the surrounding area. Overnight the mill village became a "miniature army camp."[8]

That afternoon the *Gazette* assumed the fulminant role it would play throughout the controversy when it printed the first of a series of advertisements—allegedly paid for by an anonymous group of "citizens of Gaston County"—denouncing Beal and endorsing vigilantism. "Every 100 per cent American man, woman, and child" should know that Beal was a "Red" and a "Bolshevik" who opposed religion and organized government, the ad warned. He had incited union members "to engage in violence and even bloodshed" and threatened "the very existence, the happiness, and the very life even of every citizen of Gaston county." Many congregants of Christian churches and members of patriotic and fraternal organizations had begun to question whether the union organizers should be run out of town, the announcement concluded.[9]

7. Beal, *Proletarian Journey*, 123–33; Salmond, *Gastonia 1929*, 19–23; Hood, "Loray Mill Strike," 34–36; *Gastonia Daily Gazette* (hereafter cited as *GG*), 2 April 1929; *DW*, 2 April 1929.

8. *GG*, 3, 4 April 1929.

9. *GG*, 3 April 1929.

The following afternoon the *Gazette*'s editor Hugh A. Query and managing editor James W. Atkins prominently featured "Mob Rule vs. Law and Order," the second installment in the anonymously sponsored advertising campaign. The ad exhorted "EVERY MAN AND WOMAN IN GASTON COUNTY [to] ASK THE QUESTION: AM I WILLING TO ALLOW THE MOB TO CONTROL GASTON COUNTY, THE MOB WHOSE LEADERS DO NOT BELIEVE IN GOD AND WHO WOULD DESTROY THE GOVERNMENT?" Readers should know, the ad continued, that the strike demands masked the real goal of the unrest: "OVERTHROWING THIS GOVERNMENT AND DESTROYING PROPERTY AND TO KILL, KILL, KILL." The dictum ominously declared that "THE TIME IS AT HAND FOR EVERY AMERICAN TO DO HIS DUTY."[10]

The Associated Press report for that day made no mention of this bloodcurdling scenario. "Everything was reported quiet today about the Loray mill of the Manville-Jenckes Company," it announced evenly. In reality Beal, a pacifist who abhorred physical violence, was laboring mightily to keep events from spiraling out of control. "Keep a block away from the mill," he enjoined the strikers. "Don't be seen talking to any national guardsmen. And don't commit any violence. That is what the Manville-Jenckes people want."[11]

On 5 April the *Gazette* published the last of the unsigned ads, this one submitted by a solitary "citizen of Gaston County." Lacking much of the hysteria of the two earlier pieces, this exposition bore the fingerprints of a more subtle and skillful propagandist. Quoting liberally from *Daily Worker* back issues, Party officials, and labor experts, it evinced the writer's connectedness to professional anticommunist activists. The author stated that communists advocated an end to racial separation and endorsed crossing the "color line" and "free love." As evidence, he extracted a notice from the *Daily Worker* publicizing an interracial mixer in New York at which "workers of all races [would] show their working class solidarity by coming together . . . and help break down capitalist-instilled prejudices and race hatreds." The specter of black men dancing with white women to music provided by John C. Smith's Negro orchestra was intended to make the *Gazette*'s white readers recoil.[12]

The next day Query decried Beal and co-organizer George Pershing's "bitter and venomous denunciation" of the Gastonia paper and declared that the "great mass of people around the cotton mills of Gaston county know that The

10. *GG*, 4 April 1929.

11. *GG*, 4 and 5 April 1929; Salmond, *Gastonia 1929*, 25; Beal, *Proletarian Journey*, 147; Hood, "Loray Mill Strike," 113.

12. *GG*, 5 April 1929.

Gazette is their Friend." He called in the heavy guns and devoted his lead story to a talk David Clark, a "widely known . . . man of character and standing in the textile world," had given in town the previous day. The *Southern Textile Bulletin*'s editor had claimed that he had closely followed the union's activities and that in a few days he would "have the records" on Beal and Pershing. The same edition of the *Gazette* also included a reprint of a telegram sent that day by Clark containing disparaging information about the two organizers.[13]

Working synergistically, the *Gazette, Southern Textile Bulletin,* and *Charlotte Observer* would form the nucleus of the union-bashing mill press and effectively shape public opinion and fuel extremism throughout the crisis. Their views would be mirrored—with few notable exceptions—by Carolina newspapers such as the *Charlotte News, Charleston News and Courier, Concord Tribune, Hickory Record, Spartanburg Herald, Wilmington Star, Durham Sun, Winston-Salem Journal,* and many others.[14]

With a circulation of little more than six thousand and without a Sunday edition, the little Gastonia daily lacked the ability to exert much influence beyond its immediate vicinity. Managing editor Atkins had recently served as president of the North Carolina Press Association, however, and undoubtedly enjoyed ties to journalists throughout the state. By greatly overemphasizing the strike's peril and by demonizing its leaders, the *Gazette* fomented conditions in which mob violence could flourish locally. The paper served as the mouthpiece for the town's establishment, and readers doing its bidding knew they operated extrajudicially and with the tacit support of the larger community. Labor journalist Tom Tippett, who reported on the crisis for the leftist Federated Press service, exaggerated only somewhat when he accused the little newspaper of going to "lengths that had never before been equaled in American yellow journalism." A *Gazette* front-page cartoon entitled "A Viper That Must Be Smashed!" exemplifies Tippett's assessment. Appearing early in the strike and allegedly drawn by a Loray operative, it pictured a poisonous snake coiled around Old Glory. The illustration's text read, "COMMUNISM IN THE SOUTH—KILL IT."[15]

Although David Clark boasted that the *Southern Textile Bulletin* had "the

13. *GG,* 6 April 1929.

14. *GG,* 12 April, 11 June, 18 and 19 July, and 16, 19, and 23 September 1929; Pope, *Millhands & Preachers,* 267; Salmond, *Gastonia 1929,* 77.

15. Tom Tippett, *When Southern Labor Stirs* (New York: Jonathan Cape & Harrison Smith, 1931), 78; Buhle, Buhle, and Georgakas, *Encyclopedia of the American Left,* 222–24; *American Newspaper Annual and Directory* (Philadelphia: N. W. Ayer and Son, 1928), 809; *GG,* 11 April 1929.

largest paid circulation in the South of any textile journal," fewer than four thousand subscribed to the Charlotte weekly. But powerful southern mill owners and superintendents, jittery about labor unrest in their own environs, certainly attended closely to his reporting and editorials. The Tar Heel textile aristocracy, which counted many powerful state leaders, including Governor Gardner, among its members, examined the publication intently while not always agreeing with its editor's policies. Clark's antipathy toward "radicals"—whom he regarded as anyone exhibiting less than absolute enthusiasm for laissez-faire capitalism—predated significantly the mania that had gripped North Carolina's American Legion and Daughters of the American Revolution in the mid-1920s for hectoring and blacklisting reformers, antimilitarists, and alleged "Bolshevists."[16]

The *Charlotte Observer,* with nearly forty thousand readers, edged just ahead of the *Raleigh News and Observer* to claim the title of the state's most widely circulated newspaper. Although it heralded itself as the "Foremost Newspaper in the Carolinas," it functioned, in theologian and labor historian Liston Pope's opinion, as "the traditional spokesman for the textile industries in the Carolinas." One authority called it "as stiff-necked as any southern journal in defense of textile operators and in condemnation of efforts to organize textile workers." The paper had supported the executions of Sacco and Vanzetti and had recently lambasted Democratic Party presidential candidate Al Smith.[17]

As the strike's early days wore on, sniping between the mill press and the wildly strident *Daily Worker* and radical and labor publications allied with it escalated into a full-fledged newspaper war. The communist organ described its editorial foes as members of "the yellow capitalist press of the state, which is completely dominated by the great Duke power and tobacco interests, the textile barons, and the open-shop railroads";[18] but despite the *Daily*'s boast that the Loray strikers eagerly read the paper and recognized it as their voice, Beal and his associates suppressed some editions. They worried that exaggerated

16. "This Firm Wanted the Facts—and Got Them!" *Southern Textile Bulletin,* 27 March 1930, 20–21; *American Newspaper Annual and Directory,* 1, 453; *N&O,* 22 April 1928; Joseph L. Morrison, *Governor O. Max Gardner: A Power in North Carolina and New Deal Washington* (Chapel Hill: University of North Carolina Press, 1971), 117.

17. Pope, *Millhands & Preachers,* 266; Jack Claiborne, *The Charlotte Observer: Its Time and Place, 1869–1986* (Chapel Hill: University of North Carolina Press, 1986), 175–76, 179; Clayton, *W. J. Cash,* 148–49; *American Newspaper Annual and Directory,* 806, 815.

18. *DW,* 16 April 1929; Buhle, Buhle, and Georgakas, *Encyclopedia of the American Left,* 174.

accounts of the unrest and propaganda designed to curry favor with Moscow, galvanize support for the Party, and facilitate its international fund-raising efforts would lead the local unionists to question their leadership's credibility.[19]

As paternalistic capitalism and "Americanism" battled world revolution and the Communist International in Gastonia, never before had such polarized economic and social forces collided south of the Mason-Dixon Line. The press's white-hot rhetoric and inflammatory reporting depleted the oxygen and created a vacuum in which lawlessness and violence could flourish. When the nation directed its gaze critically to "the South's City of Spindles," the innate provincialism of its inhabitants metastasized into xenophobia. No one from outside the region—no federal official, magazine or big-city newspaper correspondent, or social reformer—stood a chance of being heard above the fray and moderating the situation. North Carolinians alone could stave off the impending explosion, and only the state's liberal press could stir them to preventive action. In the days that followed, "Battling" Nell Lewis and a tiny handful of Tar Heel journalists worked to defuse the crisis, defend the strikers from both harm and exploitation, and elucidate the context and root causes of the unrest.[20]

Lewis weighed in on the controversy in the 14 April 1929 edition of "Incidentally." The sarcasm she employed to deprecate the alarmists' and doomsayers' warning of a communist-inspired apocalypse would have surprised none of her readers. Satire served as her most dependable weapon. She used the occasion to downplay events in Gastonia and to belittle one of her favorite bugbears, the Daughters of the American Revolution (DAR). She had ardently studied the organization for many years and rarely passed up the opportunity to lampoon it. Aware of the descendance of many of the region's textile operatives from patriots in the American Revolution, Lewis proposed forming chapters of the DAR and the Sons of the American Revolution at mills throughout Dixie. "Such organization as I suggest would mean a complete transformation of the Southern textile worker," she explained. A worker joining one of these patriotic societies would subordinate his interests and individual rights: "The Flag of capitalistic imperialism would become more important to him than a living wage or decent hours of labor or the development of his children, and with the clarity of patriotic vision he would see that what in his error he had

19. *DW*, 12 April 1929; Weisbord, *Radical Life*, 202; Tippett, *When Southern Labor Stirs*, 85.

20. *N&O*, 22 April 1928.

regarded as reasonable demands for human rights were the evil machinations of the enemies of the State."[21]

As the heady first days of the strike passed, comparative order prevailed in Gastonia, and large numbers of workers filtered back into the mill or moved on, looking for work elsewhere. The union's die-hard strikers, particularly the intergenerational women belonging to what southern scholar Jacquelyn Dowd Hall terms the "venerable tradition of 'disorderly women,'" continued to contest, through strategies ranging from flirtation and mockery to aggressive self-defense, the attempts by the "Nasty Guardsmen" to constrain the protesters' rights to assemble peaceably. Many men refused to demonstrate unarmed; thus, women and children acted as the principal members of the picket lines formed to keep scabs from entering the mill.[22]

Just when it seemed that the national attention directed at Gastonia had begun to wane and production at Loray would soon revert to its previous level, a sensational act of terrorism exposed the smoldering rancor and the fragility of order in the textile town and breathed new life into the strike. In the early hours of 18 April a mob estimated variously at fifty to five hundred masked men—armed with pistols, shotguns, and rifles and equipped with wrecking tools—expeditiously overpowered ten union guards and razed the wooden shack that served as their organization's headquarters. The uproar roused curious townspeople and attracted their presence from blocks around but failed to disturb the three companies of National Guardsmen encamped just a few hundred yards away at the mill. As the last getaway car drove off, Major Stephen B. Dolley, a former commander of the American Legion's Gaston Post, and his troops came running and arrested the strikers who had been guarding the union hall.[23]

This violent act and the law authorities' response undoubtedly account for Lewis's traveling to the area a few days later. She devoted virtually all of her

21. *N&O*, 14 April 1929.

22. *N&O*, 7 April and 5 May 1929; Jacquelyn Dowd Hall, "Disorderly Women: Gender and Labor Militancy in the Appalachian South," *Journal of American History* 72, no. 2 (September 1986): 356; Weisbord, *Radical Life*, 185–86, 191–92; Salmond, *Gastonia 1929*, 31–34; *GG*, 4 and 5 April 1929; John H. Owens, "Strike Vignettes," *Labor Defender* (May 1929): 101; Pope, *Millhands & Preachers*, 258; Dee Garrison, intro. to *Strike!* by Mary Heaton Vorse (Urbana: University of Illinois Press, 1991), xvi.

23. *GG*, 18 April 1929; Salmond, *Gastonia 1929*, 41–42; Tom Tippett, "Bosses Pit Violence against Loray Solidarity" (Federated Press), 22 April 1929, ACLU Papers; *New York World*, 19 April 1929; Joseph H. Separk, *Gastonia and Gaston County, North Carolina: Past, Present, Future* (Kingsport, Tenn.: Kingsport Press, 1936), 75.

28 April "Incidentally" column to the deteriorating situation. In "The Governor and the Mob" she censured North Carolina's popular chief executive for dispatching troops so precipitously. They had proven ineffectual and had inflamed the feelings of the unionists, who believed that the guardsmen operated at the behest of the textile establishment. She informed the governor that his ownership of a rayon mill made him "in a private capacity, a member of one of the warring groups" and—perhaps unfairly—a dubious figure in the eyes of many workers. He could redeem himself "by using all the weight of his office to secure justice for the strikers and the conviction of their lawless foes."[24]

In her editorial "Whose Fault Is It?" Lewis charged that the state's industrialists could have averted the unrest in Gastonia if they had not "given an earnest, if inadequate, imitation of Gold Almighty." She, along with numerous progressive North Carolina women leaders, had for many years lobbied energetically for a systematic survey of the conditions under which female industrial workers labored. Manufacturers had bitterly opposed and frustrated their efforts. When the University of North Carolina's Institute for Research in Social Science had attempted a similar effort, it had run into a stone wall, and mill owners had exerted formidable political pressure on the college's administration. She declared that the communist sally into the region provided liberals "with a golden opportunity . . . to say, 'We told you so!'" "Consider it said herewith," she added emphatically, "through a megaphone!"[25]

In "Wounded in the House of His Friends" Lewis could not resist taunting the *Charlotte Observer,* which she labeled "The Manufacturers' Pride and Joy." Hastily sworn in special deputy sheriffs had replaced the National Guard troops three days after the attack on the union hall and commissary. Authorities had drafted many of these deputies from the ranks of Gastonia's zealous legionnaires and imported others—not inaccurately described by Tom Tippett as "plug uglies"—from the surrounding area. On the afternoon following the Guard's withdrawal, fifty lawmen and special officers armed with billy clubs, pistols, and bayoneted rifles conveniently supplied by the departing militia enforced an anti-parade ordinance the city council had rushed through. They charged into several hundred strikers marching to protest the injunction, punched and kicked them, and beat many with rifle butts. During the melee

24. *N&O,* 28 April 1929; Jeremy Brecher, *Strike!* (Cambridge: South End Press, 1997), 280; Morrison, *Governor O. Max Gardner,* 42.

25. *N&O,* 28 April 1929.

one deputy swung his Springfield and knocked the *Charlotte Observer*'s star reporter, LeGette Blythe, unconscious. Another officer pistol-whipped Blythe while he lay in the street. (The mill promptly provided legal counsel for the assailants and hired them as guards.) How "much more fitting and so much less amusingly ironical," Lewis concluded acidly, "if the official blackjack had laid out" Robert E. "Fleet" Williams, the erudite veteran reporter who had covered the unrest with great balance and thoroughness for her own paper, which she dubbed "The Workers' Friend."[26] *Gazette* editor Hugh Query preferred another cognomen for the *Raleigh News and Observer,* which he accused of engaging in a "systematic campaign of long-distance denunciation of a situation about which it apparently knows nothing." He charged the capital daily of once again living up to its old nickname, the "Raleigh News and Disturber."[27]

Two events threatened to escalate the violence further. First, the Communist Party predictably subordinated syndicalism to propaganda and ideological orthodoxy. The Party had rushed to Loray an array of office functionaries and representatives from its many affiliated organizations, including the Worker's International Relief (WIR), the International Labor Defense Press Service, the Young Communist League, Young Pioneers, and the *Daily Worker.* Although some members of this formidable apparatus provided vital services—as did Vera Buch, who frequently assumed day-to-day command of the strike, and Amy Schechter, representing the WIR—others such as Pershing, NTWU secretary-treasurer Albert Weisbord, and *Labor Defender* editor Karl Marx Reeve made only brief forays into Gastonia and issued provocative statements perfectly suited for the radical press but also made to order for the mill owners' publicists. The handful of organizers who came and stayed displayed great courage and conviction, but among them all only Beal consistently placed the strike's success above the party line.[28]

26. Morrison, *Governor O. Max Gardner,* 59; *GG,* 9 and 23 April 1929; *NYT,* 10, 11, and 15 April 1929; Tom Tippett, "Reign of Violence against Gastonia Strikers" (Federated Press), 25 April 1929, ACLU Papers; *N&O,* 28 April and 5 May 1929, 28 January 1934; Salmond, *Gastonia 1929,* 45–46; Hood, "Loray Mill Strike," 90–92.

27. Many North Carolinians also referred to the paper as the "Nuisance-Disturber," although its maverick editor, Josephus Daniels, who had instigated and weathered a staggering number of political and journalistic brawls, promoted his journal as "The Old Reliable." *GG,* 25 April 1929; *Wall Street Journal,* 17 May 1965; *N&O,* 14 August 1904, 6 June 1926, 17 August 1930; Morrison, *Josephus Daniels,* 24–49.

28. *Charlotte News,* 14 July 1935; Tippett, *When Southern Labor Stirs,* 79–80, 85–86; Salmond,

Weisbord and other leaders' insistence on "complete solidarity of all workers regardless of color" created a breach between the union and its Piedmont rank and file. A correspondent representing the *Nation* observed that the strikers remained "wholly unconverted to the idea of race equality." One informed him that "the Nothun folks cayn't tell us how to run the nigguhs; we know how to do that ourselves." The Party's irreligion created another cleavage. Located in the heart of the Bible Belt, militantly Protestant Gaston County contained 120 places of worship, and churches lined the City of Spindles' streets. "One can hardly get from under the shadow of their towering spires," bragged its Chamber of Commerce president.[29]

The ascendancy of the "Committee of One Hundred" at Loray also foreshadowed mayhem. Tippett believed that Manville-Jenckes established the vigilante organization from its workforce to operate as a private militia the day after the guardsmen decamped. But it seems almost certain that the committee—perhaps in a formative stage—destroyed the union buildings. Indeed, on the morning of the attack the mill had temporarily ceased operations. According to one disgruntled worker, management enlisted "bosses, bosses' pets, and a lot of special guards, spies and pimps" to staff the organization. The committeemen upheld a strict code of silence in talking to reporters and investigators, but they boasted about their membership to townspeople, and virtually everyone in the community must have known of their affiliation.[30]

"Barbarous Gaston," Lewis entitled an editorial in her 5 May column. In her commentary she appropriated the rhetoric of nativists who privileged Anglo-Saxon culture as she attempted to shame Tar Heels into protecting the strikers' rights. "As surprising and humiliating as it may be," she wrote,

---

*Gastonia 1929*, 34–35, 52–55; Vorse, "Gastonia," 702; Garrison, *Strike*, xi–xii; Bernstein, *Lean Years*, 22–23; Pope, *Millhands & Preachers*, 242–48; Beal, *Proletarian Journey*, 139–40, 155; Weisbord, *Radical Life*, 175, 183, 206–8; Hood, "Loray Mill Strike," 82–83, 127–31.

29. Karl Reeve, "The Awakening South," *Labor Defender* (May 1929): 91; Owens, "Strike Vignettes," 101; Karl Reeve, "Gastonia Sees and Learns," *Labor Defender* (June 1929): 117; Paul Blanshard, "Communism in Southern Cotton Mills," *Nation*, 24 April 1929, 501; Salmond, *Gastonia 1929*, 67; Pope, *Millhands & Preachers*, 97, 245–48; Hood, "Loray Mill Strike," 97, 106–7, 127–31; "Gastonia, North Carolina: The South's City of Spindles (Three Radio Talks Made over Station, WBT, Charlotte, N.C., May 14, 1930)."

30. Pope, *Millhands & Preachers*, 255; Tippett, *When Southern Labor Stirs*, 89; Tom Tippett, "Bosses Pit Violence against Loray Solidarity" (Federated Press), 22 April 1929, ACLU Papers; Dunne, *Gastonia*, 57.

> it seems that we have a county in North Carolina which is in a condition of virtual barbarity—Gaston, of course. It is characteristic of a barbarous community that it is not ruled by law and that the conception of civil liberty which men have slowly evolved through the centuries, often in desperate encounters, and upon which our English-derived civilization especially prides itself, is unintelligible to it. In such a community violence is unrestrained.
>
> Unquestionably Gaston qualifies. In this interesting district, the machinery of law is worse than impotent for it has become the instrument of lawlessness itself. Members of a mob are allowed to do whatever violence they please and it is impossible to apprehend or punish them. Unarmed citizens, including women, are attacked by official ruffians with bayonets and blackjacks. Persons are slammed into jail on the flimsiest pretext. Under the pretense of keeping it, the peace is continually broken, and the county insolently thumbs its nose at the law.
>
> It is clear that, regardless of the letter, the spirit of civil liberty is now being violated in Gaston with impunity and, so far, without punishment, to the disgrace not only of the county but the whole state.[31]

The next afternoon a Gastonia magistrate issued a decision requiring strikers to vacate their company-owned houses or pay a bond of an entire year's rent and utilities. Deputies enthusiastically began enforcing the order the following morning, and by evening they had ousted more than fifty people and dragged their belongings into the street. As authorities evicted the strikers, they admittedly devoted their attention first to the most militant protesters, such as J. A. Valentine, whose six-year-old daughter, Sylvia, lay in bed recovering from smallpox. "She's all right now; ain't any temperature," said Dr. Lee Johnson, the company physician, as he approved the family's expulsion. "This ain't a smallpox-quarantine state."[32]

That Sunday Lewis devoted her lead editorial, "The Whip-Hand," to the evictions. Southern boosters had long vaunted their supposedly compliant Anglo-Saxon workforces in attempts to lure northern industry to Dixie. The *News and Observer* columnist suggested to the region's pitchmen a fresh sell-

31. *News and Observer*, 5 May 1929.

32. *GG*, 6 May and 12 October 1929; Salmond, *Gastonia 1929*, 56; Vorse, "Gastonia," 707–8; *DW*, 9 May 1929; Hood, "Loray Mill Strike," 104–5.

ing point inspired by the recent events in Gastonia. She authored an advertisement employing this boon:

BRING YOUR MILL TO NORTH CAROLINA

The State with All the Advantages

LONG HOURS—LOW WAGES—PURE, NATIVE-BORN, WELL-BROKEN

ANGLO-SAXON LABOR

MINIMUM LEGISLATIVE INTERFERENCE

Night Work for Women Eleven Hour Day for Children

COMPANY-OWNED VILLAGES

Where, if the workers get heady, you can turn them out of house and home.

Lewis declared that at every juncture the heavy-handed tactics of Loray's managers had increased public support for the union: "Give these mill boys rope enough and they are going to hang themselves. . . . They have played steadily into the strikers' hands. The evictions make a fine climax. I say—just give them rope enough—just give the giant intellects of North Carolina industry a chance."

In an editorial entitled "Q. and A." she professed great admiration for the sagacity of sob sister and advice columnist Dorothy Dix and newspaper commentator Reverend Dr. S. Parkes Cadman, who had embarked on a campaign to save students "from the beliefs preached by H. L. Mencken." (The *News and Observer* ran both columns.) Lewis announced she had decided to feature in "Incidentally" a regular section containing "not only advice but prophecy."[33] One anonymous correspondent allegedly had already sought her counsel. "I am naturally a friendly person," he confided. "I like people and lots of them like me. I want to be on good terms with everybody and I hate to offend folks. How can I extricate myself from the embarrassing situation in which the Gastonia strike has placed me?" None of her readers would have missed this dig at affable Governor Gardner, who styled himself as "the friendly governor" and, according to his biographer, displayed a "genius for friendship." Lewis declined

33. Mark Sullivan, *Our Times: America at the Birth of the Twentieth Century*, ed. Dan Rather (New York: Scribner, 1996), 675; Robert B. Downs and Jane B. Downs, *Journalists of the United States: Biographical Sketches of Print and Broadcast News Shapers from the Late 17th Century to the Present* (Jefferson, N.C.: McFarland & Co., 1991), 10, 152–53.

to "presume to advise so high a public official other than to say, let your conscience be the guide."[34]

"Governor Gardner Faces Jeers of State's Radical Editors with the Calmness of Assurance," a *Gazette* front-page headline shouted on 11 May. Its subheads declared, "Daniels and His Ilk Fail to Stir Governor's Ire," "Fortitude under Unjust Criticism Widely Admired," and "Pays No Attention to Snarls of Prejudiced Writers." The state's liberal and mill press had previously exchanged gibes over the strike—as when David Clark wrote, "The fact that the strike leaders are communists who are opposed to all religion, believe in free love, negro equality and openly advocate the overthrow of our Government seems to make no difference to the *News and Observer*"—but rival editors and journalists to this point had avoided denouncing each other by name.[35]

Query and Atkins now began to personalize their attack: "The most severe critics of Governor Gardner have been *The Greensboro News, The News and Observer*, of which Josephus Daniels is editor, and Nell Battle Lewis, free-lance critic and reformer, who writes for *The News and Observer.*" The article took Lewis to task for objecting to the governor's decision to deploy National Guard troops to Gastonia. The insinuation that his ownership of a textile mill accounted for his failure to condemn the mob violence more vigorously and investigate it aggressively had "undoubtedly cut him deeply." The *Gazette* surmised that the governor would soon refute these charges made "by omniscient editorialists, but that he is biding his time to call their hands."[36]

As the Gastonia daily reported, the *News and Observer* and the *Greensboro Daily News*, the state's third most circulated newspaper, conformed in their reproof of the state's chief executive. Under the leadership of editor Earle Godbey, his former associate editor Gerald W. Johnson, and his present collaborator Lenoir Chambers, the *Daily News* had earned a well-deserved reputation as a consistently literary and liberal publication. Throughout the crisis the two journals would repeatedly buttress each other and articulate parallel views.[37]

On 19 May "Incidentally" featured a cartoon drawn by Lewis. It pictured a

34. *N&O*, 12 May 1929; Morrison, *Governor O. Max Gardner*, 43, 52.

35. *GG*, 11 May 1929; "The Right of Violence," *Southern Textile Bulletin*, 25 April 1929, 30–31.

36. *GG*, 11 May 1929; Morrison, *Governor O. Max Gardner*, 58–59.

37. Fitzpatrick, *Gerald W. Johnson*, 29, 41; Leidholdt, *Standing before the Shouting Mob*, 19; Thad Stem Jr., *The Tar Heel Press* (Charlotte: Heritage Printers, 1973), 172; Michael W. Frye, "The Loray Strike Viewed by Six North Carolina Newspapers" (master's thesis, University of North Carolina, 1972), 61; Gerald W. Johnson, "Journalism below the Potomac," in *South-Watching: Selected Essays by Gerald W. Johnson*, ed. Fred Hobson (Chapel Hill: University of North Carolina Press, 1983), 78–79;

top-hatted, cigar-smoking mill executive holding up a Confederate battle flag titled "states' rights" to screen a factory from a camera lens labeled "proposed federal investigation." Behind the banner stood a woman operator, a baby in her arms, with a caption reading: "night work for women," "60-hour week," and "low wages." A girl beside her bore the inscription "11-hour day for children 14–16." Lewis entitled the two workers "99 44/100 Pure Anglo-Saxons." Southern boosters frequently employed this figure, borrowed from a famous Ivory soap advertising campaign, to promote to northern investors the insusceptibility of southern textile workers to foreign-born labor radicalism.[38]

Lewis continued her attack on mill owners in her lead editorial, "Some Missing Exhibits." She told of having attended the North Carolina Industrial Exposition, which Raleigh had recently hosted, and having searched there in vain for displays that she believed would have more accurately depicted the state's labor relations. These, she said, might have included wreckage from the NTWU's looted headquarters, union organizers in an iron cage with a "Beware the Communists" warning sign, and a tableau of Gastonia policemen with fixed bayonets entitled "Law and Order."[39]

Despite Lewis's advocacy, it seemed virtually certain that the strike had failed. Authorities upheld a city ordinance forbidding parades and enforced it with a steep fifty-dollar fine or a thirty-day jail or chain gang sentence. Productivity and staffing at the mill approached pre-walkout levels; only a small but resolute core of militant strikers remained.[40] Beal and his associates hunkered down and strove to maintain morale. The strikers resourcefully rented a parcel of land with a brook running through it and constructed a new headquarters from rough lumber. The WIR purchased tents and rushed them to Gastonia. The NTWU secured relief supplies and kerosene stoves and built a playground for children. Residents christened the community "New Town" and named its thoroughfares "Union Street" and "Workers International Relief Street."[41]

Ella May Wiggins, a feisty spinner and single mother from nearby Bessemer City, whose racial progressiveness (born of an impoverished existence that

---

Dabney, *Liberalism in the South*, 406–7; Mims, *Advancing South*, 124; *American Newspaper Annual and Directory*, 810.

38. *N&O*, 19 May 1929.

39. *N&O*, 19 May 1929.

40. Salmond, *Gastonia 1929*, 64–65; Weisbord, *Radical Life*, 216–17.

41. *DW*, 24 and 25 May 1929; Weisbord, *Radical Life*, 211–12, 219.

forced an unusual close personal and working association with blacks) and dissatisfaction with exploitative industrialization well preceded the NTWU's incursion into the South, became the strikers' minstrel and a principal figure in the tent city. Wiggins's "song ballets" (ballads) chronicled the causes and key events of the labor unrest and expressed her deep faith in the union. In her full-throated and untaught voice she intoned the lyrics she had written, such as those for her sentimental "Mill Mother's Lament."[42]

After completing their new headquarters, the workers sent Governor Gardner an open letter imparting rumors of a plot by the mill owners to wreck the building and the strikers' intention to defend it "at all costs." Newspapers around the state reprinted the missive. The unionists did not exaggerate the threat. A police officer known for his brutality attended the "jollification" celebrating the building's completion and allegedly predicted that it would stand no longer than a week.[43]

A rally by the strikers on the evening of 7 June 1929 began a calamitous sequence of events that ignited the tinderbox. Beal stayed at the National Textile Workers Union headquarters, while Vera Buch and Amy Schechter led a small group of marchers—composed entirely of women, teenagers, and children—in the direction of the factory. Less than one hundred yards from the union headquarters, a handful of cursing "laws" scattered the procession by choking Buch and beating many of the picketers, including an elderly woman.[44]

As the shaken protesters dispersed and straggled back to the colony, a car bearing patrolmen passed them and drove into the center of the union redoubt. Police chief Orville Aderholt and four deputies emerged from the vehicle. A union sentinel demanded to see a search warrant (none existed), and when a deputy attempted to wrest away another guard's firearm, gunfire on both sides broke out. The melee ended with Aderholt, who had generally com-

42. Smith and Wilson, *North Carolina Women*, 262–65; Jacquelyn Dowd Hall et al., *Like a Family: The Making of a Southern Cotton Mill World* (Chapel Hill: University of North Carolina Press, 1987), 226–29; Salmond, *Gastonia 1929*, 59–63; Margaret Larkin, "Ella May's Songs," *Nation*, 9 October 1929, 382–83; Margaret Larkin, "The Story of Ella May," *New Masses* (November 1929): 3–5; Weisbord, *Radical Life*, 217–18; Beal, *Proletarian Journey*, 159; "Dean Graham's Picture of Ella May Wiggins," *Southern Textile Bulletin*, 10 April 1930, 22.

43. "Who Are the Gastonia Prisoners," 172; Hood, "Loray Mill Strike," 112–15; Beal, *Proletarian Journey*, 154–55, 157; Salmond, *Gastonia 1929*, 60–61, 64, 70; *DW*, 21 and 27 May 1929; Weisbord, *Radical Life*, 219.

44. Weisbord, *Radical Life*, 220–21, 276.

ported himself professionally throughout the strike, mortally injured and three deputies and one striker wounded. Antithetical accounts by witnesses about who fired the first shot would emerge during court testimony later.[45]

Major Alfred Lee Bulwinkle, an attorney and former congressman, who helped head the Committee of One Hundred, assumed leadership of a frenzied effort by police, hastily sworn in deputies, and townspeople to round up the unionists. A few hours after the shooting, the Gastonia jail contained over fifty strikers. Among the strike leaders only Beal escaped, although authorities soon arrested him in nearby Spartanburg, South Carolina, and transported him back to Gastonia in a harrowing journey that nearly culminated in his lynching.[46]

Three days after the shooting, the strident *Gazette* tore into the *Raleigh News and Observer* and the *Greensboro Daily News*. Both of the papers had cautioned that the details surrounding the shooting remained unclear, and both had counseled against rash action. Query contrasted these tempered comments with the sharpness with which the state's two principal liberal presses had criticized the textile town's law authorities for failing to protect the strikers' safety, property, and civil liberties. Singling Lewis out for special criticism, he reprinted her "Barbarous Gaston" column from the previous month. Why, he asked, had Aderholt's death not outraged her to the same degree as the violence she alleged vigilantes and law authorities had committed against the strikers? Why had she refused to condemn the carnage?[47]

That Sunday Lewis responded to the murder. In "When the Law Fails" she unequivocally condemned the crime, although she suggested that a clearer account of the incident's provocation might later emerge. She reviewed the key events of the disturbance. The governor had unjustifiably called out the militia to Gastonia in response to the unionists' peaceful protest. She strongly suspected that the troops had connived with the Committee of One Hundred to wreck the strikers' headquarters and commissary. Law authorities had in effect, she wrote, condoned the vigilantism by refusing to bring mob members to justice. "What is there in that record to have made the strikers think that they could secure justice under the North Carolina law?" she demanded.

45. Weisbord, *Radical Life*, 277–78; Salmond, *Gastonia 1929*, 72–73; *CO*, 6–8 September and 5, 8, 10, 11, 16, 18, and 19 October 1929.

46. Salmond, *Gastonia 1929*, 74–75; Beal, *Proletarian Journey*, 170–74; *GG*, 8 June 1929.

47. *GG*, 10 June 1929.

"When the law fails, as it has done in Gaston, what can we expect? When the enforcement of the law itself is prejudiced and violent, what can we expect but more violence from people who rightly believe that they have been discriminated against? Very reasonably, indeed, we may expect murder."[48] Historian John A. Salmond, the author of the unrest's definitive study, writes that "passionate, angry columns" such as this one would earn Lewis "great calumny in some North Carolina circles, but they stand out today as reflecting a courageous, balanced engagement with the wider issues of class and economic hegemony that lay at the strike's core."[49]

Predictably, Lewis's commentary outraged the *Gazette*. Query castigated her. "None are so Blind," he titled his lead editorial. Readers could have anticipated outrageous and irresponsible accusations from a "writer of Nell's stamp," he charged. Her "ignorance, prejudice and bias stuck out" of her piece "When the Law Fails." The *Gazette*'s editor realized, however, that his reproof would have little effect on Lewis because of her "empty ears and non-understanding mind." He wished only that she would spend a week in the textile town to observe firsthand the "conditions about which she writes so glibly and intelligently." Query also lambasted Lewis for her elitism. Influenced by the "renowned Mencken," she discerned "nothing in this hick town to admire or to respect."[50]

Charlotte attorney Thomas A. Jimison, a native North Carolina liberal, succeeded in freeing nearly half of the incarcerated unionists by issuing writs of habeas corpus, which forced the prosecution to acknowledge that it had no evidence against many prisoners accused of complicity in the shooting. Jimison—who displayed remarkable courage and tenacity in his defense of the strikers, a command of millworkers' vernacular, and a folksy but acid wit—had passed the bar several years earlier, after quitting a career as a Methodist minister.[51] Prosecutor Clyde Roark Hoey, however, a skilled and flamboyant lawyer and the brother-in-law of the state's current chief executive, attracted the most attention of the many attorneys assembling in the Queen City. Grandly turned out in flowing silver locks, high-topped shoes, a frock coat with wing-

48. *N&O*, 16 June 1929.

49. Salmond, *Gastonia 1929*, 78.

50. *GG*, 17 June 1929.

51. Salmond, *Gastonia 1929*, 29, 85; Weisbord, *Radical Life*, 187; Tom P. Jimison, "Mill Hands and the Law," *Labor Defender* (July 1929): 138–39.

tip collar, and a red boutonniere, the teetotaling, Sunday school–teaching Hoey evoked an earlier era.[52]

At a preliminary hearing in Charlotte on 18 June Hoey presaged the cast of future legal proceedings. Over defense's objections he bellowed at Amy Schechter, demanding to know whether she believed in God and if she wished the United States to adopt a Soviet form of government. She admitted her atheism and professed her desire that political power should reside in "a majority of the people, which happens to be the workers and the farmers." Under Hoey's cross-examination Edith Miller, who had overseen the political education of children within the tent city, divulged that she did not believe the Bible represented the inspired word of God. At the conclusion of the proceedings Judge W. F. Harding made clear his support for the prosecution and ordered fourteen defendants—including Beal and three women, Buch, Schechter, and nineteen-year-old Sophie Melvin, a member of the Young Communist League who had worked with the children in the tent city—placed in jail without bond to await trial for Aderholt's murder.[53]

Five days after the Charlotte hearing Lewis excoriated Hoey in "Who Is on the Lord's Side?" "Of course [the prosecutor's] object in playing upon [the atheism of the union leaders] is perfectly obvious," she fumed. "It was, in brief, to prejudice public opinion against these people even more than it is already prejudiced—and that is a plenty—by creating the impression that they are all wild-eyed atheists. If we may take Mr. Hoey's cross-examination of the strikers . . . as indicative of the motif of the prosecution in the coming trial we may as well get set for a sweet little inquisition which is likely to include everything from Jonah and the whale to the Hebrew children in the fiery furnace."[54] That Sunday Lewis augmented her journalistic advocacy with personal activism sure to arouse controversy. In "Help from Home" she notified her readers of the fund-raising activities of the International Labor Defense (ILD) in the North and Midwest. "Why," she asked, "should this help come from outside this State while we sit back in fear and trembling lest some manufacturer say 'Boo!' at us? A fine lot of rabbits we are!"[55]

52. Douglas Carl Abrams, *Conservative Constraints: North Carolina and the New Deal* (Jackson: University Press of Mississippi, 1992), 220; *DW*, 15 June 1929.

53. Salmond, *Gastonia 1929*, 60, 86–87; Beal, *Proletarian Journey*, 174–76; *GG*, 19 June 1929.

54. *N&O*, 23 June 1929.

55. *N&O*, 23 June 1929.

Lewis noted that most of the incarcerated strikers hailed from the South; without question they deserved able counsel. Even the militant outsiders, who made up the union's leadership, had the same right. Judging by the events that led up to the shooting, she wrote, "secur[ing] a fair trial is going to be no child's play." She then stepped directly into the fray: "From several expressions I have heard recently I am quite sure that there are a number of people in North Carolina who would like to do something to help the accused strikers; who while deploring their radical leadership and unequivocably condemning the murder of Chief Adderholt [*sic*], nevertheless, wish to express their sympathy with the strikers' fundamental aims which are nothing more or less than better conditions of labor and life; and who are interested in seeing that they have a just trial. As a nucleus for the active expression of this proper feeling I herewith open The North Carolina Strikers' Defense Fund by a contribution of $10.00."[56]

On 7 July Lewis devoted nearly all of "Incidentally" to the impending trial in Gastonia. In "The Strikers' Counsel" she applauded the decision by Jimison to include native North Carolinian Frank Carter, a highly respected former judge, on the defense team, which he would now direct. Neighboring Tennessee's John Randolph Neal, who had appeared with Clarence Darrow at the Scopes "Monkey Trial," and two of Jimison's Charlotte colleagues also agreed to defend Beal and the other prisoners. The prosecution assembled a phalanx that, in addition to Hoey, included Bulwinkle; county solicitor John Carpenter; R. Gregg Cherry, who commanded the state's American Legion; and virtually the entire Gastonia bar. "Five of us [will] meet the seventeen who represent the Philistines," Jimison jauntily announced to Forrest Bailey, the executive director of the American Civil Liberties Union (ACLU), which along with the ILD sponsored the defense.[57]

In the same edition of her column Lewis included excerpts from three letters of widely varying literary quality written by Gastonia mill hands, lauding her strike fund and expressing appreciation for her activism. One correspondent, a female textile worker married to another operative, had enclosed a dollar: "i wisht we could spare more money to help the strikers. i aint agoing to sign no name because the ole man is afeard Mr. Bullwinkel and them hundred men that arests peepel will get after us. we shore want you to write some

56. *N&O*, 23 June 1929.

57. *N&O*, 7 July 1929; Salmond, *Gastonia 1929*, 84–86, 91.

more in the raleigh paper for them strikers." A second missive had declared that the "working people of Gastonia stand with you 'Heart and Soul'" and that many mill employees desired to contribute to her fund but lacked the financial means to do so. The final letter stated that most operatives distrusted the radical union that had orchestrated the strike but agreed with its demands for improved wages and living conditions. "Go to it, Miss Lewis, the mill workers are with you," its author urged.[58]

In her lead editorial that day, "Remove the Trial from Gaston County!" Lewis led the charge among the state's liberals for a change of venue. To try the case in Gaston County, "whose legal officers have been the open enemies of the strikers and where mob violence is sanctioned," she wrote, would result in a travesty of justice. No possibility existed that officials there could impanel an objective jury, and jurors with the courage to side with the defendants might face dangerous consequences. The trial would assume historic proportions not just because of the large number of defendants facing the death penalty but also because it focused on labor, the most important and explosive issue in North Carolina and one that the state's leaders obstinately refused to examine systematically. "Unchallenged and unquestioned," she proclaimed, "the Industrial Revolution has taken place among us, while, in general, we have shut our eyes to the great social questions which it has raised."[59]

In the editorial Lewis foretold with great accuracy the tenor of the forthcoming legal proceedings and presciently warned of the consequences of the prosecution's injecting religion into the trial: "There are serious indications that this trial will be much more than a trial for homicide. Not only the history of the strike, but the attitude of the prosecution exhibited at the habeas corpus hearing suggest that it may very likely turn into a heresy trial—a trial based primarily on grounds of opinion. In every period in which they have occurred such trials have been a stench and a stain. The precedent of a trial of this sort in North Carolina related to this particular question would fetter Labor here for years to come, and should shame the State which allowed it."[60]

On 21 and 28 July Lewis augmented her plea for a change of venue with an array of impressive letters she had solicited for "Incidentally" from the state's foremost leaders, including a virtual Who's Who of Tar Heel liberals. Prominent religious and judicial figures such as Bishop Cheshire, Assistant Attorney

58. *N&O*, 7 July 1929.

59. Salmond, *Gastonia 1929*, 92–93; *N&O*, 7 July 1929.

60. *N&O*, 7 July 1929.

General Walter D. Siler, and Kemp D. Battle, a highly respected attorney related to Lewis by her father's first marriage, advised sparing no effort to ensure that the Gastonia defendants received a fair hearing. Notable journalists W. O. Saunders, Louis Graves, and Oscar Coffin vehemently called upon authorities to move the trial from Gastonia. A dozen preeminent academic leaders and professors, including William Poteat, Frank Graham, and Harry Chase, urged that the defendants' religious and political views play no role in the impending trial. Leaders of the state's many women's organizations and prominent businessmen also spoke out and cautioned that North Carolina's good reputation hinged on the impartiality of the impending proceedings.[61]

Lewis's ability to muster on short notice such a remarkable range of testimonials likely stemmed in part from her charter membership in the newly organized North Carolina Committee of Liberals, whose formation the ACLU had endorsed to counterbalance the radical rhetoric spread by the ILD, but it also powerfully bespoke her personal connectedness to other liberals and her unquestioned arrival at age thirty-six as a leader in the state's progressive community.[62]

Late in the month Lewis accepted the *Gazette*'s invitation to visit Gastonia. She arrived in the textile town the weekend preceding the opening of the trial on 29 July and went directly to the county jail to interview Buch, Schechter, and Melvin. The Gastonia prisoners had only the most rudimentary understanding of the extent of the fratricide that had torn apart the Communist Party, USA, since their arrest. Infighting within the Party had sent the leaders of the two principal factions scurrying to Moscow to denounce one another before an "American Commission." Joseph Stalin deposed Jay Lovestone, the leading proponent of the doctrine of "American Exceptionalism," but refused to endorse the leader of the other major faction, William Z. Foster, who became an increasingly marginalized figure.[63]

Within this tempestuous context Party officials subordinated the fate of the Gastonia defendants to mobilizing a strident mass defense. The grandstanding and polemics associated with this approach drove a wedge between

61. *N&O*, 21 and 28 July 1929; Wilson, *University of North Carolina*, 422.

62. Salmond, *Gastonia 1929*, 111–12.

63. Edward P. Johanningsmeier, *Forging American Communism: The Life of William Z. Foster* (Princeton: Princeton University Press, 1994), 246–48; Buhle, Buhle, and Georgakas, *Encyclopedia of the American Left*, 237–38, 462; Weisbord, *Radical Life*, 234.

the ILD and the ACLU, which had retained Jimison and his local staff of attorneys. The *Daily Worker*'s incendiary rhetoric and outlandish commentary prejudiced the surrounding community and rankled the ACLU and Jimison's team, and the attempts by the ILD and the Party to exert control over the defense strategy threatened to tear apart the tenuous coalition of militants and liberals working to free the defendants. Indeed, this tension led to Judge Carter's resignation four days before the trial got under way.[64]

When Lewis called at the jail, the *News and Observer* reported, she "found that her fame had preceded her." The jailer had left strict instructions to his staff to refuse to allow anyone to speak to the women inmates. A colleague of Lewis's attempted to intervene on her behalf. "This is Miss Nell Battle Lewis of the *News and Observer,* and she wants to say a few words to the women prisoners," he announced. "Well," replied the keeper, looking at Lewis sourly, "she can't do it. She's done said too much already." The columnist laughingly departed and for the remainder of her life relished telling the story of her reception in Gastonia.[65]

Approximately five hundred spectators packed the main floor and the balcony in the little brick courthouse on the steamy Monday morning of the trial's beginning. The attire and appearance of Buch, Schechter, and Melvin and the attorneys' garb and comportment added a human interest element to many of the day's press accounts, but the explicit and eminently fair charge that Maurice V. Barnhill, the tall and lean young superior court judge from Rocky Mount hearing the case, delivered to the jury formed the lead for most of the stories filed that afternoon and evening. "There is but one issue to determine and that is 'are the defendants guilty as charged?'" he instructed. Shortly thereafter, Barnhill granted a change of venue from Gaston to Mecklenburg County.[66]

From her return to Raleigh until the 26 August opening date of the new trial, Lewis worked tirelessly to galvanize North Carolina's liberal community to demand that the prosecution not railroad the defendants. She also assailed the Party and the ILD as they attempted to exert control over Jimison and his team and as they mounted their noisy mass defense, a strategy she be-

64. Salmond, *Gastonia 1929*, 95; *GG*, 25 July 1929.

65. *N&O*, 30 July 1929, 11 April 1937, 6 June 1947.

66. *GG*, 27 and 29 July 1929; Salmond, *Gastonia 1929*, 98–101; Forrest Bailey, "Gastonia Goes to Trial," *New Republic*, 14 August 1929, 334.

lieved would alienate potential jurors and further exacerbate bias within her state against the accused unionists.[67] On 11 August she urged her readers to consider the fate of the often-overlooked native southerners awaiting trial for Aderholt's murder. She dubbed them "The Forgotten Eight." Caught between the militants and the "Right-Thinkers and Civilization-Savers . . . rallying to the defense of God and our Native Industries," she wrote, "eight young men whose identity and interests have been almost completely lost in the shuffle are sitting in jail probably wondering what it's all about." For these defendants "Karl Marx, if anything, is a name only; a 'class war' is foolishness; and martyrdom is not attractive." An understandable desire for better wages and working conditions had motivated their entry into the strike, which had culminated in the tragic shooting of the sheriff.[68]

Lewis had earlier stated that the southern defendants, caught amid the antipodal forces battling one another in Gastonia, found themselves in danger of becoming "pretty well flattened out between the upper and the nether millstones." She now discovered herself in the same predicament. As the *Gazette* impugned her as a "champion" of the communists, the *Charlotte News* dismissed her as growing "more and more laughable," and the *Southern Textile Bulletin* upbraided her for writing "disgusting articles," the communists now took her to task.[69]

The *Daily Worker* to this point had conceded that the liberal Tar Heel press—the *News and Observer* in particular—had conducted an intrepid battle against the state's textile establishment and its apologists and that North Carolina liberals had acted in the Gastonia defendants' best interests. On numerous occasions that summer the communist sheet commended the editorial stance adopted by Daniels and Lewis and remarked on the "open combat" that existed between the Raleigh morning paper and supporters of the state's mill owners. William J. Dunne, the communist organ's editor, remarked approvingly on Lewis's activism and even insinuated that she came close to understanding the elements of class struggle inherent in the dispute. Juliet Stuart Poyntz, the erudite executive secretary of the International Labor Defense, readily acknowledged that Lewis "helped [the ILD] a lot at Gastonia." From his jail cell in July, Beal differentiated the *News and Observer* and the *Daily News* from the "lying newspapers which were and are now entirely on the side of the

67. *N&O*, 4 August 1929.

68. *N&O*, 11 August 1929.

69. *N&O*, 11 August 1929; *GG*, 10 and 12 July and 14 August 1929.

manufacturers," and he attended eagerly to Lewis's commentary. Nearly fifty years after the strike, Buch recalled that Lewis had "forcefully" opposed the violence perpetrated by the vigilantes.[70]

The 25 August "Incidentally" column preceded the opening of the legal proceedings in Charlotte by a day. Having exhausted nearly every imaginable rational appeal to persuade North Carolina's citizenry that the NTWU's radicality—particularly its controversial social views and the irreligion of many of its members—should play no role in the impending trial, with tongue in cheek Lewis twitted her readers regarding the incendiary nature of Christianity. She could think of nothing more explosive to insert in labor disputes than the four Gospels. "All the other revolutions would look like child's play," she noted, if society embraced "the principles of the Agitator of Judea, that member of the laboring class, friend of the despised and the humble, who said it is easier for a camel to go through the eye of a needle than for a rich man to enter the Kingdom of God, and who promulgated the Golden Rule."[71]

An aside in that Sunday's "Incidentally" likely puzzled those who were not regular readers of the column. Lewis alluded to the "profound humility and considerable pain" with which she regarded judicial matters, "being still groggy from last Monday's knock-out." Six days before the column appeared, she had taken and passed the North Carolina Supreme Court bar examination in Raleigh. During her reading of the law over the past three years, she had mentioned her study in "Incidentally" only sporadically and briefly.[72]

One marvels at Lewis's vitality. In addition to her duties as a columnist, the leadership she displayed in galvanizing North Carolina's liberal community to attempt to prevent a railroading of the Gastonia defendants, and her legal studies, she had in late July published in the influential *Baltimore Evening Sun* an extensive two-part article examining the court proceedings and accepted a commission to cover the landmark case for the *Nation.* By the time *News and Observer* subscribers turned to her column that final Sunday in July, she likely had entrained for Charlotte or just arrived in the bustling textile city.[73]

70. *DW,* 15 and 19 June and 20 July 1929; Dunne, *Gastonia,* 45–46; Weisbord, *Radical Life,* 235; *N&O,* 9 August 1931, 6 March 1938, 7 December 1951; Buhle, Buhle, and Georgakas, *Encyclopedia of the American Left,* 631–32; "Building the I.L.D.," *Labor Defender* (May 1929): 109; Weisbord, "Gastonia, 1929," 193.

71. *N&O,* 25 August 1929.

72. *N&O,* 23 June, 25 August, and 5 September 1929; *GG,* 5 September 1929.

73. *Baltimore Evening Sun,* July? 1929.

Inside the jammed and steamy Mecklenburg superior courtroom, she joined the swarm of journalists positioned behind and to one side of the long semicircle of the sixteen defendants that arched across the floor. To the left of Judge Barnhill and directly in front of some of the accused sat the many members of the prosecution, headlined by Hoey, Carpenter, and E. T. Cansler, a renowned Charlotte criminal lawyer. Lewis labeled them "staunch defenders of the faith—faith in the unquestionable rightness of the industrial *status quo.*" Led by Jimison and Neal and buttressed by the last-minute arrival of Arthur Garfield Hays, the defense, which also included experienced Charlotte attorney Thaddeus Adams and two of Jimison's law partners, sat on the opposite side of the room. At the behest of the ILD, Leon Josephson, a young communist attorney from Trenton, also represented the accused.[74]

Unlike many of her journalistic peers, Lewis followed the trial's preliminary activities avidly as the attorneys exercised their generous rights to dismiss potential jurors peremptorily and for cause. In her *Nation* article, "Tar Heel Justice," she described the numerous "half-anxious, half-curious" strikers and their families attending the opening day's proceedings "to see what the law would do to the defendants who had roused them to demand better conditions of labor and life." A number, she noted, "were men in overalls . . . [and] some were women with thin, strained faces and babies in arms—ignorant of the deeper significance of the case, but knowing well that working hours are long and wages meager, and that the accused men and women had tried to help them."[75]

The newly minted attorney delighted in the opportunity to observe at close quarters her state's premiere legal talent vying with two of the country's foremost liberal lawyers. Hays—the ACLU's general counsel and a veteran of many high-profile courtroom battles, including the infamous Scopes and Sacco-Vanzetti trials—made himself available to Lewis for a personal interview. Reconciled to the inevitability of the native New Yorker's participation, she attempted to humanize him for her column's readers. She wrote that

74. Nell Battle Lewis, "Tar Heel Justice," *Nation,* 11 September 1929, 272–73; *N&O,* 1 September 1929; Salmond, *Gastonia 1929,* 113–16; *New York Evening World,* 28 August 1929; Weisbord, *Radical Life,* 249–50.

75. William Rollins Jr., "A Gentleman's Game," *New Masses* (October 1929): 3–4; *N&O,* 1 and 5 September 1929; *GG,* 4 September 1929; Salmond, *Gastonia 1929,* 113–16; Lewis, "Tar Heel Justice," 272–73.

he saw "neither Communism, Socialism nor any other ism as a cure-all for human life."[76] Of all her impressions of the trial's early activities, however, Barnhill's fairness and judiciousness stood out the most. The moderation and firm hand of the quiet young judge seemed to her to bode well and filled her with pride in her native state. Lewis informed her readers that Barnhill's initial rulings would displease extremists in both camps who wished to hijack the trial and infuse social and religious issues into the proceedings. The judge's decisions would silence "much potential thunder," she predicted.[77]

One of the few moments to break the tedium of voir dire had occurred several days earlier, during the examination of venireman J. G. Campbell, a diminutive and puckish *Charlotte Observer* newsdealer. During Adams's questioning Campbell had kept the courtroom in an "uproar," the *Gazette* reported. He made fun of the lawyers he knew; mentioned that he had joined the Presbyterian, not the Baptist, church because of his fear of water; and when identifying his occupation, parodied his vocation's salesmanship by showily thrusting a newspaper at Adams and bidding him a hearty "good morning." Despite Campbell's eccentricity his assurance—in the midst of the strong bias expressed by many veniremen against the defendants—that he would weigh the evidence "and nothing but" impressed the defense, which regarded him as one of the more intelligent potential jurors.[78]

"An air of expectancy, in contrast to the previous languid air, hung over the court room," the *Gazette* reported on 5 September as the prosecution readied itself that morning to present its case. Just before the examination of the state's witnesses began, defense attorney Adams announced that it was his "honor, privilege, and particular pleasure" to swear Lewis into the bar. She rose and stepped forward as the dignified-looking lawyer introduced her. As sunlight streamed through the wide shuttered windows and illuminated the packed courtroom, Barnhill and Adams administered Lewis's oath, and she kissed Adams's Bible. Lewis's numerous detractors attending the proceedings must have clucked over the fact that her swearing-in coincided with the commencement of the most dramatic trial in the state's history. Some undoubtedly believed that she had an insatiable appetite for the limelight. Instead of rejoin-

76. *N&O*, 1 September 1929.

77. *N&O*, 27, 28 August and 1 September 1929.

78. *GG*, 29 August and 10 September 1929.

ing her fellow journalists, Lewis further raised her critics' hackles by accepting Adams's invitation to join the defense in the front of the courtroom.[79]

Solicitor Carpenter chose that moment to upstage the event. He escorted Aderholt's widow, Mamie, shrouded in mourning dress and veil, and her stylish dark-haired daughter, Ethel, described by one newspaper as a "striking brunette," to a row of seats directly behind the prosecution and in front of the jury box.[80] After this theatrical moment Barnhill redirected his attention to Lewis. Her ancestry, he said, had contributed notably to the state, and she had earned a name for herself. Although many of the observers who filled the courtroom that morning undoubtedly held strong and polarized opinions about Lewis, no one could dispute the truthfulness of Judge Barnhill's carefully chosen remarks. Privately Barnhill, as he sucked on an unlit cigar, appraised the thirty-six-year-old, blue-eyed brunette *Raleigh News and Observer* reporter skeptically. The local newspapers had impugned her so thoroughly that he wondered "what type of animal" she was.[81]

The unexpected entrance of the Aderholts established the theatrical tone the prosecution had selected for the trial. Carpenter and his colleagues quickly proved themselves ham-handed showmen. During his examination of his first witness, the young physician who had treated Aderholt after his shooting, the solicitor gave a prearranged signal. With what the *Charlotte Observer* described as "surprising suddenness," the deputy sheriffs serving as attendants wheeled into the courtroom a tall object draped in black cloth. Carpenter hurriedly unpinned the covering and exposed a life-sized, flesh-colored wax model of Aderholt.[82] As Jimison, Hays, and the defense leapt to their feet to object fiercely, the clearly irritated Barnhill demanded that the figure be removed. The prosecution argued that the model would illustrate that Aderholt had received all of his wounds in his back. While his team stalled, Carpenter smoothed a crease in the effigy's coat, aligned its collar, and adjusted its hat. "Take it out now," the judge commanded.[83]

Throughout the next several days the state introduced and examined a se-

79. *GG*, 5 September 1929; *N&O*, 5 September 1929.

80. *GG*, 29 July and 5 September 1929; *DW*, 6 September 1929; *CO*, 6 September and 17 October 1929.

81. *GG*, 5 September, 17 October 1929; M. V. Barnhill to Nell Battle Lewis, 15 February 1954, NBL Papers; NBL passport, KPL Papers.

82. Salmond, *Gastonia 1929*, 117; Beal, *Proletarian Journey*, 188–89; *GG*, 5 September 1929; *N&O*, 6 September 1929; *CO*, 6 September 1929; Weisbord, *Radical Life*, 253–54.

83. *NYT*, 6 September 1929; *New York Telegram*, 6 September 1929; Beal, *Proletarian Journey*, 189.

ries of witnesses who provided an implausibly consistent account of the events on the night of the shooting. Arthur Roach—a mill special policeman who had received multiple buckshot wounds at the camp that night—maintained that after the struggle between the officer and the sentinel, unknown parties from the union hall had shouted, "Shoot him, damn them, shoot him." Policemen Tom Gilbert, who had also received wounds at the camp that night, and Adam Hord, who had emerged from the melee uninjured, supported virtually all of Roach's testimony.[84]

The cross-examination of the policemen discredited their testimony by revealing that most of them had long and prolific histories of thuggery, scrapes with the law, and intemperance. By the time Barnhill adjourned the trial late Saturday for the Sabbath, most experienced observers, such as Lewis's colleague "Fleet" Williams, concluded that the prosecution would have to produce considerably stronger evidence than it had over the past three days in order to convict the defendants.[85]

Jimison's team, however, would have no further opportunity to establish the innocence of the defendants; the trial ended freakishly and abruptly. "Juror Is Crazy; Mistrial Is Ordered," blared the *Gazette*'s Monday headline. A deputy sheriff had called Barnhill to Campbell's room at dawn on Monday to observe his bizarre demeanor. He begged for the deputy's revolver to shoot the defendants and to commit suicide. Delighted to see Barnhill, he patted the judge's shoes and babbled, "Here is our good old judge." It required four deputies to transfer the banty man to a padded cell in the courthouse.[86]

As Lewis sat in the crowded and buzzing courtroom, she could see the many young defendants, whom Williams had described as resembling a "group of college boys and girls," sink into their chairs as they realized that the proceeding might end without the acquittal they had anticipated. Barnhill alone seemed unaffected by the turmoil. "I would rather the defendants be turned loose without trial than have them convicted by an insane man," he said as he pronounced a mistrial.[87]

Gastonia's many patriots seethed with frustration. Late Monday afternoon

84. *CO*, 6–8 September 1929.

85. *CO*, 6–8 September 1929; *Seattle Industrial Worker*, 5 August 1929; *DW*, 18 July 1929; *GG*, 6 September 1929; Salmond, *Gastonia 1929*, 119–20.

86. *GG*, 9 September 1929; *NYT*, 10 September 1929; *New York Herald Tribune*, 10 September 1929; *DW*, 10 September 1929; *CO*, 10 September 1929.

87. Salmond, *Gastonia 1929*, 99; *CO*, 10 September 1929; *NYT*, 10 September 1929.

a crowd began to form to prevent a rumored rally of the union. When the meeting did not materialize, members of the crowd cried out, "Run them out of town."[88] A horde of men estimated at between three and five hundred converged at a Gastonia rooming house where union organizers and Party functionaries frequently stayed. Singing the opening line of the doxology, "Praise God, from Whom all blessings flow," one hundred men burst through the front door. Once inside, the chorus segued into "My Country, 'Tis of Thee," as it rounded up a trio of NTWU officials and supporters, including British communist Benjamin Wells. The mob shoved its captives into separate automobiles, and the drivers of the procession of over one hundred vehicles turned their machines due east in an audacious attempt to overrun North Carolina's second-largest city.[89]

The main body of raiders overran Charlotte at eleven o'clock. Advance troops identified themselves to the *Observer*'s city editor as Gastonia policemen. Leaders made it clear that they intended to lynch not only the Gastonia prisoners but also Jimison, Dunne, and Hugo Oehler, Beal's replacement as the NTWU's southern organizer. Several hundred men assembled at the courthouse and surrounded the adjacent jail with the intent of occupying it and seizing the unionists, but the mob lost its courage when it eyed the heavily fortified building. Across the street intruders broke into the law offices of Jimison and his partners and the headquarters of the ILD and ransacked both facilities.[90]

In "Gastonia Goes Wild," Lewis's lead editorial in the 15 September *News and Observer*," she lambasted the town's authorities. A probe conducted by Carpenter into the pandemonium had resulted in the filing of warrants against only fourteen suspects, but it nevertheless threatened to rip the cover from the Committee of One Hundred, implicate it in the violence directed at the unionists since the strike's beginning, and reveal the ties of the organization

88. *CO*, 10 September 1929; *DW*, 12 September 1929; *New York World*, 11 September 1929; Pope, *Millhands & Preachers*, 290–91.

89. *CO*, 14 September 1929; *NYT*, 11 September 1929; *DW*, 12 September 1929; American Civil Liberties Union, *Justice—North Carolina Style, The Record of the Year's Struggle for Unions in Gastonia and Marion, April 1929 to April 1930* (New York: American Civil Liberties Union, 1930), 6; *GG*, 12 September 1929.

90. *CO*, 10 September 1929; *New York World*, 11 September 1929; *NYT*, 11 September 1929; Nell Battle Lewis, "Anarchy vs. Communism in Gastonia," *Nation*, 25 September 1929, 321; Jessie Lloyd, "Gastonia Mob Leader Investigates Reign of Terror" (Federated Press), 11 September 1929, ACLU Papers; *GG*, 17 September 1929.

to the Loray Mill establishment and its lackeys. "Police officers who were in the June 7 raid have been arrested as members of this mob, as well as several officials and employees of the . . . mill, practically all of whom are said to be witnesses for the State," she wrote. Although the vigilantism had at long last taught her the meaning of that "vague but familiar term, '100 per cent Americanism,'" she could discern no more difference between it and "100 per cent Bolshevism at its worst than between two excessively rotten apples."[91]

The anarchy that flourished in Gastonia following the mistrial reached its apex as Lewis filed her copy on Saturday for her mid-September "Incidentally" column. Several hundred men—including many Loray Mill workers released from their duties for the afternoon and helpfully equipped by the factory with pistols and ammunition—patrolled the town's streets to thwart a mass meeting the NTWU had scheduled. The fifty police and special officers mustered for the occasion in no way interfered with the vigilantes and instead made preparations to help turn back the unionists.[92]

In her second *Nation* article in two weeks, "Anarchy vs. Communism in Gastonia," Lewis updated her earlier piece and provided a comprehensive accounting of what had transpired that afternoon. Party leaders, who had become aware of the dangerous situation in Gastonia, decided at the last moment to call off the rally. Many who planned to participate, however, did not learn of the cancellation. Ella May Wiggins, the strikers' minstrel, and two dozen other union members riding in the back of a hired truck found the way to the rally blocked by a band of heavily armed men. Although the vehicle's operator complied with their demand that he reverse course, the vigilantes decided to terrorize the unionists further. They piled into a large caravan of automobiles and followed their prey closely, cursing and trying to intimidate them.[93]

Five miles south of Gastonia, an Essex sedan separated from the pack, sped forward, and suddenly blocked the highway. The truck's driver slammed into the stopped car. The collision threw many of the union supporters onto the ground, but Wiggins remained in the back of the truck. At that moment gunmen fired, and a bullet struck her just below her collarbone, tearing into her

91. *N&O*, 15 September 1929.

92. Salmond, *Gastonia 1929*, 127; *DW*, 14 September 1929; Lewis, "Anarchy vs. Communism in Gastonia," 321–22.

93. Lewis, "Anarchy vs. Communism in Gastonia," 321–22; *NYT*, 16 September 1929; *New York Evening Post*, 17 September 1929; *N&O*, 15 September 1929; Salmond, *Gastonia 1929*, 128.

heart and spinal cavity. The truck driver and a handful of other unionists carried Wiggins's body to a cabin where blacks resided. She, almost alone among the Carolina strikers, had transcended the powerful prejudice that had confined the union's membership to whites only, and she rightly rested in this humble and integrated setting until authorities transported her body to the morgue.[94]

Across the nation reporters and editorialists denounced North Carolina and the lawlessness that flourished in Gastonia. It remained for Lewis, however, to write arguably the most moving and human memorial to Wiggins. "Ella May" appeared in "Incidentally" the week following her murder. Lewis's signature sarcasm manifested itself only in the caustic subtitle she chose for the editorial: "A Triumph of North Carolina's Industrialism."[95] The columnist explained that by the time of Wiggins's death at age twenty-nine, she had given birth to nine children, only five of whom survived. Her husband had deserted her, and she worked twelve-hour shifts, often during the night, to support her family. Never had she earned more than nine dollars a week. "When Ella came home dog-tired . . . there were a thousand things to do: supper to get, dishes to wash, clothes to mend, the house to keep decent," Lewis recounted. "Day after day the same exhausting, life-sapping grind—day after day, day after day." She told her readers that Wiggins had joined the NTWU for her children.

> But soon there was trouble. Police with blackjacks broke up the union parades. Some of the women who marched were choked. One old woman was knocked to the ground, and there was another woman with blackened eyes and a swollen face. Neighbors whispered of a "Committee" that would "get you" if you stuck to the union. Soldiers came to protect the mill. A mob wrecked the union headquarters. Then there was shooting in the night, and a dead police officer. Sixteen of Ella May's friends were in jail—thirteen of them to be tried for their lives. That was the end of her old union now, some people said. She'd be in jail, too, the first thing she knew. But Ella May stuck. "They'll have to kill me to make me give up the union," she said defiantly.

94. *CO,* 16 September and 6 November 1929; *NYT,* 16 September 1929; Salmond, *Gastonia 1929,* 51, 128.

95. *N&O,* 22 September 1929.

In the wake of the mistrial, Lewis continued, the committee and the mob had run amok, vandalizing the union headquarters and beating an organizer. Strikers who continued to support their organization took their lives into their own hands. Many considered whether they should turn their backs on Beal and the other prisoners, return to the mills, and accept their lot in life.

> People had a right to hold meetings, didn't they? Then, come on! Ella May climbed into a truck with other union members and they started. In the mill section they were met by a gang of angry, threatening men armed with guns. Frightened, the driver of the truck turned back. "Look behind—they're after us!" The driver began to speed. A line of cars was in mad pursuit. The truck dashed on still faster, with the cars chasing it furiously.
>
> A sharp halt. A volley of shots. Agony tearing suddenly through Ella May's breast. The children . . . . . . The baby . . . . . . Dear Jesus, what will happen to them now? . . . . . .

"Ella May" predictably outraged the mill press. The *Gazette* believed that Lewis had sunk so low that it now coined a new pejorative that amalgamated her with its foremost bugbear. The little paper labeled its opponents "Mencken and Nell Battle Lewis type[s]." Lewis's editorial, however, stirred Frank Graham, who had attained growing prominence within the university and throughout the state. The modest but exuberant professor of history wrote a long letter for publication in "Incidentally," which Lewis reprinted in its entirety the following week. The two liberal reformers had countless bonds in addition to their progressive agenda and admiration for one another. They shared an abiding devotion to the university, fondness for trustee and publisher Josephus Daniels, and abundantly overlapping friendship and kinship networks.[96]

Graham's eulogy of Wiggins in "Incidentally" proved almost more than David Clark, editor of the *Southern Textile Bulletin*, could bear. After smearing the balladeer, he extended his attack to her extollers. "Miss Nell Battle Lewis of . . . the *Raleigh News and Observer*," he charged, "gave the communists much

96. *GG*, 19 and 23 September 1929; Snider, *Light on the Hill*, 203–6; Ashby, *Frank Porter Graham*, 71–77; David Clark letter, 31 January 1930, FPG Papers; *CO*, 18 February 1930; *Southern Textile Bulletin*, 10 and 17 April 1930.

aid while they were creating disturbances at Gastonia and as an appreciation of one of her efforts she received a letter from Frank Graham . . . of the University of North Carolina and published it." Clark believed that Graham's effusive letter provided convincing evidence of his alignment with the communists.[97]

The final trial of the Gastonia defendants, which began on 30 September, proceeded much more routinely and expeditiously than the mistrial. The communists had ended their agitation in Gastonia, and the NTWU, belatedly conceding that the mill had broken the strike, abandoned the tent city and its headquarters. The prosecution surprised many by freeing nine of the defendants—including the three women—and by reducing the charges against the remaining seven unionists to second-degree murder. Carpenter consolidated the murder accusations with a blanket second indictment of assault with intent to kill the deputies. All of the nol-prossed defendants, with the exception of the women, were native southerners.[98]

The ILD, which had consolidated its control over the defense and demoted Jimison—replacing him as chief counsel with his law partner, J. Frank Flowers—observed that the prosecution's action boded poorly for the defendants. Without the abundant preemptory challenges the defense had enjoyed in the mistrial, it had little chance of obtaining a sympathetic jury. Barnhill unintentionally made matters worse by disallowing any jurors from Charlotte. He had noticed in the previous trial that many of the most prejudiced veniremen lived there. Within only four days the judge had assembled a panel overwhelmingly made up of middle-aged, landowning farmers.[99]

Hardly had the trial gotten under way when, two days later, violence erupted in Marion some fifty-five miles northwest of Gastonia. On the morning of 2 October 1929, outside the main gate to the Marion Manufacturing Company, the town sheriff and his deputies fired into the backs of unarmed unionists, killing six and wounding twenty-five. "I think the officers are damned good marksmen," the mill manager told a reporter. "If I ever organize an army they can have jobs with me."[100]

97. *Southern Textile Bulletin*, 10 April 1930.

98. Salmond, *Gastonia 1929*, 134–35, 138; Pope, *Millhands & Preachers*, 295; *NYT*, 30 September and 1 October 1929.

99. Salmond, *Gastonia 1929*, 137; *NYT*, 30 September and 1 October 1929; Margaret Larkin, "Small Farmer Jury to Try Gastonians" (Federated Press), 4 October 1929, ACLU Papers; *DW*, 3 October 1929; *GG*, 3 October 1929.

100. *Asheville* (N.C.) *Citizen*, 4 October 1929; Benjamin Stolberg, "Madness in Marion," *Nation*,

"Hurrah for the mills," Lewis jeered four days after the shooting, in "Reaping the Whirlwind." "Hurrah for the new prosperity. Hurrah, oh, three times three, for the almighty dollar." The Marion strikers' blood, she declared, cried out to "every man and woman of heart in North Carolina."[101]

Lewis posited the maxim that should guide all labor relations in the mechanized era: "MAN—his health, his happiness, his opportunity for development—is always more important, infinitely more precious in fundamental value, than ever the machine or any of its products could be." From this indisputable premise she derived her policy prescriptions for her state's industrial ills. First, she proposed a thorough overhaul of the "notoriously defective" laws that permitted sixty-hour workweeks; twelve-hour days; women to work night shifts; and children between the ages of fourteen and sixteen, who had completed four years of education, to work more than eight hours a day. She also advocated a reorganization of the State Department of Labor that would include within that agency a newly created women's bureau and provide mechanisms for effective enforcement of stiffened labor laws. Finally, all North Carolinians should accept the rights of workers to organize and of the citizenry to investigate and find fault with the way mill owners operated their factories.[102]

Lewis followed "Reaping the Whirlwind" with "Comedy in a Churchyard," Gerald Johnson's eloquent commentary on Wiggins's life and the injustice of her murder. The editorial had appeared several weeks earlier in the *Baltimore Evening Sun,* whose leadership three years earlier, at Mencken's behest, had persuaded the native North Carolinian to leave his Chapel Hill teaching post and join the publication's editorial staff as an associate editor. From his perch in "Bawlamer," Johnson would solidify his reputation as the most perceptive national observer and critic of Dixie.[103]

Through her own writing in "Incidentally" Lewis opened the eyes of, sometimes influenced, and often infuriated many members of her immediate audience, which in addition to liberal supporters and rank-and-file readers

---

23 October 1929, 462–64; NBL, "Timeline of North Carolina Textile Strikes," October? 1929, NBL Papers; Tippett, *When Southern Labor Stirs,* 109–55.

101. *N&O,* 6 October 1929.

102. *N&O,* 6 October 1929.

103. Fitzpatrick, *Gerald W. Johnson,* 61–64, 83–85; Mencken, *Thirty-Five Years of Newspaper Work,* 306; *Baltimore Evening Sun,* 19 September 1929.

included many of her state's most powerful politicians, businessmen, and religious leaders. But she also used her column with great frequency to broadcast throughout North Carolina the views of Johnson, Graham, labor journalist and proletarian novelist Mary Heaton Vorse, and other prominent liberal and leftist journalists and social activists, whose prestige and support for her agenda buttressed her own credibility and strengthened her advocacy. Showcased within the conspicuous and agenda-setting capital daily, which provided many citizens, including opinion leaders, with their only exposure to journalism, Lewis's column served as a venue for progressive critics and infused the public sphere with their commentary.[104]

Lewis almost certainly did not attend the retrial of the Gastonia defendants. Exhausted by her personal involvement in the earlier court cases and her frenetic publication schedule and likely demoralized by the inability of North Carolina's liberal community to stem the bloody backlash directed at the unionists in Gastonia and Marion, she journeyed out of state for a much-needed rest. She may have gone, as she often did for respite, to the University of Virginia, where her brother Ivey and his family resided in a pavilion that adjoined the Rotunda and abutted the academical village's storied lawn. While there, she may have visited *Virginia Quarterly Review* editor Douglas Southall Wilson. Despite its association with the traditional university, the fledgling quarterly had begun to establish a liberal reputation by regularly focusing on controversial southern issues and publishing thought-provoking articles. Wilson had engaged Lewis to author an essay on the labor unrest in North Carolina for his journal's next edition.[105]

The prosecution began to build its case on 4 October. With the exception of some sharp sparring between opposing counsel, the next several days featured nearly all of the same witnesses as the mistrial and at first developed almost identically to it. The two trials differed, however, in several crucial respects. Arthur Garfield Hays had opted out, stating publicly that he had other com-

104. Hobbs, *North Carolina: Economic and Social*, 272; *N&O*, 19 October 1930; Paul Starr, *The Creation of the Media: Political Origins of Modern Communications* (New York: Basic Books, 2004), 23–24.

105. FPG to NBL, 28 October 1929, FPG Papers; "Pavilion Residents, 1895–1995" (cited 20 March 2006), www.virginia.edu/100yearslawn/html/pavilions.html; Edward L. Ayers, "A Southern Chronicle: The *Virginia Quarterly Review* and the American South, 1925–2000" (cited 20 March 2006), www.vqronline.org/viewmedia.php/prmMID/8057; Gerald W. Johnson, "A Tilt with Southern Wind-Mills," *Virginia Quarterly Review* 1, no. 2 (July 1925): 184–92; Broadus Mitchell, "Fleshpots in the South," *Virginia Quarterly Review* 3, no. 2 (April 1927): 161–76; Nell Battle Lewis, "North Carolina at the Cross-Roads," *Virginia Quarterly Review* 6, no. 1 (January 1930): 37–47.

mitments but confiding to friends that the Gastonia case "was the most trying situation" he had encountered in his legal career.[106] On 9 October Carpenter and his colleagues abruptly rested their case. The defense had not had the opportunity to present its witnesses during the mistrial, and despite the conservative composition of the jury, Flowers and Jimison's team remained hopeful regarding the trial's outcome. Besides calling into question the veracity of the law officers, it had established that all of the state's other witnesses had ties to the Loray Mill. That afternoon the defense called a score of witnesses, nearly all of whom had worked at the mill or as union organizers. Much of their testimony focused on the brutality of the police, Gilbert and Roach's drunkenness, and the fact that the lawmen had shot first.[107]

In its cross-examination Carpenter's contingent attempted to appeal to the jury's prejudices by boring into the testifiers' political, racial, and religious beliefs; probing their sexual histories; and playing to the distrust many of the region's residents held toward outsiders. North Carolina rules of procedure afforded attorneys great liberty to impeach witnesses with these sorts of questions.[108]

On 10 October, in his interrogation of a young female striker, Jake F. Newell demanded to know if the ILD, which had provided the witness with assistance throughout the unrest, served as an arm of the Communist Party. Barnhill excused the jury and brought the proceeding to a halt. Newell's associate, E. T. Cansler, cited the Sacco-Vanzetti case as one of numerous precedents that upheld the prosecution's line of questioning. The reference to the anarchist trial caused a sensation in the courtroom. The state had for months promised it would not conduct itself as its counterpart had in the infamous Massachusetts trial. Barnhill did not permit the question, but he borrowed the attorney's law books to study the matter further and reserved his right to change his mind regarding the permissibility of this kind of inquiry.[109]

The following day Barnhill, still undecided about whether he would allow questions focusing on the defendants' political beliefs, had to act again to rein

106. Salmond, *Gastonia 1929*, 137–39; Terry Teachout, *The Skeptic: A Life of H. L. Mencken* (New York: HarperCollins, 2002), 225–28; Kevin Boyle, *Arc of Justice: A Saga of Race, Civil Rights, and Murder in the Jazz Age* (New York: Henry Holt, 2004); *CO*, 5 October 1929.

107. Pope, *Millhands & Preachers*, 296; Salmond, *Gastonia 1929*, 139–42.

108. *NYT*, 12 October 1929.

109. *GG*, 10 October 1929; *New York World*, 11 October 1929; *New York Herald Tribune*, 11 October 1929; *New York Evening World*, 11 October 1929.

in Newell. The combative attorney attempted to impeach a defense witness by charging that he had appeared at a rally alongside a black organizer and had advocated "social equality" between the races. The jury again departed the courtroom as Carpenter, Cansler, and Newell approached the bench. They testified that the speakers at the gathering had not merely endorsed the strike but had also attempted to foment violence by inciting "the negroes on the farms of the South to rise against the whites." This argument did not persuade the judge. "I rule against you, gentlemen," he informed the prosecution.[110]

On the morning of 14 October Beal took the stand, where he would remain throughout the entire day's session. At midmorning Cansler began his cross-examination. A few minutes into his inquiry he asked Beal about his association with the Socialist Party earlier in the decade. Barnhill sustained an objection and dismissed the jury, while counsel again debated the admissibility of testimony surrounding the witnesses' political affiliations and beliefs and their views on racial issues.[111]

The dispute finally forced Barnhill to render a ruling on the contentious issue. He crafted a tortured compromise between the positions staked by the opposing counsel. The judge interdicted entirely any inquiry that focused on the witnesses' racial views and forbade interrogation regarding their membership in communist organizations. He maintained that discussion of these volatile issues would make it impossible for the jurors to rule fairly. Only if testifiers volunteered without solicitation their affiliations with radical groups could the state pursue the matter. But Barnhill dismayed the defense by permitting the prosecution to ask questions regarding the witnesses' personal political beliefs so that the panel could better assess the credibility of the testifiers. He did not at this point render a decision as to whether he would allow witnesses who did not believe in God to testify. A rarely invoked and controversial North Carolina statute dating back to the Revolutionary War mandated that they could not.[112]

Beal displayed intelligence, a quick wit, and extraordinary evasiveness regarding his political beliefs and emerged from Cansler's five-hour cross-examination virtually unscathed. Despite the fact that throughout the unrest the mill press had portrayed the district organizer as a fiend, the *New York*

110. *GG*, 11 October 1929; *NYT*, 12 October 1929.

111. *CO*, 15 October 1929.

112. *CO*, 15 October 1929; *NYT*, 15, 27 October 1929; *New York World*, 15 October 1929; *New York Herald Tribune*, 15 October 1929.

*World* stated that in his testimony he projected an appearance "as one of the mildest agitators that ever led a strike."[113]

The next witness, twenty-year-old Edith Miller, a doctrinaire communist and the wife of one of the defendants, made no attempt to hide her radical convictions. Like all of the testifiers, as she took the witness stand she swore an oath to tell the truth and sealed it by kissing the Bible. Sporting a short—almost masculine—hairstyle that set her apart from most southern women, she coolly and articulately responded to Newell's grilling. Miller stated that she did not believe in a Supreme Being that rewarded good acts and punished bad ones. The defense objected strongly regarding this inquiry into the witness's religious beliefs, but Barnhill allowed it and instructed the jury that although Miller had the "right to believe as she may please," the panel could take her heresy into account as it evaluated her credibility and to "determine what sanctity, if any, she attached to the oath that she had taken." When the witness stepped down, Newell, who regularly taught a Bible class, smiled triumphantly at his colleagues.[114] "I shall always believe that the testimony of Edith Miller weighed more heavily against us than all the other matter presented before the jury," Beal later wrote in his memoirs. He believed that Miller cared more about winning the approval of "Stalin's lackeys in New York and Moscow" than the lives of the seven defendants, whom Party representatives after much debate had counseled to avoid using their testimony to propagandize communist principles.[115]

On 17 October the prosecution and defense began their summations. Hoey and Newell sought to portray the defendants variously as revolutionaries, emissaries of the Communist Party, murderers, and atheists. Carpenter concluded the trial the following afternoon with a remarkable display of histrionics. As gape-mouthed jurors and snickering reporters looked on, the solicitor reenacted Aderholt's shooting. Carpenter lay on the floor and shouted out a description of the mortally wounded man. He rose and spoke to the weeping widow: "I want you, Mrs. Aderholt, to take the coat of your husband to your home. Take it as an emblem of the very personification of the truth and honesty that was your husband's." He walked over to the weeping widow and pre-

113. *New York World*, 15 October 1929; *New York Herald Tribune*, 15 October 1929.

114. *CO*, 16 October 1929; *NYT*, 16 and 27 October 1929; *New York World*, 16 October 1929; Beal, *Proletarian Journey*, 200; Weisbord, *Radical Life*, 270–71.

115. Beal, *Proletarian Journey*, 196, 200; Pope, *Millhands & Preachers*, 298–99; Weisbord, *Radical Life*, 286; Salmond, *Gastonia 1929*, 145–46.

sented her with the bloody and shot-ridden garment. As he took her hand into his, the defense roared an objection, and Barnhill ordered the state to stop its grandstanding. His admonition had little effect. The irrepressible attorney knelt before the jurors and assumed the role of Mamie Aderholt tending to her dying husband. Still on his knees, Carpenter placed his arms on the jury box and sobbed out the police chief's last words. In his finale he implored the panelists to "do your duty, men. In the name of justice, do your duty."[116]

Immediately following this performance, Barnhill recessed for the weekend. On Monday morning he cautioned the panelists to disregard much of the prejudicial material the prosecution had introduced and declared that the defendants had a legal right to participate in the strike. The fact that several of the accused men came from states other than North Carolina should not in any way influence the impending judgment. The liberal young justice instructed the jurors to ignore the prosecution's questions directed at Beal regarding whether he had sought to overthrow the government violently. The judge also stated that Miller had a right to her own religious beliefs. Members could take into account her lack of faith in a Supreme Being only to evaluate her credibility. Barnhill ended his lengthy charge with an emphatic command to the jurors: "You should lay aside and disabuse your minds of all extraneous matter and determine this case in a fair and impartial manner upon the testimony."[117]

The jury returned to the packed courtroom in less than an hour, declaring that it had found all of the accused men guilty of second-degree murder. The sweeping judgment surprised many of the journalists and attorneys—perhaps even the judge. Numerous observers had expected the jurors would absolve some of the strikers.[118] The judge cast aside any appearance of fairness by sentencing the northern defendants most severely. Beal smiled faintly as he and the three other unionists from the North earned prison terms of seventeen to twenty years at hard labor in the Raleigh penitentiary. The trio of prisoners from the Carolinas received various periods of incarceration ranging from five to fifteen years. Barnhill incongruously set extraordinarily low bonds of just

116. *DW*, 18 and 21 October 1929; *NYT*, 18 and 19 October 1929; *New York World*, 19 October 1929; *CO*, 18 and 19 October 1929; *GG*, 18 October 1929; Pope, *Millhands & Preachers*, 302–4; Beal, *Proletarian Journey*, 206–7.

117. *CO*, 22 October 1929.

118. *GG*, 21 October 1929; *NYT*, 22 October 1929; *New York World*, 23 October 1929.

a few thousand dollars on each of the defendants as they awaited their appeal in North Carolina's supreme court. Beal wondered if the state's authorities wanted "us to 'skip' bail."[119]

Lewis ended her two-week interruption of "Incidentally" the Sunday following the verdict. All four of her editorials in the 27 October *News and Observer* zeroed in on the Gastonia debacle. In "The Gaston Mind" she upbraided the county grand jury for its failure several days earlier to charge anyone for Wiggins's murder or the three union organizers' kidnapping. After examining over seventy witnesses to Wiggins's shooting, the jury had announced that it did not have sufficient evidence to indict any of nine Loray Mill employees accused of killing the strikers' minstrel. "Nothing so shamelessly contemptuous of the rudimentary standards of public decency has taken place within my memory," Lewis thundered. The grand jury had sent a series of resounding messages to the world: "To hell with the orderly processes of civil government which men have set up for their mutual protection! To hell with the ideal of justice and all the sacrifices which through the centuries men have made to establish it! To hell with the theory of democracy in which the rights of the poor and humble are equal to those of the rich and the proud!" The jury's failure to indict a single individual, she charged, had signaled to the public that men could murder with impunity in Gaston County and that within that vicinity "the concept of law is a brutal travesty and the Christian religion is a joke." The mention of the word *civilization* in the county provoked the "sound of diabolical laughter—the laughter of the demon and the beast which have stalked in madness [there]."[120]

Despite Lewis's opinion that the unionists' conviction would be overturned, the following summer the state supreme court sustained Barnhill's ruling and affirmed his sentencing. The decision mattered little to the defendants. The same day the court announced its judgment in the appeal, the *News and Observer* revealed that it had authoritatively determined that Beal and four of the other appellants had fled to the Soviet Union. The remaining defendants and Edith Miller soon joined them. According to Beal's accounts of his Soviet experiences, he and most of the unionists observed and endured misery aplenty

119. "Aderholt Murderers Convicted," *Southern Textile Bulletin*, 24 October 1929, 26; Beal, *Proletarian Journey*, 208–9; *NYT*, 22 October 1929; *CO*, 22 October 1929; *GG*, 22 October 1929.

120. *N&O*, 27 October 1929; Salmond, *Gastonia 1929*, 155; *NYT*, 25 October 1929; *GG*, 24 October 1929.

and soon found the workers' paradise a hell on earth. Only the Millers appear to have thrived in the USSR. Beal and several of the other men would eventually escape to the United States.[121]

In mid-November 1929, a month after the verdict in the Charlotte trial of the Gastonia defendants and the county grand jury's failure to charge anyone for the murder of Wiggins or the kidnapping of organizers, Lewis reflected in "Incidentally" on her involvement in the disastrous labor unrest. "During recent months," she wrote, "I have understood as never before the travail out of which all progress comes. What a bitter struggle it is, what a passionate clash of opinions! The flame that is to light the years ahead of us is obscured by so much smoke in our own day. I suppose this has always been so. Looking through Marion and Gastonia one sees history not as a dry tale that [is] told but as a living, continuous process in which human advance has come slowly and very painfully, wrought of conflict and confusion, with blood and sweat and countless sacrifices and great patience,—and faith."[122]

Lewis's involvement in the Loray Mill strike and its aftermath—capped by the publication of her article "North Carolina at the Cross-Roads" in the January 1930 issue of the *Virginia Quarterly Review*—marked the high point but not the end of her journalistic career and her leadership role in southern liberalism. Nell Lewis had not exhausted her championship of fair play, and she had yet to put to use her new admission to the North Carolina bar.[123]

121. *NYT*, 21 August 1930; Beal, "I Was a Communist Martyr," 40–45; Salmond, *Gastonia 1929*, 167–73; Beal, *Proletarian Journey*, 348–49; Bernstein, *Lean Years*, 27–28.

122. *N&O*, 17 November 1929.

123. Lewis, "North Carolina at the Cross-Roads," 37–47.

Dr. Richard H. Lewis, Nell's father, achieved national renown in the field of public health. Early in Nell's career, her feminism and temperament sometimes created discord with Dr. Lewis, who held traditional views regarding women's roles. (Courtesy of the North Carolina Office of Archives and History, Raleigh, North Carolina.)

Ivey F. Lewis, Nell's half brother, served as dean of the University of Virginia and helped furnish the "scientific" rationale for the commonwealth's racial integrity movement. The prominent biologist later became Nell's confidant during the South's massive resistance to public school integration. (North Carolina Collection, University of North Carolina Library at Chapel Hill.)

Kemp P. Lewis, Nell's half brother, a leading textile executive, supported her throughout her many bouts of mental illness. The problems he and his elder brother, Richard Jr., faced with unionization likely contributed to Nell's political reversal. (North Carolina Collection, University of North Carolina Library at Chapel Hill.)

Nell as a student at Raleigh's St. Mary's School, which she attended from 1907 through 1911. Her behavior did not always rise to the institution's genteel standards. "I wasn't very good," she later confessed. (Courtesy of the North Carolina Office of Archives and History, Raleigh, North Carolina.)

Nell, the editor-in-chief of St. Mary's literary magazine and yearbook, meets with her staff in 1911. She is pictured at the head of the table. (Saint Mary's School, Raleigh, North Carolina.)

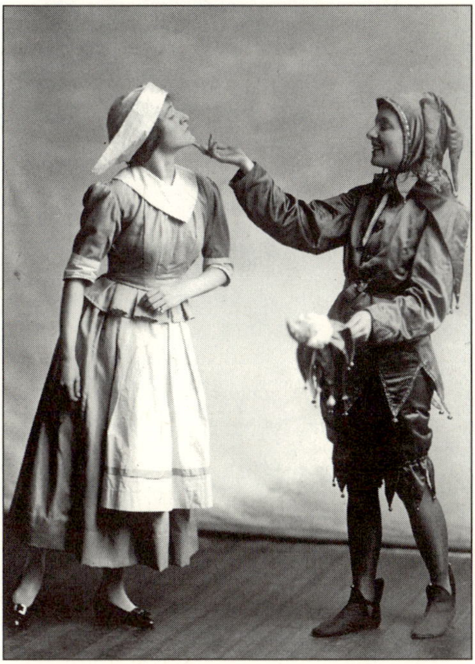

Nell as the wise and ironical fool Feste in Smith College's 1917 production of Shakespeare's *Twelfth Night*. She returned to Raleigh from the northern school "filled with liberal ideas," a niece later recalled. (Sophia Smith Collection and the College Archives, Smith College, Northampton, Massachusetts.)

Lewis, in her YMCA uniform, and her beau Lenoir Chambers in Nice, France, in 1919. Her father apparently, under mysterious circumstances, played a prominent role in ending her love affair. (Southern Historical Collection, Wilson Library, The University of North Carolina at Chapel Hill.)

The Gastonia defendants in 1929. Fred Beal stands in the front row, second from left. As the South's leading female liberal journalist, Lewis crusaded on behalf of the imprisoned members of the communist-controlled union. She would later recant her progressive activism. (Courtesy of the North Carolina Office of Archives and History, Raleigh, North Carolina.)

Lewis, one of North Carolina's pioneering female attorneys, prepares to argue for the Samarcand defendants, who were accused in 1931 of burning down two buildings at the state "detention home and industrial school for immoral, neglected, and wayward [white] girls." (Courtesy of the North Carolina Office of Archives and History, Raleigh, North Carolina.)

Lewis taught English, history, and Bible at St. Mary's 1937 through 1944 and again in 1954. Despite her political metamorphosis, many students considered their teacher "quite avant-garde" because of her individuality and directness. (Courtesy of the North Carolina Office of Archives and History, Raleigh, North Carolina.)

Frank P. Graham *(seated top left)* confers—probably in 1947—with future Progressive Party presidential candidate Henry Wallace. Lewis, as the associate editor of the *Raleigh Times*, dubbed the former vice president "Red Hank" and lambasted him. (Southern Historical Collection, Wilson Library, The University of North Carolina at Chapel Hill.)

Jonathan Daniels *(right)* meeting with President Harry S. Truman. Daniels directed the *Raleigh News and Observer* after the death of his father, Josephus, in 1948. Lewis's conservatism and her resentment of her liberal new editor must often have frustrated Jonathan, but he nevertheless afforded his opinionated columnist a high degree of autonomy. (Associated Press.)

Senator Frank P. Graham campaigns during North Carolina's bitterly contested 1950 Democratic Party primary. Lewis opposed her former liberal ally's candidacy and stumped for one of his opponents, Willis Smith. (Southern Historical Collection, Wilson Library, The University of North Carolina at Chapel Hill.)

# 6 IN DESPERATION

Illness removed Lewis from the next clash between North Carolina's mill establishment and the state's progressive community, diminished her connectedness to her Tar Heel allies, and forced her dependence in a fragile condition on her brothers. In January 1930 she departed Raleigh for Charlottesville, where for the next four months she resided with Ivey and perhaps occasionally with relatives living nearby. She received medical treatment, but no existing correspondence suggests that her brothers believed she was suffering from another severe bout of mental illness such as the one they had perceived a decade earlier. A sweet taste in her mouth defied diagnosis and worried her greatly.[1]

During her stay in Virginia, Lewis deferred her authorship of "Incidentally." Recessing her column not only removed her from her principal platform but also cut into her finances. In the early years of the Great Depression she undoubtedly relied increasingly on the twenty dollars she received for each of her columns to meet her living expenses. Despite her friendship with Josephus Daniels, the newspaper paid her only for completed work.[2] For "Battling Nell" to have withdrawn from the fight that North Carolina liberals were waging to better the working conditions of textile workers and stifled her irrepressible voice, a serious ailment must have plagued her during the first half of 1930. She cryptically informed her readers two years later that she "had no control [over] the long blank stretches in 'Incidentially'" and that these gaps could be considered "autobiographical."[3]

"It's fine to be back in Grandole N.C.!" Lewis wrote on 1 June as she resumed her column. She acknowledged that much had changed in her beloved state during her "long vacation." Authorities had disgracefully acquitted all of the men accused of murdering Ella May Wiggins, Lewis's mentor and close friend Kate Burr Johnson had resigned her directorship of the State Board of Public Welfare to superintend the New Jersey State Home for Girls,

1. Mitchell, "Nell Battle Lewis," 78–79; NBL to KPL, 24 July 1931, IFL to KPL, 19 March 1932, NBL to RHL Jr., KPL, IFL, and Isaac Manning, 12 May 1933, all in KPL Papers.

2. RHL Jr. to IFL, 29 July 1932, KPL Papers; Frank Smethurst to NBL, 21 December 1930, NBL Papers.

3. *N&O*, 4 September 1932.

and Jonathan Daniels—whom the columnist would increasingly regard with distaste—seemed poised to assume expanding levels of authority at the paper.[4]

University of North Carolina (UNC) president Harry W. Chase had announced his intention to resign, and on 9 June the institution's board of trustees unanimously drafted as his successor Frank Porter Graham, who, in addition to his duties as a history professor, headed the state's conference for social service. In her lead editorial, "The Right Man," six days later, Lewis applauded the board's decision. She recounted a recent conversation with a "capitalistic friend," who had remarked to her, "Now that we have a Bolshevik at the head of the University, I assume you're pleased." "Believe me," she apprised her readers, "I certainly am! It suits me right down to the ground."[5]

While still in a weakened state, Lewis learned that the Depression had wrought havoc with her inheritance. The Atlantic Coast Realty Company, with which the Lewis siblings had contracted to develop Cloverdale into a residential community, lapsed into receivership. The sizable amount of preferred stock that the four Lewises had acquired for participating in the venture had become tied up in legal wrangling. The company had recently defaulted twice on dividend payments, which formed a crucial part of Nell's income.[6]

Nell had expressed her lack of confidence in the proposition since its inception three years earlier. She now confided to Ivey that Kemp had botched the deal. With Kemp's permission and the counsel of attorney and family friend Joseph B. Cheshire Jr., throughout the summer she applied her legal abilities and much of her energy to attempting to resuscitate the endeavor. Also during this period, Nell busied herself with planning a new career. She had reversed her earlier decision not to practice law and now made plans to open her own office.[7] Her anxiety regarding her health, however, ended her direct oversight of the Cloverdale matter. From Ivey's home in November, she apologized to Cheshire and one of his colleagues for having forgotten about an important meeting of the directors the previous month.[8]

4. *N&O,* 1 June 1930; *Chapel Hill Weekly,* 17 October 1941; NBL to Mrs. Whitley, [1946?], NBL to IFL, [1954?], James J. Kilpatrick to NBL, 16 July 1956, all in NBL Papers.

5. *N&O,* 15 June 1930.

6. Joseph B. Cheshire Jr. to KPL, 23 June 1930, NBL Papers.

7. KPL to NBL, 24 June 1930, J. W. Ferrell to KPL, 13 May 1927, NBL to IFL, 11 July 1930, all in NBL Papers; Mitchell, "Nell Battle Lewis," 80–81.

8. NBL to Joseph B. Cheshire Jr. and Paul F. Smith, 18 November 1930, NBL Papers.

Little documentation exists regarding the nature of Lewis's illness then, but a letter written to her in late October by a friend expressed hope that the columnist would soon recover from her appendectomy. She did not recuperate quickly, and the obscure and upsetting problem with her mouth continued to puzzle her physicians. She returned to Raleigh around the New Year and heralded her homecoming in "Incidentally" on 4 January. After spending well over half of the previous year ill and away from home, able to furnish only sporadic installments of her column and fixated on her deteriorated finances, she bade "good riddance" to 1930, even though she had spent much of it "in the shadow of Mr. Jefferson's beautiful Rotunda," where a succession of nurses had overseen her rehabilitation. She revealed to her readers that she had come "precariously close to dying."[9]

The *News and Observer* announced in early March the opening of Lewis's law office on the sixth floor of Raleigh's imposing twelve-story North Carolina Bank and Trust Building. The newspaper remarked that she held the distinction of being only the second woman to practice law actively in the capital city. During the initial weeks of her new career, she handled several routine legal matters, including an attempt to collect money owed a northern publishing firm and a divorce and custody suit. By April, however, a spectacular case with lurid undertones fell into her lap: heading up the defense of sixteen teenage girls facing electrocution for setting fire to two residential dormitories at Samarcand Manor, the state "detention home and industrial school for immoral, neglected, and wayward [white] girls."[10] Lewis's bountiful ties to North Carolina's "organized women"; her work for the State Board of Charities and Public Welfare; and her deep and abiding interest in criminology, penology, mental health, and related issues—particularly as they applied to girls and women—made the case irresistible for her. "The whole problem of crime and delinquency interests me tremendously," she wrote to Lisbeth Parrott,

9. Lucy Lay to NBL, 27 October 1930, NBL Papers; *N&O*, 4 January 1931; NBL to RHL Jr., KPL, IFL, and Isaac Manning, 12 May 1933, KPL Papers.

10. *N&O*, 1 March 1931; Norman D. Anderson and D. T. Fowler, *Raleigh: North Carolina's Capital City on Postcards* (Dover, N.H.: Arcadia Publishing, 1996), 33; "East Lawn Bulletin," 15 March 1931, KPL Papers; Mitchell, "Nell Battle Lewis," 83; Newsome, *North Carolina Manual, 1929*, 284–86; NBL to Janie Carlyle Hargroves, 29 April 1931, NBL Papers; Susan Cahn, "Spirited Youth or Fiends Incarnate: The Samarcand Arson Case and Female Adolescence in the American South," *Journal of Women's History* 9, no. 4 (winter 1998): 152.

who held the position Lewis had previously occupied at the board. "I hope to make it my specialty."[11]

Lewis knew Samarcand well. Five years earlier she had profiled the reformatory, located fifty miles southwest of Raleigh, in "Samarcand Not Different from World of Humanity," a *News and Observer* feature article. She had attempted to ameliorate the "prevalent" perception "that [the institution] is a social sink full of scarlet women." She lauded the current superintendency of Agnes MacNaughton, who fostered the "good spirit which pervades the institution" and administered it along "efficient and useful lines." Under MacNaughton's leadership the two hundred–plus girls and young women there busied themselves at an exhausting array of wholesome activities. They attended school and received vocational training in subjects such as dressmaking and basketry. They operated the laundry, tended the animals and the garden, took regular physical training, played sports, and sang in the chorus and glee clubs.[12] A subsequent article in the *News and Observer*, authored by a male reporter, hinted at the behavior that spurred authorities to confine the girls and young women, whose ages averaged fourteen. "Samarcand is a training school for girls who have taken the one misstep that the world regards with the least charity," he euphemized.[13]

On 12 March 1931 inmates at Samarcand set afire two of the facility's oldest buildings. The fact that they had to ignite each of the structures twice indicated their determination to destroy the two cottages entirely. Chiefly on the basis of their alleged confessions to Estelle Stott, a trained nurse who served as MacNaughton's secretary, authorities charged sixteen teenagers—all under the age of eighteen and at least one as young as thirteen—with the capital crime of first-degree arson and transferred them to the jail in Lumberton, the seat of nearby Robeson County.[14] Lewis did not directly involve herself until two weeks after the conflagration, when an acquaintance from the women's movement retained her for a nominal fee to provide the defendants' "case a more thorough investigation and deeper interest than it could receive from

11. Susan Pearson, "Samarcand, Nell Battle Lewis, and the 1931 Arson Trial" (honors essay, University of North Carolina, 1989), 39; NBL to Lisbeth Parrott, 2 May 1931, NBL Papers.

12. *News and Observer*, 20 November 1926.

13. *News and Observer*, 1 April 1928.

14. Pearson, "Samarcand, Nell Battle Lewis, and the 1931 Arson Trial," 47–48; Roberta King to NBL, 12 May 1931, NBL to Kate Burr Johnson, 26 May 1931, both in NBL Papers; *N&O*, 20 May 1931.

an attorney appointed by the court." She began to prepare for the legal action with her usual zeal.[15]

On 15 April, a month prior to the beginning of their trial, the Samarcand arsonists seized the limelight again when a half-dozen of the teenagers set fire to their beds, shattered light fixtures and windows, and broke up their furniture. The Associated Press reported that when the jailer released the girls into a hallway to prevent their asphyxiation, they attacked him with shards of glass and window sashes they had torn loose. Firemen, law officers, and the county solicitor rushing to the scene reportedly faced a similar onslaught. Authorities finally subdued the culprits and transferred them to the jail in Carthage, a few miles from Samarcand. The other defendants remained incarcerated in Lumberton.[16]

Lewis expressed sympathy for even the most "disreputable" of the girls and believed strongly that all of them had "been handicapped by society." She nevertheless confided to George W. McNeill, who along with another court-appointed attorney in Carthage would assist her in the case, that she was finding the Samarcand girls "very troublesome and embarrassing clients, and [that she was] much tempted to lose patience with them."[17] She suspected that at least four of the defendants suffered from mental problems and arranged for Dr. Harry W. Crane, a member of the university's Department of Psychology and a part-time member of the Board of Charities and Public Welfare, to examine them. She also solicited "interested ladies" in the vicinities of the jails that housed her clients to see that her charges appeared in court "dressed as neatly and modestly as possible."[18]

Despite Lewis's efforts, the girls continued to defy authority and wreak mayhem. On 30 April they staged another spectacular revolt. According to the report of the incident in the *News and Observer* the following day, the girls awaiting trial in Carthage virtually replicated their pandemonium of

15. Pearson, "Samarcand, Nell Battle Lewis, and the 1931 Arson Trial," 49–50; NBL to Janie Carlyle Hargroves, 29 April 1931, NBL Papers.

16. Pearson, "Samarcand, Nell Battle Lewis, and the 1931 Arson Trial," 48–49; *Elizabeth City* (N.C) *Daily Advance*, 16 April 1931; *N&O*, 2 May 1931.

17. NBL to Lisbeth Parrott, 2 May 1931, NBL to George W. McNeill, 2 May 1931, both in NBL Papers.

18. Newsome, *North Carolina Manual, 1929*, 156–57; Wilson, *University of North Carolina*, 444; NBL to Harry W. Crane, 25 and 29 April 1931, NBL to Janie Carlyle Hargroves, 29 April 1931, all in NBL Papers.

two weeks earlier. When they ignited two bunks in their fireproof cell, the town's fire department raced to the scene. Released into the corridor outside their cell, the girls allegedly kicked out windows and armed themselves with pocketknives, which they wielded to threaten the hose company. A town barber attempting to comply with the sheriff's order to give the young prisoners a "good drenching" received a cut on his arm.[19] McNeill provided Lewis with an eyewitness account of the disturbance. When he reached the jail, he observed the girls "acting like raving maniacs, smashing and breaking windows in the runaround, and perfectly nude."[20]

The *News and Observer* on 2 May published a story in which the young prisoners contested authorities' accounts of the "rampage." Josephine French explained that the jailer's wife released the girls nearly every day and sometimes allowed them to play a Victrola and dance. When the woman did not discharge them for recess at the usual time, Josephine and several of her friends had burned a mattress "to bring somebody up to let us out." "We just have to do something to get a thrill," they explained. "Starting a fire is about the best way."[21]

Several days later Lewis traveled to the reformatory to gather evidence. Despite the glowing picture she had once painted of the facility and despite her close personal ties to its sponsors, she began to surmise that "something is very decidedly wrong there." She apparently confirmed her suspicions with a former Samarcand employee, who identified for her numerous informants who could testify on the malfeasance and maltreatment that existed there.[22]

To gather information about MacNaughton and her disciplinary policies, Lewis energetically visited and corresponded with many women who had previously worked for the superintendent. Lewis also asked a physician who had earlier overseen the girls' medical care his "opinion of the methods of dealing with the venereal diseases at Samarcand and . . . of the methods of punishment of inmates."[23] As the 19 May trial date neared, she received a flood of letters documenting abuses that had existed under MacNaughton and Stott's stewardship. Former teachers at the reformatory chronicled the ineptitude,

19. *N&O*, 1 May 1931.

20. George W. McNeill to NBL, 30 April 1931, NBL Papers.

21. *N&O*, 2 and 20 May 1931.

22. NBL to George W. McNeill, 6 May 1931, NBL Papers.

23. Pearson, "Samarcand, Nell Battle Lewis, and the 1931 Arson Trial," 56; NBL to Mary Ellen Skelley, 7 May 1931, NBL to C. W. Durham, 7 May 1931, both in NBL Papers.

vindictiveness, caprice, and cruelty with which the two women had run the institution. The physician echoed the complaints of the teaching staff.[24]

Throughout her trial preparation Lewis detailed in her casebook background information about the defendants, including their sexual histories. She hoped that by delving into these private matters, she would uncover negligence in the treatment of venereal disease at the reformatory and buttress her ability to argue that environmental deprivation accounted for the misconduct, sexual and otherwise, in which the girls had engaged.[25] The most damning evidence Lewis uncovered involved the punishments MacNaughton and Stott had dispensed to the inmates. Sometimes they had ordered staff to lock disobedient girls in their rooms in the bedbug-infested disciplinary dormitory for periods of up to several months or to shear their hair. A teacher wrote of beatings of seventy or more licks with long hardwood switches, in one case producing "big black and blue stripes across the back of a youngster about nine years old."[26] Lewis apparently also conducted personal interviews with several former teachers living in the vicinity of Raleigh. She learned that MacNaughton discharged patients infected with venereal disease from the facility's hospital after only two weeks and housed them with uninfected residents, with whom the recovering inmates lived in close contact and shared bathroom facilities.[27]

On 19 April Lewis and her cocounsel, in an arrangement negotiated in advance with the county solicitor, entered pleas of guilty to a reduced charge of attempted arson for fourteen of the defendants. Judge Michael Schenck nol-prossed charges against the other two girls and released them to their parents and relatives. As a result of the plea bargain, the defendants accused of attempted arson faced penalties of imprisonment from four months to ten years.[28] Lewis's attempts to ensure that the girls projected decorous images to the public and the judge met with mixed success. The *News and Observer* reported that as the "bright faced young defendants in attractive silk and cotton prints" arrived in the school bus that transported them to the trial, they sang

24. Georgia Piland to NBL, 9 May 1931, C. W. Durham to NBL, 11 May 1931, Roberta King to NBL, 12 May 1931, Charlotte Tedder to NBL, 14 May 1931, all in NBL Papers.

25. Cahn, "Spirited Youth or Fiends Incarnate," 159, 172, 176; *N&O*, 20 May 1929.

26. Georgia Piland to NBL, 9 May 1931, Roberta King to NBL, 12 May 1931, both in NBL Papers; *Elizabeth City (N.C) Daily Advance*, 19 May 1931; *N&O*, 20 May 1931.

27. *N&O*, 20 May 1931.

28. Blackwell P. Robinson, ed., *The North Carolina Guide* (Chapel Hill: University of North Carolina Press, 1955), 373, *N&O*, 1 September 1946; *Greensboro Daily News*, 20 May 1931.

lightheartedly and "hurled insults" at a photographer attempting to take their pictures.[29]

Despite the guilty pleas entered by the defense, the judge ordered the prosecution to present its case. He stated that he would sentence the defendants the following day; if insufficient evidence existed to convict any of the girls, he would dismiss their charges.[30] During the morning the state called its witnesses. MacNaughton—whom Lewis suspected of suffering from "rapidly failing mental health"—conspicuously failed to take the stand, and it fell on Stott and another Samarcand staff member to provide much of the incriminatory testimony. Both alleged that the girls had confessed to setting the reformatory fires. During her cross-examination Lewis attempted to disparage the judgment of the two women and to reveal their cruelty. She charged that the reformatory's administration had failed to establish sound disciplinary policies and relied instead on brutal whippings dispensed by MacNaughton or the two witnesses. Schenck refused to allow Lewis to pursue this line of questioning as vigorously as she wished because he maintained it did not pertain specifically to the charges directed at the defendants.[31]

That afternoon the defense examined many of the defendants. Margaret Abernethy provided a particularly poignant chronicle of her upbringing and her life at Samarcand. Prompted by her mother's death and her father's conviction for committing incest against her, authorities had confined the sixteen-year-old to the facility two and a half years earlier. She claimed that she had endured four beatings there, two for running away and two for behaving rudely to teachers. Staff had locked her in a room in vermin-filled Chamberlain Hall for periods of up to three months. Although on cross-examination Margaret admitted that she told investigators she had set fire to the building, the teenager declared her innocence and claimed she had confessed only because she believed it would provoke officials to incarcerate her someplace other than Samarcand.[32]

The other girls who testified told similar stories about their backgrounds and their treatment at the reformatory. They described the many beatings they had suffered as they lay on a rug in the disciplinary hall. All insisted that they either had not admitted to burning the dormitories or had provided false

29. *N&O*, 20 May 1931.

30. *Elizabeth City* (N.C) *Daily Advance*, 19 May 1931; *Greensboro Daily News*, 20 May 1931.

31. *N&O*, 20 May 1931, 21 June 1953; NBL to Kate Burr Johnson, 26 May 1931, NBL Papers.

32. *N&O*, 20 May 1931.

admissions of guilt to escape the institution. The psychologist revealed that his testing had determined that the four girls he had examined—all in their mid-teens—had mental ages of approximately nine to eleven years and consequently little ability to distinguish right from wrong.[33]

Lewis pulled out all the stops for her summation, which later in her life she would regard as the most eloquent and moving speech she had ever delivered. She charged that the state, which had imposed itself in her clients' lives in order to provide them with the guidance and direction they had not received at home, had failed miserably to do so and now intended to penalize them further. The defendants had a right to discipline based on a compassionate understanding of their many problems. "I am not saying they should not be punished," she continued, "but I am saying that half-grown girls in a civilized community should not be laid on a whipping carpet, when flogging has been abolished in chain-gangs." She concluded by expressing her certainty that God would not judge them as guilty. Knowledgeable spectators believed the judge would administer lenient sentences.[34]

On the morning of 20 May Lewis, wearing a businesslike checked suit and cradling her brief in her left arm, posed outside the courthouse for a photograph that would appear on the front page of her newspaper the next day. The cameraman captured another image that the capital daily would feature next to hers: one of the defendants looking decidedly unladylike, puffing on a cigarette as she walked to the trial.[35] The newspaper related that the girls—who included "mental defectives, the daughter of a prostitute, the daughter of an insane mother, the daughter of a man now serving a term for a crime against his own child, and the daughter of parents who had died in her infancy, leaving her a piece of unwelcome human driftwood"—listened raptly to the beginning of the judge's remarks; but when he sentenced a dozen of them to serve sentences of one and a half years in the state penitentiary, they began to wail violently. Schenck warned them that if they did not abide by the rules in prison, he would extend their sentences to periods of up to five years. Two girls received suspended sentences.[36]

Authorities escorted the twelve defendants convicted of attempted arson

33. *N&O,* 20 May 1931.

34. *N&O,* 20, 21 May 1931, 1 September 1946; NBL to Kate Burr Johnson, 26 May 1931, NBL Papers.

35. *N&O,* 21 May 1931.

36. *N&O,* 21 May 1931.

to a school bus that conveyed them to cells in the state prison's only fireproof wing, which the girls would share with the inmates beneath them on death row, awaiting electrocution. Lewis would visit the girls—half of whom she felt certain had played no part in the burning of the dormitories—on at least one occasion.[37]

Her assault on Samarcand's administration and her exposé of its cruelty alienated her from numerous former colleagues within the State Board of Public Welfare and from acquaintances and associates in the women's movement, who construed her zealous defense as an attack on their progressive agenda and the institution per se, one of their proudest monuments. A segment of these detractors undoubtedly believed that a desire to achieve celebrity had inspired the aggressive tenor of her defense.

The case opened a cleft within the state's feminist community, undermined its moral authority, and embarrassed its leadership. The publicity had thrust onstage and humiliated many prominent members of the state's organized women. Annie Kizer Bost, a women's club leader, had replaced Johnson as commissioner and headed the predominately female staff of the board, which supervised the institution. Dr. Elizabeth Delia Dixon-Carroll—one of the first members of her sex to practice medicine in the state—who between 1930 and 1934 directed the Federation of Women's Clubs, served as president of the board of managers for Samarcand, which she had helped found. The matter involved women at other levels, including those who had overseen the daily management and instruction at the reformatory.[38] Lewis had known that her fierce advocacy would antagonize many of her supporters, but she would not moderate her indictment. "I have been sharply criticized for my connection with this case," she had written to Parrott in the midst of the attorney's courtroom preparation, "but I am thoroughly satisfied about it in my own mind."[39]

Lewis had few close friends in whom to confide. "Mowed down by the distressing Samarcand arson case," dispirited by her deteriorating finances, and increasingly panicked by her mouth problems, she vented to Johnson in faraway Trenton, New Jersey: "The State Board of Public Welfare has construed my defense of these girls (who originally were to be tried for their lives) as an attack on the Board. I am now regarded by former allies as an enemy of the

37. *N&O*, 21 May 1931; NBL to George W. McNeill, 19 June 1931, NBL Papers.

38. Smith and Wilson, *North Carolina Women: Making History*, 180, 221, 330; Powell, *Dictionary of North Carolina Biography*, 2:80–81; *N&O*, 1 June 1930, 13 January 1935.

39. *N&O*, 21 May 1931; NBL to Lisbeth Parrott, 2 May 1931, NBL Papers.

welfare work." Bost, who had replaced Lewis's mentor as the most eminent woman within North Carolina's government, confronted Lewis and implied that she had grandstanded and behaved irresponsibly. "Would you have acted like this if Mrs. Johnson had been Commissioner?" she demanded.[40]

Although Lewis felt demoralized over the case's resolution, the "sweet talking in a circle and general passing of the buck" among members of the board, and her belief that the mismanagement of Samarcand would "be beautifully whitewashed," her spirited defense and the concomitant press coverage helped ameliorate at least temporarily many of the reformatory's abuses. In the weeks following the defendants' sentencing, the institution's board of managers abolished the practice of whipping inmates, and Bost mandated that the facility employ an assistant superintendent to establish and oversee its disciplinary procedures.[41] In 1953 Lewis reflected on the case in an editorial in "Incidentally," which she entitled "North Carolina at Its Worst." Explaining that illness had prevented her from remaining in contact with her clients following the verdicts, despite her wish to do so, she grimly told her readers: "I know the fate of only one of the sixteen, one of the four who got off. She killed herself. Hurrah for North Carolina!"[42]

Throughout her illness Lewis consulted Dr. Isaac Manning, dean of UNC's two-year medical school. Manning had married her older sister, Pattie, who died during Nell's early adolescence. She revealed to him that during the previous months she had received treatment from a half-dozen dentists, none of whom could provide relief from the strange taste in her mouth. The dean recommended rest, diversion, and help from her brother Kemp to relieve her anxiety over her lack of income, which she had divulged consisted of "nothing." Despite the fact that the Depression had played havoc with the Lewis brothers' resources and their belief that their sister had "never known the value of Money," they made immediate plans to come to her aid.[43]

At the Johns Hopkins Hospital Dr. B. Lucien Brun, an oral surgeon recom-

40. NBL to Kate Burr Johnson, 26 May 1931, NBL Papers; *N&O*, 9 August 1931; RHL Jr. to IFL, 25 June 1931, NBL to KPL, 24 July 1931, NBL to IFL, 30 July 1931, Claiborn M. Carr to Peggy Logan, 27 June 1932, all in KPL Papers.

41. NBL to Kate Burr Johnson, 26 May 1931, NBL to George W. McNeill, 19 June 1931, both in NBL Papers.

42. *N&O*, 21 June 1953.

43. Isaac Manning to KPL, [July 1931?], RHL Jr. to IFL, 25 June 1931, IFL to KPL, 19 March 1932, Beverly R. Tucker to IFL, 10 March 1932, all in KPL Papers.

mended by Kemp, operated on Nell's jaw in June 1931, to excise what he diagnosed as infected bone. At his request she also had her adenoids removed. To pay for the operations and her travel expenses, Nell spent much of one thousand dollars she had recently borrowed. Although the oral surgeon assured her that he had effectively treated her teeth and jawbone, she informed Kemp, "I left Baltimore with my mouth worrying me as much as ever."[44]

Nell then traveled to Richmond, where she underwent a complete battery of medical tests at the hospital of Dr. John Shelton Horsley, a distinguished physician recommended by Ivey. The facility's medical staff failed to identify a specific cause for her difficulty but surmised that her illness the previous year had affected her salivary glands. The hospital's physicians or others Nell consulted apparently believed that menopause, which her father had predicted many years earlier would exacerbate the emotional disturbance he perceived in his daughter, factored prominently in her problems. If she had begun to undergo natural menopause at age thirty-eight, it occurred very prematurely, well before the average age of fifty, and it seems highly unlikely that she experienced this change as a matter of course.[45]

After her examination in Richmond, Nell began to receive continuous treatments of ovarian extracts, also known as "organotherapy," a forerunner of modern hormone replacement therapy. Surgery may have motivated Lewis's doctors to place her on this regimen. A letter Kate Burr Johnson would write to Kemp in 1933 supports this theory. "Regardless of her mouth, Nell would have had a hard time these past few years," Johnson concluded. "The operation that she underwent is always followed with serious consequences to the nervous system and emotional state."[46]

Perhaps during Nell's extended stays with Ivey in 1930, she received an ovariectomy or related surgery before entering menopause. She may have undergone this procedure instead of or in addition to the appendectomy she reported. Some physicians associated ovarian dysfunction with neurosis and

44. NBL to KPL, 24 July 1931, RHL Jr. to IFL, 31 July 1931, both KPL Papers.

45. Robert Berkow, Mark H. Beers, and Andrew J. Fletcher, eds., *The Merck Manual of Medical Information Home Edition* (New York: Pocket Books, 1997), 1178–80; NBL to KPL, 24 July 1931, NBL to IFL, 30 July 1931, IFL to KPL, 4 October 1931, 19 March 1932, all in KPL Papers.

46. Judith A. Houck, *Hot and Bothered: Women, Medicine, and Menopause in Modern America* (Cambridge: Harvard University Press, 2006), 21–24, 43; Elmer L. Severinghaus, "The Relief of Menopause Symptoms by Estrogenic Preparations," *Journal of the American Medical Association*, no. 104 (February 1935): 624; NBL to IFL, 30 July 1931, Kate Burr Johnson to KPL, 18 September 1933, both in KPL Papers.

posited that ovariectomies might in some cases restore their patients' mental health. In Nell's correspondence she later identified a professor of clinical surgery and gynecology as having served as one of her principal physicians at the University of Virginia Hospital and having discussed her mental distress with her.[47] Weighed down by health and financial worries and the verdict and aftermath of the Samarcand trial, she also perhaps confronted the reality that she would never have children and that marriage had become increasingly improbable. She must have frequently felt isolated; her illnesses and the trial had severely circumscribed her social support system outside her family.

Throughout July and August Nell's regular physician, Dr. Hubert Haywood, oversaw her medical care and dispensed the remedies prescribed in Richmond. He also, at Manning's behest, began to administer to her injections for trench mouth, which Haywood did not believe she had. She suffered bouts of extreme despondency but late in July reported to Ivey, "'Incidentally' resumed this Sunday. The life-saving galleon progresses apace."[48] In early September, however, she telephoned her brother Dick and informed him that she had suffered another nervous breakdown. She told him that Haywood had advised her not to live alone and counseled her to stay with Ivey for a prolonged period.

Nell made plans to proceed to the University of Virginia after first entraining for Baltimore to consult a "nerve specialist," who did not hold a medical degree. She revealed to Dick that during an earlier trip to Charlottesville a neurologist at the university hospital had also expressed concern about her living by herself and recommended that she receive treatment as a resident patient at a Richmond sanatorium operated by Dr. Beverly R. Tucker, a founder of the Department of Neurology and Psychiatry at the Medical College of Virginia. She had responded "indignantly" to the neurologist's implication that she suffered from mental illness.[49] Despite her angry rejection of the sugges-

47. NBL to KPL, 15 October 1933, KPL Papers; Alfred Danby and Kathleen Sykes, "A Case of Chronic Mental Disease Associated with Ovarian Dysfunction," *Lancet*, no. 216 (1929): 129; American Medical Association, comp., *American Medical Directory, 1931* (Chicago: American Medical Association, 1931), 1601; Houck, *Hot and Bothered*, 65.

48. NBL to KPL, 24 July 1931, NBL to IFL, 30 July 1931, RHL Jr. to IFL, 31 July 1931, all in KPL Papers.

49. RHL Jr. to KPL, 3 September 1931, KPL Papers; American Psychiatric Association, comp., *Directory of Fellows and Members of the American Psychiatric Association* (New York: American Psychiatric Association, 1941), 423; Joseph E. Barrett, "Psychiatric Facilities in Virginia and Some Neighboring States," *American Journal of Psychiatry*, no. 97 (March 1941): 1229–30.

tion, her family and physicians grew increasingly convinced that mental illness had precipitated her breakdown. Almost certainly she had suffered an episode of major depression, possibly linked to bipolar II disorder.

In her classic study *Touched with Fire: Manic-Depressive Illness and the Artistic Temperament* Kay Redfield Jamison enumerates the challenges biographers face in the retrospective diagnosis of bipolar disorder but identifies numerous etiological elements and behavior patterns that allow researchers to make guarded determinations of the disease's presence. Many of these factors, manifested with varying degrees of certainty in Lewis, suggest that she may have suffered from the disorder. These include most significantly a family history of the illness, particularly its existence in a first-degree relative, such as its alleged presence in her mother. Lewis may have displayed additional characteristics discussed by Jamison. The onset of the disease may have accounted for her disastrous experience at Goucher College, and the chaotic interpersonal relationships she experienced with her father and siblings in 1920 may have stemmed in part from mania following recovery from an apparent episode of severe depression prompted by the ending of her romance.[50]

Jamison reviews the work of other psychiatric authorities, who have discovered that in artists, musicians, and writers, "the rhythm of the [mood swings] can be read from the dates of the beginning and cessation of productive work." Perhaps Lewis's cycling through the illness accounted not only for what she referred to as the "autobiographical" gaps in the publication of "Incidentally" but also for a portion of her spectacular energy and productivity. The columnist's periods of elation and of despondency during the several years immediately preceding her debilitating breakdown in 1931—her impassioned journalistic and personal advocacy during the Gastonia unrest, her collapse in 1930, her fervent defense of the Samarcand defendants, and her subsequent severe depression—suggest the classic cycles of euphoria and despair that characterize manic-depressive illness. During these phases Lewis evinced the explicit swings in mood, energy, thinking, and behavior associated with bipolar disorder.[51]

In her study Jamison notes that somatic components (such as Lewis's perplexing problem with her mouth) may accompany the onset of the depressive phases of bipolar disorder. Numerous researchers have observed that at these turning points individuals suffering from manic depression often complain of

50. Kay Redfield Jamison, *Touched with Fire: Manic-Depressive Illness and the Artistic Temperament* (New York: Free Press, 1992), 17, 58–59.

51. Jamison, *Touched with Fire*, 15, 58–59; *N&O*, 4 September 1932.

poorly defined afflictions and sometimes develop symptoms of hypochondriasis, which may prompt them to "undergo extensive and unwarranted medical evaluations, spend a great deal of money, and suffer physical complications."[52]

At the beginning of October Nell returned to Raleigh. She remained physically and psychologically frail, focused on her mouth, and unable to author her column. She had a dentist remove her upper teeth, regardless of Manning's conviction that the procedure would provide her with little relief from her problems. Deeply despondent, she turned to the church for comfort. Despite her rejection of organized religion a decade earlier, she now began to attend Sunday school at Raleigh's Church of the Good Shepherd. She also took in a young woman as a roomer.[53] At some point during the fall or early winter Nell admitted to her siblings that she "was going into melancholia" and that she had begun to have recurrent thoughts of suicide. Spurred by these disclosures, her weight loss, the drugs she had begun to take in order to sleep, and her difficulty in leaving her bed, her brothers engaged a registered nurse to oversee their sister's care. Although under this care Nell seemed to improve somewhat, Haywood believed that without extensive treatment by a skilled psychiatrist she had little hope of recovering.[54]

As 1931 drew to a close, Nell agreed to enter the Tucker Sanatorium. She provided Dick with unrestricted power of attorney and requested that if she required commitment to a mental asylum, her brothers place her in the State Hospital at Morganton, also known as Western Hospital for the Insane. She undoubtedly wished to avoid the embarrassment of being committed to the State Hospital at Raleigh, North Carolina's other public inpatient facility that cared for whites suffering from mental illness. Nell also asked that Dick continue her payment of one dollar per day to a Christian Science practitioner in New York who had recently begun to provide her with "absent treatment." Shortly after Christmas, Ivey met Nell at the sanatorium and assisted in her registration.[55]

52. Jamison, *Touched with Fire*, 15; E. Fuller Torrey and Michael B. Knable, *Surviving Manic Depression: A Manual on Bipolar Disorder for Patients, Families, and Providers* (New York: Basic Books, 2002), 31; Hales and Hales, *Caring for the Mind*, 64, 466–67.

53. RHL Jr. to KPL, 3 October, 4 November 1931, KPL to NBL, 4 November 1931, all in KPL Papers; Anderson and Fowler, *Raleigh*, 42.

54. RHL Jr. to IFL, 1, 8 December 1931, RHL Jr. to KPL, 28 December 1931, Alma Scoggin to KPL, 5 December 1931, NBL to RHL Jr., [February 1932?], all in KPL Papers.

55. RHL Jr. to KPL, 28 December 1931, IFL to KPL, 28 December 1931, both in KPL Papers; Stephen Gottschalk, *The Emergence of Christian Science in American Religious Life* (Berkeley: University of California Press, 1973), 227; Newsome, *North Carolina Manual, 1929*, 259–62.

In the trough of the Great Depression the Lewis brothers braced themselves to provide for their sister's care. The economic crisis had devastated the state's textile industry, and Dick and Kemp tried mightily to keep the mills they managed from going under. In January 1932 Dick saw his five thousand–dollar salary at Oxford Cotton Mills cut by 10 percent. Kemp earned considerably more than his older brother, but his six plants also operated under "terrible conditions." The academic salary that Ivey earned as a senior faculty member probably provided him with slightly greater resources than Dick to devote to Nell's hospitalization.[56] With the private nurse Nell retained, her bill at the Tucker Sanatorium averaged $125 per week. Dick oversaw the sale of several of her stocks to finance the initial period of her therapy. He warned his brothers that they should monitor their sister's spending carefully because "she is very careless of her money matters, and has very expensive tastes, which she gratifies if she can get the money."[57]

Nell's illness made it difficult for her to write, but in February she reported to Kemp that Tucker anticipated she would stage a gradual but complete recovery. She admired Tucker's skill as a physician and his genial manner. The psychiatrist attempted to persuade her to forgo her fixation on her problems and advised her that if the sweet taste she perceived in her mouth continued, she would have to learn to accept it without worry.[58]

Tucker and Dr. Howard R. Masters—a staff psychiatrist at the sanatorium and a Medical College of Virginia faculty member, who also treated Nell—almost certainly believed that menopause contributed to her illness and probably continued her regimen of ovarian extracts. In "Nervous, Mental and Endocrine Manifestations at Menopause," an article Masters had authored a number of years earlier, he discussed the symptoms of natural and artificial menopause. He had concluded that the condition often triggered or worsened psychological problems in women susceptible to mental illness. In some of these cases full-fledged psychosis could develop. "Mental symptoms such as depression, excitement, visual and auditory hallucinations, delusions of per-

56. John L. Bell Jr., *Hard Times: Beginnings of the Great Depression in North Carolina, 1929–1933* (Raleigh: North Carolina Department of Cultural Resources, 1982), 21, 27–30; Glass, *Textile Industry in North Carolina*, 60–62; KPL to W. A. Erwin, 3 January and 9 February 1931, RHL Jr. to KPL, 12 January 1932, KPL to RHL Jr., 20 April 1932, IFL to RHL Jr. and KPL, 22 October 1933, all in KPL Papers.

57. RHL Jr. to IFL, 7 January 1932, KPL Papers.

58. Beverly R. Tucker to IFL, 18 and 26 February and 10 March 1932, NBL to KPL, [February 1932], NBL to RHL Jr., [February 1932], all in KPL Papers.

secution, sense of unworthiness, suicidal tendencies, violence and maniacal states have been observed," he reported.[59]

According to the article, female "castrates," women who had undergone ovariectomies or whose ovaries had failed prematurely, experienced exaggerated symptoms. Castrates, regardless of their age, faced a bleak prognosis: "In those who have a mental disturbance there is a tendency to recurrence or a continuation of the psychic instability with the development of a psychoneurosis, and recovery in most cases is slow."[60] Masters recommended "organotherapy" for women experiencing difficulty with menopause. The medical staff at the sanatorium administered hypodermic injections of ovarian extracts three to seven times a week to its patients for several weeks and then prescribed the extract in tablet form for a number of months.[61]

Nell found her accommodations and treatment "very comfortable—and expensive." The sanatorium sponsored many activities to keep its patients entertained. She bowled and made linoleum cuts. She also developed an interest in soap carving, which she would retain for the remainder of her life, and sculpted figurines of the founding fathers and a crucifix. Each day she and her nurse traveled into the city. She reported that her illness had prompted "a great sifting of friends" and that "I don't like to read at all now."[62]

In mid-March Dick and Ivey visited their sister at the sanatorium and discovered that her recovery had stalled, despite the marked progress they believed she had made during the past ten weeks under Tucker's care. They acceded to her request to go to Columbia, South Carolina, to stay with Anne Perry and her family. Perry, a former classmate of Nell's from Smith College, had recovered from a nervous breakdown several years earlier and believed that a busy regimen of work, exercise, and interaction with others would promote her fellow Smithee's recovery. "The whole emphasis is upon *self-forgetfulness*," Nell informed Dick, after arriving in South Carolina. "No drugs, no doctors." The improvement she experienced during her initial weeks in Columbia led her to anticipate that she could return to her home in Raleigh in late spring and resume her previous life. Her brothers feared, however, that her dire financial condition, from which they had partially shielded her, would

59. Howard R. Masters, "Nervous, Mental and Endocrine Manifestations in Menopause," *Virginia Medical Monthly*, no. 50 (August 1923): 318–19.

60. Masters, "Nervous, Mental and Endocrine Manifestations in Menopause," 318.

61. Masters, "Nervous, Mental and Endocrine Manifestations in Menopause," 320.

62. NBL to RHL Jr., [February 1932], NBL to KPL, [February 1932], both in KPL Papers.

not allow her to maintain a household and might cause a relapse.[63] While visiting Charleston with Nell the following month, Perry contracted influenza and, wanting to protect Nell from further exposure, requested that she return alone to Columbia. Without supervision and distraction Nell lapsed into preoccupation with her health and sent for a Christian Science practitioner.[64]

In late April she arrived at Ivey's home in Charlottesville for a stay of several weeks before her anticipated homecoming. Ivey reported to his brothers that her episodes of depression seemed fewer and less severe. Nevertheless, the two siblings had a stormy interaction. Nell insisted that Ivey wire Dick for money to finance a trip to Boston so that she could receive counseling from the Reverend Elwood Worcester, whom her oldest brother derided as "another specialist of the 'faith healing' type."[65]

When Ivey received a letter from Dick several days later, Nell demanded it be read aloud and discovered that her brothers had requested information regarding her possible admission to Broadoaks Sanatorium in Morganton. She made clear that she would forcefully resist any attempt to place her in the institution, which ranked considerably beneath Tucker's facility in quality and presumably cost significantly less. Possibly as a result of the derision her proposed excursion to Massachusetts had provoked, she temporarily abandoned the idea. She continued to focus on her mouth, however, and she entrained for the Johns Hopkins Hospital in Baltimore for another consultation with Dr. B. Lucien Brun.[66]

En route to Maryland, Nell spent the night of 28 April in a Washington hotel and telegraphed Ivey to request that Dick "halt all negotiations relative to Broad Oaks immediately and finally." That evening she wrote to her brothers and stressed that if necessary she would take legal action to prevent her confinement in another sanatorium. She insisted that she had not lost her sanity and would ultimately recover. Faith—not medicine—would play the most im-

63. IFL to KPL, 19 March 1932, NBL to RHL Jr., 19, 28 March 1932, NBL to KPL, 21 March 1932, KPL to RHL Jr., 20 April 1932, all in KPL Papers.

64. Anne Perry to IFL, 24 April 1932, IFL Papers.

65. RHL Jr. to IFL, 27 April 1932, IFL to KPL, 29 April 1932, both in IFL Papers; Sanford Gifford, *The Emmanuel Movement (Boston, 1904–1929): The Origins of Group Therapy and the Assault on Lay Psychotherapy* (Boston: Francis Countway Library of Medicine, 1997; distributed by Harvard University Press), 1–2; Katherine McCarthy, "Psychotherapy and Religion: The Emmanuel Movement," *Journal of Religion and Health* 23, no. 2 (summer 1984): 92–105.

66. RHL Jr. to IFL, 27 April 1932, IFL to Anne Perry, 29 April 1932, IFL to RHL Jr., 29 April 1932, all in IFL Papers; IFL to KPL, 28 April 1932, KPL Papers.

portant role in her rehabilitation. Since her departure from Richmond, she divulged, "a new religious light has dawned on me which, if the Christian religion is true, is the brightest I have seen yet, i.e. the old story: *Jesus* saves." Ivey could aid her recovery best by praying for her.[67]

In mid-May Nell returned home for the first time in six months and, displaying great force of will, resumed her column. Although its quality after the long intermission bore no indication of her mental distress, its content sometimes reflected embarrassment over some of her former exuberance and revealed changes in her outlook. Recanting her youthful activism would increasingly become a leitmotif for her.[68] Regardless of the success she encountered in resuming her column, the effort of renewing her earlier life unnerved her. In a letter to Anne Perry in mid-June Nell confessed that she had lost hope of recovery and intimated that she might commit suicide if her friend did not intervene. As a result of the letter, Perry invited the columnist to join her for a brief visit. She intended to comfort her former classmate and dispatch her back to Raleigh but discovered a pistol in her suitcase. Understandably anxious, the South Carolinian contacted Dick Lewis and implored him to accompany his sister on her trip back. In the interim Perry requested that a family friend, who supervised Columbia's insane asylum, examine Nell.[69]

Dick informed his brothers that the superintendent "felt Nell should be confined, though . . . if we cared to take the risk, [he] thought it was [all right] to let her come back to Raleigh and try again." Both women pleaded with Dick that a sanatorium would exacerbate Nell's condition and that she should return home. Perry cautioned him, however, that attendants should monitor Nell constantly within her residence. Perry extracted a pledge from Nell that she would stay continuously in the company of others and not discuss her physical or mental problems.[70]

Back home and under the supervision of an elderly woman whom Dick had engaged to care for her, Nell seemed at first in better spirits but soon complained again of insomnia and the sweet taste in her mouth. Fearing another breakdown, Dick confiscated her revolver.[71] Almost immediately, Nell grew distressed and admitted herself to Watts Hospital in Durham for several

67. NBL to IFL, 28 April 1932 (telegram and letter), IFL Papers.

68. *N&O*, 22 May 1932.

69. RHL Jr. to IFL, 17 June 1932, KPL Papers.

70. RHL Jr. to IFL, 17 June 1932.

71. RHL Jr. to IFL, 17 June 1932.

days. While there, she received several counseling sessions from a neurologist and psychiatrist, Dr. Mabel E. Goudge, who suggested to her patient "that her present condition began in her childhood and was the natural outcome of it." This theory upset Nell tremendously, and she quickly checked herself out of the hospital.[72]

On 26 June Dick placed her in Broadoaks Sanatorium. Unlike the selective Tucker Sanatorium, whose clientele principally suffered from "nervous diseases," Broadoaks also accommodated alcoholics, drug addicts, and the insane. The facility's superintendent, psychiatrist James W. Vernon, confined Nell in a locked section of the asylum, where she could hear the screams and ravings of deranged patients. Despite the advertisements for Broadoaks, claiming that it offered residents "Billiards, Tennis and other diverting amusements," Nell had nothing to do but focus on her misery. "I am *desperately* unhappy," she informed Kemp the day following her arrival. "*Do not let me go mad,*" she pleaded. "In all reverence, Kemp, I say to you if you have any affection for me, for *Christ's* sake—and I mean for the sake of the compassionate Jesus, come and take me out of this hell."[73]

Vernon reported to Dick that "Miss Lewis has been much agitated" and had asked to transfer to Tucker's facility and that he supported the request. His letter concluded ominously: "Miss Lewis is definitely suicidal, admits to us that she is; and today has asked for sharp-pointed scissors."[74] After only three days of her stay in Morganton, Nell's oldest two brothers transported her back to the Tucker Sanatorium. She thanked them profusely, apologized for the difficulties she had caused them, pledged to become a compliant patient, and immediately settled into the choicest room in the gracious facility. Tucker placed no restrictions on her movement, and she often went into the surrounding area to purchase cigarettes and attend movies.[75]

Although Tucker found Nell's status unchanged since her departure from his sanatorium four months earlier, she had improved enough to maintain her column from the capital of the Confederacy. For the remainder of the summer

72. RHL Jr. to KPL, 20 June, 6 July 1932, KPL to RHL Jr., 22 June 1932, Isaac Manning to KPL, [June 1932], NBL to KPL, [June 1932], all in KPL Papers; American Medical Association, *American Medical Directory, 1931*, 1207.

73. American Medical Association, *American Medical Directory, 1931*, 1196b, 1201, 1213; NBL to KPL, 27 June 1932, NBL to Isaac Manning, 27 June 1932, both in KPL Papers.

74. James W. Vernon to RHL Jr., 27 June 1932, KPL Papers.

75. NBL to KPL, 1 July 1932, Beverly R. Tucker to RHL Jr., 27 July 1932, IFL to RHL Jr., 5 August 1932, all in KPL Papers.

and throughout the early fall she continued to author highly cogent and topical columns from the Tucker Sanatorium. For reference material she walked three blocks to the brand-new Richmond City Library, which served white patrons only. The lucidity of "Incidentally," which she had continuously authored since her return to Raleigh in May, baffled her brothers.[76]

In "High Point's Dissatisfied Labor," written in July, she commented on the labor unrest sweeping through the North Carolina piedmont, where roaming mobs of strikers protesting wage cuts drove to mills, severed their electricity, and encouraged their workforces to walk out. Sensitive to the economic crisis and the hardships facing Kemp and especially Dick, who had seen his salary cut by yet another five hundred dollars, and perhaps consciously or unconsciously influenced by her dependency on their largesse and emotional support, she declared: "With millions now unemployed, a worker with a job even poorly paid is lucky. It is also a fact that there are a number of mills running at a loss in order to give their operatives something to live on. Few owners, hard-boiled though some may be, are the ogres of Communist imagining."[77] She did not approve of the intrusion of state policemen into the disturbance, but she castigated the National Textile Workers Union's attempt to exploit the spontaneous strike: "Communists do nothing but becloud issues already too cloudy and incite to violence when peaceful methods have much greater chance of success. They have a bad effect on all concerned, especially the police, who in trying to suppress them almost always violate Constitutional rights of free speech and free assembly."[78]

Tucker and Masters provided Nell's brothers with regular reports of her vacillating condition. During episodes of depression she became emotional, self-absorbed, and fixated on her mouth. At other times she seemed cheerful and confident and showed interest in others and her occupational therapy. It became clear to her siblings that their sister would require treatment far into the future.[79] That summer Dick emptied Nell's house, stored her belongings,

76. Marie Tyler-McGraw, *At the Falls: Richmond, Virginia, and Its People* (Chapel Hill: University of North Carolina Press, 1994), 247–48; Workers of the Writers' Program of the Work Projects Administration in the State of Virginia, comp., *Virginia: A Guide to the Old Dominion* (Richmond: Virginia State Library and Archives, 1992), 295–96; IFL to RHL Jr., 5 August 1932, KPL Papers.

77. Brecher, *Strike*, 163–64; Bell, *Hard Times*, 35–40; *N&O*, 31 July 1932; RHL Jr. to KPL, 8 August 1932, KPL Papers.

78. *N&O*, 31 July 1932.

79. Beverley R. Tucker to RHL Jr., 27 July 1932, Howard R. Masters to IFL, 5 August, 16, and 23 September, 7 and 14 October 1932, Beverly R. Tucker to IFL, 6 and 14 July 1932, all in KPL Papers.

and contracted with a rental agency to lease the property. The brothers began to consider mortgaging or selling her residence to finance her protracted stay in the sanatorium. Although she had provided Dick with power of attorney, Joseph Cheshire advised Kemp that a judge would have to declare her incompetent and appoint a legal guardian for her before they could proceed with their plans. Kemp believed this humiliation would impede his sister's progress and that no court would declare her mentally unsound, given the clear-headedness she exhibited in writing her column.[80]

In October Nell despaired of recovering further at the Tucker Sanatorium. Her interest in obtaining counseling from the Reverend Worcester revived, and she eagerly lobbied her brothers to allow her to go to Massachusetts to consult the elderly clergyman. Dick and Kemp opposed the plan, but Ivey saw no harm in allowing his sister to consult with the minister and calculated that her living expenses in Boston would amount to much less than her care in Richmond.[81]

Worcester had served as rector of Boston's prestigious Emmanuel (Episcopal) Church, earned a doctorate in psychology in 1889 at the University of Leipzig, and later earned great acclaim through articles in influential publications for his acknowledgment of the difficulties many women faced in their private lives and his ability to treat their nervous conditions. By redirecting their attention to providing service for others; exercising, breathing, and sleeping properly; and praying, he believed sufferers might overcome their difficulties. He particularly emphasized harnessing the power of the subconscious mind through relaxation techniques and autosuggestion to promote spirituality and mental and physical well-being. By the time Nell sought his assistance, Worcester had augmented this regimen with Freudian techniques and spiritualism. He and others had founded the Boston Society for Psychical Research (BSPR).[82]

Nell undoubtedly found herself drawn to Worcester not only for his renown as a psychologist but because of his interest in spiritualism. She had attended closely to magician Harry Houdini's denouncement of medium Mina

80. RHL Jr. to KPL, 12 July 1932, KPL to Joseph B. Cheshire Jr., 15 October 1932, both in KPL Papers.

81. NBL to IFL, [October 1932], IFL to KPL, 31 October 1932, both in KPL Papers.

82. McCarthy, "Psychotherapy and Religion," 94–97; Gifford, *Emmanuel Movement*, 1–2, 16–19, 68; Elwood Worcester, *Life's Adventure: The Story of a Varied Career* (New York: Charles Scribner's Sons, 1932), 275–337.

Crandon's claim of communicating with the dead and to the formation of the BSPR. Shortly following Houdini's death in 1926, the columnist had lamented in "Incidentally" his blanket hostility to psychic perception and had expressed her belief in the genuineness of some spiritual phenomena.[83]

Nell arrived in Boston in late October and began receiving treatment from Worcester. She underwent a typically intense program of psychoanalysis, meeting with the psychologist for four one-hour sessions each week, at a weekly cost of fifty dollars. He communicated to her that he anticipated she would require a year of therapy. Gradually, the unconscious and unremembered experiences of her childhood—particularly her interactions with her stepmother, Annie Blackwell Lewis—began to emerge as a central issue in Nell's analysis. By uncovering her long-repressed relationship with Annie, Worcester and his analysand hoped to explicate her mental distress.[84]

Nell's decision at the beginning of 1933 to terminate the psychoanalysis undoubtedly did not surprise her brothers. They had renewed their discussion of selling her house to finance her expensive treatment, which they regarded dubiously, and must have felt relieved when she told them that the income from her column and renting her house would allow her to live comfortably in Boston.[85] From the "Hub of the Universe" she posted "Incidentally" home to Raleigh and received correspondence from her Tar Heel readers. Her columns sometimes evoked the agenda of the previous decade's Battling Nell, although they displayed little of her verve. She urged that the South abolish county chain gangs; jeered at David Clark, the Daughters of the American Revolution, and North Carolina's domineering power and tobacco interests; lauded Texan Jessie Daniel Ames's formation of the Association of Southern Women for the Prevention of Lynching; and condemned the death penalty.[86]

Throughout the winter and spring she attempted to recover on her own in Boston, anticipating a return to Raleigh later in the year. Her friends in Boston noticed, however, that her moods fluctuated frequently. She would show little indication of depression for several days, but the despondency would re-

83. Gifford, *Emmanuel Movement,* 7, 16; *N&O,* 28 November 1926; William F. Williams, ed., *Encyclopedia of Pseudoscience* (New York: Facts on File, 2000), 40, 204–5.

84. KPL to RHL Jr., 2 January 1933, KPL to IFL, 6 January 1933, RHL Jr. to KPL, 7 January 1933, all in KPL Papers.

85. NBL to RHL Jr., KPL, and IFL, 12 January 1933, KPL Papers.

86. *N&O,* 13 November 1932, 15 January, 26 February, and 23 April 1933; Jacquelyn Dowd Hall, *Revolt against Chivalry: Jessie Daniel Ames and the Women's Campaign against Lynching* (New York: Columbia University Press, 1993), 159–91; Wilson and Ferris, *Encyclopedia of Southern Culture,* 1569–70.

turn, and she would contemplate suicide.[87] In May the Lewis males and Manning received a hopeful and somewhat triumphant letter from Nell, informing them that Dr. Margaret Kleinert, an ear, nose, and throat specialist at the New England Hospital for Women, might have established that Nell had not imagined the debilitating problem in her mouth. Kleinert had removed a cyst high on her patient's gum that perhaps had contributed to her baffling malady. Several days later, however, Nell became upset when she noticed no improvement. Kleinert only then learned of her patient's psychiatric history. She regretted the surgery she had performed and had one of Nell's friends escort her to an experienced psychiatrist, Dr. Marianna Taylor.[88]

After her initial interaction with Nell, Taylor, who specialized in analytical psychotherapy, expressed certainty that her new patient suffered from "conversion hysteria" and explained that her physical symptoms stemmed from repressed subconscious strife. The major psychiatric literature of the day espoused the application of Sigmund Freud's theories in treating this condition, now known as "conversion disorder." According to Freud, "the malady is the result of the conflict between the libido and . . . sexual repression." He held that individuals suffering from conversion hysteria transformed the emotions and feelings associated with this conflict into physical symptoms. Today psychiatrists and psychologists believe that people affected by a number of common mental illnesses such as major depression may develop conversion disorders, which are characterized by symptoms lacking a physical cause, and may become deeply distressed when they ruminate over their perceived physical problems.[89] Nell wrote to Dick that "at last somebody is making a thoroughly intelligent effort to get at the root of the trouble." Taylor's optimism, however, regarding the prospects for Nell's recovery faded quickly. In late June she suffered a relapse and abruptly terminated her therapy and residence in Boston.[90]

Ivey requested that his sister come to Charlottesville, where she stayed with one of her Gordon relatives. At midnight on 27 June she placed a long-

87. KPL to NBL, 4 April 1933, NBL to KPL, 24 April 1933, Kenneth L. Moore to KPL, 20 July 1933, all in KPL Papers.

88. NBL to RHL Jr., KPL, IFL, and Isaac Manning, 12 May 1933, Kenneth L. Moore to KPL, 20 July 1933, both in KPL Papers; American Medical Association, *American Medical Directory, 1931*, 745, 753.

89. NBL to RHL Jr., KPL, IFL, and Isaac Manning, 16 May 1933, KPL Papers; White, *Outlines of Psychiatry*, 117–18, 343–48; Hales and Hales, *Caring for the Mind*, 481–85; American Psychiatric Association, *Directory of Fellows and Members of the American Psychiatric Association*, 412.

90. NBL to RHL Jr., 20 May 1933, Kenneth L. Moore to KPL, 20 July 1933, both in KPL Papers.

distance call to Kemp in Durham. Completely distraught, she pleaded with him to finance her treatment at the Bloomingdale Hospital in White Plains, New York. Although she had informed Dick several days earlier that Taylor "does not think that I am an institutional case," Nell reported to Kemp in her telephone conversation and in a subsequent letter that her psychiatrist "definitely felt that I should be in an institution where, as at Bloomingdale, a definite regime of [occupational therapy] is enforced, in addition to the analytical treatment."[91]

Kemp decided to lend Nell sixty-five dollars a week for her treatment at the three hundred–bed private facility, which had earned a reputation as one of the nation's premier mental health institutions. Dick accompanied his sister north and, upon his return to Oxford, reported on the impressive amenities he had encountered there, including tennis courts and a golf course. "It is the last move for her as I see it," he told his brothers, "and if these people can't cure her, it is hopeless."[92] Kemp must have felt pushed to his limits when he received a letter written by Nell the morning after her admission. "Confinement in this institution is absolutely hell," she railed. "If I stay I am certain to go insane. . . . For God's sake take me out right away." That afternoon and the following day she wrote again to her middle brother, apologizing for her outburst and expressing gratitude for his generosity. Her confinement behind "the bolts and bars" had prompted her earlier reaction. She implored Kemp to ignore what she said in her "bad moods" and resolved "to stick this out and . . . to emerge an adult."[93]

Dr. Gerald Jameison, who directed the women's division, and his medical staff may have believed that menopause had aggravated Nell's mental illness. The medical director and his Bloomingdale colleague Dr. James Hardin Wall had the previous year published an article on this phenomenon in the *American Journal of Psychiatry.* In "Mental Conditions at the Climacterium" the two authors had observed that menopause could trigger a range of psychoses, including "schizophrenia, paranoic conditions, manic-depressive psychoses, the psychoneuroses and a number of border line states." Sexual difficulties appar-

91. NBL to RHL Jr., 23 and 25 June 1933 (telegrams and letter), KPL to IFL, 27 June 1933, NBL to KPL, 28 June 1933, all in KPL Papers.

92. RHL Jr. to KPL, 1 July 1933, KPL to IFL, 27 June 1933, KPL to Dorothy Saunders Burdick, 1 September 1933, all in KPL Papers; Samuel W. Hamilton, "The Psychiatric Resources of New York," *American Journal of Psychiatry,* no. 90 (March 1934): 1102–3.

93. NBL to KPL, 1, 2 July 1933, both in KPL Papers.

ently provided a predictor and possible partial cause of such problems when faced by women at menopause. In an analysis of four representative case studies the two psychiatrists implied that their patients' virginity or incapacity to participate enthusiastically in sexual relationships with men factored into the women's subsequent mental problems.[94]

Although Nell remained at Bloomingdale for the rest of the summer, she rebelled against the rules and frequently expressed her intention to leave. She took comprehensive notes during her residence there and looked forward to her release so that she could author a "knock-out" exposé of the institution.[95] On 9 September she left the hospital without notifying her doctors. She telegraphed Kemp that she planned to go to Charlottesville but changed her mind and entrained for Trenton, New Jersey, to visit her friend Kate Burr Johnson. The Lewis males began to make plans to commit their sister to an institution.[96]

Johnson at first had no idea how to deal with Nell and observed her closely for several days. The superintendent asked her resident physician, a general practitioner with considerable experience in interacting with psychologically disturbed patients, to consult with Nell. The physician and Johnson soon grew convinced of the authenticity of the problem in their guest's mouth. Johnson arranged for an oral surgeon at the New Jersey State Hospital at Trenton to examine Nell. The hospital specialized in providing treatment for physical diseases of the mentally ill.[97]

On 18 September Johnson reported to Kemp that the oral surgeon had determined that Nell had rough bone in her mouth and an infected sinus that required draining. Johnson believed that the constant annoyance in Nell's mouth, in conjunction with the stress she had endured over the past few years and the psychological consequences of the operation she had undergone several years earlier, had profoundly impaired her mental condition. Johnson

94. Lloyd Thomson and Winfield Scott Downs, eds., *Who's Who in American Medicine, 1925* (New York: Who's Who Publications, 1925), 766–67; American Medical Association, *American Medical Directory, 1931*, 1040, 1192; Isaac Manning to KPL, 9 June 1934, KPL Papers; G. R. Jameison and James H. Wall, "Mental Reactions at the Climacterium," *American Journal of Psychiatry*, no. 88 (March 1932): 895–909; Houck, *Hot and Bothered*, 45.

95. KPL to Kenneth L. Moore, 11 September 1933, NBL to KPL, 7 August 1933, NBL to RHL Jr., KPL, and IFL, 11, 23 August 1933, all in KPL Papers.

96. NBL to RHL Jr., KPL, and IFL, 1 September 1933, KPL to NBL, 11 September 1933, both in KPL Papers.

97. Kate Burr Johnson to KPL, 18 September 1933, KPL Papers; Hamilton, "Psychiatric Resources of New York," 1123.

underscored, however, that Nell had suffered from instability throughout her life: "We must also bear in mind that the symptoms that she has had with the exception of her mouth she has always had to some degree."[98] Nell underwent the operation several days later, and throughout September and early October she stayed in Trenton. It soon became apparent, though, that her doctor there could not provide her with any relief. Kemp implored her to reenter Bloomingdale, but she adamantly refused.[99]

She arrived at Ivey's home around 8 October and a week later beseeched Kemp to help her. "I am in terrible shape," she wrote. "I have been going from bad to worse and cannot make a go of it outside an institution." She requested that Kemp finance her care at the Phipps Psychiatric Clinic at the Johns Hopkins Hospital. She promised to "stick it out this time." He agreed, but Nell soon changed her mind and decided that Bloomingdale offered the best chance of recovery.[100] With Cheshire's guidance and Nell's consent, her brothers initiated court proceedings in Raleigh that would enable Dick to become his sister's legal guardian. The four men endeavored to protect her privacy during the impending hearing. A week after writing to Kemp, Nell asked Ivey to return her to Bloomingdale, which she conceded had provided her with excellent care. She agreed at Ivey's insistence to forgo the voluntary revocable commitment she had previously insisted on and gave him permission to commit her.[101]

Jameison reported to Dick in early November that Nell seemed compliant and engaged willingly in occupational therapy, but she did not remain acquiescent for long. In early January 1934 she wrote Kemp six letters in a two-day period, entreating him to allow her to leave Bloomingdale. Her sessions with Dr. Dorothy Saunders Burdick angered Nell, who called psychiatry "the world's worst bunk." By "constantly turning the patient's attention back on herself it intensifies the introversion of a person already distressingly self-absorbed." She asked that her middle brother allow her to transfer to a Christian Science sanatorium.[102] Later in the month Kemp requested a change of doctors, and Dr. Edward Bartlett Allen began to supervise her care. Allen dis-

98. Kate Burr Johnson to KPL, 18 September 1933, NBL to KPL, 18 September 1933, both in KPL Papers.

99. NBL to KPL, 18 September 1933, KPL Papers.

100. NBL to KPL, 15 October 1933, IFL to RHL Jr. and KPL, 22 October 1933, KPL to Kenneth L. Moore, 30 December 1933, all in KPL Papers.

101. IFL to RHL Jr., 20 October 1933, IFL to RHL Jr. and KPL, 22 October 1933, Joseph B. Cheshire Jr. to IFL, 20 October 1933, all in KPL Papers.

102. American Medical Association, *American Medical Directory, 1931*, 1192; Mortimer W. Raynor to RHL Jr., 3 November 1933, KPL to Kenneth L. Moore, 5 January 1934, both in KPL Papers.

continued the psychotherapy and placed Nell on an experimental treatment of theelin, which Parke, Davis & Company manufactured from the urine of pregnant women and would later market as estrogen. The previous year, in an important study documented in the *Journal of the American Medical Association*, theelin had shown great promise in treating "female castrates."[103]

As summer approached, Nell convinced her brothers to let her return to her rooming house in Boston to consult a Christian Science practitioner, who almost certainly had her patient study Bible passages and testimonies of persons purportedly healed by Christian Science. The practitioner likely discussed with Nell her "false" beliefs regarding her condition and attempted to replace them with the spiritual truth. "Divine Love" could then enter Nell's consciousness and effect physical healing.[104] But by late July Nell had grown disillusioned with her new treatment. She felt lonely and became anxious to return to North Carolina. Hoping she could board with Manning in Chapel Hill, she wrote to Frank Graham, seeking employment at the university. He informed her that no opportunities currently existed but that he would notify her the moment an opening developed.[105]

At Kemp's request, in early August Johnson urged her friend to join her in Trenton. To entice Nell, Johnson offered to pay her to author the annual report for the State Home for Girls. Nell soon arrived in New Jersey but in all probability provided little assistance in preparing the home's report. Finding that Nell had "deteriorated greatly" in the preceding year and becoming "quite hopeless" about her friend's mental health, Johnson apparently contacted Ivey, who volunteered to care for his sister temporarily. In the early fall Johnson accompanied Nell on the train trip to Charlottesville.[106]

It had become apparent that she required a level of care well beyond the

103. KPL to Gerald Reid Jameison, 27 January 1934, Mortimer W. Raynor to KPL, 7 February 1934, both in KPL Papers; American Medical Association, *American Medical Directory, 1931,* 1192; Houck, *Hot and Bothered,* 21, 51; August A. Werner and W. D. Collier, "The Effect of Theelin Injections on the Castrated Woman," *Journal of the American Medical Association* 100, no. 9 (March 1933): 633–40; Clement D. Veler, Sidney Thayer, and Edward A. Doisy, "The Preparation of the Crystalline Follicular Ovarian Hormone: Theelin," *Journal of Biological Chemistry* 87, no. 2 (June 1930): 358–59.

104. Isaac Manning to KPL, 9 June 1934, KPL Papers; Mary Baker Eddy, *Science and Health: With Keys to the Scriptures* (Boston: First Church of Christ, Scientist, 1994); Gottschalk, *Emergence of Christian Science,* 227–30.

105. KPL to Kate Burr Johnson, 1 August 1934, KPL Papers; NBL to FPG, 4 August 1934, FPG to NBL, 28 September 1934, both in FPG Papers.

106. Kate Burr Johnson to KPL, 31 July and 13 November 1934, Kate Burr Johnson to NBL, 2 August 1934, all in KPL Papers.

capabilities of Ivey and his wife, Margaret. In October Ivey committed Nell to Western State Hospital in nearby Staunton, a 1,700-bed institution that had opened in 1828 as the Western Lunatic Asylum of Virginia. Nell predictably rebelled against the hospital's rules and in a flurry of cogent and persuasive letters, beseeched her siblings and Manning to secure her immediate release. "She has written repeatedly of the very bad effect on her of living with actively insane people and having to listen to a terrible type of obscenity and profanity, and the whole thing has been most distressing," Kemp wrote to Johnson.[107] In November Manning and his wife, Mary, agreed to allow Nell to live in their home in Chapel Hill for a one-month trial period. Dick and Kemp conferred with the Mannings to make certain they fully understood the extent of Nell's illness and the challenges they would face in living with her.[108]

Nell must have arrived in Chapel Hill in fragile condition. Her residence in the college village would extend to nearly a year. Defying predictions, she began a slow recovery. Her ordeal instilled in her an acute sensitivity to the prejudice the mentally ill encountered and the inhumane and archaic treatment they received in most hospitals and other institutions. In the spring of 1935 she wrote a letter of congratulation to her friend Louis Graves, whom Governor J.C.B. Ehringhaus had recently appointed to a commission to study the care and treatment the state provided for its mentally ill residents.[109] In great detail she impressed on Graves the need for the members of his committee to initiate a public education campaign to bring about a sea change in her fellow citizens' viewpoints. "Nervous and mental illness is *illness*," she emphasized, "and it should be regarded as no more shameful, no more humiliating than physical illness."[110]

107. Virginia Department of Mental Hygiene and Hospitals, *A Directory of Mental Hygiene and Psychiatric Facilities in the Commonwealth of Virginia and Historical Summary* (Richmond: Virginia Department of Mental Hygiene and Hospitals, 1951), 6; IFL to RHL Jr. and KPL, 22 October 1933, KPL to Christian Science Publishing Co., 12 October 1934, KPL to Kate Burr Johnson, 15 November 1934, KPL to Robert W. Glenn, 9 November 1934, KPL to S. S. Bost, 30 October 1934, all in KPL Papers.

108. KPL to Kate Burr Johnson, 15 November 1934, KPL Papers; Powell, *Dictionary of North Carolina Biography*, 4:212–13.

109. NBL to Louis Graves, 23 April 1935, NBL Papers.

110. NBL to Louis Graves, 23 April 1935, NBL Papers.

# 7 "A POOR BURNT CHILD"

Lewis cherished Chapel Hill and its venerable university, which she and her ancestors and relations had nurtured and promoted from its earliest days. Her parents had named her for her father's deceased first wife, Cornelia "Nellie" Battle Lewis, the oldest daughter of University of North Carolina president Kemp Plummer Battle. Lewis recalled well her childhood visits to his home and her walks with the elderly man around the charming village. Her father had attended the university and had served as a trustee for more than three decades and as a member of its influential executive committee for many years. All three of her brothers had earned degrees there. From 1927 into 1932 Dick had continued Dr. Lewis's service on the board of trustees. Kemp had joined the board in 1931 and would remain a member for a dozen years. Some prominent figures associated with the institution had regarded Ivey as a possible president. Nell's brother-in-law, Isaac Manning, had graduated from the university and had, like his father, risen to become a dean at their alma mater. Manning's father, John, had introduced in the state legislature the first bill that provided the University of North Carolina with an annual appropriation.[1]

Twenty years earlier Lewis had delighted in attending soirees at Chapel Hill, where she had danced the bunny hug to "Alexander's Rag Time Band" into the wee hours and from an overlook on the outskirts of campus had watched the sun rise. Her optimism and youth had now long since faded, and she returned to the campus infirm and forlorn. One can imagine that she would have contrasted the buoyancy and hopefulness she had felt during that earlier time with her current condition.[2]

Manning—a private man, who rarely socialized with his faculty or the university's leadership—devoted himself completely to his wife, Mary, and their three children and to fostering his academic program. The nation's dozen two-year medical colleges had become anachronistic, and the dean faced fierce opposition and many challenges as he sought to expand his course of study to four years. He apparently believed that the university's new chief executive

1. "Biographical Note," KPL Papers; Powell, *Dictionary of North Carolina Biography,* 4:60, 63, 212–14; Wilson, *University of North Carolina,* 312; Janis Holder, letter to author, 28 July 2006.

2. *N&O,* 6 January 1935.

did not advance the interests of the School of Medicine as actively as had his predecessor. In a history of medical education at the university Manning observed that in the early years of Frank Porter Graham's presidency, "it is possible that [the needs of the medical school] were presented and worked for less enthusiastically than heretofore."[3]

In the fall of 1933 exposure of Manning's admission policies tarnished the liberal university's reputation and thrust him into the national spotlight. When Graham overrode Manning's refusal to admit a student because of his religious affiliation, it provoked the dean to step down from the administrative position he had occupied for more than twenty-five years. Lewis arrived in the immediate wake of the controversy and undoubtedly observed sympathetically and in intimate detail the impact Graham's decision had on her close relative and guardian, whose compassion and devotion had delivered her from the misery she had experienced at Western State Hospital.

Manning, who unilaterally oversaw admissions to his program, had for more than a decade accepted only four Jewish students into each year's incoming class of forty. Many colleges and universities, following the example established by Harvard in the early 1920s, set similar quotas. Manning faced a difficult task in placing the handful of Jews in his school—virtually all of them in-state students drawn from North Carolina's tiny Jewish population—into four-year medical programs, a number of which had established quotas similar to his own. Each summer he had worked tirelessly to see that all of his senior students transferred into schools where they could complete their clinical training.[4]

In 1933 Morris Krasney, a Jewish undergraduate at the University of North Carolina—who had begun to study at the institution as an out-of-state student but who subsequently married a resident of Durham and now lived in that city—learned that Manning had refused to consider his application. The dean explained to Krasney that four of his coreligionists had received notification of their acceptance into the program. Manning would consider admit-

3. Edward C. Halperin, "Frank Porter Graham, Isaac Hall Manning, and the Jewish Quota at the University of North Carolina Medical School," *North Carolina Historical Review* 67, no. 4 (October 1990): 389–91; Edward C. Halperin, "The Jewish Problem in U.S. Medical Education, 1920–1955," *Journal of the History of Medicine and Allied Sciences* 56, no. 2 (April 2001): 144–45; W. Reece Berryhill, William B. Blythe, and Isaac H. Manning, *Medical Education at Chapel Hill: The First Hundred Years* (Chapel Hill: University of North Carolina School of Medicine, 1979), xix–xx, 36.

4. Leonard Dinnerstein, *Anti-Semitism in America* (New York: Oxford University Press, 1994), 84–87; Halperin, "Frank Porter Graham, Isaac Hall Manning, and the Jewish Quota," 394.

ting him only if one of these students withdrew. Krasney hired a lawyer. He also obtained the signatures of many alumni from Durham on a petition endorsing his entry and forwarded the document to Graham.[5]

The president's assistant, Robert B. House, examined the petition and telephoned the dean to request that he admit Krasney, but the dean refused to budge. The next day he met with Graham in his office, an encounter he later described as a "brief but frank and friendly discussion of the problem." The president, who had friendly relations with the Mannings and prominent members of Durham's well-organized Jewish community, underscored that he would not countenance denial of admission "to a Jew because he was a Jew." Manning responded that "if it was the policy of the University to fill up the vacancies in the classes in the medical school with Jews . . . the Medical School had just as well close its doors, as with a preponderance of Jews in the School the Gentiles would not come to it." The dean remained obstinate, and Graham overruled him and mandated Krasney's acceptance. In October 1933 Manning resigned his leadership of the school.[6]

The exposure of Manning's policies and resignation occurred in the midst of widespread media coverage of Nazi outrages committed against German Jews. Manning's dispute with Graham received coverage in newspapers ranging from the *New York Herald Tribune* to the little *Danville* (Va.) *Register.* Lewis's own paper printed an editorial entitled "No Aryan Doctrines at Chapel Hill." "The true essence of the spirit of the University of North Carolina is liberalism," declared Jonathan Daniels, who had assumed the editorship of the *News and Observer* upon his father's appointment as ambassador to Mexico the previous spring. "There is no place there for any Aryan doctrines now so familiar in Germany. Any discrimination between Jews and Gentiles in its student body would be a repudiation of its ideals."[7]

Ivey Lewis, who had been appointed dean of the University of Virginia in 1934, must have commiserated with his brother-in-law and Mary—a strong-willed woman with a temper, who developed an animus against Frank

5. Berryhill, Blythe, and Manning, *Medical Education at Chapel Hill,* 36–37; Halperin, "Frank Porter Graham, Isaac Hall Manning, and the Jewish Quota," 394–95.

6. Halperin, "Frank Porter Graham, Isaac Hall Manning, and the Jewish Quota," 397–99, 402, 408; Ehle, *Dr. Frank,* 54–55; Eli N. Evans, *The Provincials: A Personal History of Jews in the South* (New York: Free Press, 1997), 84; Ashby, *Frank Porter Graham,* 128–29; Snider, *Light on the Hill,* 218–19.

7. *NYT,* 2, 6, 15, 21, 29, and 30 August, 11 September, and 13 October 1933; Halperin, "Frank Porter Graham, Isaac Hall Manning, and the Jewish Quota," 399–401; *New York Herald Tribune,* 1 October 1933; *N&O,* 1 October 1933.

Graham—and shared with the other Lewis siblings his thinking on the controversy. Historian Gregory Michael Dorr, who has carefully studied the prominent biologist's enduring belief in eugenics and the impact it had on his students, the administration of his university, and the commonwealth, labeled Ivey a "virulent anti-Semite." Following Harvard's lead, Mr. Jefferson's University had in 1920 erected quotas that limited the number of Jewish students it enrolled, and without question Ivey supported this discrimination at his place of employment and at his Carolina alma mater. Although he admired the highly principled Graham, Ivey must have regarded him as lacking in sympathy for the pressures Manning faced and ignorant of the role Ivey believed that eugenics should play in admissions policies.[8]

Ivey's older brother had also grown increasingly critical of Graham's leadership. In a letter to Ivey in April 1933, Kemp Lewis confided that he had undergone a "decided weakening in my interest in the University because of the attitude of Frank Graham and his professors of actively fostering and promoting the Socialistic cause in this country." The prominent textile executive must also have experienced resentment and perhaps some humiliation when he and the other members of the board of trustees received notice of Manning's resignation. Kemp may now have perceived his family's influence as waning at the university, and Dick, the most conservative of the Lewis brothers, likely felt the same way. Graham's controversial plan to preserve the amateur quality of the university's sports program, added to his other perceived transgressions, eventually led Nell Lewis's principal benefactor to lobby for Graham's resignation.[9]

8. Edward C. Halperin, letter to author, 8 August 2006; Halperin, "Frank Porter Graham, Isaac Hall Manning, and the Jewish Quota," 405–6; Dorr, "Assuring America's Place in the Sun," 273; IFL to John Lloyd Newcomb, 31 January 1939, John Lloyd Newcomb to IFL, 5 June 1940, both in Papers of the President, Special Collections, University of Virginia Library; Virginius Dabney, *Mr. Jefferson's University: A History* (Charlottesville: University Press of Virginia, 1981), 410; Dinnerstein, *Anti-Semitism in America,* 85–86. For insight into the experience of Jewish students at the University of Virginia during Lewis's deanship, see Edward N. Calisch to IFL, 15 December 1938, 3, 6 January 1939, Norman P. Cohen to IFL, 6 August 1940, IFL to Norman P. Cohen, 28 August 1940, IFL to Albert M. Lewis, 24 May 1941, all in Correspondence of Dean of the University and Dean of the College of Arts and Sciences, Special Collections, University of Virginia Library.

9. KPL to FPG, 14 May 1931, FPG to KPL, 15 December 1931, KPL to O. Max Gardner, 7 November 1932, KPL to IFL, 6 April 1933, "Biographical Note," all in KPL Papers; Sellars, "South Saver," 53; Ashby, *Frank Porter Graham,* 131–36; Snider, *Light on the Hill,* 219–21; Dolores E. Janiewski, *Sisterhood Denied: Race, Gender, and Class in a New South Community* (Philadelphia: Temple University Press, 1985), 86, 211; *NYT,* 16 February 1936.

Upon her return to North Carolina in the fall of 1934, Nell must have heard plenty about her family's growing dissatisfaction with the university and its president, whose espousal of academic freedom and social justice would soon earn him a reputation as the region's foremost liberal. Mary Manning, who closely supervised Nell in her debilitated condition, and Kemp, who had assumed the principal financial responsibility for his sister's support, perhaps expressed their discontent the most emphatically. Kemp would continue to augment his sister's income significantly for the remainder of his life. Dick contributed sporadically, although his lesser earnings made it impossible for him to match his younger brother's degree of assistance. After Nell's return to Chapel Hill, Ivey, without explanation, permanently stopped sending her money, a behavior that puzzled and disconcerted Nell. All three brothers generously ignored her frequent inability to send them payments for her house, which her expensive illness and travels had finally forced them to mortgage. Although she owed much more to Kemp than to her other siblings, he encouraged her to repay him only nominal sums and persistently endeavored to reassure her about his ability and willingness to help provide for her.[10] Nell also undoubtedly learned more about how the labor activism she had fearlessly promoted throughout the preceding decade had two months earlier distressed and embarrassed Kemp, when his own workforce at Erwin Mills had eagerly participated in the general textile strike of 1934, the largest industrial conflict involving organized labor in the nation's history.

"Code chiselers," many of whom ran marginal mills, had soon exploited loopholes in Roosevelt's National Industrial Recovery Act and subverted its intent. Manufacturers employed the stretch-out to compensate for their reduced hours and rebuffed attempts at collective bargaining. Nearly four thousand letters of complaint mailed between August 1934 and August 1935 to the Cotton Textile National Industrial Relations Board resulted in a single finding in favor of labor. Angry workers swelled the ranks of the United Textile Workers (UTW) and deluged the Roosevelt administration with intensely personal and highly moving accounts of abuses and exploitation.[11]

On 16 August 1934 the UTW rank and file voted overwhelmingly to strike. A week later two thousand workers assembled at West Durham High School

10. NBL to KPL, 14 July 1940, 9 and 10 March 1945, all in KPL Papers.

11. Hall et al., *Like a Family*, 290, 293–319, 325–26; Glass, *Textile Industry in North Carolina*, 75–76; Brecher, *Strike*, 184.

and with flawless precision planned a walkout. Two weeks later organizers posted placards throughout the city to signal the strike's beginning: "Send the battle cry, NOW OR NEVER!" An uneasy peace ensued the following day, when for the first time nervous manufacturers kept their factories closed for Labor Day. Well before sunrise the next morning, however, twenty-five hundred strikers formed picket lines at the entrances to the city's seven textile mills.[12]

On the night of 3 September, Labor Day that year, Kemp assured the *Durham Morning Herald* that "the gates will be opened at our mills as usual and the workers will be given an opportunity to work." Despite his vow to conduct business as usual, the forward-thinking textile leader, who adhered to modern industrial and management practices, encountered what the newspaper described as an "impregnable barricade" of picketers surrounding the Erwin Mills the next morning. He found it "galling . . . to have a mob refuse to allow him entrance into his office" but wisely did not escalate the situation by summoning law authorities, which might have resulted in the city's "being torn up with bitter antagonisms, leading to disorder and crime."[13] The strike ended three weeks later, when the Board of Inquiry for the Cotton Textile Industry, which the president had convened upon the protest's beginning, issued a report detailing its recommendations. The UTW declared victory and ordered its affiliates to return to work. At its peak nearly a half-million workers throughout the eastern United States had participated in the confrontation.[14]

Frank Graham had incensed Tar Heel conservatives and members of the state's textile establishment such as Kemp Lewis during the strike. The liberal leader volunteered to make bond for the young director of the state's Socialist Party, Alton Lawrence, whom authorities had charged with trespassing in High Point. "JUST HEARD OF YOUR ARREST. GLADLY GO ON YOUR BOND. CONFIDENT YOU HAVE COMMITTED NO CRIME," the university president telegraphed his institution's former student. Tar Heel newspapers reprinted the cable on their front pages, and—Lawrence's eventual exoneration to the contrary—Graham's many enemies perceived his intervention as incontrovertible proof

12. Hall et al., *Like a Family*, 341; Janiewski, *Sisterhood Denied*, 160; *Durham Sunday Herald-Sun*, 12 August and 2 September 1934; *Durham Morning Herald*, 18, 24, and 31 August, 1 and 4 September 1934.

13. *Durham Morning Herald*, 31 August and 4 September 1934; Janiewski, *Sisterhood Denied*, 77, 106–8, 122–23, 160.

14. Brecher, *Strike*, 191–92.

of his radicalism. Jonathan Daniels defended his friend on the *News and Observer's* editorial page.[15]

Although thousands of Durham's workers celebrated their perceived triumph with a boisterous parade down Main Street, close inspection of the government report would reveal that the board had made no tangible recommendations to improve the lives and working conditions of textile operatives but had merely advocated further study by various government agencies and panels. The sweeping scale of the participation of the city's workforce in the strike prevented extensive firings and retribution, but several months later Kemp made clear to his stockholders that he would continue to manage his factories with the utmost efficiency by modernizing his plant, increasing his workers' duties, and firing unneeded employees.[16]

It is unclear whether during the general textile strike of 1934 Dick faced an increasingly assertive workforce in the mill he managed in nearby Oxford. The local newspaper, the *Public Ledger,* placed a moratorium on coverage of the far-reaching unrest and advised its readers that "strikes are un-holy, un-Christian and are like so much poison to the recovery program, which is Americanism."[17]

Nell Lewis's illness, insolvency, and psychological neediness mandated her near-total reliance on the Mannings and her brothers. The extent to which their personal opinions and political and economic beliefs planted the seeds for her gradual rejection of many aspects of her earlier progressivism provides fertile ground for conjecture. Beyond a doubt, however, her growing conservativeness often received praise and support from members of her immediate family.

One wonders, too, how widely rumors regarding her mental problems had circulated throughout North Carolina. Despite attempts by her immediate family to protect her privacy, many people within the greater Raleigh area had observed Lewis throughout her breakdown and had noted her instability. She had achieved celebrity status, most significantly through her activism during the Gastonia strike and her defense of the Samarcand girls; gossip regarding

15. Ashby, *Frank Porter Graham,* 142–43; *Washington Post* (hereafter cited as *WP*), 7 September 1934.

16. *Durham Morning Herald,* 5 September 1934; Brecher, *Strike,* 191; Janiewski, *Sisterhood Denied,* 160–61.

17. *Oxford* (N.C.) *Public Ledger,* 20 July 1934; KPL to RHL Jr., 23 May 1945, KPL Papers.

her psychological condition, prolonged absences, and repeated institutionalization must have spread throughout the state, especially among her former liberal allies and members of the Tar Heel business and political establishments. The columnist surely knew that a resumption of her liberal crusading would stoke a whispering campaign among her most vociferous critics, such as David Clark. Might this awareness have consciously or unconsciously lent weight to her changing politics? To subject oneself knowingly to such maliciousness during an era when many regarded mental illness as disgraceful would have required tremendous strength. By echoing in her column the traditional beliefs of the bulk of her readers, she preempted the derision that her championing of unpopular positions would have provoked.

"Incidentally" resumed on 6 January 1935. From Chapel Hill, where Lewis would remain until the fall, she heralded her return. "It's grand to be back," she declared. She proceeded to catalog in decidedly romantic terms the southern delights she had missed the most: "Back to pines and broomsedge and 'chanyberry' trees and mules; back to cracklin' bread and spareribs and sillibub; back to deferential Negroes who salute you in passing whether they know you or not; back to 'warn't' and 'you all'; back to hordes of kinfolks and friends; . . . back, in brief, to The Neighborhood and all its informal charm."[18]

In a series of columns written during her Chapel Hill residency, Lewis highlighted her aging and her displeasure with literature that critically appraised her homeland. In "The Pendulum Swings Back" she applauded Howard Mumford Jones's recently published article in the *Virginia Quarterly Review*, in which he assailed the enthusiasm of the region's authors for social realism alone. She said that she suffered from "a sort of hardening of [her] arteries" and had grown bored with the surfeit of tawdry tales of Dixie. She, like Jones, would "welcome with cheers a good oldfashioned Thomas-Nelson-Page Confederate colonel, and . . . thrill to a curls-and-crinoline heroine, a dashing young officer with romantic eyes, and a rose-covered white-pillared mansion." Her weariness with the fad for realism, she contended, came from "the more balanced judgment that almost everyone gets in middle age."[19]

In "An Extremity to a Hullabaloo" Lewis tore into Gertrude Stein after the author's reading at the university. Stein's often-baffling writing, which fre-

18. *N&O*, 6 January 1935.

19. *N&O*, 23 June 1935; James D. Hart, ed., *The Oxford Companion to American Literature* (New York: Oxford University Press, 1995), 336; Howard Mumford Jones, "Social Notes on the South," *Virginia Quarterly Review* 11, no. 3 (July 1935): 451–57.

quently depended on the sound and rhythm of words, not their customary meaning, left the columnist cold. Her mind had wandered as Stein, who had coined the phrase "lost generation," stood "talking and talking and talking about . . . about? . . . well, about just nothing at all." Age, Lewis explained, accounted for her impatience with the avant-garde. The "extreme Left" that Stein represented remained incomprehensible and ludicrous to Lewis, who had "trained in a Victorian literary tradition" and esteemed more accessible writers such as Dickens and Thackeray. She marveled that the "local intelligentsia," including a gaggle of professors, listened avidly to Stein and applauded her.[20]

The following year Lewis would discover a writer much more to her liking in the person of Margaret Mitchell, an exponent of romantic realism. The two women had much in common. Shortly after Lewis's graduation from Smith, Mitchell had arrived in Northampton, Massachusetts, where she completed a year of study. The Atlanta native then secured employment in the Georgia capital for three years as a reporter and feature writer for its dominant afternoon newspaper, the *Journal*. After leaving the paper in 1926, according to Mitchell's many contradictory accounts of her often-clandestine writing of *Gone with the Wind*, she worked from one to ten years on what would become American publishing's fastest-selling novel.[21]

Lewis began her column-length review of *Gone with the Wind* with a rebel yell, "Yee-aay-ee." She labeled the literary phenomenon "the best book about the South during the Civil War and Reconstruction that I've ever read." She especially appreciated Mitchell's rendering of her needy and intensely human protagonist, Scarlett O'Hara, a character Lewis described as "selfish, unscrupulous, passionate, earthy and strong, the antithesis of the conventional fictional portrait of the Southern lady of the period, one whom every right-thinking heroine of Thomas Nelson Page would cut dead."[22] The columnist posted a copy of her review to the author, and Mitchell responded by expressing her great pleasure that an authority on the South such as Lewis admired the book. The Atlantan had "laughed and laughed at the cleverness" that the feminine ideals of traditional southern fiction would have spurned Scarlett.

20. *N&O*, 17 February 1935.

21. Pyron, "Nell Battle Lewis," 77; Darden Asbury Pyron, *Southern Daughter: The Life of Margaret Mitchell* (New York: Oxford University Press, 1991), 81–99, 142–79, 228–29; Hart, *Oxford Companion to American Literature*, 437.

22. *N&O*, 13, 20 September 1936; Pyron, *Southern Daughter*, 260–83.

This exchange of letters began an occasional correspondence between the women that would continue for several years.[23]

While in Chapel Hill, Lewis seemed increasingly nettled by what she perceived as the university's propensity to abandon its traditions. In an 11 August 1935 lead editorial, "Alma Mater and Her Baby Boy," she accused the institution's administration of coddling students by dropping a long-standing requirement that freshmen take a mathematics course. "The colleges now are full of students who have no business there," she charged. "It looks to me as if we have, not too little education, as the eager educators cry, but too much—or rather, that we are trying to educate a lot of inferior material that just won't educate."[24]

Her editorial in the capital daily must have mildly troubled Frank Graham, who throughout the Depression had waged a brave and unremitting fight to promulgate to Tar Heel solons and their constituents the indispensable nature of the university's mission, but much of his friend's gibe seemed too playful to warrant a presidential response. University News Service director Robert W. Madry, however, penned a good-natured letter to Lewis, explaining that many leading colleges and universities had adopted a similar policy. He had read "Incidentally" for many years and conveyed surprise that "a liberal, a progressive," such as she, would exaggerate the significance and consequences of such a minor change.[25]

Later that month, in "The Chapel Hill Dynamite Case" and "The Chapel Hill Dynamite Case (Continued)," Lewis pressed on with her frivolous crusade. She suggested that her earlier editorial had struck a spark that threatened to explode the placid-seeming campus. She claimed that many members of the academic community had expressed to her their disapproval of the new policy and that her reproof had sent executive secretary Robert House scurrying "to explain to the State that everything at the University was just dandy, and that the changed curriculum was in line with the most fashionable educational trends." She apprised the university news director of her conversion: "It is an occasion of sorrow to me to have disillusioned Mr. Madry in regard to my 'progressive' or 'liberal' tendencies. But the sad truth, alas, is that 'the girl grew older,' and—from where Mr. Madry sits—more reactionary. After forty-two years I have discovered that a good deal of nonsense not infrequently masquer-

23. Margaret Mitchell to NBL, 17 September 1936, NBL Papers; Pyron, "Nell Battle Lewis," 77.

24. *N&O*, 11 August 1935.

25. *N&O*, 11, 18 August 1935.

ades as 'liberalism,' and that considerable foolishness is committed from time to time in the name of 'progress.' In other words, I have found that sometimes to be what is called 'progressive' is to be lacking in sound judgment; and that occasionally to be what is known as 'liberal' is to be a trifle half-baked."[26]

By early September Lewis seemed spoiling for a fight with the university's administration, albeit not yet with its chief executive. In "Prejudice Confessed" she alleged that its news director had "publicly tagged [her] as reactionary" (he had done nothing of the sort), and she "pled guilty to the charge." She felt relieved "not to have to try to be broad-minded anymore" and free to "express all sorts of middle-aged, Victorian prejudices and animadversions." Having generated a casus belli, she expressed further pique at the institution. She found the currency of the term *the social sciences* on campus irksome. Lewis propounded that to regard as sciences "subjects such as history, sociology, economics and government, in which our knowledge so far is largely amorphous and more often than not warped and colored by the passions and prejudices of men, is little short of absurd." She remained particularly contemptuous that sociology might lay claim to definitive knowledge. "The term, 'social science,' is largely a synonym for hooey—or, if you prefer, the bunk," she concluded. Many members of the state's powerful business establishment, including Kemp Lewis, must have noted with approval her harsh criticism of Dr. Howard W. Odum's sociology department and, by inference, the many activist scholars he had attracted to the university.[27]

If Lewis in her revived column espoused a crabbed and hidebound attitude toward modern literary, cultural, and academic trends, she now advocated great tolerance for accounts of psychic phenomena. In February she introduced in "Incidentally" a feature she entitled "Now You Tell One!" The section, which would appear regularly for the remainder of the column's life, sprang from a conversation she had at a Chapel Hill luncheon with other women, who volunteered stories of inexplicable and seemingly supernatural occurrences. Much later in her career, she claimed that "Now You Tell One!" had "far and away" explored "the most important subject to which this column has ever addressed itself."[28] Lewis's childhood imaginings of spirits and sprites, her adolescent exposure to ghost stories, and her father's quiet interest in psychic research, as well as her encounters during her most recent severe

26. *N&O*, 18, 25 August 1935.

27. *N&O*, 8 September 1935.

28. *N&O*, 10 February 1935, 7 September 1952.

depression with Worcester and other Boston Society for Psychical Research luminaries and with astrologers and Christian Science practitioners, had instilled in her an expanding belief in the paranormal.

The creation in 1935 of the Duke University Parapsychology Laboratory by psychologists William McDougal and Joseph Banks Rhine, who had popularized the term *extra-sensory perception*, provided Lewis with further impetus and grist for her series. Despite Rhine's integrity, he remained at times overly credulous. To assess scientifically the purported mind-reading abilities of the horse Lady Wonder, the researcher had in the winter of 1927 pitched a tent next to her barn, just outside of Richmond, where for six days he conducted tests. Soon thereafter he published a paper extolling the animal's telepathic abilities, which she had demonstrated for him by touching children's alphabet blocks with her nose to spell out the answers to questions. Rhine's subsequent discovery that Lady's owner cued the mare by wagging a whip, body movements, and voice inflections embarrassed the scientist but did not diminish his belief in animals' mind-reading and prescient abilities. At Duke Rhine would earn much of his reputation through his quantitative analysis of series of laborious card-guessing exercises, which the former marine believed proved the existence of psychic powers.[29]

Despite the notable changes in "Incidentally"—its growing espousal of traditionalism and regionalism and the prevalence of editorials devoted to the paranormal—important vestiges of its earlier progressivism remained. Lewis would never lose what Darden Asbury Pyron describes as her "virtual obsession with prisons and confinement." For the remainder of her journalistic career Lewis prolifically, and with erudition and great passion, sought to reform North Carolina's mental institutions, penitentiary, and work camps, and she lobbied forcefully to end the death penalty.[30] In "You Can't Budget Insanity," written in early March, just a few months after Lewis's release from Western State, she attempted to educate Tar Heels about the pressing need for greatly increased expenditures for the state's mental hospitals. She understood the

29. *N&O*, 23 June 1935; Joe Nickell, "Psychic Pets and Pet Psychics," *Skeptical Inquirer* 26, no. 6 (November–December 2002): 12; J. B. Rhine, *Extra-Sensory Perception* (Boston: Boston Society for Psychic Research, 1934); Williams, *Encyclopedia of Pseudoscience*, 302–3; Denis Brian, *The Enchanted Voyager: The Life of J. B. Rhine* (Englewood Cliffs: N.J.: Prentice Hall, 1982), 15–6, 34–47, 59–66; "Lady Wonder" (cited 1 September 2006), www.randi.org/encyclopedia/Lady%20Wonder.html.

30. Pyron, "Nell Battle Lewis," 74; *N&O*, 26 April 1925, 19 June and 8 October 1927, 15 March 1931, 21 August 1932, 15 January 1933, 3 February and 17 March 1935; *Baltimore Evening Sun*, 7 December 1936.

public's inclination to avert its gaze from what transpired within the institutions. "Here are the darkest dregs of our society," she declared. "Here is something we do not wish to see, much less stir up—something too painful, too tragic, too hopeless, too horrible." This heedlessness, however, had resulted in the "neglect of the most helpless group in all our population, the people who have absolutely no voice; whose statements, even if they had voice, would be discounted. Yet their lot is dreadful beyond description; their sufferings incredible to the mind in health." Her readers might naturally devolve the issue to their politicians and public health officials and expect them to act compassionately. "BUT," she emphasized, "WE ARE THE PEOPLE IN CHARGE."[31]

The following week, in "Just One of Those Mysteries," Lewis derided J. B. Roach, the superintendent of the state's penal system. Roach had just exonerated the Mecklenburg prison camp supervisor, who had enchained two black convicts in an unheated cell for such a prolonged period that their feet had required amputation. Although Roach's investigation found no "irregularity" in the facility's management, he expressed bafflement about why camp employees had not administered medical care to the prisoners before their condition reached such a dire stage. Lewis's response to the superintendent's bewilderment dripped with sarcasm: "Just one of those mysteries, Mr. Roach, just one of those mysteries. Or, maybe, just the contrariness of niggers who insist upon getting gangrenous feet in spite of all that diligent guards and camp superintendents can do to prevent it, just natural contrariness that prefers to go stumping through life with both feet cut off."[32]

Upon Lewis's return to Raleigh in the early fall of 1935, which coincided with her column's fourteenth birthday, she began immediately to recant much of her earlier activism and continued to develop and refine a series of narratives to explain her reversal's motivation. On 8 September she acknowledged in "Anniversary" that "Incidentally" had become "decidedly more conservative than it used to be" and that it no longer seemed "pale pink." She believed that "perhaps [she] should lament this as a sign of age, as part of time's toll, along with gray hair and the middle-aged spread." She did not, however, regret her metamorphosis. "I'm not sad about it: it's so much more comfortable not to feel compelled to tear your shirt and get all worked up into a lather about this

31. *N&O*, 3 March 1935.
32. *N&O*, 10 March 1935.

and that. Then (perhaps to rationalize further), I trust that some of the 'liberalism' which Incidentally has lost is a sort of sophomoric cocksureness. I don't feel nearly as capable of directing the operation of the universe as I did several years ago. In fact, let me make Incidentally's most significant admission: there really are quite a lot of things that I don't know."[33]

In uncharacteristically rambling prose she dismissed her ability to serve as a social analyst. Incredibly, "Battling Nell" maintained that her motivation for her activism throughout the 1920s and early 1930s had not derived from outrage over the many injustices she observed or a desire to give voice to powerless and exploited Tar Heels. She implied that a psychological need to counteract her deep sense of inferiority impelled her many liberal campaigns.

The following week she devoted her entire column to "Home," an editorial reminiscing about her life in Raleigh and describing her feelings upon returning there. In the most complete extant description of her upbringing, she painted an idyllic picture of her childhood. Nell as a toddler had played on the Capitol Square in the middle 1890s, supervised by her "mammy" and other subservient "ladies of the old school." Lewis neglected to mention the bloody white supremacist campaign Democrats orchestrated in the statehouse around that time, which ensured the party's hegemony within North Carolina and which soon expelled black legislators and terrorized and disenfranchised black voters. In great detail she recounted her girlhood at Cloverdale, where she had participated in a plethora of pastoral enjoyments, under the supervision of her handicapped and doting father. Dr. Lewis had insisted that she receive an experience in democracy by enrolling her in public schools, where she studied with Tar Heel children of various social classes. During her education at St. Mary's she had not understood the institution's emphasis on religion and had balked at attending devotions every morning and evening. As an adult, however, she realized the wisdom of her alma mater's policies; she had committed the chapel services to memory.[34]

Pyron correctly observes that by this time Lewis had become "virtually a caricature of the ideas and forces in southern life that she had built her reputation attacking. If she had played the archetypal rebel, heretic, and bad little girl before, she now assumed the opposite mien: the political reactionary, the racist bigot, the submissive lady, the literary romantic, the religious mystic,

33. *N&O*, 8 September 1935.

34. *N&O*, 15 September 1935; Crow, Escott, and Hatley, *History of African Americans*, 114–18.

and the devotee of ghosts and spirits."[35] With increasing directness and forcefulness, "Incidentally" conflated mental illness with the desire of individuals to engage in progressive action. In 1938 Lewis reflected on her earlier crusading and declared, "The violent urge to reform society is in nine (perhaps ten) cases out of ten a projection of one's inner difficulties, inner confusion, inner disorder upon one's environment." She now had but a single object of reformation, "N. B. Lewis," and felt certain that addressing her own troubles would prove more productive than attacking the ills she perceived in the world around her.[36]

Lewis may have in fact, perhaps unconsciously, associated the anguish she underwent in the first few years of the 1930s with her own crusading liberalism. The summit of her activism immediately preceded her spiral into severe depression. In her quest to understand her distress, she may have mistakenly construed a cause-effect relationship between the politics she had so fiercely espoused during a hypomanic phase of her apparent bipolar disorder and her subsequent profound melancholia. Might a faction of the legion of psychiatrists and other medical doctors—many of them male—from whom she received treatment during her depression have suggested or reinforced this thesis? Perhaps some of these authorities inculcated in her, during a time of heightened suggestibility, the closely related proposition that a woman's activism and rejection of established gender roles provided evidence of a disturbed mind. Members of Lewis's immediate family may have advanced and reinforced sentiments such as these.

Lewis frequently employed another account to explain her reversal. Unmindful of the deep skepticism she had displayed regarding the political agenda of the National Textile Workers Union and the Communist Party, USA (CPUSA) during the Gastonia strike, she now stated that she had unwittingly served as a radical dupe amid the unrest. She explained to her column's readers that she "was one of that motley crowd of 'liberals' from here, there and yonder who were all worked up about a bunch of bums, several of whom were accused of killing the Gastonia Police Chief." In 1937 Governor Hoey treated Lewis at the soda fountain of Brantley's drugstore, where the chief executive took his Coca-Cola break every morning. She joked with Hoey about the jailer, who had refused to allow her to speak to the female prisoners because

35. Pyron, "Nell Battle Lewis," 76.

36. *N&O*, 1 May 1938.

he believed she had "said too much already." Lewis and the governor laughed over the incident. A decade later, in "A Few Remarks by a Burnt Child," Lewis deplored her earlier incarnation as a "puerile pink," when she had carried the "torch for 'liberalism'" during the infamous trial. "Who," she asked, "beat the tom-tom louder for the poor oppressed laboring man as represented by the Gastonia defendants (as Red as your Uncle Joe Stalin, as it turned out) than the deluded editor of this column? Who, even, was nut enough to raise a fund for their defense?" She compared herself to a "poor burnt child who dreads the fire" and emphasized the significance that the historic incident had on her present politics: "I learned my lesson eighteen years ago—and I mean *I learned it!*"[37]

The fusion of the dramatic but improbable account Lewis constructed to explain her repudiation of progressivism with the fury she felt over having served as a cat's-paw for radicals would produce an extraordinary diatribe in a 1951 "Incidentally" column: "When I was completely taken in by the Communist agitation at Gastonia in 1929, there wasn't a bigger jackass or a more gullible sap in the State of North Carolina than I was. I knew absolutely nothing about what I was talking about, as I whooped it up continually in this column in support of the murderous Gastonia defendants. My experience in the bloody Gastonia business is THE thing of all others which has done most to make me distrust so-called 'liberalism,' which so often, like mine was then, is not only ignorant and neurotic, but very dangerous." How deeply Lewis believed in these narratives makes for interesting conjecture; clearly, however, they filled her writing with passion, provoked discussion about the columnist, and delighted conservative readers.[38]

In all likelihood an interplay of many factors contributed to Lewis's apostasy. Kate Burr Johnson's departure to New Jersey and Lewis's alienation from many members of the state's organized women as a result of her attack on Samarcand severely curtailed her connectedness to the Tar Heel progressive community and embroiled her in a clash with many of her former allies—a situation that her mentor might have mediated had she remained nearby. Lewis's reclusiveness, perhaps partially a consequence of her mental illness, prevented her from reestablishing a strong liberal support system.

Throughout her recent episode of severely debilitating mental illness,

37. *N&O*, 11 April 1937, 6 July 1947; Perkins, *News & Observer's Raleigh*, 185. Italicized words appeared in boldface type in original.

38. *N&O*, 16 December 1951.

members of her conservative and opinionated family had filled the vacuum this rift created and generously and lovingly sustained her. They also undoubtedly communicated to her often, during a period of great vulnerability, their traditional political and social beliefs and showed her how the platform of the state's liberals—in particular, its support for labor unionization and the progressive agenda that flourished at the University of North Carolina—had embarrassed and distressed her closest kin. But regardless of her profession that middle age had mellowed her, she remained for the duration of her career Battling Nell and would settle scores and tear into real or imagined foes. In the years that followed her recovery in Chapel Hill in the mid-1930s, she would direct some of her harshest invective toward individuals she believed had slighted her family and dishonored its reputation and legacy.

The celebrity Lewis had earned as a principal figure pioneering the southern cultural renaissance throughout the 1920s had faded, and the influence of Mencken, who had helped direct national attention to her, had waned. The heady days of her directing the *Reviewer* belonged to an earlier era. The stout and gray-headed woman, whose illness made her appear much older than her chronological age, may have returned to North Carolina embittered by her supersedence and increasing irrelevance.[39] Alcoholism as well as mental illness may have played a role in Lewis's metamorphosis. Some time after her return to Raleigh, she began to drink sherry heavily. She did not believe she could become addicted to the fortified wine, but in 1936 her drinking required medical treatment. Kemp's youngest daughter, Martha, recalled that her father "sent me over to pick her up from the hospital when I was seventeen because she and I got along just beautifully. She was very strong and opinionated. If she liked you, that was wonderful. But if she didn't, you had a hard time handling her. Fortunately she and I got along fine."[40]

Might Lewis—feeling tired, ill, and frustrated by her marginal success as a reformer—have decided calculatedly to go with the prevailing conservative flow? This course of action would not only assuage her loneliness but would, as at least one historian has suggested, jump-start her sagging career, expand her audience, and enable her to participate more meaningfully in her state's politics. Such an explanation, however, would contravene her well-documented integrity and the appraisal of several knowledgeable former allies who, while disagreeing strongly with the views she increasingly espoused, never ques-

39. Charles Angoff, *H. L. Mencken: A Portrait from Memory* (New York: Thomas Yoseloff, 1956), 205–16; Teachout, *Skeptic*, 276–97.

40. Stanley, interview.

tioned her sincerity. Lewis would not have propounded positions in which she did not earnestly believe. Although factors such as those suggested here may have influenced her unconsciously, she surely had become convinced of the rightness of her new orientation.[41]

Whatever the equation of catalysts effecting Lewis's repudiation of her earlier activism and political beliefs, she relished taunting her former allies with her conversion. In January 1937 she waved a red flag in their faces while simultaneously wrapping herself in it. She told readers of "Incidentally" that the flying of the Confederate colors on Robert E. Lee's birthday filled her with veneration for the "conquered banner." "The Confederate flag is a beautiful flag," she proclaimed, "the most moving in the world. How about that, 'Liberals'? Isn't it distressing to see a person who ought to know better attached with such rank sentiment to the reactionary past!"[42]

During this time Lewis sometimes positioned her transformation within the parallel changes she had perceived in the state's political atmosphere since the Loray textile strike. In March 1938 she provided examples of the growing conservativeness around her in "A Different North Carolina," an "Incidentally" editorial prompted by union organizer Fred Beal's subdued but nevertheless dramatic surrender to authorities in Raleigh the previous month.[43] After his escape from the Soviet Union and surreptitious return to the United States in early 1934, Beal had remained underground. During this time he had excoriated the Stalinist nation in magazine articles and through the serialization in the Hearst press of his biography, *Proletarian Nation.* Authorities arrested him in January 1938, when he visited his brother in Massachusetts. Although Hoey and his attorney general, Aaron A. F. Seawell, announced that the "State positively is making no deal with Beal," who had waived extradition, some behind-the-scenes maneuvering had taken place. The former labor organizer's attorney referred to a conference his client had arranged with Hoey, and Seawell indicated that he had received advance information that Beal would give himself up in Raleigh.[44]

At Beal's request playwright Paul Green, who had corresponded for sev-

41. Elizabeth Gillespie McRae, "To Save a Home: Nell Battle Lewis and the Rise of Southern Conservatism, 1941–1956," *North Carolina Historical Review* 81, no. 3 (July 2004): 286; *N&O,* 28 November 1956; *Carolina Israelite,* March–April 1956.

42. *N&O,* 24 January 1937.

43. *N&O,* 6 March 1938.

44. Salmond, *Gastonia 1929,* 170–71; Beal, *Proletarian Journey,* 338–52; *N&O,* 15, 16, 17 February 1938.

eral years with the fugitive renegade, reserved a hotel room at the Hotel Sir Walter from which to stage the submission. Green asked Frank Graham and Jonathan Daniels to join him there, and on 16 February the quartet walked the short distance up Fayetteville Street toward the governor's mansion. Green recalled many years later that Hoey welcomed his visitors genially and chatted politely with his erstwhile nemesis. (Beal's vehement anticommunism prompted widespread support for his pardon, and the leader of the ill-fated Loray strike earned parole early in 1942. His attorney informed reporters that Graham, Green, and Daniels had played important roles in securing the prisoner's release.)[45]

In "A Different North Carolina" Lewis revealed that she had heard from three sources, whom she did not identify, that Beal had inquired about her. She had refused, however, to call on the prisoner: "I should hesitate to resurrect by such a visit even the memory of the great social reformer that I was in 1929. I am quite willing to let dead 'liberals' bury their dead."[46]

In the spring of 1937 Lewis returned to St. Mary's to fill a temporary vacancy within its high school. She undoubtedly felt fortunate to secure the position; her teaching salary in conjunction with the income she received from her column helped end her financial dependency on her brothers' largesse. In early June she told readers of "Incidentally" that the job placed her in front of her favorite audience—adolescent girls—-and that despite the hard work of preparing her classes and communicating the material, she found her new employment enjoyable and interesting. She ached throughout the semester to convey to her students the painful knowledge that she had acquired during the past few years, lessons they would not learn in their schoolbooks. She said that she often thought: "Oh, if there were only some way by which I could tell them, so that they would really listen, what I have learned, sometimes so bitterly! . . . If only something I say might save them some measure of grief which their own experimentation will bring them!"[47]

The administration must have assessed her teaching positively because it renewed her contract. She taught English, history, and Bible at the institution through 1944—when she resigned because of another apparent episode of manic depression—and again in 1954. If during her initial semester she had

45. Salmond, *Gastonia 1929*, 172; Fred Beal, *Red Fraud: An Expose of Stalinism* (New York: Tempo, 1949), 75, 78–81; *N&O*, 17, 18 February 1938; *NYT*, 9 January 1942.

46. *N&O*, 6 March 1938.

47. *N&O*, 6 June 1937.

checked her desire to share with her students her personal philosophy and politics, it seems unlikely that she exercised similar restraint throughout her tenure at the school. In her history of St. Mary's Martha Stoops recounts the indelible, and perhaps sometimes frightening, impression Lewis made on her charges: "A solidly built woman, she would stride briskly into the classroom, briefcase in hand, and arrange her papers. Then leaning back in her chair, she would say, 'Now girls, catch these pearls from my lips. You can think what you want to think, but on tests you had better give back to me what I tell you.'"[48]

Stoops observes that Lewis's students respected her intense spirituality and appreciated the enthusiasm she devoted to her Bible class, for her the most important course she taught. St. Mary's had indeed become the focus of her religious reawakening. She authored for her pupils a series of uplift pamphlets; numerous brochures for the Sunday school classes she taught at the institution; and *The Way: Studies in the Teachings of Jesus of Nazareth*, a privately printed textbook.[49]

In "A Letter to Bible Students," which served as *The Way*'s preface, Lewis identified the causes of the modern era's "appalling moral confusion." She maintained that Charles Darwin's publication of *The Origin of the Species* had provided the impetus for many people to reject not just outdated theological dogma and superstition but religious faith itself. She did not denounce the science that Darwin personified, and she respected the order it had brought to the investigation of physical phenomenon. Nevertheless, Lewis believed that modern scientific inquiry privileged both the philosophic doctrine of materialism and materialism in the more general sense of the word.[50] She saw a parallel between the laws that had brought order to the study of science and the spiritual laws promulgated by Jesus. Christians should dedicate themselves to an abiding quest to discern the truths espoused by the Savior. "We must set about learning for ourselves from the greatest Teacher who ever lived . . . those SPIRITUAL LAWS which govern our inner lives." Contravening these spiritual tenets inevitably provoked "pain and confusion" (perhaps a reference to the tra-

48. Stoops, *Heritage*, 251; "Nell Battle Lewis," *Saint Mary's School Bulletin* 28, no. 2A (March 1939): 6–7; Powell, *Dictionary of North Carolina Biography*, 4:62; NBL to KPL, 9 March 1945, KPL Papers.

49. Stoops, *Heritage*, 251–52; Pyron, "Nell Battle Lewis," 78–79; *Belles of St. Mary's*, 26 January 1940; Nell Battle Lewis, *The Way: Studies in the Teachings of Jesus of Nazareth* (privately printed, [1942]); *N&O*, 13 September 1942.

50. Lewis, *Way*, 5, 8–9.

vails she had undergone during the preceding years as a result of her mental illness). Observance of these religious laws would result in "happiness and success."[51]

Pyron concludes that St. Mary's came to represent for Lewis her mother, Mary. Certainly, Mary epitomized for her daughter the "propriety, respectability, [and] desirable decorum" that she associated with the institution in a recurring dream. The portrayal of Mary in her death notice—"she was absorbed in a life of obedience to God and 'Christian Endeavor' was her watchword"—now depicted her daughter perfectly. But if Nell unconsciously sought to transfigure herself as a Southern Lady and thus earn the approval of her dead mother, a paragon of Ladydom, the columnist turned schoolmarm set herself up for failure.[52]

As she had observed fifteen years earlier in "Incidentally," she could never perform the "stimulating" but somewhat "taxing" part as "Your Mother's Daughter" completely convincingly. Certain aspects of the characterization admittedly came to her naturally. She had always had Mary's artistic sensibility and wit. Other of her attributes Nell acquired. As a result of her recent metamorphosis, she now internalized her mother's role as a "religieuse" and a defender of magnolia-scented traditions. But try as she might, Lewis could not for any great duration stay in character as a Southern Lady. Regardless of the contortions she underwent to conform to this icon, her psychology and combative and opinionated nature ensured that Battling Nell would make many entrances in the years that followed.[53]

As the decade proceeded, Lewis underwent another transformation. Observing Adolf Hitler's rise to power and militarism, she, like many contemporary American intellectuals and journalists, gradually reconsidered the pacifism that she had developed in the beginning of the 1920s while appraising World War I's purposeless slaughter. In the wake of her "Y-girl" service "over there," she lamented becoming a dupe of Allied propaganda and the naïveté she had exhibited during her earlier enthusiastic support for the war effort. In 1924 she wrote: "One of the regrets of my life is that I didn't have sense enough to be a pacifist during the last war, instead of hopping over to France as fast as I could get there. Nobody is going to beat a drum and wave a flag at me and get me all worked up for slaughter again! I am getting into training every day

51. Lewis, *Way,* 11.

52. Pyron, "Nell Battle Lewis," 78–80; *N&O,* 3 September 1905.

53. *N&O,* 6 May 1923.

now to be the most belligerent sort of pacifist when the next war comes. I am looking forward with keen interest to being snugly in jail yet, and I shall certainly be disappointed if I am not branded as a 'Red.'"[54]

But as the 1930s wore on and Lewis, during its final years, viewed with horror the German dictator's relentless and defiant march to war—the ceding of the Sudetenland, the pogrom orchestrated against Jews on Kristallnacht, and the annexation of the remainder of Czechoslovakia—she became what she described as a "back-sliding pacifist." Her close reading of *Mein Kampf* removed for her any confusion regarding its author's murderous intentions. On 23 April 1939, in an "Incidentally" editorial entitled "Condemned by His Own Words," Lewis extracted quotes from his screed. The Nazi leader had called Jews a "spiritual pestilence" and "seducers of our people" and had claimed that their "smell made me ill." He regarded his persecution of members of that faith as the "Lord's work." He sanctioned the use by his followers of "physical terror against the individual and the masses" and described Christianity as "spiritual terror." Proponents of democracy were, he claimed, "stupid good-for-nothings and babblers."[55]

On 3 September 1939, as Britain and France formally declared war on Germany after that nation's refusal to halt its blitzkrieg against Poland, Lewis urged a speedy military buildup by the United States. She believed, however, that this strategy alone would not halt the global conflict. In "We Should Still Pray" she pleaded for her readers to commune fervently with God. Only by seeking the Lord's intervention could her countrymen prevent themselves from being swept into the ever-widening carnage. She realized that this recommendation would draw mockery from the bête noire against whom she had contraposed herself since her return to North Carolina five years earlier. "What do you think of that, you scientific materialists?" she demanded. "How's that for pathetic naivete? She believes in prayer—thinks prayer could prevent or shorten a war! Ho! Ho! And she supposedly educated, too!"[56]

Lewis did not confine her stricture to the Nazis and the modernists represented by the Chapel Hill social scientists. She also lambasted American religious leaders, whom she charged thought in "ostrich fashion . . . that the ho-

54. *N&O*, 4 May 1924; Wm. David Sloan, ed., *The Media in America: A History* (Northport, Ala.: Vision Press, 2002), 332–34; Deborah E. Lipstadt, *Beyond Belief: The American Press and the Coming of the Holocaust, 1933–1945* (New York: Free Press, 1986), 137.

55. *N&O*, 23 April 1939; Adolf Hitler, *Mein Kampf* (Boston: Houghton Mifflin, 1943).

56. *N&O*, 3 September 1939.

locaust will not harm this land." She explained in many subsequent editorials on this topic that she did not advocate that the church take sides in the new world war. Instead, she implored the religious community to instigate a spiritual awakening that would bring about world peace and promote love.[57]

At least one of Lewis's prayers was answered during the period of American neutrality in World War II. Josephus Daniels returned to Raleigh in November 1941. The arthritis and eyesight of his wife, Addie, had worsened to the point that the seventy-nine-year-old editor and statesman had requested earlier that autumn that President Roosevelt appoint a new ambassador to Mexico. The columnist looked forward to Josephus's reinstatement behind his desk in the *News and Observer*'s front office, despite the fact that she may have felt somewhat apprehensive about whether he would continue to provide "Incidentally"—whose conservativeness stood out markedly from the remainder of the liberal newspaper—with the near-total editorial autonomy it had always enjoyed. Although Jonathan had headed the paper for eight years, Lewis had increasingly regarded the third Daniels son critically and his authority dubiously.[58]

She hinted at her uncertainty in "'The Old Man' Comes Home" in the 23 November edition of "Incidentally": "For twenty years Mr. Daniels has been my boss, and never once during all those years, though often I must have tried his patience sorely, has he been anything but kind and cordial in his relations with me. Nearest to impatience with me that he ever came was when, about fifteen years ago, he said, 'Nell, I wish you would get married; maybe then you wouldn't be so heady.' . . . Always he has allowed me extraordinary freedom in the expression of my views in this column, and I should be very ungrateful if I did not sincerely appreciate it. Needless to say, I do."[59]

Louis Graves had repeated in his *Chapel Hill Weekly* a month earlier a conversation a friend had overheard in which the senior Daniels expressed his views on the politics of "Incidentally." "I'm surprised at your keeping Nell Battle Lewis on your paper, since she is against so many of the things you are for," a subscriber to the capital daily remarked to the ambassador. "That's one of the reasons I want her to keep on writing for us," he responded. "It's a good thing for our readers to get opposing points of view." Graves noted that Jonathan Daniels seconded that opinion. "It is fortunate for the reading public

57. *N&O,* 3, 10, and 17 September, 24 December 1939, 9 February 1941.

58. Morrison, *Josephus Daniels,* 219–25.

59. *N&O,* 23 November 1941.

in the *News and Observer*'s orbit that the bosses' spirit of tolerance permits Miss Lewis to go on writing what she pleases regardless of whether or not they agree with her. Certainly she imparts an element of spice to the paper, and no two men know the high value of spice in newspaper writing better than Daniels father and Daniels son."[60]

Jonathan, who regarded Lewis as "one of the most interesting figures in Southern literary criticism in the 1920s," must have marveled over the unlikely direction her life had taken since then. Both journalists had received prominent mention in February 1941 in Charlotte newspaperman and free-lance magazine writer W. J. Cash's classic exegesis of southern history, culture, and psychology, *The Mind of the South*. In his book, which received overwhelmingly positive reviews, Cash had lauded Lewis's attacks on the Klan and fundamentalism in the early 1920s and her bold advocacy during the Gastonia unrest. Cash had praised the liberalism of the *News and Observer* under its young editor but had taken a gentle dig at him by accusing him of "sometimes waxing almost too uncritical in his eagerness to champion the underdog: surely a curious charge to bring against a Southern editor."[61]

The Danielses' seemingly unlimited tolerance of Lewis to the contrary, her column must have often exasperated and occasionally infuriated members of the family that owned the *News and Observer*. Her harsh review in an October 1941 "Incidentally" of Jonathan's most recent book, *Tar Heels: A Portrait of North Carolina*, without question reddened its author's face. Despite the fact that Gerald Johnson, the nation's leading commentator on the South, and the *New York Times* had hailed the editor's impressionistic treatment of his state, Lewis trounced it in "A Portrait with a Spotty Background." She grew most critical when she assessed the chapters devoted to the University of North Carolina and the state's public health activities. She bristled that Jonathan had glorified Graham, Odum, and Green without acknowledging the contributions of earlier generations of the institution's leaders. The author's failure to pay homage to her father's pioneering accomplishments nearly took her breath away. "If I hadn't read them myself," she gasped, "I could not have believed that anyone with any pretension to knowledge of North Carolina could write fifteen printed pages about the public health work in this State without once mentioning the name of the man who labored unselfishly for years to

60. *Chapel Hill Weekly*, 17 October 1941.

61. Pyron, "Nell Battle Lewis," 63; Cash, *Mind of the South*, 339, 354, 373; Clayton, *W. J. Cash*, 164–69, 183–87, 190–91.

lay its foundations and who brought it its first national recognition in spite of the meagreness of its early appropriations, the patriotic doctor who was its father—and mine."[62]

She may have felt some triumph in giving Jonathan his comeuppance in his own paper, but she knew that the young editor, ten years her junior, had published four celebrated books and many articles in prominent magazines and had established the sort of national reputation as a writer and a liberal that she had at one time seemed destined to achieve. Although many citizens of Lewis's native state regarded her as "North Carolina's most cultured woman," and she enjoyed literary talent in abundance, among her many book projects—including her treatise on the southern woman movement; her biography of Dorothea Dix; and her explorations of the lives of Elizabeth Cady Stanton and physician and humanitarian Elizabeth Blackwell, the first woman in the United States to graduate from medical school—only her biblical textbook privately printed for St. Mary's and the history of St. Mary's that she coauthored would ever see fruition.[63]

In mid-September 1942 Josephus Daniels, who had resumed his editorial leadership of his newspaper when Jonathan joined the military effort soon after America's entry into World War II, sent Lewis an affectionate tribute acknowledging the anniversary of "Incidentally." "I am a little late," the "Old Man" announced, "but am none the less sincere, in congratulating you upon the celebration of your twenty-first birthday as North Carolina's first columnist."[64] Although Daniels made clear the constancy of his unconditional devotion to Lewis, he beseeched her to reconsider her increasingly reactionary politics. "I loved you when you were so radical that I could not go all the way with you," he declared. "I loved you when you were a real liberal and a militant progressive. I love you still, despite your lapse into a conservatism where I cannot follow you. Come back to the liberalism that I still believe [is] in your

62. Morrison, *Josephus Daniels,* 272; *N&O,* 5 October 1941; *Chapel Hill Weekly,* 17 October 1941; *NYT,* 5 October 1941; Jonathan Daniels, *Tar Heels: A Portrait of North Carolina* (New York: Dodd, Mead & Co., 1941).

63. "Nell Battle Lewis," *Saint Mary's School Bulletin* 28, no. 2A (March 1939): 7; Powell, *Dictionary of North Carolina Biography,* 4:62; NBL to KPL, 12 March 1945, KPL Papers.

64. Morrison, *Josephus Daniels,* 224–25; Charles W. Eagles, *Jonathan Daniels and Race Relations: The Evolution of a Southern Liberal* (Knoxville: University of Tennessee Press, 1982), 86–120; "Biographical Note," Jonathan Daniels Papers (hereafter cited as JD Papers), Southern Historical Collection, Wilson Library, University of North Carolina at Chapel Hill; Josephus Daniels to NBL, 18 September 1942, NBL Papers.

heart, even if you seem sometimes to stray from the fountain of equality and real democracy."[65]

Lewis featured Daniels's letter in the next installment of her column. In "Congratulations with a Sigh" she reciprocated the warm feelings the dean of southern liberal newspapermen had expressed for her. Nevertheless, she told her readers that his note left her feeling a "trifle sad." She thought that she "had been learning some sense," whereas her elderly editor had implied she had "been falling from grace."[66] She acknowledged that she "must, indeed, seem very different now from what Mr. Daniels too kindly calls the 'real liberal'—and I consider the half-baked reformer—who wrote this column in the '20's." During that time she had "found it extremely easy to be a reformer: about all you had to do was open your mouth and holler about what ailed the world. But I have found it extremely hard to be reformed—and, of course, am still a long way from being. If that's conservatism, lamentable from Mr. Daniels' point of view, I guess I'll just have to bear the stigma."[67]

65. Josephus Daniels to NBL, 18 September 1942, NBL Papers.

66. *N&O*, 27 September 1942.

67. *N&O*, 27 September 1942.

# 8 NEW BATTLEGROUNDS

Nell Lewis praised God in her 19 August 1945 installment of "Incidentally" as she marked the yielding by Japan five days earlier to the Allies' terms of surrender. She expressed her deep gratitude to the Lord for the "inestimable blessing of peace which has come at last to the tortured world" and for the "victory of the forces of freedom." The columnist also continued to advance her frequently invoked thesis that mankind's transgressions had "brought upon us the unparalleled catastrophe of this war," and she implored the Supreme Being to "grant that we may never again repeat those sins."[1]

During the war Lewis had written to her friend Frank Porter Graham in Washington to learn more about his views regarding various postwar international organizations. Franklin D. Roosevelt had appointed Graham to the National War Labor Board, which the president created to settle industrial disputes that might impede the military effort. The commander in chief's selection outraged several ultraconservative congressmen, who resented the southern liberal leader's ties to a myriad of progressive organizations. Regardless of his many professional responsibilities, the University of North Carolina's chief executive remained virtually incapable of declining to lend his support to any assemblage advocating social, political, and economic justice in the South.[2]

Graham's impeccable liberal credentials and his inspirational delivery of the opening address at the initial convention of the Southern Conference for Human Welfare (SCHW) in Birmingham in November 1938 had resulted in his election to serve as that organization's chairman. Born of the response by idealistic southerners to Roosevelt's declaration several months earlier that the "South presents right now the Nation's No. 1 economic problem," the SCHW staged in the red brick Municipal Auditorium and other venues in the industrial city—a bastion of Jim Crowism and the focal point of the Communist Party, USA's activities in Dixie—a remarkable interracial gathering of more than twelve hundred delegates and many other attendees, including several communists.[3]

1. *N&O*, 19 August 1945.

2. NBL to FPG, 12 August 1943, FPG Papers; Ashby, *Frank Porter Graham*, 154, 174–91.

3. *Birmingham News-Age Herald*, 20 November 1938; *WP*, 6 July 1938; *NYT*, 23 and 24 November

Before leaving the convention on its second day to attend another meeting, Graham had insisted that he would under no circumstances serve as the permanent chairman of the newly formed organization. Two days later, as arch-segregationist and New Deal antagonist Martin Dies, the Birmingham City Commission, the Alabama Council of Women's Democratic Clubs, and numerous conservative southern newspapers commenced a concerted attack on the SCHW, Graham learned of his election to the post he had declined. In spite of the opprobrium he knew he would face, he accepted the lightning rod position and expressed his willingness to work in conjunction with others "who appreciate the South and can take it on the chin if necessary for the region and the people they love the most."[4]

Graham soon learned that despite the small size of the communist contingency, it contained influential members. In a series of letters that he wrote to these individuals, he attempted to persuade them to disclose any connections they had to the Communist Party. He did not request that they resign from the conference but urged a complete and truthful disclosure of their allegiance to the Party in order to allay rumors and negative publicity and to ensure their aboveboard participation at the SCHW biennial convention, which would assemble in April 1940 in Chattanooga, Tennessee. All of his correspondents denied having communist ties.[5]

At the Chattanooga convention Graham prevailed in a bitter fight against the conference's communists and fellow travelers and played a prominent role in authoring and securing the adoption of an amendment that "deplore[d] the rise of dictators anywhere, the oppression of civil liberties, the persecution of minorities, aggression against small and weak nations, the violation of human rights and democratic liberties of the people by all Fascist, Nazi, Communist, and imperialist powers alike which resort to force and aggression instead of the processes of law, freedom, democracy, and international cooperation."

---

1938; Linda Reed, *Simple Decency & Common Sense: The Southern Conference Movement, 1938–1963* (Bloomington: Indiana University Press, 1991), 15–19; Thomas A. Krueger, *And Promises to Keep: The Southern Conference for Human Welfare, 1938–1948* (Nashville: Vanderbilt University Press, 1967), 20–39; Morton Sosna, *In Search of the Silent South: Southern Liberals and the Race Issue* (New York: Columbia University Press, 1977), 91–96; Buhle, Buhle, and Georgakas, *Encyclopedia of the American Left*, 86–88.

4. *Birmingham News*, 24 and 26 November 1938; Ashby, *Frank Porter Graham*, 158; Krueger, *And Promises to Keep*, 37–39.

5. Ashby, *Frank Porter Graham*, 161–63; Krueger, *And Promises to Keep*, 82–83; Reed, *Simple Decency & Common Sense*, 22–23.

By the time of the organization's biennial meeting in 1942 in Nashville, it had effectively eliminated suspected communists from its leadership and had adopted rules barring the membership of anyone espousing violent overthrow of the United States or belonging to organizations advocating that goal.[6]

The red-baiting of the SCHW went into remission as the United States, the Soviet Union, and the other Allies battled the Axis powers. But with the war's conclusion, as Russia drew an iron curtain across Europe and that nation and the United States confronted one another in a cold war, anticommunists—ranging from extremist evangelical Christians and conspiracy theorists to well-informed American Catholic intellectuals, liberal internationalists, socialists, former communists, and labor leaders—expressed growing alarm regarding the dangers of communism. The domestic political climate turned more conservative, and intolerance of leftists grew much more severe. "In the South," southern scholar John Egerton writes, "anticommunism raced through the culture like an electrical current."[7]

The region's political leaders stoked a heady southern white backlash that powered this charge. Bristling at the criticism leveled at their homeland by northerners during the years surrounding World War II, the federal government's alleged intrusions in their native states, and blacks' demands—mounted most vehemently from outside the region—that the United States live up to its wartime rhetoric and end the fascism that existed in the South, demagogues from below the Mason-Dixon Line attempted to turn the clock back on the tentative steps made toward racial justice during this period and fortified themselves to repel any incursions against Jim Crow. These protectors of the "southern way of life" vilified their foes as "reds" or "pinks" and fueled the anticommunist delirium.[8]

The war further heightened racial tensions, as already overcrowded stateside metropolitan areas became unbearably swollen with war workers and military men, many of them seeking to prove their masculinity. In 1943 alone, according to Fisk University sociologist Charles S. Johnson, 242 "racial battles"

6. *Chattanooga News-Free Press,* 15 and 17 April 1940; Ashby, *Frank Porter Graham,* 164–66; Krueger, *And Promises to Keep,* 60–64, 76–87, 92.

7. Egerton, *Speak Now against the Day,* 443; Richard Gid Powers, *Not without Honor: The History of American Anticommunism* (New Haven: Yale University Press, 1998), 191–92; John Earl Haynes, *Red Scare or Red Menace? American Communism and Anticommunism in the Cold War Era* (Chicago: Ivan R. Dee, 1996), 89–112.

8. Howard W. Odum, *Race and Rumors of Race* (Chapel Hill: University of North Carolina Press, 1943), 13–21; Egerton, *Speak Now against the Day,* 10.

took place in forty-seven cities. In June white soldiers and sailors in Los Angeles battled youthful gangs of zoot-suited blacks and Hispanics, and in Beaumont, Texas, tales of blacks accosting a white girl and woman incited a white mob to raze the black section of the city. That same month nine whites and twenty-five blacks died in Detroit in a clash between recently arrived black workers and aggressive white mobs and policemen. Two months later a false report that a white policeman had killed a black soldier by shooting him in the back caused New York's Harlem to boil over.[9]

In the midst of this racial turbulence the Supreme Court's striking down in 1944 of Texas's all-white primary in *Smith v. Allwright* presaged meaningful black political participation throughout the largely one-party South. Near the end of his life special counsel to the National Association for the Advancement of Colored People (NAACP) Thurgood Marshall regarded this victory as the greatest in his storied career. Marshall and the association's leaders particularly relished the triumph because it humiliated one of their arch-foes, Congressman Dies, who represented the Lone Star State.[10]

The resolution by black leaders to end racial discrimination and perhaps even racial separation met not only with vehement resistance from virtually the entire southern white rank and file and its political representatives but with rebuke from many of the region's leading liberal newspaper editors. In *Southern Liberal Journalists and the Issue of Race* journalism historian John Kneebone describes the wartime reaction of these influential opinion leaders. In 1942 Mark Ethridge, the newly appointed publisher of the *Louisville Courier-Journal* and *Louisville Times* and chairman of the Fair Employment Practices Committee, put blacks on notice that "there is no power in the world—not even in all the mechanized armies of the earth, Allied and Axis—which could now force the Southern white people to the abandonment of the principle of social segregation." The next year the *Birmingham Age-Herald*'s John Temple Graves, who wrote a daily column widely subscribed to by southern papers, declared: "Segregation is not an argument in the South. It is a major premise."

9. Hebert Shapiro, *White Violence and Black Response: From Reconstruction to Montgomery* (Amherst: University of Massachusetts Press, 1988), 310–37; Walter White, *A Man Called White* (New York: Viking Press, 1948), 224–41; W. Augustus Low and Virgil A Clift, eds., *The Encyclopedia of Black America* (New York: Da Capo, 1984), 238; Kenneth Robert Janken, *White: The Biography of Walter White, Mr. NAACP* (New York: New Press, 2003), 275–76; Leidholdt, *Editor for Justice*, 417–19.

10. Juan Williams, *Thurgood Marshall: American Revolutionary* (New York: Times Books, 1998), 109–12; Kermit L. Hall, ed., *The Oxford Companion to the Supreme Court of the United States* (New York: Oxford University Press, 1992), 800–801.

In 1943 *Richmond Times-Dispatch* editor Virginius Dabney authored an influential article entitled "Nearer and Nearer the Precipice" for *Atlantic Monthly.* In his essay he took aim at "extremist Negro leaders and Negro newspapers . . . demanding an overnight revolution in race relations."[11]

Contemporaneously to the publication of Dabney's article, NAACP executive secretary Walter White published "Decline of Southern Liberals," an exposition for the *Defender* and the *Negro Digest.* Although the nation's most prominent civil rights leader conveyed his frustration with Dabney, Graves, Ethridge, and *Atlanta Constitution* editor Ralph McGill, he noted that Graham had not wavered in his support for blacks. White expressed hope that Jonathan Daniels would not abandon his comparatively enlightened racial views, as had so many of his journalistic peers.[12]

Nell Lewis had observed the activism of the SCHW and the NAACP with concern during the years leading up to World War II and throughout the global conflict. The application in late 1938 by a black woman, Pauli Murray, for admission to the University of North Carolina's graduate school elicited a stern response in "Incidentally" early the following year. Murray resided in New York but had grown up and completed high school in Durham, where her many demeaning encounters with Jim Crow had left a lasting impression and helped inspire her to become a civil rights pioneer.[13]

Lewis commended Governor Clyde Hoey's recent response to the Supreme Court's *Gaines v. Missouri* decision, which had dismissed that state's offer to fund the legal education of a black student elsewhere and regarded skeptically the state's professed intention to develop within its borders a law school for blacks equal in quality to its all-white university in Columbia. Hoey had requested that the General Assembly provide additional resources to both North Carolina's College for Negroes and its black Agricultural and Technical College to enable them to provide postbaccalaureate offerings.[14]

Lewis also cheered the governor's simultaneous emphatic avowal that Tar Heels do "not believe in social equality between the races and will not tolerate mixed schools for the races." "The policy of strict racial segregation which we have always followed in this state has the soundest biological basis," she declared, "and there is no chance that it will be modified—or so I believe and

11. Kneebone, *Southern Liberal Journalists,* 196–214; Virginius Dabney, "Nearer and Nearer the Precipice," *Atlantic Monthly,* January 1943, 94–100.

12. Walter White, "Decline of Southern Liberals," January 1943, *Negro Digest,* 43–46.

13. *N&O,* 15 January 1939; Crow, Escott, and Hatley, *History of African Americans,* 117–18, 162.

14. *N&O,* 15 January 1939.

hope." She professed astonishment and irritation that a poll of Chapel Hill graduate students had revealed that a majority of them favored admitting Murray, whom the columnist termed the "New York Negress," and other black students seeking advanced degrees. "This indication of our new 'liberalism' is not too reassuring to me," she fretted. Although in the spring the General Assembly passed an enabling act permitting the state's black colleges to offer graduate and professional programs, it allocated no funding to support this end.[15]

The Raleigh journalist's vehement support for continued segregation, coupled with increased expenditures to afford blacks more equal opportunities for graduate and professional education, differed little from the positions adopted by most white southern liberals. Graham, however, despite not publicly challenging separate but equal educational systems, had begun to feel increasingly uncomfortable with this aspect of Jim Crow. After Murray learned of her rejection, she initiated a correspondence with him. He pledged his efforts to ensure that Murray and other members of her race received enhanced educational opportunities at black colleges within his state and promised that he would begin to seek "the next possible advance."[16]

Like Graham, Daniels was becoming more uneasy with unequivocal social separation between blacks and whites. Speaking on his alma mater's campus as debate raged among its students and faculty regarding Murray's application, he announced, "I don't see how anybody can object to taking a graduate course with a Negro." But regardless of Daniels's growing sensitivity to racial injustice, he did not urge an end to Jim Crow. It would take another fifteen years and the imprimatur of the Supreme Court's unanimous decision in *Brown v. Board of Education* before he and a courageous handful of his peers in the southern press would endorse ending segregation. And even then, this vanguard of liberal journalists would base their lonely stands on the "law of the land," not on the inequity of second-class citizenship. Despite Daniels's and Graham's tentative and highly moderate racial attitudes at the time of *Gaines*, they nevertheless made headlines in southern newspapers and aroused the wrath of the region's many racial traditionalists.[17]

In 1942 Lewis echoed Dabney's, Graves's, and Ethridge's anxieties about growing black militancy. In "Right Down Hitler's Alley" she charged northern

15. *N&O*, 15 January 1939; Egerton, *Speak Now against the Day*, 233.

16. Pauli Murray, *Song in a Weary Throat: An American Pilgrimage* (New York: Harper & Row, 1987), 109–24; Ashby, *Frank Porter Graham*, 227–28; Egerton, *Speak Now against the Day*, 233.

17. Murray, *Song in a Weary Throat*, 121, 167; Eagles, *Jonathan Daniels and Race Relations*, 68–69, 158, 169; Egerton, *Speak Now against the Day*, 232–33, 250.

black extremists and white demagogues from her region with fomenting racial animosity that played into the hands of America's enemies. She conceded that blacks throughout the region faced economic hardship and racial prejudice: "It is only the blindest and most prejudiced Southerner who will deny the [racial] shortcomings of the South . . . or who will not admit many injustices from which the Negro in the Southern States still suffers." But, she insisted, wise native leaders remained best qualified to deal with the problems in their homeland. She evoked memories of the Reconstruction era and its "tragic consequences for both races." Outsiders meddling in the affairs of Dixie begot this "darkest decade of Southern history." Intense criticism of the South by northerners might force those "most friendly to the advance of the Negro" to sever their support for the race.[18]

Global tensions further unsettled Lewis around this time. Immediately following the war's ending, she noted with alarm the gains socialists and leftists had made in Western Europe. "Very likely we'll soon see a Communist Europe with a Socialist Britain and a China at least half Communized, while we're left as the only major capitalistic nation and one in which all socialistic trends have been increased," she predicted. Over the next two years Lewis looked on in dismay as the Soviet Union expanded its dominance throughout Eastern Europe, turned its back on the Yalta Conference provisions to allow free elections within that region, and engaged in a range of nefarious activities. She chronicled for her readers Russia's menacing military buildup and its installation of communist regimes in Bulgaria, Hungary, Poland, Romania, and nearby nations; intrigue in Greece, Iran, and Turkey; establishment of a Canadian spy ring charged with stealing U.S. atomic secrets; and obstructionist tactics within the United Nations.[19]

Inconceivably and indefensibly to Lewis, many Americans and their leaders turned a blind eye to the dire threat she perceived. Henry A. Wallace, whose advocacy for blacks and sharecroppers during his service as vice president had earned the Iowan the enmity of powerful southern Democrats, personified for Lewis negligence bordering on treason. She referred to him variously as "Heneree" and "Red Hank." At the behest of party leaders, in preparation for the 1944 election, Roosevelt had replaced Wallace with Harry S. Truman, who hailed from Missouri, a state that had added a star to the Confederate flag.[20]

18. *N&O*, 27 September 1942.

19. *N&O*, 19 August 1945, 3 August 1947.

20. Dewey W. Grantham, *The South in Modern America: A Region at Odds* (New York: HarperCollins, 1994), 186; *N&O*, 6 July 1947; *Raleigh Times* (hereafter cited as *RT*), 26 July 1948.

As Truman's inherited secretary of commerce, Wallace disagreed with the fledgling president over the hard line he took with the Soviet Union and expressed racial views that infuriated many white southerners. In the fall of 1946, in a speech entitled "The Way to Peace," which the idealistic secretary delivered at a Congress of American-Soviet Friendship at Madison Square Garden, he decried the racial hatred that had fueled the recent grisly execution of two black men—one a war veteran—and their wives by a white mob of Georgians. Wallace devoted most of his remarks, however, to criticizing what would soon become known as the Truman Doctrine, the containment of Soviet expansionism by supplying aid to noncommunist nations such as Greece and Turkey. He warned that a "get tough with Russia" policy would result only in the Soviets becoming more antagonistic toward the United States. "I am neither anti-British nor pro-British," he declared, "neither anti-Russian nor pro-Russian."[21]

Truman exploded and fired his idealistic cabinet member, and the erstwhile secretary soon began to entertain presidential ambitions. Tapping the enthusiasm many Americans held for continuing the New Deal and the spirit of the Popular Front, which had battled fascism and united many liberals, progressives, and communists, Wallace embarked on a national speaking tour, charging that Truman's loyalty program, confrontation with the Soviet Union, and abandonment of New Deal reforms had given rise to fascism in America. Communists and their supporters within leftist labor unions provided the candidate-in-the-making with a bedrock of support.[22]

Lewis could not contain herself when, in the late spring of 1947, Wallace's Crusade for Peace invaded her state at the behest of the Southern Conference for Human Welfare's Committee for North Carolina and its student chapter at the University of North Carolina. Her ensuing heady crusade against Wallace, the SCHW, and Graham would resurrect "Battling Nell" and begin her reemergence as a powerful and articulate adversary of the forces seeking to bring social and racial justice to the South. She must have found the attention her campaign earned gratifying. After the renown she had achieved early in her career, she had for fifteen years, in the wake of her breakdown, func-

21. *WP*, 13 September 1946; *NYT*, 27 July and 13 September 1946; William Manchester, *The Glory and the Dream: A Narrative History of America, 1932–1972* (Boston: Little, Brown, 1973), 1:503–7; Buhle, Buhle, and Georgakas, *Encyclopedia of the American Left*, 37.

22. David McCullough, *Truman* (New York: Touchstone, 1992), 515–18; Manchester, *Glory and the Dream*, 507–8; *NYT*, 13 September 1946; Powers, *Not without Honor*, 200–201; Buhle, Buhle, and Georgakas, *Encyclopedia of the American Left*, 636–37.

tioned as a marginal and occasionally eccentric journalistic figure. Many factors, however, in addition to a possible desire for celebrity, sparked her attack.

"Man of the Courage of His Convictions," Josephus Daniels's editorial encomium of Wallace in the 5 June *News and Observer,* in which the elderly editor announced the former vice president's arrival in Raleigh and advertised the speeches he would make that day at Chapel Hill and in the capital, mortified and outraged the columnist. Aggravating Daniels's offense for Lewis, he had extended Wallace an invitation, which Wallace had accepted, to spend the night before his addresses at Wakestone, the Danielses' family home.[23] The next morning the Old Man undoubtedly had second thoughts about the hospitality he had extended. His guest implied to journalists at a press conference at Wakestone that he might challenge Truman in the Democratic primary or run against him at the head of a third-party ticket. Although Daniels admired Wallace's commitment to peace and to continuing Roosevelt's agenda, the *News and Observer*'s editor, an unwavering proponent of a unified Democratic Party, generally supported Truman and later expressed his regret over his guest's "ill-advised candidacy."[24]

Graham had deeply desired to have Wallace speak at Chapel Hill that day but knew that extending an official invitation would outrage conservative trustees and members of the state's business establishment. The university president therefore asked Junius Irving Scales, who helped head the SCHW's Committee for North Carolina, to invite Wallace to deliver an address on campus. "He is a dear friend," Graham told the industrious student leader. "I know I can count on you."[25]

The afternoon of the press conference Graham introduced Wallace to a capacity crowd at the university as a "champion of justice, freedom and peace among all nations of the world." The featured speaker then warned his listeners, "We can't fight Communism with force," and urged that the United States respond to the communist government coup in Hungary by endeavoring to "woo" that nation with aid. At a reception following his address, the progressive luminary shook hands with hundreds of admirers. Graham's effusive remarks lauding Wallace and the warm reception the presumptive presidential candidate earned at Chapel Hill undoubtedly turned Lewis's stomach. Since

23. *N&O,* 5 June 1947; Morrison, *Josephus Daniels,* 260–61.

24. *N&O,* 6 June 1947; Morrison, *Josephus Daniels,* 260–61, 274.

25. Junius Irving Scales and Richard Nickson, *Cause at Heart: A Former Communist Remembers* (Athens: University of Georgia Press, 1987), 183.

assuming the university's leadership, Graham had repeatedly slighted Lewis's family and alienated them from the institution with which they so powerfully identified. The complicity of the university's administration in furnishing the controversial Wallace with a pulpit from which he could proselytize a rising generation of North Carolina leaders provoked an irrevocable break between her and her former friend and liberal ally.[26]

Elated by the success of the reception Scales had organized, Graham invited the young leftist to drive with the university president and Wallace to Wakestone for an early dinner with Daniels. Graham occasionally drew Scales into the conversation, but for the most part the young man listened respectfully as his three elders discussed the pressures liberals faced in the postwar years.[27] In the evening Wallace addressed a large integrated audience at Raleigh's Memorial Auditorium. With glamorous movie star and North Carolina native Ava Gardner perched behind him on the speaker's platform, he praised Graham, Daniels, and Claude Pepper, the liberal senator from Florida. Wallace assailed the Truman Doctrine and "reactionary" southern congressmen. The crowd interrupted his speech with applause nearly thirty times.[28]

Smitten by Gardner's beauty, Scales, who sat on the stage with her and Daniels, attended little to Wallace's remarks. After the speech, the young man introduced the actress to a group of workers striking the enormous R. J. Reynolds factory in Winston-Salem that produced Camel and other cigarette brands. Gardner shook hands with each of the members from Local 22 of the Food, Tobacco, Agricultural, and Allied Workers union. Then she requested a cigarette from the affiliates of the interracial and militant labor organization. "Anything but a Camel will do," she said, thrilling her audience. In the hubbub after the speech Scales searched for some of his classmates who had offered him a ride home. As the student leader noticed one of the students standing on her tiptoes scanning the auditorium for him, Josephus Daniels stepped behind the attractive young woman and pinched her bottom. Thus ended Lewis's miserable day, which had consisted for her of a galling succession of events in which "Red Hank" had bamboozled not only her employer and Graham but also thousands of her friends and neighbors.[29]

26. *N&O,* 6 June 1947.

27. Scales and Nickson, *Cause at Heart,* 183; Curtis D. MacDougall, *Gideon's Army,* vol. 1: *The Components of the Decision* (New York: Marzani & Munsell, 1965), 164.

28. *N&O,* 6 June 1947.

29. Scales and Nickson, *Cause at Heart,* 183; Robert Korstad and Nelson Lichtenstein, "Oppor-

That Sunday the columnist tore into Wallace. In "Came the Dawn" she employed her signature sarcasm to mock the presumptive presidential candidate. "As you're doubtless aware," she told her readers, "the New Day broke in Raleigh and Chapel Hill last Thursday, the bright new day of human brotherhood and non-segregation and peace-on-earth and fellow-traveling in a big way and, in general, what-have-you. It was, indeed, a rosy dawn. Mr. Henry A. Wallace, former Republican, who, apparently, is now preparing to ease out of the Democratic Party into a third party of his own, gave us the benefit of his views." Lewis encouraged the subject of her editorial to form a new party. This would save her from forgoing voting or from even casting her ballot for the "Republican candidate, as we most assuredly would do and no I-reckon about it."[30]

Her spirits lifted one week after Wallace's North Carolina speeches, when the House Un-American Activities Committee (HUAC) issued a *Report on Southern Conference for Human Welfare.* The report alleged that the "conference actually is being used in devious ways to further basic Soviet and Communist policy. Decisive and key posts are in most instances controlled by persons whose record is faithful to the line of the Communist Party and the Soviet Union." The South's most eminent liberal figure received prominent discussion in the report: "Frank P. Graham, head of the University of North Carolina, was the first chairman of the Southern Conference for Human Welfare and today remains as its honorary president. He is not a Communist and no doubt on occasion has had some differences with the Communist Party. He is, however, one of those liberals who show a predilection for affiliation with various Communist-inspired front organizations." A listing of a dozen of these associations followed.[31]

On 15 June, three days after HUAC issued its report admonishing Graham, Lewis's oldest brother died unexpectedly while vacationing in the mountains of North Carolina. Dick had served as a father figure for Nell. The conservative former member of the university's board of trustees and textile executive, who had resided in the little textile and tobacco town of Oxford for the past four decades, must have shared with his sister his distaste for his alma mater's

---

tunities Found and Lost: Labor, Radicals, and the Early Civil Rights Movement," *Journal of American History* 75, no. 3 (December 1988): 801–3.

30. *N&O,* 8 June 1947.

31. *Congressional Record,* 80th Cong., 1st sess., 1947, 93, pt. 6, 7068; Krueger, *And Promises to Keep,* 167–73; Ashby, *Frank Porter Graham,* 233.

politics. The radical and dangerous direction that Nell believed Graham obstinately continued to chart for the university seemed to her not only to imperil young Tar Heels but also to betray the memory of her dead brother, father, and paternal grandfather, all graduates of the university, and of Isaac Manning, who had died the previous year. Undoubtedly, as the remaining members of the Lewis clan assembled in Oxford for Dick's funeral, they discussed the controversy swirling about Graham and the university.[32]

Kemp, who had taken about all he could stand of the leftist philosophy that he believed permeated the thinking at Chapel Hill, may have commiserated with Nell at the memorial service. As he continued to confront intractable and seemingly interminable labor problems at his mills, he had recently received condescending correspondence from the University of North Carolina chapter of the SCHW castigating him for his labor policies. The student writing to the eminent industrial leader condemned Erwin's negotiations with its unionized employees as "pernicious" and accused the former trustee of abdicating his "responsibilities . . . to the american [*sic*] people." The young student forwarded his letter to the press. Kemp complained to Graham about the "very vicious letter of abuse."[33]

On 6 July Lewis praised the committee's censuring of the SCHW. In an editorial entitled "A Few Remarks by a Burnt Child" she—without mentioning Graham—excoriated the organization. She again confessed her naïveté during the Loray textile strike and apologized for having mocked an earlier generation of anticommunist activists. "I was so 'progressive,' so 'liberal,' that I jeered at the Red-hunt of the 20's," she recalled. "I simply couldn't believe that the noble labor leaders at Gastonia were Communists; and, even if they were, should we all not cultivate the wonderful virtue of tolerance? Oh, sho! sho!" She volunteered some advice to the "fuzzy-minded, well-meaning, ill-informed natives, such as I was in 1929, who are all for 'progress' and will hop on almost any band-wagon that seems to be headed in the general direction of Utopia." These dupes should withdraw from the conference and had "better watch their step lest before long they look like monkeys—or worse."[34]

32. *N&O*, 17 June and 24 August 1947; *Oxford* (N.C.) *Public Ledger*? 17 and 20 June 1947.

33. KPL to W. M. McLaurine, 9 June 1939, KPL to Clyde R. Hooey, 28 March 1940, KPL to Stockholders and Directors of Erwin Cotton Mills Co., 25 January 1941, KPL to George R. Cowden, 15 April 1941, KPL to Clarence E. Boesch, 20 October 1941, KPL to RHL Jr., 20 April 1945, Jack B. Shelton to KPL, 13 December 1945, KPL to Kemp D. Battle, 19 December 1945, all in KPL Papers; James A. Hodges, *New Deal Labor Policy and the Southern Cotton Textile Industry, 1933–1941* (Knoxville: University of Tennessee Press, 1986), 172–75.

34. *N&O*, 6 July 1947.

Two weeks later, in "Unfitting and Undesirable," Lewis commenced her long-aborning attack on Frank Porter Graham. She did not assail Graham aggressively but expressed her hope that he would at once resign his honorary presidency of the SCHW. "Nobody thinks that Frank Graham is a Communist," she granted. "Most people who know him consider him entirely sincere in his own individual brand of liberalism and humanitarianism. But, even so, for him to continue to lend his influence to this now officially Red-tagged Conference does neither him nor our University any good. In fact, I think it does the latter harm—and his first responsibility, of course, is to that."[35]

Three days later HUAC exposed a Red cabal in Lewis's backyard. Called before the committee to testify on communist infiltration within the Congress of Industrial Organizations (CIO), Winston-Salem resident Anne Matthews charged that the majority of the officers of Local 22 of the Food, Tobacco, Agricultural, and Allied Workers union, a CIO affiliate, had communist ties. Matthews had until recently served as an office secretary for the local, which had after an epic struggle secured a contract to represent workers at the R. J. Reynolds manufacturing facility, the biggest tobacco factory in the world and the South's largest employer of blacks. She also revealed that she had previously functioned as the CPUSA's treasurer for its Carolinas' District.[36]

In the process of querying Matthews about the local, Mississippi congressman John E. Rankin asked if the communists sought to establish a Soviet state within the South. The organizer accurately explained the Party's far-fetched goal between 1930 and 1943 of "self-determination in the black belt," in which a series of contiguous and predominantly black counties extending from Texas to Virginia would achieve political autonomy. Having evoked this specter, Matthews informed the committee that Chapel Hill harbored a nest of communist students led by Scales. Asked by the press to respond to the charges against him, the war veteran and campus leader would only say, "I believe that the slandering tactics of this committee should not be dignified by a reply from anyone who believes in the traditions of American liberty."[37]

Matthews's revelations, added to Graham's failure to respond to "Unfit-

35. *N&O*, 20 July 1947.

36. *NYT*, 24 July 1947; *WP*, 24 July 1947; Scales and Nickson, *Cause at Heart*, 184; Robert Rodgers Korstad, *Civil Rights Unionism: Tobacco Workers and the Struggle for Democracy in the Mid-Twentieth-Century South* (Chapel Hill: University of North Carolina Press, 2003), 270–71, 323–25, 338.

37. *WP*, 24 July 1947; Harvey Klehr, *The Heyday of American Communism: The Depression Decade* (New York: Basic Books, 1984), 324–27; Buhle, Buhle, and Georgakas, *Encyclopedia of the American*

ting and Undesirable," incensed Lewis. "What about This, Dr. Frank P. Graham?" she entitled her lead editorial in the 27 July installment of her column. "I don't see any use beating around the bush about this thing any longer," she seethed.

> What about it, Dr. Frank P. Graham? We want to know—lots of us who pay taxes to support the University of North Carolina and to whom the institution belongs. We want to know what's going on there. We want to know whether our money is being spent to provide a comfortable nest for Muscovite fledglings. We do not want and we do not propose to have at our most important State educational institution a branch of a foreign revolutionary political party which is violently opposed to the principles of Democracy. We want it rooted out right away. We want the nest emptied of Uncle Joe Stalin's little fledglings. We want the pinkish curtain of "Liberalism" torn away and these little Kremlin characters put into their place, which we trust is a very considerable distance from Chapel Hill.[38]

Away on vacation—with his wife, Marian, at their cottage in then remote Nags Head—Graham did not reply. Even if he had been present on campus, however, he would not have responded to Lewis's shrill attack. Many of his admirers rose to support him, but it fell on the shoulders of Kemp D. Battle, who was one of Graham's closest friends and foremost defenders, a university trustee, and a relative of the columnist, and who enjoyed detailed knowledge about her professional accomplishments and private life, to administer the most articulate and withering scolding of Lewis.[39]

Within hours after reading Lewis's column, the Rocky Mount attorney posted his contradiction to his cousin. He began by conveying the "sense of shock [he felt] at both the tone and substance" of her attack on Graham and by deploring her condescension: "You speak as one on a high eminence of moral superiority calling to task a wicked and slothful servant who is wasting the

---

*Left*, 93–94; David C. Roller and Robert W. Twyman, eds., *The Encyclopedia of Southern History* (Baton Rouge: Louisiana State University Press, 1979), 263–64; *N&O*, 27 July 1947.

38. *N&O*, 27 July 1947.

39. FPG to John A. Park, 4 September 1947, FPG Papers; Aidan Smith, letter to author, 7 February 2007.

money of you down-trodden taxpayers. The role does not become you. I look back with nostalgia to your salad days when you flashed a hot and generous sword in defense of what you then thought were the rights of the oppressed laboring man. You think now you were misguided then, but your heart was in the right place."[40] Battle ended his letter by appealing to Lewis's earlier advocacy for workers and her love for North Carolina: "Surely every drop of blood in your veins should cry out for you to stand by him on such an issue. It will be a sad day for this state if he fails." Graham's removal from the university, "a center of enlightenment in the South," would thrust the "institution and the state into a reactionary control which would throw its blight on the future and on the things we hold dearest. What a tragedy if in that great struggle your talent should be on the wrong side!!"[41]

The red-baiting by "Incidentally" spurred a number of letters to the paper's "People's Forum." One reader asked, "What's criminal about Communism?" and berated Lewis because she projected the attitude that "she is divinely ordained [as] the Lord's prime dispenser of His truth." Another correspondent feigned "shock" upon learning of the columnist's Episcopalianism. Did Lewis know that HUAC had determined that the editor of the Episcopal paper, the *Churchman*, belonged to nearly two dozen communist front organizations? "How can patriotic Miss Lewis belong to a church dominated by Red Fascists?" the writer wondered.[42]

In Lewis's 10 August lead editorial in "Incidentally," "What about This, Dr. Frank P. Graham? (Continued)," she reminded her readers of Matthews's testimony that an organized group of communist students existed at Chapel Hill. Although she allowed that Party membership violated no law, she refused to dismiss the radicalism at the university as harmless youthful experimentation and exuberance. "There are many people in the Communist Party quite different from 'silly boys,'" she expounded; "there are determined, adroit (to speak euphemistically), Kremlin-commanded regulars as well. How do we know that some of the latter may not operate among and behind the 'silly boys'?" Speaking on behalf of "the people of North Carolina," Lewis demanded, in boldface print: "*What about this, Dr. Frank P. Graham? Is there or isn't there a branch of the Communist Party at our University? If there is, what are its activities, so far as you know?*"[43]

40. Kemp D. Battle to NBL, 27 July 1947, NBL Papers.

41. Kemp D. Battle to NBL, 27 July 1947, NBL Papers.

42. *N&O*, 6 and 9 August 1947.

43. *N&O*, 10 August 1947; italicized text in boldface type in original.

Lewis's crusade to rout out the communists at Chapel Hill evoked a letter to her from a young veteran studying there. He confirmed for her that "hundreds" of his peers—including many "misguided liberals"—sympathized with communism's goals. The correspondent discussed the difficult nature of identifying Party "professionals." The FBI had begun an investigation on campus in an effort to learn more about the activities of these individuals, he said, but it had failed to take any significant action.[44]

In addition to rank-and-file readers of the *News and Observer*, other editorial writers throughout the region attended closely via newspaper exchange agreements to Lewis's developing campaign against Graham and directed their gaze toward Chapel Hill. The *Savannah Morning News*, one of Georgia's largest papers, echoed Lewis's concerns, and the *Fayetteville Observer* weighed in on the issue. John A. Park Sr., the ebullient and conservative editor of the *Raleigh Times*, the city's afternoon daily, approved of the columnist's attempt to shine a bright light on the collegiate radicals.[45]

Still in Nags Head, Graham continued his golden silence regarding the escalating controversy. His failure to comment exasperated Lewis. In her 17 August column's lead editorial, "What about This, Dr. Frank P. Graham? (No. 3)," she dryly maintained that the "grave is noisy" compared to the office of the university president. She again demanded a response to Matthews's charge. In an adjoining editorial the columnist insisted she did not intend to force the retirement of her former liberal ally; she simply had decided to exercise her rights as a taxpayer to demand an accounting from a public official. Elsewhere in her column Lewis featured the letter from her student informer. What he had shared regarding the breadth of support that communism enjoyed at the university and the FBI's concomitant interest there had rendered a great service, she said. She found Graham's reputed ignorance about these matters "interesting and important."[46]

Lewis's campaign reached its zenith the next week, when she devoted her entire column to "An Open Letter to Governor [R. Gregg] Cherry," a former prosecutor of Beal and the other Gastonia defendants, now halfway through

44. William F. Patterson to NBL, 10 August 1947, NBL Papers.

45. *Savannah Morning News*, 29 July 1947; *N&O*, 16 March 1956; John A. Park to FPG, 19 August 1947, FPG Papers; William H. Richardson, "Plenty of Obstacles and Some Mistakes Could Not Keep John A. Park from Becoming One of the South's Outstanding Publishers at Age Forty," *Southern Advertising and Publishing*, September 1926, 15, 18; Powell, *Dictionary of North Carolina Biography*, 5:15–16.

46. *N&O*, 17 August 1947.

his gubernatorial term. She explained to the governor that Graham had failed to comment on the issue and that she anticipated he would continue his silence. His behavior necessitated her appeal to a higher authority: "I herewith address myself to you, sir, as the Chairman of the University's Board of Trustees and express to you my most earnest hope that the trustees will look into this important matter at the earliest opportunity and that they will take whatever steps may be necessary to clarify the situation at Chapel Hill and, if it needs cleaning up, clean it up."[47]

Having embroiled the governor directly in the controversy and emphasized to the readers of the state's most influential press his ultimate responsibility for dealing with the matter, she established her warrant. She informed Cherry that inside the University's Memorial Hall, which contained a double-columned panel displaying the names of the alumni who had sacrificed their lives for the Confederacy, hung a tablet devoted to her paternal grandfather, "the first of the four Richard Henry Lewises in my immediate family who in successive generations have attended and loved the University." Countless other of her kinsmen, she explained, had also gone to college there, including her brothers and Isaac Manning. The institution's administration had acknowledged the outstanding accomplishments of her father and her brother Ivey by awarding both men honorary degrees.[48] Right after the "Confederate War" and just before the university's closing during Reconstruction, she divulged, her father had resided in storied Old East, the campus's first building. He grew enamored of his room's fireplace, which functioned particularly well. Many years later Dr. Lewis had painstakingly gathered the dimensions of the structure and insisted that the builders of Cloverdale reproduce it in the sitting room.[49]

After easily understanding the first portion of the open letter, Cherry must have puzzled over the rather strange direction it had taken. Lewis, however, quickly made clear the purpose of her digression:

> Around that fireplace in Old East, during my father's student days, he and his cronies, undoubtedly, often sat and swapped yarns and discussed the various aspects of "life" on which youth always has such clear and weighty opinions, probably expressing sometimes the normal

47. *N&O*, 24 August 1947.

48. *N&O*, 24 August 1947; Wilson, *University of North Carolina*, 383.

49. *N&O*, 24 August 1947; Wilson, *University of North Carolina*, 31.

"radicalism" of Tarheel collegians at the close of the tragic '60's. I am frank to tell you, Governor, that, assuming that, even with steam heat, that fireplace in Old East still exists, it makes me very sick, indeed, to think that around it recently there may have gathered collegians of such a different stripe. I have no stomach whatever for the thought that around it Mr. Viroffsky and Mr. Ivanovich, of Brooklyn, N. Y., but late of the Ukraine, operating under Anglicized aliases, and Mr. Thus-and-so and Mr. What-have-you, of God-knows-where, together with their youthful naive dupes, may have been discussing and planning—or shall I more accurately say, "plotting"?—to disseminate ideas inimical to democracy and the safety of this country, laughing the while up their sleeves at the gullibility and naivete of North Carolinians who with their lazy and mistaken "tolerance" allow them to do so. I repeat: that is a thought which makes me sick; and my nausea, I assure you, sir, is extreme.[50]

Lewis's letter perplexed Cherry, who responded by inviting her for a meeting. He stated that although he had read her petition with a "great deal of care," he nevertheless remained confused: "I am not certain that I clearly understand the purpose of your letter to me." On 28 August she called on the governor, who cordially listened to her complaint but did not provide her with any ammunition for "Incidentally." The conservative governor certainly shared her antipathy toward communism, but he also envisioned an expanded role for North Carolina's colleges and universities in educating the swarms of veterans inundating the state's campuses. He may have viewed in Lewis's attack a potential distraction from the larger goals of his administration.[51]

As Lewis began to wind down her campaign, she dedicated her 31 August lead editorial to her growing collection of statements and articles authored by FBI director J. Edgar Hoover. She devoted particular attention to his HUAC testimony, in which he had confessed that he felt great fear when he thought about the "hoodwinked and duped" liberals and progressives who through their membership in front organizations aligned themselves with communists. She singled out the SCHW as an obvious example of such a facade and

50. *N&O*, 24 August 1947.

51. Hugh Talmage Lefler and Albert Ray Newsome, *North Carolina: The History of a Southern State* (Chapel Hill: University of North Carolina Press, 1954), 589; Powell, *North Carolina through Four Centuries*, 509; R. Gregg Cherry to NBL, 26 August 1947, NBL Papers; *N&O*, 7 September 1947.

pleaded guilty to having once played the role of one of the "completely duped little humanitarian helpers." During the Gastonia unrest and trials she had served as an "innocent and gullible ally of the Communists." Her ignorance then formed the only factor she could discern that partially exonerated her. Although Lewis did not mention Graham by name in her editorial, she made it clear that Hoover, too, deplored academic administrators who furnished environments in which Scales and his ilk could flourish.[52]

In early September Graham returned from his vacation and became aware of the magnitude of the onslaught that Lewis had helped foment. He found on his desk a letter from editor John A. Park written two weeks earlier and demanding an immediate explanation regarding the "attitude of liberalism at Chapel Hill." The university's leader, presumably tanned and rested—but also slightly wounded, having sustained yet another of the innumerable blows his lifework would provoke—politely but tersely relayed that he had "no comment to make at this time but when appropriate [would] report the University policies to the University Board of Trustees."[53]

Graham provided a more complete discussion of the matter to a friend who had told him that she shared with his "thousands of friends righteous indignation at Nell Battle Lewis for her personal attack." In his response he acknowledged that the university had long had a number of leftist students. He hoped that during their study at Chapel Hill the "free and democratic process [would] become a part of their thinking." He pointed out that communist students attended many colleges and universities, including Harvard and the University of Illinois, whose presidents had expressed no great concern about this issue. "It is not unlawful to be a Communist in the United States, or Britain, or France, or Canada, or Australia, or in any modern democratic country," he observed. "The way to win the youth of America is through a program of positive democracy; not by suppression of freedom but by improvement of democracy; by enlarging the meaning of freedom and equal opportunity for all people."[54]

How Graham regarded Lewis's attack must remain a subject for conjec-

52. *N&O*, 31 August 1947; Ashby, *Frank Porter Graham*, 237–38, 361–62; John Edgar Hoover to NBL, 19 August 1947, NBL Papers; Federal Bureau of Investigation, *Menace of Communism, Statement of J. Edgar Hoover, Director, before the Committee on Un-American Activities, House of Representatives, March 26, 1947* (Washington, D.C.: U.S. Government Printing Office, 1947).

53. John A. Park to FPG, 19 August 1947, FPG to John A. Park, 4 September 1947, both in FPG Papers.

54. Pauline Smith to FPG, [21?] September 1947, FPG to Pauline Smith, 23 September 1947, both in FPG Papers.

ture. He had known her and her family since her adolescence. Along with his close friends and supporters—among them Paul and Elizabeth Green and Louis and Mildred Graves—he knew well her complicated personal history and the many possible contributing factors that in addition to her ardent anti-communism might have induced her condemnation. Characteristically of Graham, however, his personal papers contain no evidence that he gossiped about Lewis or impugned her motives.

Her disparagement notwithstanding, Graham continued to demonstrate his willingness to "take it on the chin" to champion human rights for his fellow southerners. Late the next month the President's Committee on Civil Rights, which included the North Carolinian among its fifteen members, issued its landmark report, *To Secure These Rights.*[55] Behind the scenes Walter White had played a major role in encouraging President Truman to convene the committee. Aroused by a horrifying spate of attacks and lynchings in the Deep South committed by white policemen and mobs against blacks, including several war veterans, White had assembled a delegation of labor, religious, educational, and racial leaders that met with Truman in the White House in the fall of 1946. The president, whose upbringing in a section of Missouri known for its adherence to Jim Crow had imbued him with many traditional racial attitudes of the South, had to this point regarded White dubiously, but he listened grimly to the details regarding the recent wave of racial violence.[56]

"Civil Rights Committee Asks Ban on Segregation," a 30 October 1947 *News and Observer* headline trumpeted. The newspaper announced that Truman had hailed the report, *To Secure These Rights,* by comparing it to the Declaration of Independence, from which it derived its name, and by referring to it as an "American charter of human freedom in our time." In reality the book-length document may have gone further than the president wished. Among its thirty-five recommendations it advocated federal laws to prevent lynching, discrimination against minority voters, and segregation in the military, interstate transportation, and the District of Columbia. Although these proposals would almost certainly infuriate the overwhelming majority of white southerners, the panel did not stop there. It endorsed the "elimination of segrega-

55. Sosna, *In Search of the Silent South,* 150–52; President's Committee on Civil Rights, *To Secure These Rights: The Report of the President's Committee on Civil Rights* (Washington, D.C.: U.S. Government Printing Office, 1947).

56. White, *Man Called White,* 330–31; McCullough, *Truman,* 588; Shapiro, *White Violence and Black Response,* 372.

tion, based on race, color, creed, or national origin, from American life," and a majority of its members urged Congress to condition "all federal grants-in-aid and other forms of federal assistance . . . on the absence of discrimination and segregation."[57]

Graham and Dorothy R. Tilly, the only other southern representative on the committee, had appealed to the other authors to moderate their indictment of Dixie. The two southerners, while favoring desegregation, objected strongly to the recommended cutoff of federal funds to states that continued to practice racial discrimination. Graham authored for the report a brief minority statement that expressed his and Tilly's aversion to "federal control over education" and his long-held belief "that the best way ultimately to end segregation is to raise the educational level of the people in the states affected; and to inculcate both the teachings of religion regarding human brotherhood and the ideals of our democracy regarding freedom and equality."[58]

That Sunday Josephus Daniels delivered a scathing editorial indictment of *To Secure These Rights.* In "Remedy Worse than Disease" he reverted to the quintessential and contradictory motifs that had stamped his remarkable and controversial career: his fierce championship of the common man and his abiding racism. He began with a disparaging paraphrasing of the report's central findings and an endorsement of states' rights. He particularly resented the recommendations that he maintained "would make of the Federal government the sort of government that Alexander Hamilton desired, minus the king he preferred, [as opposed] to the sort of government Washington, Jefferson, and Madison set up—one that has been an indissoluble Federal government with fixed and limited power, with sovereign indestructible States functioning in all fields not assigned to the central government." Seeking to shield Graham from the sharp criticism Daniels knew he would face, the editor expressed his wish that the report had identified the panelists who had dissented from the majority opinion that Congress withdraw funding from states practicing discrimination and segregation.[59]

Daniels admitted that southern whites had "not always done as well by the

57. *N&O,* 30 October 1947; President's Committee on Civil Rights, *To Secure These Rights,* 151–73.

58. President's Committee on Civil Rights, *To Secure These Rights,* 166–67; Ashby, *Frank Porter Graham,* 224–25; Sosna, *In Search of the Silent South,* 150–52.

59. *N&O,* 2 November 1947; C. Vann Woodward, *The Strange Career of Jim Crow* (New York: Oxford University Press, 2002), 90–93; Joseph L. Morrison, *Josephus Daniels Says . . . An Editor's Political*

Negro as they should," but he advised that other regions of the country first address the racial problems that existed in their own backyards before criticizing Dixie. The wartime riot in Detroit, the redlining of blacks in Harlem, and many other incidents of racial bigotry in the North made hypocritical the singling out of the South with "such exaggerated and prejudiced statements." The authors of *To Secure These Rights* had failed to recognize the "many conspicuous actions of officials in the Southern States to uphold all the laws and secure the civil and other rights of Negroes in the South." Although the editor believed that the report justifiably denounced lynching, he charged, "There is no word of condemnation of those guilty of the rapes for which the crime has most frequently been resorted."[60]

As Lewis on 11 January described her agenda for her column in 1948, the seemingly immortal Josephus Daniels lay on his deathbed, and Lewis knew that her own life would change irrevocably during the new year. In identifying her goals, she first pledged to battle the communist infiltration of American institutions relentlessly, particularly penetrations in North Carolina. Democracy and communism, she avowed, could never be reconciled, and proponents of the latter philosophy always sought the elimination of the human freedoms associated with democracy. Lewis then announced her intention to campaign for transforming the United Nations into a genuine world government replete with a military force. Her third aim for "Incidentally" consisted of promoting America's ties to other English-speaking nations, presumably in an attempt to form a bulwark against Soviet aggression.[61]

Josephus Daniels died four days later. Lewis authored a highly personal eulogy. In "My Friend, Mr. Daniels" she described the autonomy he had afforded her. Even during her heyday as a rabble-rousing feminist in the mid-1920s, the editor had steadfastly refused to rein her in. She repeated her fond recollection that in the midst of this controversy, he had joked, "Nell, I wish you would get married; then maybe you wouldn't be so heady!" The editor had then leaned back in his chair in the paper's front office and guffawed. "I must have been 'heady' to a degree obnoxious," Lewis reflected, and "it must have taken a deal of patience to put up with me. But Mr. Daniels only laughed and wished—

---

*Odyssey from Bryan to Wilson and F.D.R., 1894–1913* (Chapel Hill: University of North Carolina Press, 1962), 23–28, 37–55, 125–28, 149–59, 224–36.

60. *N&O*, 2 November 1947.

61. *N&O*, 11 January 1948.

without too much hope—for a curbing marital yoke for me—and continued to give me my head, swelled and muddled though it was." She recalled that she had enjoyed an unparalleled level of freedom as a columnist, despite the fact that her employer at the time of his death remained the last nationally known editor practicing personal journalism and continued to imbue every page of his newspaper with his character.[62]

Lewis's editorial did not mention the frustration and resentment that had occasionally also marked her relationship with the elderly editor and his sons. She begrudged the fact that the paper's management had reduced her salary after reviving her column in 1935. "I've finally got those 'friends of labor,' the Danielses, to put the pay for *Incidentally* back where it was before I was sick—after *ten* years," she complained to Kemp in 1945. Pride had made her conceal the fact that she sometimes lacked the financial means to pay her debts. "I certainly would never tell a Daniels that!" she bristled. That same year Lewis confessed to her middle brother that she never could read Josephus's commentary, "The Old Codger," which she regarded as "terrible tripe." She told Kemp that liberality alone did not account for her employer's support for her column. "He's a good newspaperman and knows that divergent views create readers' interest."[63]

In a letter written to an ardent fan who particularly admired the paranormal subject matter in "Incidentally," Lewis confessed that her column faced an uncertain future and that she regarded the new leadership of the *News and Observer* dubiously. "Frankly, I don't know what may happen to 'Incidentally,'" she vented. "I need tell you, in complete confidence, that none of Mr. Daniels's sons is in any way his equal and that Jonathan, who now edits the paper does not like me and, I think, would be glad to get rid of me." Lewis could only discern one way to proceed, to "go on as I have done for the past twenty-six years, writing the truth as I see it. The first word that any of the Daniels boys says to me as to how I should write the column, in view of their father's complete tolerance of my views, I shall construe as a request for my resignation, which will be immediately forthcoming." If she had to terminate her relationship with the newspaper, she felt sure some other publication would provide her with a venue for expression. She had never written "Incidentally" to satisfy any of the Danielses but only for the Lord, to whom she prayed "it might help in bringing in His kingdom."[64]

62. *N&O*, 16, 18 January 1948.

63. NBL to KPL, 22 January, 10 March, and 4 May 1945, all in KPL Papers.

64. NBL to Mrs. R. T. Whitley, [January? 1948], NBL Papers; *N&O*, 27 February 1938.

Lewis had to wait only two weeks to witness a major change at the *News and Observer.* Its new editor, knowing full well the animosity he would face, endorsed with few reservations Truman's request that Congress adopt many of the recommendations of his Committee on Civil Rights. The president surprised legislators by proposing in early February a ten-point human rights charter, which included provisions that would furnish federal protection against lynching, eliminate the poll tax and ensure fuller protections of voting rights, and prohibit discrimination in interstate travel. He also instructed his secretary of defense to end all prejudicial policies in the armed forces. Truman's civil rights program greatly exceeded all previous proposals designed to ensure minority rights.[65]

As southern representatives raged, Daniels glibly attempted to downplay the groundbreaking nature of the president's charter and to shield his friend Graham from even more invective. The most significant aspect of the proposals, in the editor's opinion, "was the complete disregard which [Truman] gave to the extreme recommendations of his Committee on Civil Rights, many of which would have been remedies worse than the disease. [This referred principally to the report's suggestion that the federal government withhold funds from states enforcing segregation laws.] Even when they were made they were accompanied by dissents from such a liberal Southern member of the committee as Dr. Frank Graham." Having, Daniels hoped, diminished passions somewhat, he stated that Roosevelt had favored similar policies and that Truman placed great faith in the ability of southern localities to resolve the "inequalities arising from segregation"—not that he had taken a seminal step toward eliminating racial separation.[66]

By today's standards Daniels's spinning, elision, and cautious praise of Truman's proposals hardly constitutes a powerful display of editorial courage, but he had nevertheless strained the levels of tolerance of most of his white readership. Harry Ashmore, who served as editorial page editor of the *Charlotte News* in the mid-1940s, recalled a half-century later, "You couldn't have stayed [in the South] and had any influence at all if you openly opposed segregation."[67]

Lewis authored an intensely sentimental response to Truman's racial charter. She devoted her entire 22 February column to a reminiscence about her

65. *N&O*, 3 February 1948; Egerton, *Speak Now against the Day*, 476; McCullough, *Truman*, 586–87; Eagles, *Jonathan Daniels and Race Relations*, 140–41.

66. *N&O*, 5 February 1948; Eagles, *Jonathan Daniels and Race Relations*, 138–39.

67. Egerton, *Speak Now against the Day*, 460–62; Harry S. Ashmore, *Civil Rights and Wrongs: A Memoir of Race and Politics, 1944–1994* (New York: Pantheon, 1994), 59–61.

family's long and affectionate ties to black servants and neighbors. "All the carrying-on about the President's civil rights program and the ugly possibilities for the South from heated controversy regarding it" provoked her nostalgia and made her pine for the harmonious racial relations that she believed had existed during her early years.[68]

Oberlin, a black settlement near Cloverdale, had housed many "uncles" and "aunts," who had worked for "Doc'r Lewis." No spot in that neighborhood had fascinated her more as a child than the nearby blacksmith's shop operated by "benign Uncle Willis." Nell recalled that her "mammy" and courteous and ladylike "Aunt Pinkin," who had meticulously polished the family's silver, came from the community. "Uncle Ed," the kind and devoted attendant to Dr. Lewis, also had lived there. In addition to employing many black servants and farmhands, her father, she recalled, had played an important role in the lives of Oberlin's upper class. Through his work at Shaw University he, along with his white peers in Raleigh's medical establishment, had trained many of Raleigh's black physicians. One of them still lived in an impressive brick house in the settlement. Her father's death had so upset these and other Oberlin residents that they had passed resolutions of respect for him. Nell and her brothers had cherished these eulogies.[69]

On 12 June the *Raleigh Times* announced that Lewis would join that newspaper as its new associate editor three days later. Publisher and editor John Park had hired her at a weekly salary of seventy dollars "with principal responsibility for the editorial page." No other woman in the state's history appears to have risen to so high a position at a daily paper.[70] The day following the statement in the *Times*, Lewis declared in "Incidentally" that she had written the last edition of her column. "It's a brutal parent," she conceded, "who slays an only child. But prepare yourself for such brutality, for today that's just what I'm getting ready to do." (In reality Lewis and her new employer had discussed the revival of her column in the fall and its possible syndication.) Although she emphasized that she and Daniels had parted on "completely amiable terms" and that he had afforded her complete editorial freedom, almost certainly their strained relationship and political differences had contributed to her decision

68. *N&O*, 22 February 1948.

69. *N&O*, 22 February 1948.

70. *RT*, 12 June and 3 July 1948; John A. Park to NBL, 9 June 1948, Virginius Dabney to NBL, 4 June 1948, both in NBL Papers.

to move just a short distance down West Martin Street to the smaller press to commence providing the *News and Observer* with its principal editorial competitor in Raleigh.[71]

That Sunday Daniels graciously bade Lewis good-bye. He admitted that "sometimes what she said [in 'Incidentally'] had only paper proximity" to the editorials his father and he had written, but nevertheless he found it a "sad task to say goodbye to Nell." He ended his farewell by putting Raleigh's residents on notice that a "lady who can work as well with a scalpel as a stylus is now at large in type six days a week." In their editorial pages Dabney and a number of his southern peers joined Daniels in celebrating Lewis's new appointment. "Newspaperwomen do not often become associate editors," the Richmonder remarked, "but there is no reason why they shouldn't, especially when they have the ability that Miss Lewis has shown. The *Raleigh News and Observer*'s loss is the *Times*' gain."[72]

Lewis undoubtedly relished her ability at the *Times* to weigh in with greater frequency on the increasingly contentious presidential race, especially the opportunity to lambaste Henry Wallace, the Progressive Party's soon-to-be presidential candidate. Upon arriving at her new job, she disparaged the size of the party's recent interracial turnout at Raleigh's Memorial Auditorium to attend a concert by Paul Robeson, the controversial black actor, singer, and activist. She predicted that the overwhelming number of Tar Heels would cast their votes for the Democrats or the Republicans, who had just nominated New York governor Thomas Dewey to head their ticket. Like many southern papers, the *Times* appraised Truman's likely nomination ambivalently and anticipated without great concern Dewey's almost certain victory.[73]

Since the president's introduction of his human rights charter, the region's proponents of racial traditionalism and states' rights—particularly in the Deep South—had angrily reassessed their ties to the Democratic Party and with increasing fervor contemplated a bolt. The president's nomination in mid-July by his party at its steamy and raucous Philadelphia convention, where the liberal wing emerged victorious with a staunch civil rights plank, instigated the storming out of all of Mississippi's and half of Alabama's delegates amid catcalls from other states' representatives.[74]

71. *N&O*, 13 June 1948.

72. *N&O*, 13 June 1948; *RT*, 3 July 1948.

73. *RT*, 23 and 25 June 1948; Egerton, *Speak Now against the Day*, 490–93, 504.

74. Egerton, *Speak Now against the Day*, 495–98.

The insurgents, joined by anyone else who wished to attend, assembled on 17 July in Birmingham's Municipal Auditorium, which ironically a decade earlier had served as the birthplace of the SCHW. As high-pitched rebel yells reverberated throughout the facility, the enthusiastic Dixiecrats waved Confederate flags and portraits of Robert E. Lee as they anointed South Carolina governor James Strom Thurmond to head their party. In his acceptance speech the ambitious former paratrooper elated the delegates by proclaiming that there were "not enough troops in the Army to force the southern people to break down segregation and admit the Negro race into our theaters, into our swimming pools, into schools and into our homes." Although Thurmond claimed that a broad concern regarding the intrusion of the federal government on states' rights motivated his candidacy, the incendiary racism advanced by other speakers had earlier led to a decision by the American Broadcasting Company to switch off its cameras.[75]

In a series of editorials that summer Lewis welcomed the entry of the Dixiecrats into the race. The *Times* explained that the "indignation" felt by many southerners regarding the flouting of states' rights at the Philadelphia convention had justifiably given rise to the new party. Although North Carolinians generally remained lukewarm to the Dixiecrats, Lewis favored the new party's attempt to supplant the Democrats. The states' righters, she said, had registered as Democrats without knowing the "South would be kicked in the teeth at Philadelphia by the big city Northern bosses et al." Thurmond's supporters had not betrayed a "principle that has been a cardinal one of the Democratic Party since its formation": to forswear "panting after the Negro vote in the cities of the North."[76]

As Wallace and the Progressives gathered for their convention in Philadelphia in late July, Lewis, in a lead editorial entitled "Warning Hereby Given to 'Red Hank' Wallace," vilified them "as the "briefest of political ephemerae—for instance, like those insects—poisonous, some of them, maybe?—whose life-span is just a day." She continued her diatribe by addressing her bête noire directly and threateningly: "But the good die young, Henry—so it looks as if there's a paradox somewhere. Still, you're a 'do-gooder,' aren't you, 'Red Hank?' As we understand it, you're all set to save us. Salvation is comparatively a simple matter, isn't it, Hank, when you have the right backing? It's been ef-

75. Kari Frederickson, *The Dixiecrat Revolt and the End of the Solid South, 1932–1968* (Chapel Hill: University of North Carolina Press, 2001), 51, 100–102, 130–42.

76. *RT*, 2, 9, and 12 August 1948; Frederickson, *Dixiecrat Revolt*, 146–47.

fected recently in several other countries, hasn't it? And you have the right backing, haven't you? Peace on earth; goodwill to the Rooshians—it's wonderful." The prominent role played by communists at the convention and the later endorsement of Wallace's candidacy by the CPUSA undoubtedly intensified the new associate editor's animosity toward the Iowan.[77]

With this editorial Battling Nell completed her political metamorphosis from the liberal reformer of her youth into a reactionary defender of the "southern way of life." One could easily imagine her harangue emanating from the *Gastonia Gazette* twenty years earlier. Indeed, her choice of imagery and her ominous tone evoked the mill town paper's printing of "A Viper That Must Be Smashed!" its cartoon portraying Beal and his fellow union organizers as a poisonous snake coiled around Old Glory. "COMMUNISM IN THE SOUTH—KILL IT," the illustration's caption had read. As the *Gazette* had provoked violence, Lewis's anti-Wallace editorials and those written by her peers in the southern press undoubtedly helped lay the groundwork for the savage reception Wallace encountered beginning the next month on his campaign tour of more than twenty cities in six southern states. Red-baiting by Dixie newspapers and their attacks on his racial progressivism, exemplified by his courageous and incendiary decisions to speak only to nonsegregated audiences and to boycott whites-only hotels during his excursion, fueled hostility and violence. North Carolina, renowned as the most liberal southern state, subjected the presidential candidate to far and away the most appalling display of viciousness.[78]

The day before Wallace's 29 August speech in nearby Durham, Lewis made much of his canceling his reservations to stay at the city's premiere hotel, the stately sixteen-story Washington Duke, and the decision by a number of white members of his staff to obtain lodging at a black facility in the city. "This cheap publicity stunt which can do nothing but stir up prejudice," she predicted, "will be regretted as much by the substantial and responsible Negroes of North Carolina as by the whites who wish to see the relations of the two races which, heretofore, have been exceptionally good in this State, remain so." Black Tar Heels had never been "troublemakers" and had displayed great patience in "trying to solve the tremendous problems that inter-racial relations present." They knew that they should keep their distance from "fanatical demagogues . . . stirring up hate and bitterness" in the South. She felt confi-

77. *RT*, 23 July 1948; Powers, *Not without Honor*, 202–3; Haynes, *Red Scare or Red Menace?* 130–31; Egerton, *Speak Now against the Day*, 501.

78. *GG*, 11 April 1929; *NYT*, 16, 31 August 1948; *WP*, 28 August 1948.

dent that when "Wallace and his cohorts attempt to break down segregation with one blow of Moscow's hammer and cut down the plant of inter-racial friendship with one stroke of Moscow's sickle, they will be regarded with disgust by the best North Carolina Negroes and whites alike."[79]

Outside the Durham Armory the next evening twenty white anti-Wallace pickets carried signs reading SEND WALLACE BACK TO RUSSIA, WE DON'T HAVE RACE PROBLEMS HERE, and WALLACE— ALLIGATOR BAIT. This group soon pushed its way into the armory to join a much larger number of hostile audience members. Notified of the trouble brewing, Wallace's party attempted without success to gain a police escort to the venue. When the delegation arrived, it managed to persuade one of the ten National Guardsmen at the site to escort the controversial presidential candidate to the stage. The sergeant drew his sidearm and led Wallace to his speaking place. "This is the most unique introduction I have ever experienced," the Iowan began. The audience heard little else of the speech he attempted to deliver for the next quarter-hour. Hecklers shouted him down, threw eggs, and set off firecrackers. A hoodlum stabbed a University of North Carolina student serving as a bodyguard twice in the arm and six times in the back.[80]

Not unexpectedly, Wallace faced only minor heckling when he spoke at Chapel Hill the next morning, but in the nearby hosiery town of Burlington the candidate's interracial caravan encountered a crowd variously estimated at five hundred to several thousand residents—most of them hostile—milling around the public square. Hooligans climbed on the arriving automobiles and rocked them back and forth. As Wallace and an aide stepped from their Hudson, eggs and tomatoes hit them. A fistfight broke out in the crowd. The mob shouted, "Get your Communists and niggers out of this town," and menacingly pressed in on Wallace. When he attempted to speak, the rabble bellowed and interrupted him. One man lifted to his shoulders his young son, who proceeded from this vantage point to throw objects at the delegation. Wallace's temper flared only once when he pulled an angry bystander to him and asked him three times, "Am I in America?"[81]

As the day wore on, Wallace met with similar receptions in Greensboro, High Point, and Winston-Salem. The next day he boarded a train for Deca-

79. *RT*, 28 August 1948.

80. Curtis D. MacDougall, *Gideon's Army*, vol. 3: *The Campaign and the Vote* (New York: Marzani & Munsell, 1965), 707–9; *NYT*, 31 August 1948; *WP*, 31 August 1948.

81. MacDougall, *Gideon's Army*, 3:711–12; *NYT*, 31 August 1948; *WP*, 31 August 1948.

tur and departed the state. He would face plenty of animosity throughout the remainder of his southern tour, but the venom and thuggery he encountered would not rise to the level he had endured in North Carolina. Although the *New York Times* reported that Truman very vigorously denounced the "acts of rowdyism throughout [the state] against Henry A. Wallace . . . as 'a highly un-American business' and as violating the national spirit of fair play," Lewis and many southern editorialists did not criticize the disorder.[82]

Lewis's newspaper appears not to have formally endorsed a presidential candidate, but it strongly commended Thurmond. The defeat of the Confederacy, she insisted, most certainly did not obviate the states' rights the insurgent wielded to rebuff Truman's racial program. She agreed with her fellow Carolinian's statement that the president's proposal "would make radical changes in the American way of life which can only lead to violence, lawlessness, and widespread racial discord." She knew that when the Dixiecrat leader came to her hometown, the many citizens of her state who shared his beliefs would stand their ground, as had the Tar Heel Confederates, and provide him with an enthusiastic welcome. Readers knowing nothing of Lewis's apostasy and transformation would have blinked in wonderment upon learning that twenty years earlier the author of this editorial had in scores of columns and magazine articles joyfully lampooned boosters, members of patriotic societies glorifying the Lost Cause, and states' righters seeking to impede social justice.[83]

Truman's victory, in November 1948, stoked by "Give 'em hell Harry's" 355-speech whistle-stop flaying of the "do-nothing 80th Congress," undoubtedly dumbfounded Lewis to the same degree that it did her fourth estate peers and the general public. The Dixiecrat revolt of four southern states—Alabama, Louisiana, Mississippi, and South Carolina—belied the traditional southern solidarity of the Democratic Party and revealed the widening fissure between the party and whites in the region's counties with high concentrations of blacks. Within the eleven states indisputably regarded as southern, North Carolina voters cast the smallest percentage of their ballots for Thurmond.[84]

82. *NYT*, 31 August and 1 September 1948; *WP*, 31 August 1948; *RT*, 3 September 1948; MacDougall, *Gideon's Army*, 3:712–20.

83. *RT*, 5 October 1948.

84. Robert A. Garson, *The Democratic Party and the Politics of Sectionalism, 1941–1948* (Baton Rouge: Louisiana State University Press, 1974), 310–14; Egerton, *Speak Now against the Day*, 508–10; Frederickson, *Dixiecrat Revolt*, 184; Key, *Southern Politics in State and Nation*, 342–44.

Henry Wallace's national showing matched the Dixiecrats' at slightly less than 2.5 percent. In North Carolina fewer than four thousand voters cast their ballots for the Progressive Party candidate. The *Daily Worker* expressed its disappointment over the poor showing of Wallace, whose supporters *Pravda*, the organ of the Soviet Communist Party, hailed as "the flower" of the United States. The always disjointed SCHW, which had further divided itself over whether to support Wallace's candidacy, soon disbanded.[85]

Coincidentally with the election, Lewis resigned her position because of "ill health." She had lasted just five months at the *Times*, where she and Park had enjoyed friendly relations and shared the same politics. Since making her bold and surprising decision to end her long association with the *News and Observer* and join Raleigh's afternoon paper, she had shown abundant initiative and energy in producing an outpouring of editorial comment—much of it passionate—on the turbulent presidential election.[86]

Little documentation sheds light on the nature of her illness, but the few clues that exist suggest another bout of severe depression that matched almost perfectly the one Lewis had undergone fifteen years earlier. In the wake of her resignation she ceased writing, ended her regular reading of newspapers and magazines, and grew anxious about her finances, especially the possibility of defaulting on her mortgage and becoming dependent on her brothers. Ivey and Kemp had long ago given up on the possibility of recovering from their sister any payment of the nearly ten thousand dollars they had expended many years earlier to purchase her home. The Lewis males, who remained characteristically solicitous of Nell, had let their notes lapse and could no longer legally collect on their investment.[87]

By late August 1949, despite her residence in Chapel Hill, where the no-nonsense Mary Manning again oversaw Nell's convalescence, she had not yet recovered. Kemp wrote to his sister at this time in a letter reminiscent of the countless ones he had written to her during her previous debilitating collapse. He protectively attempted to assuage her financial concerns and expressed

85. *NYT*, 7 November 1948; "1948 Presidential Election Results" (cited 12 June 2007), www.uselectionatlas.org/RESULTS/national.php?f=0&year=1948; Krueger, *And Promises to Keep*, 186.

86. *N&O*, 1 January 1950; 25 March 1956; "Some Saint Mary's Alumnae of Note," *Saint Mary's School Bulletin* (June 1953): 41; "Nell Battle Lewis, 1911," Nell Battle Lewis Papers, Saint Mary's School Archives.

87. KPL to NBL, 23 August 1949, NBL Papers; *N&O*, 13 August 1950.

his "satisfaction that you are coming through in excellent shape." The tone of her voice during a telephone conversation the previous day, he told her, had "thrilled" him. The false optimism her brother conveyed almost certainly masked his deep concern over the prospects of her recovery.[88]

88. KPL to NBL, 23 August 1949, NBL Papers.

# 9 FANNING THE FLAMES

"Hark from the Tomb," Lewis entitled her resurrection of "Incidentally" in the *News and Observer* on New Year's Day at the century's midpoint. Despite their often flinty relationship, Jonathan Daniels had expressed to her the previous spring his willingness to renew his publication of her column. From Chapel Hill in December she notified the editor that her health had improved to the point that she could begin writing again. Although it undoubtedly galled Lewis that the restoration of her journalistic career relied heavily on Daniels's largesse and that he would exercise ultimate supervision over her column, she had few options. Her experience at the *Times* had emphasized her frailty and her incapacity to practice rigorous journalism on a daily basis, and previous attempts to interest other newspapers in "Incidentally" had failed.[1]

Daniels surely lacked the affection his father had felt for Lewis, but the ties their two families shared perhaps influenced somewhat his decision to renew her column. More important, however, Lewis attracted conservative readers to the paper and provided the highly partisan liberal sheet with at least some semblance of balance. Daniels had faced no shortage of criticism for his support for Truman's civil rights program and his antipathy to demagogic politicians seeking to exploit the Cold War. Possibly he permitted the return of "Incidentally" to reduce complaints from subscribers and legislators regarding his editorial high-handedness and his progressive views. Daniels knew that Lewis would at times exasperate him and that her views would often not coincide with his. After expressing her delight over returning to her old paper and sharing with her readers how much she had missed surrendering her byline when she had joined the *Raleigh Times*—"my narcissism just couldn't stand the anonymity of editorial writing"—she proceeded to tweak Frank Graham and, by extension, her editor.[2]

The previous March, North Carolina governor W. Kerr Scott, an economic progressive and racial moderate, had at the behest of his wife and Daniels be-

1. *N&O*, 4 September 1932, 1 January 1950; NBL to Jonathan Daniels, 6 December 1949, Jonathan Daniels to NBL, 10 December 1949, both in JD papers.

2. *N&O*, 1 January 1950.

gun to consider Graham to replace the recently deceased Senator J. Melville Broughton. For eleven days Daniels and Scott lobbied the university president, who repeatedly accepted and declined the position. In the end Graham found it impossible to withstand the frustrated editor's call to service. "Your state, your country, your commander-in-chief need you there," he demanded, banging the Grahams' dining room table as the populist cigar-smoking governor looked on.[3] As Graham, conflicted over his irrevocable break with the university, packed his office, he paused to gaze out the window, which looked over the campus. "I'm leaving here now, and I carry a lot of scars," he remarked pensively in an unusual moment of personal candor.[4]

An ultra-conservative contingency of Graham's soon-to-be colleagues wasted no time in inflicting another wound upon him. Ohio Senator John W. Bricker, the *New York Times* reported, threw the body "into heated controversy" the day following the announcement by demanding from the floor of the Capitol an investigation of Graham. Bricker referred to a dispute regarding whether Graham posed a risk to the nation's security. A year and a half after Nell Lewis's attack on her former liberal ally in the summer of 1947, conservative radio commentator Fulton Lewis Jr. had uncovered discord within the Atomic Energy Commission regarding the academic leader's suitability to serve as the first president and chairman of the board of the Oak Ridge Institute of Nuclear Studies. The commission had ignored its security board's objections to providing Graham with complete access to atomic secrets and subsequently awarded him full clearance.[5]

By the time of Lewis's latest editorial revival the clamor regarding the appointment of Graham had subsided, and he had begun to build during his ten months in the Senate a reputation for thoughtfulness, eloquence, and collegiality. Although he supported much of Truman's agenda, including many aspects of his civil rights program, Graham's opposition to affording compulsory powers to a proposed permanent federal Fair Employment Practices Commission (FEPC) surprised many of his northern admirers. More knowledgeable observers of the new senator, however, saw his stance as entirely consistent

3. Powell, *North Carolina through Four Centuries*, 514–15; Julian M. Pleasants and Augustus M. Burns III, *Frank Porter Graham and the 1950 Senate Race in North Carolina* (Chapel Hill: University of North Carolina Press, 1990), 243–44; *N&O*, 8 January 1950.

4. Ehle, *Dr. Frank*, 150.

5. *NYT*, 24 March 1949; *WP*, 24 March 1949; Ashby, *Frank Porter Graham*, 237–38.

with the brief minority report he had authored for *To Secure These Rights*, in which he had favored the elimination of segregation but had opposed the use of federal sanctions to meet this goal.[6]

When reporters asked the North Carolinian what his friend Truman would think of Graham's incomplete support, he replied, "I don't think he is going to like it." Although the senator's stand on the FEPC frustrated the president and many liberals, his declaration that he would not participate in the probable filibuster on the bill rankled virtually all of his southern peers, including Hoey. The *News and Observer* reported that the senior Tar Heel senator, who intended to obstruct the "unfair and vicious" legislation, felt certain that if it reached the floor, it would pass. As a matter of principle, Graham believed that parliamentary maneuvers should not be allowed to prevent votes on any issue. "Graham is turning into a Washington paradox," the paper concluded: "He can't be counted upon doing anything that he sincerely doesn't believe to be right, certainly a new approach to politics on Capitol Hill."[7]

The odd pairing of the Tar Heel senatorial duo provided much of the grist for Lewis's "Hark from the Tomb." She used one of her father's favorite stories to analogize the relationship between Graham and Hoey. Dr. Lewis enjoyed telling the tale of a farmer who had lost his plow horse. To get his planting done, he improvised by harnessing himself to a small male cow he owned. The animal proceeded to drag the farmer to many unintended environs. "I trust that the Frankolaters (pronounced like idolaters) will forgive me," the columnist taunted, "when I say that these days Senator Hoey seems to me not unlike the man hitched up with that little steer. Forgive me, excuse me, do! No offense, no offense at all, really!" With her mocking editorial Lewis signaled to her readers and editor that her hiatus had not reduced her antagonism toward the personification of southern liberalism.[8]

Without question many of the *News and Observer*'s readers welcomed the revival of *Incidentally* and its aggressive defense of the southern way of life. With the violent postwar backlash directed toward the Communist Party, USA (CPUSA) furnishing a catalyst, an ever-expanding number of rank-and-file residents of Dixie demonstrated their intensified opposition to the targets of Lewis's midcentury editorials: the NAACP and proponents of Truman's racial

6. Pleasants and Burns, *Frank Porter Graham*, 56–57; President's Committee on Civil Rights, *To Secure These Rights*, 166–67; *N&O*, 8 January 1950.

7. Pleasants and Burns, *Frank Porter Graham*, 57; *N&O*, 8 January 1950.

8. *N&O*, 1 January 1950.

policies, leftist unions, and progressives attempting to bring social and economic justice to the South.

Although the columnist would intermittently continue to link these organizations and individuals to a potent domestic communist conspiracy, the CPUSA was nearing collapse. Many internal as well as external factors accounted for its decline, including the American public's growing conservativeness and fearfulness of an aggressive and expansionistic Cold War foe equipped via espionage with secrets to the atomic bomb, the demoralization of leftists after Henry Wallace's trouncing in the recent presidential election, the conviction of many Party leaders under the Smith Act's sedition section, FBI infiltration of the organization, and its continued alienating obsequiousness to the Soviet Union. In this hostile environment the CPUSA turned on itself and purged a third of its membership (including large numbers of homosexuals and bisexuals), deemed inadequate to face the impending struggle for existence. Those who remained readied themselves to join various layers, including underground and overseas levels designed to function throughout the crisis and rebuild the Party should authorities outlaw it.[9]

Reeling from the increasing success of R. J. Reynolds in enervating Winston-Salem's radical Local 22 by laying off black workers, hiring whites from surrounding counties, and exploiting the charged racial and political postwar environment (the local would in 1950 lose a close National Labor Relations Board election) and from the demise of the Southern Conference for Human Welfare, North Carolina's beleaguered communists struggled in the face of intense enmity to eke out a victory. As Junius Scales, chairman of the Carolinas District of the Communist Party, prepared himself to assume the OBU (operational but unavailable) leadership status he would soon adopt, he and his comrades in the late 1940s turned their eyes toward Durham's Erwin Mills in an audacious but impractical attempt to supplant the large Textile Workers Union of America (TWUA) local that represented workers there.[10]

Working with a "handful of students and ex-students"—presumably some from the University of North Carolina—Scales researched the company, whose board of directors Kemp Lewis chaired. (Upon resigning his presidency of the mills in 1948, Kemp had created and assumed the chairmanship.) Several stu-

9. Buhle, Buhle, and Georgakas, *Encyclopedia of the American Left*, 152–53, 636–37, 755–56; Scales and Nickson, *Cause at Heart*, 217–24; Haynes, *Red Scare or Red Menace*, 163–82.

10. Korstad and Nelson, "Opportunities Found and Lost," 801–4; Krueger, *And Promises to Keep*, 191; Scales and Nickson, *Cause at Heart*, 231, 244.

dents obtained jobs at Erwin and established contact with militant workers discontented with the moderate TWUA. The presence of communist organizers within the business to which he had devoted his entire professional life did not escape Kemp's attention. Company spies and FBI informants infiltrated the "Erwin Mills textile club," which began in 1949 to publish and distribute within the factory a mimeographed newspaper that mocked the company's executives and union leaders and lauded the Soviet Union and its role in spreading peace throughout the world.[11]

While Lewis prepared "Hark from the Tomb," Eleanor Roosevelt and Daniels exchanged letters regarding Graham. The former first lady had heard rumors that her friend would face opposition in May's Democratic primary, which in the largely one-party state would determine whether the two Tar Heel members of the Upper House would continue their federal service.[12] According to historians Julian M. Pleasants and Augustus M. Burns III, who closely studied the 1950 Senate race in North Carolina, Daniels, through his essential role in selecting Graham, had signaled his intention to transcend his position as a journalist and author and become "a mover and a shaker—a politico." The former academic leader's "success in the Senate would now become, in some degree, Daniels's success." His impressive Washington résumé, which included stints as press secretary to presidents Roosevelt and Truman, afforded him extensive access to national leaders. Then nearing completion of a biography of the nation's chief executive, Daniels corresponded on a frequent basis with the White House's present occupant.[13]

Daniels informed Mrs. Roosevelt that his candidate would prevail, barring a particularly vicious contest. "The only danger we face," he conjectured, "is that Frank may be put in a difficult position in connection with the civil rights program of the President." Graham would retain his seat unless a "horrible nigger-Communist campaign" emerged. He requested that when the former first lady came to Chapel Hill in late January to deliver a series of talks on the United Nations as part of the Weil Lecture on American Citizenship—which the family of feminist and reformer Gertrude Weil had endowed—she highlight Graham's support for the international organization and world peace.[14]

11. Scales and Nickson, *Cause at Heart,* 244–45, 275; "Biographical Note," KPL Papers.

12. Eleanor Roosevelt to Jonathan Daniels, 20 December 1949, 7 January 1950, Jonathan Daniels to Eleanor Roosevelt, 27 December 1949, both in JD papers.

13. Pleasants and Burns, *Frank Porter Graham,* 17; Jonathan Daniels to Harry S. Truman, 14 January 1950, JD papers.

14. Jonathan Daniels to Eleanor Roosevelt, 27 December 1949, JD papers.

The Senate primary that winter developed within a context publicized by the *News and Observer* and its state peers as they persistently broadcast heady news events centering on race and Russian espionage: Truman pressed Congress hard to pass his civil rights program, which included his FEPC bill; Senator Joseph McCarthy brandished (but did not release) a list of communists employed by the State Department; J. Edgar Hoover charged that British scientist Klaus Fuchs had revealed portions of the design of the atomic and hydrogen bombs to the Soviet Union; and, largely on the basis of testimony of onetime Soviet spy Whitaker Chambers, a jury convicted former State Department official Alger Hiss—who allegedly had functioned as a communist agent—of perjury.[15]

Tar Heel newspapers also informed their audiences that racial activism and the Cold War would in accelerated form affect local conditions and perhaps their daily lives. Black students had begun a lawsuit to gain admission to Chapel Hill's law school, and the trustees redoubled their efforts to crack down on communists within the academic community. In this atmosphere millionaire alumnus Gordon Gray accepted in early February the presidency of the Consolidated University of North Carolina. Despite his heirship to the R. J. Reynolds fortune, Gray had recently dedicated himself to public service, as illustrated by his present duty as secretary of the army. The sizable contingency of trustees estranged by Graham's activism and unwavering defense of civil liberties rejoiced in the selection of the new leader. As the university's acting president announced Gray's appointment, he assured the trustees that only a court decision or an act of the general assembly would enable blacks to attend the university and that careful vetting prevented the hiring of new faculty members with communist sympathies. In "A Capitalist for Chapel Hill" Lewis voiced her satisfaction—no matter "what the Comrades think of it"—over the appointment.[16]

The decision by conservative corporate attorney Willis Smith in late February to run against Graham provided him with serious and well-financed competition and transformed the Senate race into a major news story. Smith claimed he had received hundreds of letters and telephone calls urging his candidacy and believed that "the majority of North Carolinians are not in favor of all the things our present incumbent Senator Graham stands for."[17] By the end of March the tenor of the race had become clear. *U.S. News & World*

15. *N&O,* 18 and 27 January, 4 and 14 February 1950.

16. *N&O,* 29 January and 7 February 1950; Snider, *Light on the Hill,* 238–41.

17. *N&O,* 18 and 25 February 1950.

*Report* revealed that clownish former senator Robert Reynolds also planned to crusade against Graham with signature color and negativism. He proposed to drive a red car and wear a matching suit as he stumped the state playing recordings of the "Internationale."[18]

While not yet mentioning Graham by name, Smith's platform tarred him indirectly and made generous use of charged language. In this document the corporate attorney identified little of what he stood for, although he made clear that he objected to a great deal: "I am opposed to socialistic and communistic trends in government, and likewise opposed to the employment of Socialists or Communists in our governmental departments, either State or National. I am equally opposed to those holding high office who condone such employment or give aid, encouragement and comfort to Socialists, Communists, and their sympathizers and fellow travelers." North Carolinians quickly found themselves surrounded by seemingly countless placards, posters, and buttons proclaiming, "Mr. Smith Is Going to Washington."[19]

The attacks by Graham's opponents placed him on the defensive. He responded by paying homage to free enterprise, underscoring his history of fighting all forms of totalitarianism, and deploring the big lie. "The basic assumption behind Nazi and Communist propaganda tricks is that if a falsehood is big enough and is repeated often enough, some people will start to believe it," he told an audience in the Piedmont town of Dunn. "Tonight I want to answer a falsehood that has been repeated over and over again about me. I have never been, am not now, and never will be a Communist or a Socialist, or a member or supporter of any organization known or suspected by me of being controlled by Communists or Socialists."[20]

Although the negativity and unanticipated closeness of the race alarmed Daniels, Nell Lewis gleefully looked forward to a battle royal. In "A Hot Time in the Old State This Spring," the lead editorial in her final column for March, she could hardly restrain her merriment: "Altogether, the outlook is a very happy one. Most fitting, indeed, that here where, as in all Dixie, politics has always been a major diversion, with the rising sap of Spring there should come this freshening excitement of what looks to be a socko-battle. I'm charmed by the prospect—charmed!"[21]

18. *N&O*, 12 March 1950.

19. *N&O*,14 and 22 March 1950.

20. *N&O*, 27 March 1950.

21. *N&O*, 26 March 1950.

In the waning days of March Daniels's editorials attempted to confute the charges leveled at his candidate. Clearly rattled, he stressed that Graham, like Reynolds and Smith, opposed the FEPC bill. The editor emphasized that in *To Secure These Rights* the future senator had made his dissent to federal sanctions "as clear as type and ink could make it." The sole purpose of the challengers' harping on the FEPC measure "would appear to be an effort to stir the furies of racial prejudice as a means of getting votes." Daniels said he had anticipated that Reynolds would stoop to this level, but the editor expressed amazement that a "gentleman" such as Smith, who before entering the contest had never exploited racial issues, would seek an advantage by instilling distrust between blacks and whites. The *News and Observer* also deplored the red-baiting of Graham "by direct charge or innuendo."[22]

Lewis, however—who had begun to regard herself as the Raleigh paper's only journalist with the courage to confront Daniels—made clear in her first "Incidentally" of April that, regardless of her employer's editorial admonition, she had no intention of downplaying the aid and comfort she believed Graham had provided Moscow. In "Replying to Yours of 1947 . . ." she showed that she had not forgotten the slight she had suffered when the university president had refused three years earlier to respond to her goading.[23]

No one in North Carolina had attended more closely to the senator's speech in Dunn than she, Lewis contended. As a result of the tightening race and to curry favor with the electorate, Graham at last had provided some of the answers she had sought so long ago. She rehashed the numerous "earnest interrogations" she had directed at him in the summer of 1947. In her testimony before HUAC Anne Matthews had raised serious questions about the Communist infiltration directed by Junius Scales at the state's foremost university. Surely the institution's administration owed the taxpayers an explanation of the dangerous situation. Graham, nevertheless, had decided that Lewis's inquiries "were beneath his notice" and maintained a "clam-like silence." Only the senator's anxiety about his prospects in the primary accounted for his long overdue clarification of his stance on communism. "Mr. Mollusk is mute no more!" she chortled.[24]

Lewis's editorial may have triggered the long-aborning explosion that occurred between her and Daniels around this time. Perhaps the columnist

22. *N&O*, 24 and 27 March 1950; Eagles, *Jonathan Daniels and Race Relations*, 148–49.

23. *N&O*, 2 April 1950; NBL to IFL, [April?] 1954, NBL Papers.

24. *N&O*, 2 April 1950.

sought to expand "Replying to Yours of 1947 . . ." into a crusade similar to her earlier attack on Graham. If so, Daniels may have decided to limit her autonomy. Sam Ragan, who after Frank Smethurst's death in 1941 had become the paper's managing editor, witnessed a public outburst in the newsroom in which Lewis screamed at Daniels, "I hope all your children have nigger babies." This imprecation undoubtedly seemed particularly vile in light of the fact that the four Daniels children were girls and that the violation of "southern womanhood" by black men contravened Jim Crow's most powerful dictum. The paucity of commentary on the election in "Incidentally" after early April—despite Lewis's fiery backing for Smith—suggests that Daniels in fact exerted his authority at this time.[25]

Several weeks later venerable feminist, labor, and racial activist Gertrude Weil, who, after trailblazing attendance at Smith College for her Tar Heel sisters, had left her fingerprints on virtually every progressive social measure that had earned her native state its reputation for liberality, administered a scolding to Lewis for her "vitriolic blast" directed at Graham. Weil remarked on the irony of Lewis's having begun her Easter column on 9 April with a quotation from the conclusion of George Bernard Shaw's *Saint Joan,* "O God that madest this beautiful earth, when will it be ready to receive Thy saints?"[26]

The malicious treatment of Graham the previous week in "Replying to Yours of 1947 . . ." had reminded Weil of the famous play, and she struggled to recall Joan's final lines before the English burned her at the stake. Lewis's Easter column, the seventy-year-old reformer claimed, had serendipitously furnished her with the precise wording. The doyenne of the state's organized women conveyed her amazement that Lewis had assumed the role of inquisitor. "Considering in retrospect what you used to stand for in the early stages of your writing," Weil remarked disappointedly, "it seems incredible that it can be you who are now lighting the fagots."[27]

In "Just an Old Medieval Fagot-Lighter!"—Lewis's lead editorial in her 23 April column—she printed Weil's chastisement and ended it with an aside for her readers: "So now, dearly beloved brethren, when you see attached to my name the letters of my new dishonorable degree you'll know what they

25. William S. Powell, *North Carolina Lives: The Tar Heel Who's Who* (Hopkinsville, Ky.: Historical Record Association, 1962), 1014; Pleasants and Burns, *Frank Porter Graham,* 117–18.

26. *N&O,* 23 April 1950, "Gertrude Weil, 1879–1971" (cited 18 June 2007), www.jwa.org/exhibits/wov/weil/over.html.

27. *N&O,* 23 April 1950.

mean: N. B. Lewis, F-L." Although Weil had provided a role model for Lewis after her return from France and throughout her liberal heyday, the columnist evinced no chagrin for her apostasy in the curt response she provided in "Incidentally"—"Dear Miss Gertrude: As to the 'incredibility' of my 'lighting the fagots,' I should certainly blush with shame to think that years and experience had brought no changes in the point of view of that ill-informed and naive ass who wrote 'Incidentally' in the 1920's. Best wishes."[28]

In May race moved increasingly into the forefront of the contest. Smith forces apparently considered making general use of previously privately circulated leaflets that had implied that Graham's liberal racial views would encourage "crossing the color line." These handbills pictured black soldiers dancing with white women in London during World War II. "Look before you vote," the text read, "and remember these persons could be your sisters or daughters under such an educational program as Graham advocates. THINK. Your decisions today will reflect in the faces of our children in the generation to come." (The disclosure by Graham operatives on 12 May that Smith enthusiasts intended to distribute this material en masse shortly before the election may have preempted the ruse.) At the same time, an unidentified party in New York City mailed to hundreds of Tar Heels postcards that seemed upon cursory inspection to have originated from the NAACP's executive secretary, Walter White. "Your vote and active support of Senator Frank Graham in the North Carolina primary . . . will be greatly appreciated," the appeal declared. Knowledgeable recipients quickly discerned the fraud when they noticed that "W. Wite" of the "National Society for the Advancement of Colored People" had sent the cards.[29]

Many voters saw through overt trickery such as this, but demagoguery exploiting an episode of Graham's racial fairness undoubtedly swayed constituents. His naming of a young black man as an alternate appointee to West Point infuriated a large percentage of the electorate. To select the most qualified applicants impartially, the senator had subjected aspirants to a civil service examination. A student at Saint Augustine's College had earned one of the top scores on the test, and Graham designated him the second alternate. Despite the fact that a white student served as the senator's first choice and, after passing an army physical, enrolled in the academy, many North Caro-

28. *N&O*, 23 April 1950.

29. *N&O*, 12 and 24 May 1950; Ashby, *Frank Porter Graham*, 262; Pleasants and Burns, *Frank Porter Graham*, 171–76.

linians seethed over the incident. A handbill circulating throughout the state the month of the election featuring a picture of the black alternate, whose hair the distributors retouched to appear particularly kinky, capitalized on the outrage felt by racial traditionalists. "This is what Frank Graham appointed to West Point," the caption read.[30]

Lewis perhaps obliquely referred to her apparent muzzling in "No Holy War," which appeared in the 7 May installment of "Incidentally." "As the campaign gains momentum and the slugging on both sides gets heavier," she remarked, "I confess I find the side-line seat which I now occupy a bit binding, much less exhilarating than the hustings upon which in 1928 I charged around in behalf of the then-current 'liberalism'—which meant the vain attempt to elect a member of the Roman Church as President of the United States." Many of her readers undoubtedly inferred from her editorial that her highly partisan editor had at long last exercised his prerogative to rein in his conservative and ultra-combative columnist.[31]

Daniels, who found himself embroiled in the political and journalistic fight of his life, displayed none of his columnist's newfound moderation. A week before the balloting, he printed in the Sunday *News and Observer* "Sound the 'Tocsin,'" the definitive editorial of his crusade. He knew that many readers might not know the meaning of the final word in the caption he had chosen, and he explained that it meant an alarm signal and that his father had frequently used the term.[32]

"His paper stands squarely by Frank Graham now," Jonathan Daniels declared.

> The voters of North Carolina have never had a chance to vote for a finer, cleaner, more Christian and more patriotic Democrat than Frank Graham. Yet such a man, in words which fall like a confession from the lips of one of the candidates against him, has been attacked and vilified by "the mean, the little and the vicious." He has been subjected in a Democratic primary to all the prefabricated smears of the Republicans used by a candidate who has denounced the national program of the Democratic party, whose nomination he seeks, as "socialism." The attacks on Frank Graham have turned this primary from an election

30. Pleasants and Burns, *Frank Porter Graham*, 175–78.
31. *N&O*, 7 May 1950.
32. Pleasants and Burns, *Frank Porter Graham*, 180; *N&O*, 21 May 1950.

> into an assault on decency, character and service in North Carolina. It is time for the "tocsin" of Democratic decency to ring across North Carolina.[33]

"Graham High Man in Senate Race," a *News and Observer* banner headline proclaimed triumphantly on 28 May. The incumbent had garnered nearly 49 percent of the total and had bested Smith by fifty-three thousand votes, nearly the number of ballots cast for Reynolds. The newspaper observed that the heady election had prompted a record turnout and had broken with the past in several other important respects. For the first time in the state's modern history a candidate had injected the "Negro question" into a Democratic primary, and never before in North Carolina had a contender for a top office labeled his opponent a "Communist dupe."[34]

A tense waiting period transpired for more than a week as Smith considered exercising the prerogative that existed within North Carolina for a second-place finisher in a race with more than two candidates to call for a runoff election when a winner had garnered less than a majority of the votes. Having expended his war chest, the challenger seemed disinclined to mount another contest after the drubbing he had suffered. Lewis, however, wasted no time in conveying her hope to Smith that he would continue his candidacy. Two days after the election she wrote to him to urge that he press on if he believed he stood any chance at all of prevailing. He offered a safe and reasonable alternative to Graham, she maintained.[35]

The runoff seemed increasingly unlikely until the Supreme Court issued three unanimous high-profile racial decisions on 5 June. In *Henderson v. United States* the federal government, represented by the attorney general and siding with black plaintiffs, persuaded the Court of the unconstitutionality of the de jure segregation that existed on southern dining cars. *Sweatt v. Painter* posed an even more dire threat to *Plessy*. The NAACP's Thurgood Marshall convinced the Court that a newly created law school for blacks in Houston in no way equaled the program in Austin at the University of Texas. In his argument Marshall moved beyond a simplistic comparison of the institutions' facilities and stated that the black school lacked extracurricular and intangible aspects such as a law review and a reputation that powerfully affected its students' and

33. *N&O*, 21 May 1950.

34. *N&O*, 28 May 1950; Pleasants and Burns, *Frank Porter Graham*, 186.

35. *N&O*, 30 May and 8 June 1950; Pleasants and Burns, *Frank Porter Graham*, 194.

graduates' success. *McLaurin v. Oklahoma State Regents for Higher Education* provided a companion case for *Sweatt.* It ended the University of Oklahoma's isolation of a black doctoral student, who—after a federal district court mandated his admission to the all-white institution—found himself forced to sit in classrooms in a separate row marked by signage stating "reserved for Negroes" and similarly sequestered in the university's library and cafeteria. As it had done in *Henderson,* the federal government in *Sweatt* and *McLaurin* filed an amicus brief in which it maintained that the "'separate-but-equal' theory of *Plessy v. Ferguson* is wrong as a matter of law, history, and policy."[36]

Jesse Helms, who would in 1972 become the first Republican senator from North Carolina in the twentieth century, played a vital role in persuading Smith to call for a runoff. Almost certainly, Lewis knew Helms. He had worked as a sports reporter for her newspaper and as assistant city editor for the *Raleigh Times.* After Japan's surrender Helms became city editor of the *Times.* At the time of the 1950 primary the young broadcaster, a close but apparently unofficial advisor to Willis Smith, served as news director for two statewide radio networks and the capital city's WRAL radio station.[37]

Helms contrived the idea of staging a rally at Smith's home, where a massive show of support from his backers might convince him to stay in the race. The day following the court decisions, Helms obtained airtime at his station and recorded an announcement urging listeners to attend the rally. The spot played repeatedly during the evening, and the *News and Observer* reported that four hundred fans mobbed the Smith residence. Lewis, who lived on the same street as the challenger and returned to her home from Chapel Hill at this time, may have attended the gathering. The following afternoon—one day before the twelve-day deadline—Smith requested that the State Board of Elections order a second primary, which would take place on 24 June.[38]

The court decisions, in conjunction with widespread reports regarding the bloc voting of Tar Heel blacks for Graham, poured gasoline on the smoldering embers that existed in the wake of the earlier primary. Race became the

36. Hall, *Oxford Companion to the Supreme Court,* 540–41, 766–67, 851; Jack Greenberg, *Crusaders in the Courts: How a Dedicated Band of Lawyers Fought for the Civil Rights Revolution* (New York: Basic Books, 1994), 72–78; Mark V. Tushnet, *The NAACP's Legal Strategy against Segregated Education, 1925–1950* (Chapel Hill: University of North Carolina Press, 1987), 72–73, 125–32.

37. Jesse Helms, *Here's Where I Stand: A Memoir* (New York: Random House, 2005), 16–34; Wilson and Ferris, *Encyclopedia of Southern Culture,* 1188; "Jesse Helms" (cited 6 July 2007), www.unctv.org/biocon/jhelms/timeline.html.

38. Pleasants and Burns, *Frank Porter Graham,* 198–99; *N&O,* 8 June and 31 December 1950; Ehle, *Dr. Frank,* 174.

foremost issue in the contest, and North Carolina found itself gripped by an extraordinary hysteria.[39] Irrespective of Smith's purported aversion to racial divisiveness, his lieutenants and especially his local supporters energetically devised dirty tricks and negative advertisements and spread rumors that drove a wedge between blacks and whites and sowed hatred between the races. Pleasants and Burns detail a profusion of these schemes. In one community a black man, ostensibly representing a "Colored Committee for Dr. Frank Graham," placed an ad in the local paper predicting a low turnout for the second primary. He encouraged members of his race to flock to the polls again and elect a senator who supported the recent court decisions. In the eastern part of the state a sedan sporting Graham banners and filled with affluent-looking blacks drove through small towns. Freelancing Smith enthusiasts, hoping to infuriate white voters, probably dreamed up and executed these hoaxes.[40]

In regions throughout the state astonishingly racist fliers materialized. One featured a photograph portraying the black representatives in the 1868 South Carolina Reconstruction legislature. The image of the interracial dancers emerged again, sometimes modified, according to numerous accounts, by superimposing a photograph of Frank Graham's wife, Marian, into the picture. "WHITE PEOPLE WAKE UP," another circular demanded. "DO YOU WANT? Negroes working beside you, your wife and daughters in your mills and factories? Negroes eating beside you in all public eating places? Negroes riding beside you, your wife and your daughters in buses, cabs and trains?"[41]

The hate-mongering resulted in the remarkable spectacle of Tar Heels repulsing the man long regarded as their state's most beloved and selfless public figure. Children chanted to him, "No school with niggers, no school with niggers." Textile workers, whose lives he had long endeavored to improve, snubbed him and even spat at him. "It is right strange to see laboring people whom I've worked for for twenty years turn against me," he told an assembly. When he tried to shake hands with one group of mill employees, they refused to extend their hands and announced, "We'll have nothing to do with nigger lovers here." Another man muttered something only Graham and his dignified spouse could discern and spat at the ground. "My God," Graham told an aide, "Did you hear what that man said?"[42]

Apparently deprived by her editor of the unrestrained forum "Incidentally"

39. Pleasants and Burns, *Frank Porter Graham*, 201, 208–9.

40. Pleasants and Burns, *Frank Porter Graham*, 219.

41. Pleasants and Burns, *Frank Porter Graham*, 220–23.

42. Pleasants and Burns, *Frank Porter Graham*, 233; Ashby, *Frank Porter Graham*, 267, 270.

had long provided her, Lewis stumped for Smith. The insurgent's camp undoubtedly could hardly believe its good fortune in being able to feature the popular journalist at its rallies. "Dice" Daniels, as Smith fans mockingly referred to Graham's foremost partisan and publicist, had become a hot-button issue in the campaign, and the widely despised editor's feisty columnist espousing a position diametrically opposed to his must have energized the crowds she addressed. (Daniels had earned his nickname as a result of his proficiency shooting craps during his student years at the University of North Carolina.)[43]

Historian Elizabeth Gillespie McRae, who has studied Lewis's ascendancy as an influential conservative figure in the 1940s and 1950s, notes the approval Lewis received for her outspoken support for Smith. As she lauded the corporate attorney's championship of traditional southern values and his opposition to the FEPC, national civil rights initiatives, and socialism, her fans expressed to her their confidence that her "opinion will carry so much weight" and "sway people toward Smith." Lewis must have enjoyed her celebrity, tweaking of Daniels, and circumvention of his will. Relegated in her column during the second primary to stoking her reader's fears that as a result of the Supreme Court decisions "the do-gooders are getting ready to ride us—the crusaders, the zealots, the fanatics, the holier-than-thous—and may God have mercy on us!" and to anticipating gleefully that Gordon Gray after his arrival in late September would crack down on the Chapel Hill communists, she could in her speeches move beyond these subordinate issues and speak her mind about the momentous election.[44]

The challenger and his inner circle must have viewed Lewis as a prized advocate; they selected her as one of a handful of orators to speak before Smith at his capstone rally in Raleigh the night before the election. The rowdy event, which featured multiple lusty rounds of "Dixie" accompanied by an organ, took place in the Wake County Courthouse packed with the candidate's supporters. A statewide radio network relayed the proceedings.[45] "Battling Nell" announced her intention to vote for Smith, a "man—not a God or a saint," in large part because he would hold back the spreading tide of socialism. As an intoxicated celebrant hollered, "Hold that line," the crowd roared, thus pro-

43. McRae, "To Save a Home," 280; *N&O*, 25 June 1950; Eagles, *Jonathan Daniels and Race Relations*, 4.

44. McRae, "To Save a Home," 280–82; *N&O*, 11 and 18 June 1950.

45. *N&O*, 24 June 1950; Pleasants and Burns, *Frank Porter Graham*, 243.

viding the interjector with the encouragement—if he required any—to echo his line throughout her speech.[46]

Lewis maintained that the election offered voters a clear choice between left and right, and she made clear which of these directions she favored. She asked the raucous audience if it wanted the "country to follow this trend to the left which even in the United States already has increased to an alarming degree or do you want to preserve that way of life which despite its many obvious imperfections gives to both individuals and states the maximum of freedom and initiative consistent with stability and order?"[47] "Our nation," she cautioned, "is the last strong bulwark of the kind of democracy which has been developed during the past 150 years and which still seems to many of us the best form of human government evolved thus far. Make your vote tomorrow not weaken but strengthen that bulwark. Such a strengthening vote I am convinced will be one for Mr. Willis Smith."[48]

The outcome of the election furnished little drama the following evening. From the moment the results began to trickle in, it became clear that Graham would suffer a defeat. Smith, in the final total, earned 281,114 votes to his opponent's 261,789.[49] Many factors contributed to the loss: Graham's failure to state clearly during his campaign where he stood on the cloture vote that would end the probable filibuster of the FEPC bill (in July he enigmatically voted nay; had he communicated the direction of his vote in May, he could very well have preempted the second primary), his naming a black alternate appointee to West Point, his membership in leftist organizations, the ineptitude of labor, and a poor black turnout all weighed against him. Daniels's and Scott's heavy-handed support became an issue and alienated some voters, and Graham's naïveté as a politician and the overconfidence of many of his supporters hurt his effort. Beyond a doubt, however, the Supreme Court rulings, which galvanized and energized Smith forces and enabled them to convulse the state with a racist backlash and scapegoat Graham as someone "who would be a party to the sabotage of southern tradition," powerfully influenced the result.[50]

At the Hotel Sir Walter in Raleigh, where both of the candidates main-

46. Pleasants and Burns, *Frank Porter Graham*, 243.

47. *N&O*, 24 June 1950.

48. *N&O*, 24 June 1950.

49. *N&O*, 25 June 1950; Pleasants and Burns, *Frank Porter Graham*, 244, 260–61.

50. Pleasants and Burns, *Frank Porter Graham*, 264–69, 275; *N&O*, 25 June 1950.

tained their headquarters, Graham issued a concession statement and visited Smith and his spouse in their headquarters to congratulate them. Future president of the University of North Carolina William Friday, then Graham's unofficial aide, drove the senator and his wife to her sister's house thirty-five miles away, in Hillsborough. After vacating the old classical revival president's mansion in Chapel Hill, the couple lacked a residence of their own in North Carolina. Friday recalled that they traveled the entire distance in stunned silence.[51]

The humiliating defeat shocked and humbled Daniels. In a letter to Harry Truman, written two days after the election, he confessed his disbelief that such a bigoted campaign "could happen in North Carolina, but I have never seen the effectiveness of race fear and race hatred in a political campaign before. . . . Nobody could measure the proportions of the bitterness which poured out of the precincts." He had discovered "this race issue is . . . pure dynamite." At this time he surrendered his ambitions to serve as a political broker and thereafter confined his principal professional energies to directing his newspaper and to his literary activities.[52]

Smith's victory, of course, elated Lewis. She had thwarted her editor and forestalled the perils she believed Graham and his liberal acolytes posed to her cherished state and to her country. North Carolina's new senator, working in conjunction with the highly conservative Hoey, posed a formidable obstacle to northerners and southern quislings seeking to alter the racial status quo in Dixie. Certainly, the ominous international situation seemed to her to cry out for the confrontational policies Smith and other no-nonsense hardliners advocated. On the very afternoon of the election a massive communist army, powerfully equipped by the Soviet Union, launched a surprise invasion of South Korea and thrust the United States into a hot war.[53]

Lewis may have gloated to like-minded friends and her family regarding the part she played in the campaign, but not until a week after the election could her readers discern for the first time in "Incidentally" a hint of the extra-journalistic role she had played in the spectacular political upset and the iden-

51. *N&O*, 25 June 1950; Snider, *Light on the Hill*, 254–55; Pleasants and Burns, *Frank Porter Graham*, 245–46.

52. Pleasants and Burns, *Frank Porter Graham*, 249; Jonathan Daniels to Harry S. Truman, 26 June 1950, JD papers; Eagles, *Jonathan Daniels and Race Relations*, 152–53.

53. Max Hastings, *The Korean War* (New York: Touchstone, 1987), 52–53.

tity of the candidate for whom she had voted. In "A Distracting Gadget," a whimsical editorial devoted to the microphone, she mentioned her considerable experience as a public speaker. Over the years she had discovered that her platform abilities improved if she established a strong and sincere rapport with her listeners. She found this difficult to do when isolated in a radio studio but apparently not the "night before the primary, when I talked at the Smith rally in Raleigh, which was on the air." She had learned that when making use of a microphone, "You've got to feel an audience: you've got to give it your whole attention, your whole self, or you don't really get across."[54] In a thank-you letter to "My dear Nell Battle" Smith left no doubt that she had come across well. He expressed the "great appreciation I have for the splendid work you did for me during the campaign" and stated that the assistance she and other friends had provided had made his victory possible.[55]

Having helped vanquish Graham, Lewis wasted no time in concocting a campaign designed to expunge the political tolerance he had bequeathed to Chapel Hill. "Clean 'em Out, Mr. Gray," she entitled her lead editorial in "Incidentally" on 30 July. She eagerly looked forward to the communists' banishment that she hoped the secretary of the army would soon order. "That place ought to be cleaned up!" she exhorted. "Our State University ought not to be allowed any longer to provide a nest for these vermin."[56] A flier distributed by the "Student Section, Carolina District, Communist Party, U.S.A." made Lewis's blood boil and provided the inspiration for a series of editorials the following week. "The U.S. is in actuality waging an unjust war of aggression against the whole people of Korea," the flier alleged. "DOES OPPOSITION TO THIS WAR PROVE DISLOYALTY TO ONE'S COUNTRY?" Scales and his comrades asked. "NO!" The bottom of the circular listed the Chapel Hill post office box belonging to the young district chairman.[57]

The return address confirmed for Lewis the continued existence of communist infiltration at the university. One of Lewis's columns on this infuriating topic appeared on the anniversary of her father's death twenty-four years earlier. "What would he think of his beloved University as a covert for conspiracy!" she demanded. "Sirs and ladies," she chastised the current board of

54. *N&O*, 2 July 1950.

55. Willis Smith to NBL, 28 July 1950, NBL Papers.

56. *N&O*, 30 July 1950.

57. *N&O*, 6 August 1950.

trustees, "why DO you hesitate to clean the communists out of our University? If you really bring your influence to bear, I know it can be done. Clean out that scum, those vermin, that riff-raff, those traitors, who have for years been poisoning the minds of North Carolina youth at Chapel Hill!"[58]

Gray did not disappoint Lewis. In his inaugural address on 10 October the fledgling president put the few possibly remaining university radicals on guard. "We shall not knowingly allow any campus to become a workshop, or laboratory, or training ground for the operations of those who are committed to the destruction of American culture and institutions," he warned. "Indeed, Communists are not welcome at any of our three institutions." Although he pledged to confront Party members and sympathizers prudently and "not be governed by hysteria," he underscored that his administration would not countenance the expansive tolerance for speech that had marked his predecessor's tenure. He dismissed out of hand Graham's deeply held belief that the openness and optimism radiated at Chapel Hill would discourage militancy within its academic community.[59]

Controverting Lewis's certainty that the "swell" inauguration speech augured well for Gray's presidency, he would prove—despite his golden résumé and considerable intelligence—an ineffectual and uninspiring academic leader, who frequently found his new position frustrating. He had no experience in higher education and found it difficult to apprehend and negotiate the individualism, free-thinking, and disputatiousness that flourishes within the professorate. "Gray was as lacking in perception of what a university is as any person I've ever seen," one professor later observed.[60]

In the spring of 1951 the university again emerged as a central issue for "Incidentally." In late March the U.S. Court of Appeals for the Fourth Circuit reversed an earlier district court decision that the unaccredited law school at the North Carolina College for Negroes offered students an education comparable to that at the University of North Carolina. After determining that the "Negro School is clearly inferior to the white," the three-judge panel, relying on the precedent of *Sweatt*, mandated that four black applicants—including future civil rights leader Floyd B. McKissick—be allowed to enter Chapel Hill's program. Contemporaneously, a special group of trustees, which at Gray's behest

58. *N&O*, 6 August 1950.

59. *N&O*, 15 October 1950; Snider, *Light on the Hill*, 240–41.

60. Snider, *Light on the Hill*, 240–41; *N&O*, 15 October 1950.

had studied the university's admissions policies, yielded to the inevitable and recommended to the board's Executive Committee that in fields of study not offered by the state's black colleges, "applications shall be processed without regard to color or race."[61]

On 1 April, in a lead editorial entitled "Heading for Rough Waters?" Lewis acknowledged that although "nobody who loves the South can contemplate the breaking down of segregation of the races in this region with anything but the most profound apprehension," the Supreme Court's recent desegregation decisions had left the Executive Committee with no other option. The sea change in the university's policy and the court of appeals' decision, she realized, ended forever the segregation of the state's public graduate and professional programs. Nonetheless, for the foreseeable future the number of black students studying with whites at the postbaccalaureate level would remain tiny. "When they increase to any appreciable degree," Lewis anticipated, "you and I . . . will be gone from here, and the children of the 'liberals' can cope with the matter."[62]

Two days after the Supreme Court on 4 June refused to hear the university's appeal, the trustees admitted the black law students. Under Gray's leadership the institution, which boasted a storied reputation for liberalism and thus enjoyed a singular position to pioneer integration in southern higher education, had lagged behind other regional universities—including stodgy University of Virginia—in admitting black professional and graduate students. Louis Austin, who fearlessly edited the black *Carolina Times*, acidly described Gray as a "slick lawyer" who desired to "keep the Negroes down, but do it as quietly as possible," a device the Durham journalist believed had long characterized Tar Heel racial relations.[63]

The black students, whom the administration initially housed together in a separate section of a dormitory, made clear that they did not intend to accept second-class status. Proscribed from using the university's recreational facilities, McKissick, fully clothed, reportedly jumped in the university nata-

61. Augustus M. Burns III, "Graduate Education for Blacks in North Carolina, 1930–1951," *Journal of Southern History* 46, no. 2 (May 1980): 215–17; Snider, *Light on the Hill*, 246–47.

62. *N&O*, 1 April 1951.

63. Burns, "Graduate Education for Blacks in North Carolina," 217; Snider, *Light on the Hill*, 247–48; Henry Lewis Suggs, ed., *The Black Press in the South, 1865–1979* (Westport, Conn.: Greenwood Press, 1984), 267–68.

torium just to claim that Chapel Hill had an integrated swimming pool. After first refusing to allow the black students to obtain passbooks to athletic contests, the administration insisted that they sit in a separate section at football games, which it considered "social occasions." The *Daily Tar Heel* editorialized against recalcitrance of this sort. "Our task is not to fight grudgingly the new social situation in which we find ourselves," its student editor advised in late September, "but to make the transition as gracefully and smoothly as possible."[64]

Attitudes such as this, which the overwhelming majority of the student body seemed to share, turned Lewis's stomach. On 7 October, in "Stay with It Boys," she commended House and Gray for their resistance to integration at football games. "You are dead right," she informed them. "Don't give an inch, not one inch! For if you once start letting down the bars in extra-educational activities, we are in for endless and inconceivable trouble. If there is to be no segregation at football games, then why at dances?" The administration should refuse to cave in to the "liberals." If they prevailed in this and subsequent disputes, "they would wreck the South, and I don't mean maybe, perhaps, or peradventure. I mean they would WRECK IT."[65]

Lewis's insistence that the university draw a line in the sand met with the approval of not only many rank-and-file readers but also Senator Hoey, who applauded "Stay with It Boys." In a letter to "My dear 'Battling Nell,'" whose column he regularly read, he conveyed his pleasure "with your treatment of so many public matters." Lewis began "Incidentally" with the ultra-conservative legislator's letter on 21 October. He agreed that—if left unchecked—liberals would ruin the region. "Some of [them] have gone literally crazy on this subject of segregation" and completely failed to realize the dire consequences this would have for the South.[66]

Despite the sentiments expressed by Lewis and Hoey, the university administration had, in mid-October, buckled in the face of negative publicity and ended its discriminatory seating policy. The columnist vented her disgust, after printing Hoey's missive, in "They Didn't Have the Guts." She bemoaned seeing "among even some of the best Southerners now an attitude of sickly resignation [regarding the inevitability of integration] that makes me want to upchuck. 'It's bound to come,' they whine, 'so we might as well accept it.' Who

64. Snider, *Light on the Hill*, 248.

65. Snider, *Light on the Hill*, 248–49; *N&O*, 7 October 1951.

66. Clyde R. Hoey to NBL, 9 October 1951, NBL Papers; *N&O*, 21 October 1951.

says 'it's bound to come'? I certainly don't, and never expect to! It will come only if enough spineless white people let it come."[67]

Editorials of this kind in late 1951, including several in which Lewis warned that terminating racial separation would fuel the rise of violent terrorist organizations such as the Ku Klux Klan, attracted the notice not only of North Carolina's senior senator but also of the Gastonia unrest's most notorious figure, Fred Beal. In the 7 December *News and Observer* there appeared a letter to the editor from Beal. The former communist communicated his sadness upon having discovered Lewis's aggressive stand for segregation. "I am sorry to learn this," he wrote. "Somewhere in the crevices of my cranium I had tagged her as a fighter for the underdog, for noble ideals, for human rights. Like many fluctuating so-called liberals of the past our Nell capitulates to the enemy when 'the hour of decision' is at hand." Her argument that integration should not proceed on the grounds that it might provoke Klan savagery seemed to him akin to saying that potential depositors should refuse to put money in banks because robbers might one day hold them up.[68]

"I'm Taking No 'Lip' Off'n Beal," Lewis entitled her rejoinder in mid-December. "Fred Beal . . . Fred Erwin Beal . . . Does that name ring a bell anywhere in your mind?" she asked. Although the title she selected for her editorial suggested a pugnacious rebuttal, she supplied an accurate biography of the labor organizer and reserved her passion for a familiar discussion of her own political reversal. During the Gastonia turmoil the communists had manipulated her and exploited her naïveté and liberalism, which was "not only ignorant and neurotic, but very dangerous." Her subsequent epiphany that Beal and his comrades had played her for a dupe furnished the overwhelming motivation for her transformation and accounted for her warning that she was "taking no 'lip' off'n him, particularly no pious 'lip.'"[69]

As the University of North Carolina begrudgingly admitted its first black students and Lewis urged her fellow Tar Heels to hold the line against substantive integration, she glorified the Lost Cause in "Incidentally" in a way that would have swollen her Yankee-hating stepmother, Annie, with pride. In early July the columnist told her readers in "A Welcome Period" that too many southerners had forgotten their heritage. She had entered a "very Confederate period" and had begun to recall many things that she had learned during

67. *N&O*, 21 October 1951.

68. *N&O*, 21 October, 18 November, and 7 December 1951.

69. *N&O*, 16 December 1951.

her youth pertaining to the war and its aftereffect. "I'm dusting off my background, so that, against it I'll be better able to judge current events," she announced.[70]

Later in the month, in "Historical Illiterates," Lewis deplored a trend she perceived among southerners who considered it "smart and 'progressive' to cut our roots and ignore our background." Her recent reading on the Civil War's aftermath had taught her lessons she wished she could impart to "every present-day Southern 'liberal,'" such as how the "Southern white people survived the frightful ordeal of Reconstruction that followed four years of devastating war and . . . saved Anglo-Saxon civilization below the Potomac," an interpretation of that complex historical period that—even at the time of Lewis's writing—historians increasingly disputed. She believed that although "many of the descendants of the Southern patriots of 1865–'75 have become pretty feeble," they would eventually steel themselves and repel the forces threatening their native way of life.[71]

70. *N&O,* 1 July 1951.

71. *N&O,* 15 July 1951; Eric Foner, *Reconstruction: America's Unfinished Revolution, 1863–1877* (New York: Harper & Row, 1989), xix–xxvii.

# 10 "WITH ALL DELIBERATE SPEED"

During the several years immediately preceding the Supreme Court's unanimous landmark decision in *Brown v. Board of Education* on 17 May 1954, which reversed *Plessy v. Ferguson* and concluded "that in the field of public education the doctrine of 'separate but equal' has no place," Lewis frequently faced disappointment and sadness. Although she refrained from writing about it, Gordon Gray's dispiriting performance as president of the Consolidated University of North Carolina must have chagrined her. Less than a year after his arrival in Chapel Hill, the *News and Observer* had lamented the "unraveling of Mr. Gray's presidency before it is well begun" and quoted one of the trustees who had nominated him as saying that the morale at the institution had "reached a low ebb."[1]

In late June 1952 Lewis's beloved brother Kemp, her steadfast and foremost protector, died unexpectedly, albeit after several years of increasingly severe and painful illness. The sensitivity, generosity, and self-sacrifice, which Ivey later recalled Kemp had exhibited in his youth, consistently marked his relations with his family throughout his life. In "Incidentally" Nell described him simply as a "hero." In his will, after providing for his wife and their four daughters, he almost certainly ensured that his sister would lead a comfortable existence for the remainder of her years. To honor Kemp's half-century of service to Erwin Mills, the company halted the operation of its machinery during his funeral.[2]

Precisely three years after his victory in the controversial 1950 primary, Willis Smith suffered an unforeseen heart attack. Rushing to Bethesda Naval Hospital to comfort his mentor, his young legislative aide, Jesse Helms, fought hard to suppress his tears until after he left the hospital room. North Carolina's junior senator died on 26 June. Although the self-made Smith had worked hard throughout his life, since his arrival on Capitol Hill he had maintained an exhausting schedule to demonstrate his diligence and perhaps to re-

1. Joseph Tussman, ed., *The Supreme Court on Racial Discrimination* (New York: Oxford University Press, 1963), 42; Snider, *Light on the Hill*, 241.

2. *N&O*, 1, 13 July 1952; *Chapel Hill Weekly*, 3 July 1952; *Durham Morning Herald*, 1 July 1952; IFL to NBL, 12 May 1954, NBL Papers.

pair his reputation after the unsavory campaign he had run against Frank Graham. Lewis recalled that during the 1950 senatorial campaign Smith "offered himself as a rallying point and champion of the overwhelming sentiment in North Carolina at that time for a turn to the Right." She, among many thousands of conservative Tar Heels, owed him a great debt "for representing so vigorously [our] honest convictions in a campaign of far too much bitterness on both sides."[3]

Lewis's eulogy for Senator Clyde Hoey appeared in "Incidentally" on 16 May 1954, as Thurgood Marshall, who had planned to travel from Mobile to Los Angeles that day to deliver a speech, received an inside tip that he might wish to appear instead at the Supreme Court the following morning. The "silver-tongued" Hoey, "an accomplished practitioner of the South's now-almost-lost art of oratory," who had died four days earlier, had closely witnessed Lewis's political conversion. She wrote that during her "befuddled 'liberal' days" at the Gastonia trials, his abilities as the most skilled and eloquent member of the prosecutorial team had "pained" her. Much later in life, he had delighted her by reading one of her columns castigating communism into the *Congressional Record*. Hoey's surprising death would deprive her of a formidable confederate in her quest to galvanize white southerners to resist the implementation of *Brown v. Board*.[4]

Lewis devoted her entire column on 23 May to the decision and featured an extensive analysis of the response by the regional press. Most of the newspapers she had read, she noted—particularly in North Carolina—urged moderation and restraint. Daniels certainly had. The morning after the verdict, he stressed that in coming to terms with *Brown*, the "South never needed wisdom more, nor fury less."[5] Many of Lewis's fans undoubtedly anticipated that *Brown* would trigger a blast in her editorial, but only in the final section of the piece did she come close to denouncing the decision. She conveyed her bewilderment that *Plessy* could be constitutional one day and not the next and that within her country's democratic government, nine unelected justices, often appointed on the basis of their partisanship, could "render a decision affecting the whole country so vitally and disrupting at one blow customs and institutions of such long standing."[6]

3. Helms, *Here's Where I Stand*, 40–41; Pleasants and Burns, *Frank Porter Graham*, 278–79; *N&O*, 5 July 1953.

4. Williams, *Thurgood Marshall*, 225; *N&O*, 16 May 1954.

5. *N&O*, 23 May 1954; Eagles, *Jonathan Daniels and Race Relations*, 169.

6. *N&O*, 23 May 1954.

Lewis's comparatively judicious reaction stimulated a number of letters to her from correspondents who may have recalled her quiescence during the latter portion of the 1950 primary and the runoff. Had Daniels muzzled her? they inquired. She informed them in early June that no censorship had occurred. The length of her *Brown* editorial had prevented her from weighing in on the judgment. Belatedly, she provided her opinion: "I am unequivocably opposed to this decision. I consider it, together with the War of the '60's, one of the two worst things that has ever happened to the South. And I cannot see how its ultimate results can be anything but the decline and deterioration of this region."[7]

The contempt Lewis expressed for the verdict and her fearful prediction of the disastrous consequences it would wreak resembled not at all the restraint Daniels had counseled. Perhaps because of the backfiring of his earlier apparent attempt to suppress "Battling Nell," he made no attempt to curb his headstrong columnist. Although she knew that her aggressive attacks accusing liberals of coddling communists and her inflammatory resistance to integration pushed Daniels to his limits, she continued to speak her mind.

Nell explained to Ivey, who had retired from his university post in 1953, that "Incidentally" derived its worth from genuinely reflecting its author's convictions. "And as long as I write it, it is not going to be anything else. (How long I'll be able to write it with Jonathan as Editor I don't know, but I'm not doing any trimming on account of that.)" The *News and Observer*, she told her brother, "is an all-out party-line Democratic sheet now edited by a character far, far inferior to the late Josephus." She believed that the major value of her column "at present is in presenting honestly a viewpoint different from that of the N. and O.'s editorial page. I think this helps to give the paper a balance which otherwise it wouldn't have and its readers a chance for fairer judgment. I am, literally, the only person on the paper now who is not a Daniels' yes-man."[8]

The editorial dissension between Daniels and Lewis unquestionably became a subject of conversation among rank-and-file readers, politicians, and journalists, including the copious number of editors from surrounding states who maintained newspaper exchange agreements with North Carolina's most eminent daily and examined its Sunday edition with particular care. This attention greatly expanded Lewis's influence and resulted in the republication of

7. *N&O*, 6 June 1954.

8. NBL to IFL, [April?] 1954, NBL Papers; Dabney, *Mr. Jefferson's University: A History*, 410.

her column in vicinities far removed from Raleigh. The columnist's sex, which set her apart from the overwhelmingly male southern press corps, provided her viewpoint with novelty and further amplified the notice she received. The South could lay claim to comparatively few female public intellectuals, and segregationist forces found in Lewis an articulate, forceful, and reliable voice.

The *Brown* decision frightened many white Tar Heel women, who expressed their objections to it in church auxiliaries, by organizing petition drives, and by lobbying the governor. They viewed racial integration as a peril to their families and communities and worried that it would place their daughters in close contact with sexually precocious blacks, that it would spawn intermarriage, and that it violated God's will.[9] Lewis capitalized on this cohort's fears and cultivated them. Her gender undoubtedly created a bond between her and her white female readers. Elizabeth Gillespie McRae observes that Lewis, unmarried and childless, had in her column long positioned North Carolina as her "metaphoric home." As she battled to stave off the menace she perceived that the Court's decree posed to her native state, many white women regarded her appreciatively as a protector of the southern way of life and the security, order, and privilege it furnished them. The columnist "lent her full sympathy and journalistic support" to these readers, and they, in turn, inundated her with praise and with schemes to preserve Jim Crow.[10]

As Lewis in the summer of 1954 formulated her stand against the Court's edict, she discussed in several editorials entitled "Along the Segregation Front" the rudiments of what would soon become known as "massive resistance" and lauded champions of the confrontational policy. In late June she also commended purportedly compliant southern blacks (who may or may not have existed) endorsing the racial status quo. These individuals, she said, depicted the feelings of the members of their racial group in the region much more accurately than did the NAACP.[11]

Following the summer of 1954, Lewis's fierce defense of segregation in "Incidentally" abated as she closely anticipated the Supreme Court's implementation order and the report of the Governor's Special Advisory Committee on Education. North Carolina's chief executive, William Umstead, had convened this body in late August to examine the impact *Brown* would have on the state's public schools and to recommend a response. Chaired by Thomas J. Pear-

9. McRae, "To Save a Home," 285.

10. McRae, "To Save a Home," 276, 283, 285.

11. *N&O*, 20 June and 4 and 18 July 1954.

sall, the former speaker of the state's House of Representatives, the nineteen-member panel included three blacks—all of whom the state employed—including the presidents of two black colleges.[12]

Shortly after Thanksgiving, in "Two Red Connections of Tarheelia," Lewis marked the death of Fred Beal in Massachusetts on 14 November and rejoiced over the FBI's arrest of Junius Scales four days later in Memphis. Lewis paid Beal, who had died from a heart attack at age fifty-seven, a reluctant compliment by conceding that after he "saw the light from actual experience of life behind the Iron Curtain, he did what he could to make up for the harm he'd done," but she heaped scorn on Scales and his supporters within the state. "Well, they got him at last," she crowed, "but no thanks are due to any of the muddle-headed 'liberals' at Chapel Hill and elsewhere in North Carolina who have protected him for so long, with his treason stinking right under their noses." (The Supreme Court would in 1957 reverse a six-year sentence Scales received under the Smith Act. Although he resigned his membership in the Communist Party after the disclosure of the charges leveled in early 1956 by Nikita Khrushchev against Stalin and his personality cult and the Red Army's suppression of the Hungarian uprising later that year, the North Carolinian was convicted in a second trial and, after refusing to name names, served fifteen months in prison.)[13]

The issuing on 30 December 1954 of the final report of the Governor's Special Advisory Committee commanded Lewis's attention and spurred her authorship of a series of editorials on race. The body concluded, "The mixing of the races forthwith in the public schools throughout the State cannot be accomplished and should not be attempted." With this in mind Tar Heel authorities were instructed to attempt to comply with *Brown* without substantially modifying or discontinuing the "present school system." Mandatory "mixing of the races in our schools on a State-wide basis and without regard to local conditions and assignment factors other than race would alienate public support of the schools to such an extent that they could not be operated successfully." The state should therefore implement legislation that furnished local school boards with the power to enroll and assign students. Governor

12. Crow, Escott, and Hatley, *History of African Americans*, 167; Powell, *North Carolina through Four Centuries*, 520–21; William H. Chafe, *Civilities and Civil Rights: Greensboro, North Carolina, and the Black Struggle for Freedom* (New York: Oxford University Press, 1980), 67–68.

13. *N&O*, 28 November 1954; *NYT*, 16 and 19 November 1954; Scales and Nickson, *Cause at Heart*, 301–415; Buhle, Buhle, and Georgakas, *Encyclopedia of the American Left*, 721.

Luther H. Hodges, who had succeeded Umstead after his death in November, endorsed the report, and in early January the General Assembly began to consider a bill based on the committee's recommendations. Although Hodges desired to ensure that North Carolina's public schools remained open and did not at this time react to the desegregation decree with the militant resistance then being formulated in the region—especially in the Deep South and Virginia—the Tar Heel governor and the designers of the pupil assignment plan clearly intended to stymie the NAACP by forcing it to finance a daunting number of local legal actions.[14]

In mid-January Lewis urged support of her state's proposed response to the "dynamite-loaded decision of the U.S. Supreme Court." The following month she lifted her gaze northward and began to profile the hotheaded defiance emerging in Virginia. On 13 February she featured a statement by a "lover of the South, a contributor to its welfare, and a friend of the Negro," her brother Ivey, who persisted in espousing the eugenical theories he had clung to throughout his professorial career. In considering the impact of integration, he asserted: "The welfare of the Negroes should be and is a major consideration. No race in history has made such rapid progress as the Negroes in the United States in the last hundred years. Enforced integration, in my opinion, would be a misfortune for them, bringing far greater ills than those now suffered." The eminent biologist made clear his tenacious support for Jim Crow: "I am unalterably opposed to integration," which he believed would lead to "miscegenation in the long run."[15]

Ivey had evoked the same arguments to oppose the integration of the University of Virginia. In the wake of *Sweatt* and with the assistance of the NAACP, Gregory Hayes Swanson, a black attorney wishing to pursue advanced legal study, had in 1950 broken the color barrier at the institution. After ordering his admission in early September, the Federal Circuit Court of Appeals for Virginia chastised the university's attorneys resisting his enrollment for using the courtroom as a public relations forum.[16] Swanson's struggle had piqued the

14. *N&O*, 16 January 1955; George Lewis, *The White South and the Red Menace: Segregationists, Anticommunism, and Massive Resistance, 1945–1965* (Gainesville: University Press of Florida, 2004), 125; Crow, Escott, and Hatley, *History of African Americans*, 167–68; Chafe, *Civilities and Civil Rights*, 67–68; Eagles, *Jonathan Daniels and Race Relations*, 176.

15. *N&O*, 16 January and 13 February 1955.

16. J. Rupert Picott, "Desegregation of Higher Education of Virginia," *Journal of Negro Education* 27, no. 3 (summer 1958): 324; Kay Bryan, "The History of Desegregation at the University of Virginia,

inchoate racial consciousness of Sarah Patton Boyle, an occasional writer for magazines and the spouse of a faculty member at the university. "If this colored boy comes here," she vowed, "I'm going to make him welcome, and I aim to make no secret of it either."[17]

Lewis's 13 February 1955 "Incidentally" featuring Ivey preceded by less than a week Boyle's sudden emergence as a southern spokeswoman on the region's race relations. The *Saturday Evening Post* entitled her essay "Southerners Will *Like* Integration." The piece included a photograph of the forty-eight-year-old activist Boyle and two University of Virginia black medical students walking in front of the Rotunda that abutted the pavilion in which Ivey and his family had resided for many years. In her article, which appeared in seventeen million American homes, Boyle recounted Swanson's experience at the university and advanced her thesis that most whites beneath the Mason-Dixon Line privately supported fairer treatment of blacks and integration but kept their views to themselves out of fear of violating southern mores.[18]

In the firestorm that ensued, Boyle faced snubs and chilly responses in Charlottesville, demands for her husband's firing, vilification in the southern press, and a continuance of the threats her work had previously provoked, and she received approximately thirty angry letters—many of them graphically obscene—for each of the next several months. In her memoir, *The Desegregated Heart: A Virginian's Stand in Time of Transition,* she recounted much of this calumny. "I did not believe that there was another American white woman with a principle as degrading as that detestable Jewess, Eleanor Roosefelt" [*sic*], one correspondent expostulated. "I hope you get all the Negro men to rape you that you seem so anxious for other people to get," another writer raged.[19]

Although Boyle confided that this vulgarity unnerved her, no attack distressed her more than the drubbing Lewis administered. "For More, No Doubt, than 30 Pieces of Silver," the columnist entitled her assault on 27 February in

---

1950–1969" (honors thesis, University of Virginia, 1979), 12–19, *Cavalier Daily*, 16 September 1950; Peter Wallenstein, *Cradle of America: Four Centuries of Virginia History* (Lawrence: University Press of Kansas, 2007), 336.

17. Boyle, *Desegregated Heart*, 51; Kathleen Murphy Dierenfield, "One 'Desegregated Heart': Sarah Patton Boyle and the Crusade for Civil Rights in Virginia," *Virginia Magazine of History and Biography* 104, no. 2 (spring 1996): 257–58.

18. Sarah Patton Boyle, "Southerners Will *Like* Integration," *Saturday Evening Post*, 19 February 1955, 25, 133–34.

19. Boyle, *Desegregated Heart*, 206–54; Dierenfield, "One 'Desegregated Heart,'" 267–69.

the *News and Observer.* The North Carolinian shared much of the Virginian's background and knew precisely how to get under her skin. As Lewis frequently did, in her article Boyle had established her southern pedigree to buttress her credibility. The author of "Incidentally" highlighted the impropriety of her northern neighbor, who had proudly recounted in the *Saturday Evening Post* that one of her grandfathers had served as Robert E. Lee's personal scout and the other had fought under Stonewall Jackson, posing for a photograph in the company of the two black students on the university's lawn. The picture's subjects formed "a jolly trio, grinning in front of the Rotunda."[20]

Lewis told her readers that Ivey had informed her that the "reaction of Charlottesville people to Mrs. Boyle's article has been 'most unfavorable.'" Some had even termed it "revolting," a response that Lewis shared. The former dean had not bothered to consult with what he described as the "small number of crackpots" within the university community who may have sided with Boyle or, apparently, with any of the city's many black residents.[21]

The title of the article, according to Lewis, greatly overstepped the magazine's discussion of a single black student's desegregation of the university's law school five years earlier. Boyle had limited her discussion of "the question of integration merely to the admission of Negroes to graduate and professional schools, now virtually settled, and wholly ignores that question as it relates to the public schools, where it is an entirely different and violently controversial matter." Her notion that most white southerners privately condoned integration flew in the face of the fact that any plebiscite within the region would result in a strong expression for continued racial separation. "Thousands of readers of [Boyle's] piece outside the South, ignorant of conditions here and mistakenly assuming that she knows what she's talking about, will be grossly misled as to the true state of Southern opinion," Lewis declared.[22]

Having refuted the substance of "Southerners Will *Like* Integration," Battling Nell now dispensed her coup de grâce. Boyle had revealed in her article that she had "felt a twisting pain" when the university administration had initially refused to admit Swanson. Lewis assured her that the "pain which twisted her then was as nothing compared to the excruciating one which I experienced upon reading her piece":[23]

20. Dierenfield, "One 'Desegregated Heart,'" 268–70; *N&O*, 27 February 1955.

21. *N&O*, 27 February 1955.

22. *N&O*, 27 February 1955.

23. *N&O*, 27 February 1955.

> This pain of mine, which was especially severe in the neck, resulted not only from the content of the Boyle article but from the humiliating memories which it revived. It recalled to me those lamentable days, now, happily, however, well in the past—when I, too, was a South-saver, though never along this particular line, the inter-racial. The smug assumption of superiority on the part of the author evident in this piece made me blush, not only for Mrs. Boyle, but for another half-baked reformer, the one I used to be.
>
> As they grow older, self-constituted reformers often gain insight into the basically neurotic nature of their ailment. And Mrs. Boyle, it would seem, is now quite old enough to know better. Forty-eight, she says she is. But, still, it's so satisfying—isn't it?—so pleasantly inflating for the ego, to lift high the torch to enlighten one's benighted fellow-countrymen: to be the inspired and inspiring herald of a bright, new day, a shining Dixie Joan of Arc, striking from the South the shackles of prejudice and leading it onward and upward![24]

Boyle's article and her prolonged civil rights campaign within Charlottesville, a vicinity with which Lewis harbored such intimate and long-standing ties, so infuriated her that on 1 March she sent the activist a letter written with her poison pen. The columnist introduced herself by way of a protracted and impressive listing of her lineage affiliated with the university and from the surrounding countryside and by revealing that she, like Boyle, worshiped within the Episcopal Church.[25] Lewis enclosed a copy of her editorial and a letter of complaint she had written to the *Saturday Evening Post*'s editor and chastised Boyle for misleading the magazine's large audience "about this most important question" and for doing the "South, the Negro, and the country definite disservice." Not content with the wide reprinting "For More, No Doubt, than 30 Pieces of Silver" would normally achieve in the regional press, Lewis mentioned in a postscript that she had mailed copies of her column to a wide range of southern newspapers, including the *Charlottesville Daily Progress*, whose publisher remained hostile to Boyle's civil rights agenda.[26]

Several days later the obliging *Daily Progress*—to Boyle's great mortification—reproduced the thirty-column-inch attack. "The humiliating effect of

24. *N&O*, 27 February 1955.

25. NBL to Sarah Patton Boyle, 1 March 1955, NBL Papers.

26. NBL to Sarah Patton Boyle, 1 March 1955; Boyle, *Desegregated Heart*, 148–49.

this kind of public insult is hard to exaggerate," Boyle recalled in her memoir. It not only made her the laughingstock of her foes but also of many of her acquaintances. The "sheer venom" of the editorial "tormented" its subject. To this point in time she had known that she would confront malice from lower- and middle-class whites but had no idea that members of her "own social group might feel so poisonously about me."[27]

Lewis received many letters from North Carolina and Virginia and additional correspondence from Georgia and Mississippi praising her editorial. An elderly physician from Richmond, Virginia, told her that after reading the piece, he had discussed it over the telephone with his boyhood friend, John Powell, the celebrated pianist and composer, who had served as the charismatic leader of Virginia's Anglo-Saxon Clubs in the 1920s. Powell, who "was having a meeting of peatriots" [*sic*], rhapsodized about the "great work of Dr. Ivey Lewis against Communism & against race mixing." The famous musician, whom Virginia had honored four years earlier by declaring 5 November "John Powell Day," had seen the editorial and hoped to obtain anything else the columnist wrote about Boyle, whom he despised and regarded as a publicity seeker. The physician implored Lewis to "keep up [her] courageous stand for America and help save the white race in the South."[28]

Lewis, however, did not emerge from her fray with Boyle entirely unscathed. A number of writers chastised her. She annotated several of these responses, apparently intending to show them later to Ivey. One Tar Heel correspondent from Roanoke Rapids compared the author of "For More, No Doubt, than 30 Pieces of Silver" to a "vulture that picks the eyes out of newborn lambs, waits for them to die, [and] then feasts on their carcasses." Beneath this text Lewis inscribed, "I strongly suspect this woman is a Negress."[29]

The *News and Observer*'s editorial department forwarded to her another letter from Charlottesville, perhaps written by the wife of a faculty member, maintaining that Boyle had a constitutional right to proclaim her convictions. Under the correspondence Lewis typed: "This letter wasn't published in N. and O., paper's policy very hush-hush on anything that would stir much talk about segregation. Would not wish to give me that much attention. Nigger-

27. *Charlottesville Daily Progress*, 4 March 1955; Boyle, *Desegregated Heart*, 226–28.

28. *N&O*, 1 January 1956; H. Norton Mason to NBL, 28 March 1955, NBL Papers; Edmunds, *Virginians Out Front*, 370–71.

29. Sue M. Denny to NBL, 28 February 1955, NBL Papers.

loving sheet, of course." Although Daniels apparently had accepted the notion that short of firing Lewis he could do nothing to limit her agitation, he had declared a near moratorium on racial issues on his editorial page to defuse tempers while the General Assembly debated how to respond to *Brown*, and he opted not to print the comments from the university town.[30]

Hodding Carter, editor of the Greenville, Mississippi, *Delta Democrat-Times*, provided Lewis with much less of a target for a campaign of vituperation than Boyle when in mid-March he published in *Look* magazine "A Wave of Terror Threatens the South." In his carefully sourced article the Pulitzer Prize winner expressed great concern over the political power the citizens' councils in his state had accumulated and their bigotry against blacks and religious minorities. He also described the attempts of the councils to bully into submission the courageous handful of individuals who opposed them and worried that the organizations might one day metastasize into terrorist organizations such as the Ku Klux Klan. "As one ineffectively protesting newspaperman in one Mississippi community, I don't like what's going on," he announced. "If I were a Negro, a Jew or even a Catholic, I might be even more disturbed, though it is uncomfortable enough to be labeled simply a 'nigger lover.'"[31]

On 13 March, in a lead editorial in "Incidentally," "St. George and the Dragon in Mississippi," Lewis conflated the Charlottesville racial activist with the Magnolia State journalist: "In addition to that inspiring Joan of Arc in Virginia, Sarah Patton Boyle, there now appears in Mississippi, in shining armor and with flashing blade, St. George—who else!—in lonely but heroic combat with the dragon of prejudice in the benighted South: Hodding Carter." Both of these liberals, Lewis implied, sought to cash in on the desire of northern publications to revile the South and exploit the racial crisis wrought by *Brown*.[32]

Then in the process of developing into an unofficial publicist for the Tar Heel citizens' council, the Patriots of North Carolina, Inc., Lewis dismissed Carter's anxiety about the organizations. (Led by eugenicist Wesley Critz George, the former president of the North Carolina Academy of Science and a professor emeritus of histology and embryology at Chapel Hill, the Patriots, which sought to sustain the "purity of the white race and of Anglo-Saxon in-

30. Nancy Bowers to NBL, 6 March 1955, NBL Papers; Eagles, *Jonathan Daniels and Race Relations*, 177.

31. Hodding Carter, "A Wave of Terror Threatens the South," *Look*, 22 March 1955, 32–36.

32. *N&O*, 13 March 1955.

stitutions," claimed numerous distinguished charter members, including several state legislators and a University of North Carolina trustee.) Lewis also renounced as overly sensational the article's title and one of its photographs, which pictured a burning cross. These criticisms aside, Lewis failed to inject into her censure of the hard-bitten newsman either her personal story or the sort of psychoanalysis that had so discomposed Boyle. Other southern newspapers undoubtedly reprinted the editorial, but it stimulated less commotion than "For More, No Doubt, than 30 Pieces of Silver."[33]

Late in the month the North Carolina General Assembly, acting on the recommendations of the Governor's Special Advisory Committee, passed a law that provided local school boards with the authority to enroll and assign students in public schools and on school buses throughout the state. Legislators also began to establish a North Carolina Advisory Committee on Education to replace the earlier task force. Seven white men, including holdover chairman Thomas J. Pearsall, would staff the new body.[34]

Early in April Lewis regarded her state's new pupil assignment law dubiously in "Not Necessarily Final." Some local systems, she worried, might break faith and comply with *Brown*, and endless litigation might occur as plaintiffs repeatedly singled out city and county school boards and brought suit against them. She advised voters to evaluate the individuals serving on these bodies carefully, presumably to ensure that they stood firm against integration. Her state's comparatively subdued response to the Supreme Court's decision dejected her. "By enacting this new law North Carolina has expressed its moderation as contrasted with some other Southern States which have taken stronger stands," she grumbled. "Personally, I'm not moderate on this subject."[35]

The following week the state legislature acted much more to her liking when it unanimously adopted a defiant resolution avowing that its public schools could not be integrated. In "A Clear Courageous Statement of Fact" Lewis told readers that the proclamation served

33. *N&O*, 13 March 1955; Francis M. Wilhoit, *The Politics of Massive Resistance* (New York: George Braziller, 1973), 116; NBL to Gardner Cowles, 16 March 1955, NBL Papers; McRae, "To Save a Home," 285; George Lewis, "'Scientific Certainty': Wesley Critz George, Racial Science and Organised White Resistance in North Carolina, 1954–1962," *Journal of American Studies* 38, no. 2 (August 2004): 227, 333.

34. Powell, *North Carolina through Four Centuries*, 521; Crow, Escott, and Hatley, *History of African Americans*, 169–70; Luther H. Hodges, *Businessman in the Statehouse: Six Years as Governor of North Carolina* (Chapel Hill: University of North Carolina Press, 1962), 81–82; *N&O*, 3 April 1955.

35. *N&O*, 3 April 1955.

> emphatic notice to various groups, hitherto blatantly articulate, that North Carolina does not propose to be high-pressured or brow-beaten on a matter so vital to the welfare of all its people as the segregation of the races, properly telling off: the integration fanatics, white and colored, both within and outside this State; the "liberals" and "intellectuals" from God-knows-where and with God-knows-what haywire notions now teaching in our Southern colleges; the Communists in this country, whose party platform, as of October 1954, calls for the end of all segregation; the politicians who would use the segregation issue to get votes in the North; and the opportunists among the clergy who couldn't leap on the brotherhood bandwagon fast enough after they got their cue from the Supreme Court.[36]

The final day of the next month, the Supreme Court issued its desegregation implementation decree, often referred to as *Brown v. Board II.* The justices directed that public school systems make a "prompt and reasonable start toward full compliance . . . with all deliberate speed." School authorities would conform to the earlier *Brown* decision; federal district judges would monitor these leaders' activities to ensure compliance in good faith.[37]

Lewis entitled a lead editorial on *Brown v. Board II* "About as Good as Could Be Expected." The Court's sensitivity to local conditions and the gradual approach that she discerned in the compliance decree suggested to her that the "nine free-wheeling social theorists who in May 1954 decided, against all precedents of their bench, to overturn at one stroke the centuries-old customs and social attitudes of a whole great section of this country may have learned something during the past year." She interpreted the Court's recent order not as a road map detailing how communities must conform to the earlier *Brown* decision but as a retreat by the justices. She suggested that galvanized resistance to the Court's activism might further intimidate it. Years—perhaps generations—would pass before Tar Heels saw an end to racial separation. Her attitude contradicted an editorial by Daniels in which he emphasized that regardless of the Court's prudent implementation order, the justices had not altered their basic position.[38]

36. *N&O,* 10 April 1955; Hodges, *Businessman in the Statehouse,* 82.

37. Crow, Escott, and Hatley, *History of African Americans,* 169; Tussman, *Supreme Court on Racial Discrimination,* 45–46.

38. *N&O,* 5 June 1955; Eagles, *Jonathan Daniels and Race Relations,* 177–78.

Throughout the summer of 1955 Lewis frequently employed "Incidentally" to spur Dixie's citizenry to stiffen its resistance to the Supreme Court's "'abominable' decision" and often continued to flout her editorial independence from Daniels. She approved the recommendation by her state's fiery assistant attorney general, I. Beverly Lake, that every Tar Heel community charter nonprofit corporations that could if necessary operate private schools. Students attending these institutions, Lake suggested, possibly would receive state tuition grants. Daniels deplored Lake's rash remarks, which the editor believed "incite[d] the extremists on both sides of the segregation question."[39]

Lewis loathed the effect that the "vociferous and aggressive Nacpee [NAACP]" had on the "moderation and common sense" of North Carolina's black leaders and fancifully hoped—as did Daniels—that Tar Heel blacks would embrace a program of voluntary segregation that Governor Hodges proposed in early August during a statewide radio and television address. "If we are not able to succeed in a program of voluntary separate school attendance," he warned, "the State within the next year or so will be face to face with deciding the issue of whether it shall have some form of integrated public schools or shall abandon its public schools." Daniels's conception of voluntary segregation—which did not rule out minimal integration—contrasted with Lewis's unrelenting and Hodges's periodic opposition to even token desegregation.[40]

Lewis expressed relief in early September that North Carolina's schools had reopened without a trace of integration, and she applauded the "good spirit" of the majority of her state's blacks, who, she believed, had taken Hodges's appeal for voluntary segregation to heart. Most Tar Heel blacks, she wrote, had "refused to let a small but aggressive minority, directed from New York, get them excited." This cooperation had for the time forestalled "the ever-present possibility of abolition of the public schools as a last resort."[41]

When in the following month Hodges recast his stance in preparation for a run for the governorship in 1956 and advocated granting local communities "the authority to run their schools the way they want to or not run them at all if they choose," Daniels denounced the proposal. Sanctioning a local option, he protested, signaled a retreat from the state's historic dedication to public

39. *N&O* 17 July 1955; Eagles, *Jonathan Daniels and Race Relations*, 178–79.

40. *N&O*, 24 July and 14 August 1955; Eagles, *Jonathan Daniels and Race Relations*, 179–82; Hodges, *Businessman in the Statehouse*, 87–89.

41. *N&O*, 11 September 1955.

education and undoubtedly would result in the closing of some school systems. Lewis viewed the governor's about-face ambivalently. She favored uniform hardcore defiance of *Brown* at the state level.[42]

Lewis's defiant stance against *Brown* grew even stronger with the arrival of the new year. On 8 January, in a lead editorial entitled "The Doctrine of Interposition," Lewis again contradicted her editor and stated her strong support for the long-forgotten and long-dismissed theory. Her inspiration derived from a heady nine-week advertising campaign then appearing on the editorial page of James Jackson Kilpatrick's *Richmond* (Va.) *News Leader*. Displaying all the restraint of an Edmund Ruffin, Kilpatrick disinterred and popularized the doctrine, which called for the invocation of state sovereignty to negate attempts by the federal government to usurp the rights that states believed the U.S. Constitution afforded them.[43] Lewis lauded Kilpatrick and called his campaign an "admirable piece of newspapering." She supported the rising interest in interposition because it demonstrated that "at least some people are aware of the 'transcendent issue' in all the anti-segregation hullabaloo, which is simply whether the U.S. Supreme Court shall be allowed to change the Constitution at will." She believed that there had "never been a more violent assault upon it than that made on 17 May 1954, and if such a wanton attack on the fundamental principles on which this nation rests is allowed to go unchallenged, the decay of constitutional government here is not only far advanced but eventually may go to unpredictable lengths."[44]

On 29 January Daniels, on his editorial page, heaped scorn on interposition, calling the doctrine "nothing more or less than defiance of the federal government." The Civil War had for him "settled the 'right' of secession in the negative for all time." He cautioned North Carolina and all other states to avoid acts of sedition and couch any protests they might have against integration within the Constitution's framework as interpreted by the Court.[45]

To Lewis's great delight, Hodges, when announcing his gubernatorial candidacy in early February, employed language that evoked interposition by de-

42. Eagles, *Jonathan Daniels and Race Relations*, 182; *N&O*, 16 October 1955.

43. *N&O*, 8 January 1956; Ronald L. Heinemann et al., *Old Dominion, New Commonwealth: A History of Virginia, 1607–2007* (Charlottesville: University of Virginia Press, 2007), 343; J. Harvie Wilkinson III, *Harry Byrd and the Changing Face of Virginia Politics, 1945–1966* (Charlottesville: University Press of Virginia, 1968), 127–29; Nunman V. Bartley, *The Rise of Massive Resistance: Race and Politics in the South during the 1950s* (Baton Rouge: Louisiana State University Press, 1969), 129–30.

44. *N&O*, 8 January 1956.

45. *N&O*, 29 January 1956.

claring his opposition to *Brown* because the decision "usurped the rights of the States and Congress." The governor continued to endorse his phantasmal "plan of voluntary choice of separate schools," according to which all parents would freely continue to enroll their children in segregated schools. This system, he said, would result in the "preservation of our public schools . . . and our traditions and customs, too." If, however, blacks refused to abide by this scheme, he warned he would introduce legislation similar to Virginia's that would provide tuition grants to enable children to attend single-race private schools.[46]

On 12 February 1956, in a lead editorial entitled "Clear, Courageous, and Cheering," Lewis commended the governor's recent statement and again conveyed her desire that he call the legislature into a special session before the beginning of the next school term. Undoubtedly, she hoped that during a hurried and excited meeting passions would prevail and the representatives would adopt an interposition resolution and other defiant and obstructionist measures similar to those being ratified by Virginia and the Deep South states. She also recommended to Hodges that during the special session he propose a referendum that would enable Tar Heel voters to make their views clear on the Court's mandate.[47]

When in a series of editorials Daniels censured the governor's fluctuating policies and increasingly hard-line stance, Hodges grew to believe that the *News and Observer* had "definitely decided to complain about almost everything I do." The governor, who suspected that the editor supported "integration but hasn't the courage to say so," nevertheless, must have derived comfort that his toughening stance met with Lewis's strong approval.[48]

Lewis devoted most of her 18 March column to praising the "Southern Manifesto," massive resistance's most significant document. One hundred and one southern congressmen—the vast majority of the region's federal legislators, including both of North Carolina's senators and all but three of its members of the House of Representatives—signed the statement, which protested the *Brown* decision's "clear abuse of judicial power." "The Supreme Court of the United States, with no legal basis for such action, undertook to exercise their naked judicial power and substituted their personal, political and social ideas for the established law of the land," the manifesto's authors charged.[49]

46. *N&O,* 12 February 1956.

47. *N&O,* 12 February 1956.

48. Eagles, *Jonathan Daniels and Race Relations,* 184–85.

49. *N&O,* 18 March 1956; Bartley, *Rise of Massive Resistance,* 116–17.

In "Southern Solons Defend the Constitution" Lewis declared that the American people should welcome the remonstrance of the region's senators and congressmen against the "wanton assault" on the Constitution. She claimed that as a result of the Court's repeated affirmation of separate but equal over many decades, the doctrine had become enshrined in the Constitution itself. "So, when in May 1954 Warren and his free-wheelers reversed all previous decisions of the Supreme Court on this subject," she argued, "their high-handed reversal was equivalent to amending the Constitution according to their own notions." The manifesto protested the "shocking abuse of judicial power and usurpation of legislative power by the Supreme Court."[50] Lewis followed her exposition on constitutional theory and civil rights with a digression into pseudoscience and civil rights. She had sent to a friend, who boasted expertise in palmistry, a newspaper picture of Autherine Lucy waving after arriving at New York's La Guardia Airport. Thurgood Marshall had brought the badly shaken Lucy to Manhattan to recuperate after her integration of the University of Alabama had provoked a series of riots in early February.[51]

Lewis reported that her friend had concluded that the length of Lucy's heart line indicated that her "emotions are unusually intense, but . . . they are not involved with an individual or with humanity but, rather with a plan or a purpose." Her commitment to this goal, however, "would be purely emotional, selfish, and probably unsuccessful, due to the shortness of the index finger in relation to the others." The shape of Lucy's thumb suggested "a lack of broadness, generosity, or reasoning power." The descending direction of her head line pointed to her "worrying or neurotic character." Finally, the short span of her fate line designated that she "will have her day in newspapers and, perhaps, in the magazines, but it will be short-lived, because she is not the material of which heroes or martyrs are made."[52]

The following month Daniels and Lewis again staked out contraposed positions when they responded to the North Carolina Advisory Committee on Education's 5 April issuance of its final report. The body recommended that local school authorities facing desegregation be given the authority to abolish their public schools and that white parents not wishing for their children

50. *N&O*, 18 March 1956.

51. *NYT*, 26 February and 2 March 1956; Diane McWhorter, "The Day Autherine Lucy Dared to Integrate the University of Alabama," *Journal of Blacks in Higher Education*, no. 32 (summer 2001): 100–101.

52. *N&O*, 18 March 1956.

to study within integrated classrooms receive state tuition grants. The committee advised that Hodges summon the legislature to a special summer session to consider the proposals and prepare a statewide referendum to amend the constitution. On 15 April Lewis devoted her lead editorial, "The Advisory Committee's Excellent Report," to praising the "honest, . . . moderate, . . . courageous, . . . informed" proposal, which she regarded as "one of the most important documents in North Carolina history." Her editor, however, deplored the reckless nature of the report and the fact that it "digs up more snakes than it kills." He predicted that once whites acknowledged the fact that blacks could attend any schools they wished, most blacks would choose to educate their children with members of their own race. The fact that the committee countenanced the elimination of public education shocked him.[53]

By the spring of 1956 Lewis—while working for the most liberal Tar Heel newspaper—could lay claim to being her state's version of Kilpatrick. Harry Golden, the publisher and editor of the highly personal *Carolina Israelite,* which counted among its subscribers not only the author of "Incidentally" but an impressive array of national literary and political figures, in his March–April edition termed her the "strongest journalistic force in North Carolina in the attempt to circumvent the Supreme Court's decisions to eliminate racial discrimination in the free public schools."[54]

Although the opinionated commentators admired one another, despite their diametrically opposed political beliefs, Golden marveled at Lewis's transformation. In a conversation he had recently had with Frank Graham, the two men had deplored her apostasy. "Ah, somewhere along the line we lost her," the pair had sighed. Golden explained to his readers that "it was Nell Battle Lewis who STOOD ALONE in North Carolina defending the right of the Gastonia strikers to a fair trial, after they had been charged with murder." Graham, in a manner exiled from his beloved native state, resided in a modest apartment in New York, where in 1951 he had begun a career with the United Nations (UN). Despite the many frustrations he faced working for the organization, he would remain based in Manhattan in the UN's employ until after Marian Graham's death in April 1967 and after suffering a heart attack

53. Lewis, *White South and the Red Menace,* 125–26; Hodges, *Businessman in the Statehouse,* 91–92; *N&O,* 15 April 1956; Eagles, *Jonathan Daniels and Race Relations,* 185–86.

54. *Carolina Israelite,* March–April 1956; Wilson and Ferris, *Encyclopedia of Southern Culture,* 957–58; Powell, *Dictionary of North Carolina Biography,* 2:313–14.

a month later, when he returned to Chapel Hill to live with his sister. He died there in 1972.[55]

In mid-May Lewis marked the two-year anniversary of *Brown v. Board of Education* by devoting her entire column to cheering the groundswell of resistance to the decision whipped up by southern politicians, citizen's councils, and journalists such as herself. After the initial shock of the decree, a growing percentage of southerners had realized that "there is nothing sacred about a judicial body of nine political appointees of fallible judgment and personal prejudice, and that there IS something which the creators of that body, the American people, can do, through their State Legislatures and their Congress to protest against the Court's usurpation of power never given it by the Constitution and to prevent recurrence of it."[56] Residents of Dixie had rejected defeatism, she announced, and now resolved to stand up to the "judicial dictatorship." It made no sense to her to respect unconditionally the authority of government. "Millions of Germans," after all, "had respect for the authority of Adolf Hitler." James Kilpatrick's powerful promotion of the doctrine of interposition, the subsequent adoption of resolutions pertaining to it by many regional legislatures, the Southern Manifesto, the passage of laws forbidding integration by many states in the former Confederacy, and the rise of organizations similar to the Patriots impressed her as "heartening signs of determination to resist the unconstitutional dictatorship of the U.S. Supreme Court."[57]

The southern backlash against the "truculent aggressiveness" of the NAACP also buoyed her. Several legislatures had outlawed the association or forbidden state and municipal governments to hire its members. She stated that despite assurance by the organization's leaders that it had no ties to the Communist Party, no one could dispute that the "results of agitation by the NAACP, which continually foments ill-will, must be highly pleasing to the Reds." Southerners could take great comfort in the fact that although two years had passed since *Brown*, public schools in Alabama, Florida, Georgia, Louisiana, Mississippi, North Carolina, South Carolina, Tennessee, and Virginia remained segregated.[58]

55. *Carolina Israelite*, March–April 1956; Ashby, *Frank Porter Graham*, 285–303, 318–30.

56. *N&O*, 13 May 1956.

57. *N&O*, 13 May 1956.

58. *N&O*, 13 May 1956.

On 17 June Lewis made clear in "Incidentally" her goal for massive resistance. She believed that the South had demonstrated the impossibility of implementing *Brown*. Two decades earlier the federal government had acknowledged the infeasibility of Prohibition by repealing the Eighteenth Amendment. Taking a swipe at the renowned Swedish economist and sociologist Gunnar Myrdal, whose *An American Dilemma: The Negro Problem and Modern Democracy* the Court had cited in a footnote, she emphasized her hope that "within a reasonable time common-sense will prevail over Swedish sociological theory, and the anti-segregation decision, in some constitutional way, [will] be reversed or rendered innocuous."[59]

A week later, in an intensely sentimental and highly personal editorial entitled "A Letter to a Friend," Lewis professed her devotion to her deceased black cook and mammy and—by inference—all members of their racial group who accepted their Jim Crow status. She addressed the letter that began "Incidentally" to her cook, Emma Walker, "Wherever-She-May-Be." Lewis, who for years had prayed for Emma "on the other side," now wished the two women could discuss the "dreadful thing that's happening to the relationship of your race and mine in the South, the increasing hostility and suspicion, and might try, together, to think of something we might do to help in checking it." While desirous of such a conversation, the columnist nevertheless expressed relief that her friend had not lived to witness the present discord.[60] Lewis asked Emma if she had known about Mammy, Margaret Selby, who had been born into slavery and who died during Lewis's girlhood. "Nothing but kindness and affection is associated in my mind with Mammy," she reminisced. "Both in instinct and behavior, she was much more of a lady than many of the white women I've known." Her death had affected Nell deeply.[61]

"Aggressive [black] extremists" in the present era, Lewis lamented, would label Emma a "handkerchief head" because of her fondness for her employer. Despite this condemnation, Lewis declared:

> there've been many happy relationships like yours and mine in the South. But that's the sort of thing which the ill-advised, hell-for-leather agitators of your race and the haywire, myopic, mushy "liberals" of mine can't understand and so don't take into consideration. Yet, in

59. *N&O*, 17 June 1956; Myrdal, *American Dilemma*.
60. *N&O*, 24 June 1956.
61. *N&O*, 24 June 1956.

> varying degrees, that's been the thing, the basic thing, the only thing—that mutual good feeling and respect, often affection—which has made possible the wonderful progress of your people in the South since their emancipation, which is so greatly to the credit of us all. If that good feeling is destroyed, something precious and irreplaceable will be lost forever, and whatever future social structure the South may build will be of "bricks without straw."
>
> So, let's both of us pray that, somehow, that goodwill may continue and increase and save the South, in which the fate of your race and that of mine are inextricably interwoven, from "chaos and the dark."

"Miss Nell" signed her letter, "With love, as always."[62]

Lewis's passionate and articulate advocacy for massive resistance so impressed the Patriots of North Carolina by the summer of 1956 that a principal figure within the council, Burlington textile executive Erwin A. Holt, sponsored at that time the printing and distribution of a pamphlet consisting of selections from a half-dozen editorials by the "Outstanding North Carolina Writer." A notice at the bottom of the brochure's final page stated that the "excerpts are printed by special permission of MISS NELL BATTLE LEWIS whose views are independent of the News & Obeserver [*sic*] Editors." (Despite the auspicious formation of the Patriots the previous year, infighting and the organization's inability to achieve a mass following would lead to its demise in 1958, earning it an embarrassing distinction as the most ephemeral of the major citizens' councils.)[63]

In early July Lewis initiated a correspondence with James Kilpatrick in order to verify the accuracy of her paper's coverage of Virginia's militant opposition to *Brown*. Along with the clippings she suspected of partiality, she included in her mailing the pamphlet Holt had published. The editor of the *Richmond News Leader* found little to quibble with in the Raleigh paper's reportage other than the "sort of bias which was to be suspected of the *News and Observer*'s staff man." The foremost propagandist of interposition expressed be-

62. *N&O*, 24 June 1956.

63. Nell Battle Lewis, "Excerpts from a Weekly Column, Appearing in the *News & Observer*, Raleigh, N.C., Titled Incidentally," [July? 1956], NBL Papers; "Description," Erwin A. Holt Papers, Southern Historical Collection, Wilson Library, University of North Carolina at Chapel Hill; Neil R. McMillen, *The Citizens' Council: Organized Resistance to the Second Reconstruction, 1954–64* (Urbana: University of Illinois Press, 1971), 111–14.

wilderment, however, regarding her editor's capacity for tolerance. "I declare," he exclaimed, "I don't see how you keep your job there. If I were Jonathan Daniels, which heaven forfend, I think I would fire you before breakfast."[64]

Lewis addressed a potent audience when "Incidentally" appeared on 22 July 1956. Legislators had convened in Raleigh for the following afternoon's beginning of the special session that almost certainly would result in the solons' finally adopting, after a two-year hiatus, a full-scale plan of massive resistance. Without question they attended closely to the state's dominant newspaper as they arrived in the capital. In "North Carolina Has Common-Sense" Lewis dismissed the charges she knew the delegates would face as they prepared the referendum to amend the constitution to allow for tuition grants for private schools and to empower local authorities to close schools in their communities and as they altered the state's compulsory school attendance law and debated the formulation of a resolution protesting *Brown*. She advised that no one give credence to the "great outcry by some of the integrationists . . . that the people who favor the proposed bills want to destroy the public schools. Nothing could be further from the truth." "The fact is, they want to save them," she declared. "The thing that would really destroy North Carolina's public schools would be to mix the races in them."[65]

In the shortest session in the history of the assembly—only five days—the Tar Heel lawmakers, despite Daniels's vehement opposition, adopted with almost complete unanimity the proposals of the North Carolina Advisory Committee on Education and a resolution of "condemnation and protest" objecting to the Supreme Court's "tyrannical usurpation of power." To protect his state's liberal reputation, Hodges called the measures "moderate" and termed them "'safety valve' legislation." The program "would not necessarily" be put into effect, he explained. It would be implemented only "if it should ever be needed," meaning, of course, if blacks eschewed voluntary segregation and initiated court action to integrate the schools. In a letter to Gerald Johnson, Daniels relayed his fear that the legislature's program formed the "first step for North Carolina along the road to Mississippi attitudes."[66]

64. NBL to James J. Kilpatrick, 16 July 1956, NBL Papers; Robbins L. Gates, *The Making of Massive Resistance: Virginia's Politics of Public School Desegregation, 1954–1956* (Chapel Hill: University of North Carolina Press, 1964), 104–10.

65. *N&O*, 22 July 1956; Hodges, *Businessman in the Statehouse*, 95–101.

66. Chafe, *Civilities and Civil Rights*, 72–77; Hodges, *Businessman in the Statehouse*, 92–97; Eagles, *Jonathan Daniels and Race Relations*, 186–90; *WP*, 29 July 1956; *NYT*, 28 July 1956.

"Didn't I tell you North Carolina had common sense?" Lewis asked in "Incidentally" a week after 8 September, when the Tar Heel electorate by a margin of well over four to one voted to amend the state constitution to place in effect the segregationist plan. In the eastern counties, which contained the highest percentage of blacks and where numerous white readers of the *News and Observer* had canceled their subscriptions in response to Daniels's editorials, the vote averaged seven to one in support of the proposals. Lewis took pride in the fact that a Virginia referendum over a tuition grant proposal had passed by a much narrower majority. The North Carolina plebiscite formed for her an "impressive vote of confidence in Governor Hodges' leadership on the segregation-integration issue in this State."[67]

Later that month she commended in "Incidentally" the Virginia General Assembly's adoption of a bastion of segregationist laws proposed by Governor Thomas Stanley. The obstructionist "Stanley Plan," orchestrated by Senator Harry F. Byrd, consisted of three principal bulwarks to integration. First, a three-member Pupil Assignment Board subsumed from local school boards the responsibility for the placement of students. Purportedly this body would act objectively, but in fact it existed solely to stymie integration. Should black litigants surmount this redoubt, they would face yet another barrier. The governor would close schools integrated via court action or appeals regarding the board's decisions. The commonwealth would then furnish funding to support the private education of students and to pay the salaries of principals and teachers assigned to closed institutions. Finally, although the city councils of communities whose schools the governor had suspended could petition him for their reopening, they could not assume that they would receive state financing. Most localities, of course, would find it impossible to operate their schools without assistance from Richmond.[68]

On 11 November, in a lead editorial entitled "'Leakage through the Dyke'?" Lewis endorsed the "trenchant remarks" made by former assistant attorney general I. Beverly Lake, her state's stoutest "advocate of undiluted segregation." Lake, undoubtedly inspired by Virginia's tenacity, warned that North Carolina's recently adopted segregationist plan required strengthening. He advocated the passage of additional massive resistance legislation and the "formulation and proclamation in clear terms of a fixed, strong, determined policy

67. *N&O*, 16 September 1956; Hodges, *Businessman in the Statehouse*, 104–5; Eagles, *Jonathan Daniels and Race Relations*, 190.

68. *N&O*, 30 September 1956; Leidholdt, *Standing before the Shouting Mob*, 78.

that, come what may, we will not integrate." He did not believe that the oath he had taken to support the Constitution bound him to "accept the sociological and psychological assumptions of the United States Supreme Court" or to "bow in humble submission before whatever command comes out of Washington" or to "urge my neighbors to acquiesce meekly in repudiation of their heritage and betrayal of their posterity." Lewis responded to Lake's defiance by ending her editorial with a single-word sentence—"Cheers!"[69]

In all probability Lewis discerned in the hotheaded lawyer an ideal successor to Hodges, whose gubernatorial term would expire in 1960. Lake's diehard opposition to even token integration and his red-baiting of the NAACP attracted the columnist powerfully to him. (He would in fact—with the support of the bungling North Carolina Defenders of States' Rights, which emerged from the wreckage of the Patriots in 1958—vie with moderate Terry Sanford in the hotly contested 1960 Democratic gubernatorial primary.)[70]

The future must have seemed bright for "Battling Nell" at this juncture. If she and other obstinate segregationists could hold Hodges's feet to the fire and persuade him and the legislature to emulate the shining example furnished by Virginia's formidable fortress against school integration and later ensconce Lake in the governor's mansion, they possibly could stave off even minimal integration. This scenario, of course, would require an aroused Tar Heel citizenry supportive of a heightened level of massive resistance, but Lewis surely took comfort in the outcome of the recent referendum and believed that she and like-minded publicists, in conjunction with the Patriots, could stoke among the rank and file an even more aggressive defiance of the Court's mandate. She undoubtedly savored the possibility of inciting this further insurgency from the pages of the despised Jonathan Daniels's *News and Observer.*

Perhaps Lewis relished some of this agenda as she drove home on the night of 26 November 1956, shortly before she stepped out of her parked automobile, with her keys and purse in one hand, and collapsed in her front yard.[71]

69. *N&O,* 11 November 1956.

70. Lewis, *White South and the Red Menace,* 143–44; McMillen, *Citizens' Council,* 114.

71. *N&O,* 28 November 1956.

# CONCLUSION

Early on the morning of 27 November 1956, a paper boy delivering the *News and Observer* discovered Nell Lewis's body in her front yard. The door to her automobile remained partly open from the night before, and she was still clutching her purse and keys. The combative columnist appeared to have died quickly and peacefully from a heart attack, a half-year shy of her sixty-third birthday.[1]

Her memorial services more fittingly reflected her pugnacious personality. She had left detailed instructions regarding her funeral arrangements. Although she had remained a member of Christ Church, where she had been baptized and confirmed and where her father for thirty-seven years had served as senior warden, she despised its rector, the Reverend Stephen Walke. Consequently, when she had attended religious services, which she normally did only on special occasions, she worshiped at Raleigh's Church of the Good Shepherd or St. Michael's, whose rector, the Reverend James Beckwith, she admired. Although Lewis mandated in her will that her funeral services take place at Christ Church, she stipulated that Beckwith preside over the ceremony and that Walke speak nary a word. Her niece, Lottie Woolen, recalled that the rites seemed to last forever and that her aunt required the mourners to stand beside her grave until attendants had spread the last shovelful of earth over it.[2]

Walke had incurred Lewis's ire by urging his parishioners to embrace the *Brown v. Board of Education* decision. She subsequently could not even bring herself to refer to the clergyman as "Father," which seemed to her "just too consanguineous." In her column, "Incidentally" she dubbed him instead "Uncle Stephen." When a lightning storm of biblical proportions had sparked a fire that razed Governor Hodges's church during the July massive resistance special session, Christ Church had emerged unscathed. Divine intervention must have accounted for its survival, Lewis jeered. Uncle Stephen perhaps had pleaded, "Remember me, Lord!" and beseeched the Creator to recall how after the Court's "anti-segregation decision," the rector "could hardly wait to

1. *N&O*, 28 November 1956.

2. Lottie Woolen, telephone interview by author, 28 November 2000; *N&O*, 27 May, 19 August, and 28 November 1956.

leap into the pulpit and, practically tearing [his] surplice, hop on the integration bandwagon and start beating a drum."[3]

Lewis left a modest estate of twenty-five thousand dollars, the bulk of which she distributed to Lottie and to Kemp's other daughters. To her other close relations, with the exception of Ivey, she bequeathed sums of one hundred to five hundred dollars. Apparently still indignant until her dying day about the lack of financial support her sole surviving brother had provided her, she bestowed upon him a single dollar.[4]

The prospect of Jonathan Daniels's appraising her life would have disgusted Lewis every bit as much as Walke's presiding over her funeral, but the responsibility for writing her obituary for the *News and Observer* nevertheless fell upon the editor's shoulders. In his brief but gracious tribute he observed—undoubtedly drawing somewhat from his interactions with his headstrong employee—that "Miss Lewis did not live quietly." The "colorful author" of the "frequently brilliant and sometimes highly controversial column" had come to his father's newspaper after World War I as the "personification of 'flaming youth.'" She had begun "Incidentally" frivolously to furnish readers with lighthearted commentary about the capital city. As she became involved in weightier matters, such as public welfare, her column changed to reflect her interests. Daniels reviewed her run for the legislature, her brief but dramatic law career, and her teaching appointment at St. Mary's.[5]

He maintained, however, that her work as a journalist provided the best reflection of her personality. Although the conservative views she had espoused in recent years contrasted powerfully with the politics she had embraced as a young woman, she had continued to "express herself with the same sprightliness and vigor which had marked her earlier writings." Her column "was always widely read and usually debated sharply," he noted. "Nell Battle Lewis made for herself a name that will be long remembered in North Carolina. Hers was a forceful personality and her high ability and complete sincerity were beyond question."[6]

Lewis reportedly did not stay buried for long. She had made it clear to many in her social circle that if she could transcend the netherworld, she would be coming back, possibly in the form of her favorite "ha'nt," a poltergeist. Six months after her death her neighbor and longtime intimate,

3. *N&O*, 19 August 1956.

4. *N&O*, 4 December 1956.

5. *N&O*, 28 November 1956.

6. *N&O*, 28 November 1956.

Margarette Smethurst, recounted in the *News and Observer* that Lewis's spirit had visited six of her friends and that it had also returned to Cloverdale, her family home. One woman could not rid her house of the ghost until she threw out every item that reminded her of the journalist. A man heard her pacing the second floor of his home. When he later divulged this experience to his wife, she asked if he had gone upstairs to confirm Lewis's presence. "I didn't need to," he explained. "I knew who it was. Nobody else ever walked as hard and as loud as Nell." Smethurst herself had encountered her old friend. Alone in her house, she had heard a familiar rapping on her dining room table and recognized "Nell's old knock—brisk, loud, distinctive."[7]

Had Lewis survived her heart attack, the decision the following year by school boards in Winston-Salem, Greensboro, and Charlotte to admit a dozen black students to previously white schools, together with Daniels's contemporaneous failed attempt to persuade Raleigh authorities to assign a black student to all-white Broughton High School, surely would have strained the columnist's weakened cardiovascular system to its limits. Had she still been alive, she would undoubtedly have attempted to rally and fortify the recalcitrant whites protesting this token desegregation.[8]

The knowledge that the General Assembly's actions during the summer of 1956 and the subsequent voter referendum marked the high-water mark of her state's massive resistance would have depressed Lewis deeply. Tar Heel political leaders had little stomach for the brinkmanship employed by the obstinate Virginians. Consequently, North Carolina endured no school closings. The actions of Hodges and the legislature during the special session nevertheless stymied meaningful integration of North Carolina's public schools for ten years. The plan developed by the North Carolina Advisory Committee on Education would be declared unconstitutional in 1966. Although integration had occurred in most of the state's school districts by 1965, complete desegregation would not occur in all communities until the 1970s.[9]

In John Egerton's monumental study of the South in the decades immediately preceding the civil rights movement, *Speak Now against the Day,* he impresses

7. *N&O,* 12 May 1957.

8. Crow, Escott, and Hatley, *History of African Americans,* 171; Powell, *North Carolina through Four Centuries,* 195–96.

9. Chafe, *Civilities and Civil Rights,* 81–82; Eagles, *Jonathan Daniels and Race Relations,* 191; H. G. Jones, *North Carolina Illustrated, 1524–1984* (Chapel Hill: University of North Carolina Press, 1983), 424; Crow, Escott, and Hatley, *History of African Americans,* 171–72.

upon his readers that well before the *New York Times* embarked on a policy of hiring female journalists in any magnitude, a number of women from below the Mason-Dixon Line had entered the male arena of the fourth estate and had established reputations for themselves. With good reason he begins his listing of five of these pioneers with Lewis.[10]

Consciously rejecting the role of Southern Lady—and seemingly constitutionally incapable of conforming to the limiting characterization—Lewis, after returning from France in 1919, chose instead to join a vanguard of remarkable women in North Carolina wresting their way into the public sphere to uphold the interests of Tar Heels theretofore bereft of voice and representation. With growing confidence and passion, throughout the 1920s and the first few years of the following decade, Lewis in her liberal iteration confronted the many problems that plagued her native region.

From the platform of one of the South's most influential presses and via prestigious national magazines and journals, she gleefully deconstructed Ladydom and skewered the racial, religious, and political intolerance that the Ku Klux Klan, biblical literalists, and patriotic societies promulgated and which formed the bedrock of southern culture. She alternately mocked and scorned her state's powerful and exploitative conservative business establishment. In her newspaper column she also relentlessly punctured boosters, Babbitts, social snobs, and eulogists of moonlight and magnolias.

During this era, however, Lewis did not limit her contribution to criticism. Through her reporting and her column, her publicity work for the pioneering State Board of Charities and Public Welfare, and her cultural and personal activism, she helped develop and advertise a series of policy recommendations, which she and her liberal allies believed would propel the South forward and benefit its most vulnerable residents. Intimately connected to the state's organized women and the epicenter of southern progressivism—the University of North Carolina—Lewis urged the adoption of specific voting, labor, and social reforms. In "Incidentally" and through her directorship of the budding *Reviewer,* she advanced literary realism and promoted the southern cultural renaissance.

Her many controversial stands won her celebrity—and notoriety—throughout the region, attracted the attention of H. L. Mencken and Edwin Mims, and earned her a well-deserved reputation as the prototype of the new southern

10. Egerton, *Speak Now against the Day,* 253.

woman. By the mid-1920s Lewis seemed well on her way to assuming national journalistic prominence. Her reputation as a crusading liberal columnist, an activist, and a breaker of gender barriers reached its apex late in the decade and in the early 1930s as a result of her trailblazing run for the state legislature, her impassioned stumping for Al Smith in the 1928 presidential election, her fierce advocacy in the Gastonia murder trials, and the ardent defense the novice lawyer—one of a handful of forerunning female Tar Heel attorneys—mounted for inmates of the Samarcand reformatory for girls. During her progressive heyday "Battling Nell" seldom prevailed in encounters with her powerful foes, but none of her defeats diminished her spirit or stilled her voice. Time and again, she placed herself in the forefront of the South's liberal press in attacking injustice.

Lewis's distinction as her state's earliest female columnist (and presumably one of the first in the South) and her outspokenness garnered attention and amplified her impact. The spectacle of one of Dixie's daughters, who boasted an impeccable southern pedigree, interrogating and often disparaging sacrosanct doctrine also attracted readers. The stylistic freedom she enjoyed as a columnist and the intensely personal nature of her writing made her column conspicuous and distinguished her from editorialists.

Besides the general readers who attended to "Incidentally," the political and business leadership and the intelligentsia of the state studied her commentary. Disseminated in many parts of the region through newspaper exchange agreements and widespread reprinting, "Incidentally" also commanded the attention of editors and opinion leaders well outside the *News and Observer*'s immediate range of circulation. Lewis magnified her column's impact by frequently using it to broadcast the viewpoints of other leading liberals to her readers, many of whom received their only exposure to journalism from her newspaper.

Her advocacy rallied and galvanized feminists and liberals and shocked and dismayed traditionalists. It also helped set an agenda and spark debate of the region's status quo. The courage she displayed as a young single woman and the vigor with which she entered public life surely inspired many female readers to question the prevailing dogma that constrained women's roles. One wonders what role Lewis might have played in the history of southern liberalism had she not encountered sexism and psychological problems when her flame burned most brightly. She undoubtedly possessed the talent and drive to direct a major liberal newspaper at a time when editors projected great influence, to establish a political career when Tar Heels mired in the Great Depression needed a champion, or to become a legal advocate for her state's many poor and powerless citizens. Yet these very obstacles contributed formidably to her sensitivity and the establishment of her progressive goals.

After battling debilitating mental illness, medical ignorance, sexism, isolation, and occasional financial hardship away from home, Lewis returned to North Carolina in late 1934 in the process of recanting many aspects of her previous activism, albeit never her concern for the inmates of prisons and mental institutions. In her column she attributed her reversal to aging and to having resolved the psychological problems she blamed for her earlier activism. She now also claimed that communists had manipulated her during the labor unrest in Gastonia.

As she struggled in the mid-1930s to recover from the most severe episode of depression in her life, many factors unmentioned by Lewis may have combined to erode her liberalism. Consumed with health and financial worries, frustrated in her publishing ambitions, and beholden to family members with whom she now resided while deprived of her former network of feminist support, Lewis surely would have been ripe for absorbing her kin's outspoken conservative ideology. She had, already in 1932, rethought her advocacy for labor, apparently when its agitation reached her brothers' mills. She now lived with her family's anger over slights by the University of North Carolina and its tolerance of communism. Continual exposure to her relatives' rancor—and sympathy for their grievances—could hardly have left her unmoved. Alcoholism might have affected her thinking, and the difficulty she would have faced in reassuming her controversial liberal persona when rumors of her mental problems had circulated throughout the state possibly reinforced her turnabout.

The racism and the glorification of the Old South and the Lost Cause imprinted on Lewis during her childhood and her brother Ivey's eugenical credo may also have contributed to her transformation. The distinguished biologist would later serve as a confidant and trusted advisor to his sister as she attempted to sustain Jim Crow. In the end exhaustion, stress, her limited success as a South saver, and her subsequent collapse may have heightened her susceptibility to the region's prevailing ideology.

For thirteen years after her return to her native state, Lewis functioned as a minor and sometimes eccentric journalistic figure. In 1947, unsettled by Soviet expansionism and intrigue, she grew consumed with fear of a widespread domestic communist conspiracy. The heightened postwar racial activism further alarmed her. Her heady attacks on presidential candidate Henry Wallace; the Southern Conference for Human Welfare; communists; proponents of increased rights for blacks; and Frank Porter Graham, the personification of southern liberalism, resurrected her career and earned acclaim from her many traditional readers and from southern politicians and business leaders. Her sex, apostasy, and compelling narrative regarding her transformation attracted attention and undoubtedly amplified her audience. Lewis's appointment as the associate editor of the conservative *Raleigh Times* broke another gender barrier in the history of North Carolina journalism and gave her the exhilarating opportunity to bore into her foes and vie editorially with her bête noire, Jonathan Daniels, on a daily basis. She seemed on the cusp of achieving prominence as a leading defender of the traditional South when illness—apparently another major episode of depression—prompted her resignation from the *Times* and temporarily halted her revival.

Upon reestablishing her column in the *News and Observer* in 1950, Lewis continued to stoke the white southern backlash against liberals and racial progressives. The striking ideological contrast between "Incidentally" and Daniels's liberal editorial page generated discussion and expanded her readership. Conservatives, including much of the state's political and business establishment, who regarded Daniels with antipathy surely relished Lewis's recalcitrance and followed her commentary closely. The decision by Willis Smith to feature the columnist so prominently in his campaign against Graham establishes her significance as an influential reactionary figure. Supreme Court civil rights decisions, a changing racial and political climate, and the incumbent's long history of progressivism doomed Graham's candidacy in the historic election, but her prolonged crusade against him and the speeches she delivered for Smith contributed to her former ally's defeat.

Lewis's reputation as a leading voice of the southern way of life peaked in the wake of *Brown v. Board of Education* as she goaded her state to join Virginia and the Deep South in their massive resistance to public school integration. No Tar Heel journalist lobbied more forcefully toward this end. The defiance promoted in "Incidentally" drew the attention of major southern editors and resulted in the column's widespread reprinting. Her editorials spurred and sanctioned hard-line resistance by the Patriots of North Carolina and other belligerent proponents of ongoing racial segregation. Although the governor and the General Assembly ultimately rejected the militant stand she urged, her agitation shortly before her death helped create a political climate conducive to the adoption of legislation that for many years prevented significant integration of the state's public schools.

Lewis's extraordinary, contradictory, and intensely idiosyncratic life's journey remains notable not just because of its connectedness to many of the convulsive events that shaped southern history in the first half of the twentieth century but also for the agency Battling Nell displayed, the gender barriers she helped to demolish, and the courage and vitality with which she asserted herself.

# BIBLIOGRAPHY


PERSONAL COMMUNICATIONS

Halperin, Edward C. Letter to author, 8 August 2006.

Holder, Janis. Letter to author, 28 July 2006.

Smith, Aidan. Letter to author, 7 February 2007.

Stanley, Martha. Telephone interview by author, 8 May 1992.

Woolen, Lottie. Telephone interview by author, 8 May 1992, 28 November 2000.

Young, Nanci. Interview by author, 17 July 2003.

PERSONAL PAPERS AND MANUSCRIPT COLLECTIONS

American Civil Liberties Union. Papers. University of Minnesota, Minneapolis.

Chambers, Lenoir. Papers (no. 3827). Southern Historical Collection, Wilson Library, University of North Carolina at Chapel Hill.

Class of 1917 Records, Smith College Archives.

Daniels, Jonathan. Papers (no. 3466). Southern Historical Collection, Wilson Library, University of North Carolina at Chapel Hill.

Correspondence of Dean of the University and Dean of the College of Arts and Sciences, MSS 3299, Special Collections, University of Virginia Library.

*Gastonia Gazette* Correspondence (no. 3867-z). Southern Historical Collection, Wilson Library, University of North Carolina at Chapel Hill.

Graham, Frank Porter. Papers (no. 1819). Southern Historical Collection, Wilson Library, University of North Carolina at Chapel Hill.

Holt, Erwin Allen. Papers (no. 3551). Southern Historical Collection, Wilson Library, University of North Carolina at Chapel Hill.

Johnson, Kate Ancrum Burr. Papers (no. 91). Special Collections Department, Joyner Library, East Carolina University, Greenville, N.C.

Lewis, Kemp Plummer. Papers (no. 3819). Southern Historical Collection, Wilson Library, University of North Carolina at Chapel Hill.

Lewis, Nell Battle Papers. North Carolina State Archives, Raleigh.

Lewis, Nell Battle Papers. St. Mary's School Archives, Raleigh, N.C.

Papers of Ivey Foreman Lewis, 1879–1959. RG-6/2/1.551, RG-6/2/1.651, Special Collections, University of Virginia Library.

Papers of the President. RG-2/1/2.491 subseries 4, Special Collections, University of Virginia Library.

Powell, John. Papers (no. 7284). Manuscripts Division, Special Collections Department, University of Virginia Library.

## BOOKS, YEARBOOKS, HANDBOOKS, AND CATALOGUES


Abrams, Douglas Carl. *Conservative Constraints: North Carolina and the New Deal.* Jackson: University Press of Mississippi, 1992.

American Civil Liberties Union. *Justice—North Carolina Style, The Record of the Year's Struggle for Unions in Gastonia and Marion, April 1929 to April 1930.* New York: American Civil Liberties Union, 1930.

American Medical Association, comp. *American Medical Directory, 1931.* Chicago: American Medical Association, 1931.

*American Newspaper Annual and Directory.* Philadelphia: N. W. Ayer and Son, 1928.

American Psychiatric Association, comp. *Directory of Fellows and Members of the American Psychiatric Association.* New York: American Psychiatric Association, 1941.

Anderson, Norman D., and D. T. Fowler. *Raleigh: North Carolina's Capital City on Postcards* Dover, N.H.: Arcadia Publishing, 1996.

Angoff, Charles. *H. L. Mencken: A Portrait from Memory.* New York: Thomas Yoseloff, 1956.

Aptheker, Herbert, ed. *A Documentary History of the Negro People in the United States.* Vol. 3: *From the N.A.A.C.P to the New Deal.* New York: Citadel Press, 1973.

Ashby, Warren. *Frank Porter Graham: A Southern Liberal.* Winston-Salem: John F. Blair, 1980.

Ashley, Perry J., ed. *Dictionary of Literary Biography.* Vol. 29. *American Newspaper Journalists, 1926–1950.* Detroit: Gale Research Co., 1984.

Ashmore, Harry S. *Civil Rights and Wrongs: A Memoir of Race and Politics, 1944–1994.* New York: Pantheon, 1994.

Astor, Gerald. *The Right to Fight: A History of African Americans in the Military.* Cambridge: Da Capo, 1998.

Bain, Robert, Joseph M. Flora, and Louis D. Rubin, eds. *Southern Writers: A Biographical Dictionary.* Baton Rouge: Louisiana State University Press, 1979.

Baker, Richard Terrill. *A History of the Graduate School of Journalism, Columbia University.* New York: Columbia University Press, 1954.

Baldwin, Marian. *Canteening Overseas, 1917–1919.* New York: Macmillan, 1920.

Bartley, Nunman V. *The Rise of Massive Resistance: Race and Politics in the South during the 1950s.* Baton Rouge: Louisiana State University Press, 1969.

Barzun, Jacques. *A Stroll with William James.* New York: Harper & Row, 1983.

Beal, Fred E. *Proletarian Journey: New England, Gastonia, Moscow.* New York: Hillman-Curl, 1937.

———. *Red Fraud: An Expose of Stalinism.* New York: Tempo, 1949.

Beardsley, Edward H. *A History of Neglect: Health Care for Blacks and Mill Workers in the Twentieth-Century South.* Knoxville: University of Tennessee Press, 1987.

Bell, John L., Jr. *Hard Times: Beginnings of the Great Depression in North Carolina, 1929–1933.* Raleigh: North Carolina Department of Cultural Resources, 1982.

Berkow, Robert, Mark H. Beers, and Andrew J. Fletcher, eds. *The Merck Manual of Medical Information Home Edition.* New York: Pocket Books, 1997.

Bernstein, Irving. *The Lean Years: A History of the American Laborer, 1920–1933*. Boston: Houghton Mifflin, 1960.

Berryhill, W. Reece, William B. Blythe, and Isaac H. Manning. *Medical Education at Chapel Hill: The First Hundred Years*. Chapel Hill: University of North Carolina School of Medicine, 1979.

Boyle, Kevin. *Arc of Justice: A Saga of Race, Civil Rights, and Murder in the Jazz Age*. New York: Henry Holt, 2004.

Boyle, Sarah Patton. *The Desegregated Heart: A Virginian's Stand in a Time of Transition*. New York: William Morrow, 1962.

Brecher, Jeremy. *Strike!* Cambridge: South End Press, 1997.

Brian, Denis. *The Enchanted Voyager: The Life of J. B. Rhine*. Englewood Cliffs, N.J.: Prentice Hall, 1982.

Buhle, Mari Jo, Paul Buhle, and Dan Georgakas, eds. *Encyclopedia of the American Left*. New York: Oxford University Press, 1998.

Cash, W. J. *The Mind of the South*. New York: Alfred A. Knopf, 1941.

*Catalogue of the University of Virginia Session of 1848–1849*. Richmond: H. K. Ellyson, 1849.

Chafe, William H. *Civilities and Civil Rights: Greensboro, North Carolina, and the Black Struggle for Freedom*. New York: Oxford University Press, 1980.

Chalmers, David M. *Hooded Americanism: The First Century of the Ku Klux Klan, 1865–1965*. Garden City, N.Y.: Doubleday, 1965.

Chambers, John Whiteclay II, ed. *The Oxford Companion to American Military History*. New York: Oxford University Press, 1999.

Claiborne, Jack. *The Charlotte Observer: Its Time and Place, 1869–1986*. Chapel Hill: University of North Carolina Press, 1986.

Clayton, Bruce. *W. J. Cash, A Life*. Baton Rouge: Louisiana State University Press, 1991.

Coates, Albert. *By Her Own Bootstraps: A Saga of Women in North Carolina*. N.p.p., 1975.

Cott, Nancy F., ed. *No Small Courage: A History of Women in the United States*. New York: Oxford University Press, 2000.

Couch, W. T, ed. *Culture in the South*. Chapel Hill: University of North Carolina Press, 1934.

Cox, Earnest Sevier. *White America*. Richmond: White America Society, 1923.

Crow, Jeffrey J., Paul D. Escott, and Flora J. Hatley. *A History of African Americans in North Carolina*. Raleigh: North Carolina Division of Archives and History, 1992.

Cullen-DuPont, Kathryn. *The Encyclopedia of Women's History in America*. New York: Da Capo, 1998.

Dabney, Virginius. *Dry Messiah: The Life of Bishop Cannon*. New York: Alfred A. Knopf, 1949.

———. *Liberalism in the South*. Chapel Hill: University of North Carolina Press, 1932.

———. *Mr. Jefferson's University: A History*. Charlottesville: University Press of Virginia, 1981.

Daniels, Jonathan. *Frontier on the Potomac*. New York: Macmillan, 1946.

———. *Tar Heels: A Portrait of North Carolina*. New York: Dodd, Mead & Co., 1941.

Dinnerstein, Leonard. *Anti-Semitism in America*. New York: Oxford University Press, 1994.

*Donnybrook Fair.* Baltimore: Norman T. A. Munder, 1912.

*Donnybrook Fair.* Baltimore: Norman T. A. Munder, 1914.

Downs, Robert B., and Jane B. Downs. *Journalists of the United States: Biographical Sketches of Print and Broadcast News Shapers from the Late 17th Century to the Present.* Jefferson, N.C.: McFarland & Co., 1991.

Dunne, William J. *Gastonia: Citadel of the Class Struggle in the New South.* New York: Workers Library Publishers, 1929.

Eagles, Charles W. *Jonathan Daniels and Race Relations: The Evolution of a Southern Liberal.* Knoxville: University of Tennessee Press, 1982.

Eddy, Mary Baker. *Science and Health: With Keys to the Scriptures.* Boston: First Church of Christ, Scientist, 1994.

Edmunds, Pocahontas Wight. *Virginians Out Front.* Richmond: Whittet & Shepperson, 1972.

Egerton, John. *Speak Now against the Day: The Generation before the Civil Rights Movement in the South.* New York: Alfred A. Knopf, 1994.

Ehle, John. *Dr. Frank: Life with Frank Porter Graham.* Chapel Hill: Franklin Street Books, 1993.

Evans, Clement A. *Confederate Military History.* Vol. 5. Atlanta: Confederate Publishing Co., 1899.

Evans, Eli N. *The Provincials: A Personal History of Jews in the South.* New York: Free Press, 1997.

Evans, Sara M. *Born for Liberty: A History of Women in America.* New York: Free Press, 1989.

Feinstein, Howard M. *Becoming William James.* Ithaca: Cornell University Press, 1984.

Fitzpatrick, Vincent. *Gerald W. Johnson: From Southern Liberal to National Conscience.* Baton Rouge: Louisiana State University Press, 2002.

Foner, Eric. *Reconstruction: America's Unfinished Revolution, 1863–1877.* New York: Harper & Row, 1989.

Frederickson, Kari. *The Dixiecrat Revolt and the End of the Solid South, 1932–1968.* Chapel Hill: University of North Carolina Press, 2001.

Garrison, Dee. Introduction to *Strike!* by Mary Heaton Vorse. Urbana: University of Illinois Press, 1991.

Garson, Robert A. *The Democratic Party and the Politics of Sectionalism, 1941–1948.* Baton Rouge: Louisiana State University Press, 1974.

Gates, Robbins L. *The Making of Massive Resistance: Virginia's Politics of Public School Desegregation, 1954–1956.* Chapel Hill: University of North Carolina Press, 1964.

Gatewood, Willard B. *Preachers, Pedagogues & Politicians: The Evolution Controversy in North Carolina, 1920–1927.* Chapel Hill: University of North Carolina Press, 1966.

Gavin, Lettie. *American Women in World War I: They Also Served.* Niwot: University Press of Colorado, 1997.

Gifford, Sanford. *The Emmanuel Movement (Boston, 1904–1929): The Origins of Group Therapy and the Assault on Lay Psychotherapy.* Boston: Francis Countway Library of Medicine, 1997; distributed by Harvard University Press.

Gilmore, Glenda Elizabeth. *Gender and Jim Crow: Women and the Politics of White Supremacy in North Carolina, 1896–1920.* Chapel Hill: University of North Carolina Press, 1996.

Glass, Brent D. *The Textile Industry in North Carolina: A History.* Raleigh: North Carolina Department of Cultural Resources, 1992.

Goebel, Julius, Jr. *A History of the School of Law, Columbia University.* New York: Columbia University Press, 1955.

Gordon, Armistead C. *Gordons in Virginia, with Notes on Gordons of Scotland and Ireland.* Hackensack, N.J.: William M. Clemens, 1918.

Gottschalk, Stephen. *The Emergence of Christian Science in American Religious Life.* Berkeley: University of California Press, 1973.

Grant, Madison. *The Passing of the Great Race.* New York: Charles Scribner's Sons, 1916.

Grantham, Dewey W. *The South in Modern America: A Region at Odds.* New York: HarperCollins, 1994.

Green, Elna C. *Southern Strategies: Southern Women and the Woman Suffrage Question.* Chapel Hill: University of North Carolina Press, 1997.

Greenberg, Jack. *Crusaders in the Courts: How a Dedicated Band of Lawyers Fought for the Civil Rights Revolution.* New York: Basic Books, 1994.

Hales, Dianne, and Robert E. Hales. *Caring for the Mind: The Comprehensive Guide to Mental Health.* New York: Bantam Books, 1995.

Hall, Jacquelyn Dowd. *Revolt against Chivalry: Jessie Daniel Ames and the Women's Campaign Against Lynching.* New York: Columbia University Press, 1993.

Hall, Jacquelyn Dowd, and Anne Firor Scott. "Women in the South." In *Interpreting Southern History: Historiographical Essays in Honor of Sanford W. Higginbotham.* Edited by John B. Boles and Evelyn Thomas Nolen. Baton Rouge: Louisiana State University Press, 1987.

Hall, Jacquelyn Dowd, James Leloudis, Robert Korstad, Mary Murphy, Lu Ann Jones, and Christopher B. Daly. *Like a Family: The Making of a Southern Cotton Mill World.* Chapel Hill: University of North Carolina Press, 1987.

Hall, Kermit L. ed. *The Oxford Companion to the Supreme Court of the United States.* New York: Oxford University Press, 1992.

Harris, Frederick, ed. *Service with Fighting Men: An Account of the Work of the American Young Men's Christian Associations in the World War.* Vol. 2. New York: Association Press, 1922.

Hart, James D., ed., *The Oxford Companion to American Literature.* New York: Oxford University Press, 1995.

Hastings, Max. *The Korean War.* New York: Touchstone, 1987.

Haynes, Earl. *Red Scare or Red Menace? American Communism and Anticommunism in the Cold War Era.* Chicago: Ivan R. Dee, 1996.

Heinemann, Ronald L., John G. Kolp, Anthony S. Parent Jr., and William G. Shade. *Old Dominion, New Commonwealth: A History of Virginia, 1607–2007.* Charlottesville: University of Virginia Press, 2007.

Helms, Jesse. *Here's Where I Stand: A Memoir.* New York: Random House, 2005.

Hewett, Janet B., ed. *North Carolina Confederate Soldiers: 1861–1865, Unit Roster*. Vol. 3. Wilmington, N.C.: Broadfoot Publishing Co., 1999.

Hitler, Adolf. *Mein Kampf.* Boston: Houghton Mifflin, 1943.

Hobbs, Samuel Huntington Jr. *North Carolina: Economic and Social.* Chapel Hill: University of North Carolina Press, 1930.

Hobson, Fred. *Mencken: A Life.* Baltimore: Johns Hopkins University Press, 1994.

———. *Serpent in Eden: H. L. Mencken and the South.* Chapel Hill: University of North Carolina Press, 1974.

Hodges, James A. *New Deal Labor Policy and the Southern Cotton Textile Industry, 1933–1941.* Knoxville: University of Tennessee Press, 1986.

Hodges, Luther H. *Businessman in the Statehouse: Six Years as Governor of North Carolina.* Chapel Hill: University of North Carolina Press, 1962.

Houck, Judith A. *Hot and Bothered: Women, Medicine, and Menopause in Modern America.* Cambridge: Harvard University Press, 2006.

Jackson, Kenneth T. *The Ku Klux Klan in the City, 1915–1930.* Chicago: Ivan R. Dee, 1992.

James, William. *The Varieties of Religious Experience.* New York: Longmans, Green and Co., 1935.

Jamison, Kay Redfield. *Touched with Fire: Manic-Depressive Illness and the Artistic Temperament.* New York: Free Press, 1992.

Janiewski, Dolores E. *Sisterhood Denied: Race, Gender, and Class in a New South Community.* Philadelphia: Temple University Press, 1985.

Janken, Kenneth Robert. *White: The Biography of Walter White, Mr. NAACP.* New York: New Press, 2003.

Johanningsmeier, Edward P. *Forging American Communism: The Life of William Z. Foster.* Princeton: Princeton University Press, 1994.

Johnson, Gerald W. "Journalism Below the Potomac." In *South-Watching: Selected Essays by Gerald W. Johnson.* Edited by Fred Hobson. Chapel Hill: University of North Carolina Press, 1983.

Jones, H. G. *North Carolina Illustrated, 1524–1984.* Chapel Hill: University of North Carolina Press, 1983.

Josephson, Mathew, and Hannah Josephson. *Al Smith: Hero of the Cities, A Political Portrait Drawing on the Papers of Frances Perkins.* Boston: Houghton Mifflin, 1969.

Keegan, John. *The First World War,* New York: Alfred A. Knopf, 1999.

Key, V. O. Jr. *Southern Politics in State and Nation.* Knoxville: University of Tennessee Press, 1984.

King, Florence. *Southern Ladies and Gentlemen.* New York: St. Martin's Press, 1975.

Klehr, Harvey. *The Heyday of American Communism: The Depression Decade.* New York: Basic Books, 1984.

Kneebone, John T. *Southern Liberal Journalists and the Issue of Race, 1920–1944.* Chapel Hill: University of North Carolina Press, 1985.

Knipp, Anna Heubeck, and Thaddeus P. Thomas. *The History of Goucher College.* Baltimore: Goucher College, 1938.

Korstad, Robert Rodgers. *Civil Rights Unionism: Tobacco Workers and the Struggle for Democracy in the Mid-Twentieth-Century South.* Chapel Hill: University of North Carolina Press, 2003.

Krueger, Thomas A. *And Promises to Keep: The Southern Conference for Human Welfare, 1938–1948.* Nashville: Vanderbilt University Press, 1967.

Lancaster, Richard C. *Serving the U.S. Armed Forces, 1861–1986: The Story of the YMCA's Ministry to Military Personnel for 125 Years.* Schaumburg, Ill.: Armed Services YMCA of the USA, 1986.

Lefler, Hugh Talmage, and Albert Ray Newsome. *North Carolina: The History of a Southern State.* Chapel Hill: University of North Carolina Press, 1954.

Leidholdt, Alexander S. *Editor for Justice: The Life of Louis I. Jaffé.* Baton Rouge: Louisiana State University Press, 2002.

———. *Standing before the Shouting Mob: Lenoir Chambers and Virginia's Massive Resistance to Public-School Integration.* Tuscaloosa: University of Alabama Press, 1997.

Leloudis, James L. *Schooling the New South: Pedagogy, Self, and Society in North Carolina, 1880–1920.* Chapel Hill: University of North Carolina Press, 1996.

Lewis, George. *The White South and the Red Menace: Segregationists, Anticommunism, and Massive Resistance, 1945–1965.* Gainesville: University Press of Florida, 2004.

Lewis, Nell Battle. *The Way: Studies in the Teachings of Jesus of Nazareth.* Privately printed, [1942].

Linder, Suzanne Cameron. *William Louis Poteat: Prophet of Progress.* Chapel Hill: University of North Carolina Press, 1966.

Link, William A. *The Paradox of Southern Progressivism, 1880–1930.* Chapel Hill: University of North Carolina Press, 1992.

Lipstadt, Deborah E. *Beyond Belief: The American Press and the Coming of the Holocaust, 1933–1945.* New York: Free Press, 1986.

Low, W. Augustus, and Virgil A. Clift, eds. *The Encyclopedia of Black America.* New York: Da Capo, 1984.

MacDougall, Curtis D. *Gideon's Army.* Vol. 1. *The Components of the Decision.* New York: Marzani & Munsell, 1965.

———. *Gideon's Army.* Vol. 3. *The Campaign and the Vote.* New York: Marzani & Munsell, 1965.

MacLean, Nancy. *Behind the Mask of Chivalry: The Making of the Second Ku Klux Klan.* New York: Oxford University Press, 1994.

Manchester, William. *The Glory and the Dream: A Narrative History of America, 1932–1972.* Vol. 1. Boston: Little, Brown, 1973.

Marshall, S.L.A. *World War I.* Boston: Houghton Mifflin, 1964.

Mason, Mary Ann Bryan. *A Wreath from the Woods of Carolina.* New York: General Protestant Episcopal Sunday School Union and Church Book Society, 1859.

McCullough, David. *Truman.* New York: Touchstone, 1992.

McMillen, Neil R. *The Citizens' Council: Organized Resistance to the Second Reconstruction, 1954–64.* Urbana: University of Illinois Press, 1971.

Mead, Gary. *The Doughboys: America and the First World War.* New York: Overlook Press, 2000.

Mencken, H. L. *Happy Days, 1880–1892.* New York: Alfred A. Knopf, 1940.

———. *Heathen Days, 1890–1936.* New York: Alfred A. Knopf, 1943.

———. *A Mencken Chrestomathy.* New York: Vintage Books, 1982.

———. *Newspaper Days, 1899–1906.* New York: Alfred A. Knopf, 1941.

———. *Thirty-Five Years of Newspaper Work.* Edited by Fred Hobson, Vincent Fitzpatrick, and Bradford Jacobs. Baltimore: Johns Hopkins University Press, 1994.

Mims, Edwin. *The Advancing South: Stories of Progress and Reaction.* Garden City, N.Y.: Doubleday, Page & Co., 1926.

Moore, Edmund A. *A Catholic Runs for President: The Campaign of 1928.* New York: Ronald Press Co., 1956.

Morrison, Joseph L. *Governor O. Max Gardner: A Power in North Carolina and New Deal Washington.* Chapel Hill: University of North Carolina Press, 1971.

———. *Josephus Daniels Says . . . An Editor's Political Odyssey from Bryan to Wilson and F.D.R., 1894–1913.* Chapel Hill: University of North Carolina Press, 1962.

———. *Josephus Daniels: The Small-d Democrat.* Chapel Hill: University of North Carolina Press, 1966.

Moton, Robert Russa. *Finding a Way Out: An Autobiography.* College Park, Md.: McGrath, 1969.

Murray, Pauli. *Song in a Weary Throat: An American Pilgrimage.* New York: Harper & Row, 1987.

Myrdal, Gunnar. *An American Dilemma: The Negro Problem and Modern Democracy.* 2 vols. New Brunswick, N.J.: Transaction Publishers, 1996.

Newby, I. A. *Plain Folk in the New South: Social Change and Cultural Persistence, 1880–1915.* Baton Rouge: Louisiana State University Press, 1989.

Newsome, A. R., comp. *North Carolina Manual, 1929.* Raleigh: North Carolina Historical Commission, 1929.

O'Brien, Michael. *Rethinking the South: Essays in Intellectual History.* Athens: University of Georgia Press, 1993.

Odum, Howard W. *Race and Rumors of Race.* Chapel Hill: University of North Carolina Press, 1943.

Olson, Lynne. *Freedom's Daughters: The Unsung Heroines of the Civil Rights Movement from 1830 to 1970.* New York: Scribner, 2001.

Perkins, David, ed. *The News & Observer's Raleigh: A Living History of North Carolina's Capital.* Winston-Salem: John F. Blair, 1994.

Pleasants, Julian M., and Augustus M. Burns III. *Frank Porter Graham and the 1950 Senate Race in North Carolina.* Chapel Hill: University of North Carolina Press, 1990.

Pope, Liston. *Millhands & Preachers: A Study of Gastonia.* New Haven: Yale University Press, 1942.

Porter, Earl W. *Trinity and Duke, 1892–1924: Foundations of Duke University.* Durham: Duke University Press, 1964.

Powell, William S. *North Carolina Lives: The Tar Heel Who's Who.* Hopkinsville, Ky.: Historical Record Association, 1962.

———. *North Carolina through Four Centuries.* Chapel Hill: University of North Carolina Press, 1989.

———, ed. *Dictionary of North Carolina Biography.* 6 vols. Chapel Hill: University of North Carolina Press, 1979–96.

Powers, Richard Gid. *Not without Honor: The History of American Anticommunism.* New Haven: Yale University Press, 1998.

Pyron, Darden Asbury. "Nell Battle Lewis (1893–1956) and the 'New Southern Woman.'" In *Perspectives on the American South.* Vol. 3. Edited by James C. Cobb and Charles R. Wilson. New York: Gordon and Breach Science Publishers, 1985.

———. *Southern Daughter: The Life of Margaret Mitchell.* New York: Oxford University Press, 1991.

*A Red Triangle Girl in France.* New York: George Doran, 1918.

Reed, John Shelton, and Dale Volberg Reed. *1001 Things Everyone Should Know about the South.* New York: Doubleday, 1996.

Reed, Linda. *Simple Decency & Common Sense: The Southern Conference Movement, 1938–1963.* Bloomington: Indiana University Press, 1991.

Rhine, J. B. *Extra-Sensory Perception.* Boston: Boston Society for Psychic Research, 1934.

Ripley, William. *The Races of Europe: A Sociological Study.* New York: D. Appleton, 1910.

Robinson, Blackwell P., ed. *The North Carolina Guide.* Chapel Hill: University of North Carolina Press, 1955.

Rodgers, Elizabeth, ed. *Mencken and Sara: A Life in Letters, The Private Correspondence of H. L. Mencken and Sara Haardt.* New York: McGraw-Hill, 1987.

Roller, David C., and Robert W. Twyman, eds. *The Encyclopedia of Southern History.* Baton Rouge: Louisiana State University Press, 1979.

Rowbotham, Sheila. *A Century of Women: The History of Women in Britain and the United States.* New York: Penguin, 1997.

Salley, Katherine Batts, ed. *Life at Saint Mary's.* Chapel Hill: University of North Carolina Press, 1942.

Salmond, John A. *Gastonia 1929: The Story of the Loray Mill Strike.* Chapel Hill: University of North Carolina Press, 1995.

Scales, Junius Irving, and Richard Nickson. *Cause at Heart: A Former Communist Remembers.* Athens: University of Georgia Press, 1987.

Scott, Anne Firor. *The Southern Lady: From Pedestal to Politics, 1830–1930.* Charlottesville: University Press of Virginia, 1970.

Seelye, L. Clark. *The Early History of Smith College, 1871–1910.* Boston: Houghton Mifflin, 1923.

Separk, Joseph H. *Gastonia and Gaston County, North Carolina: Past, Present, Future.* Kingsport, Tenn.: Kingsport Press, 1936.

Shapiro, Herbert. *White Violence and Black Response: From Reconstruction to Montgomery.* Amherst: University of Massachusetts Press, 1988.

Shortall, Katherine. *A "Y" Girl in France, Letters of Katherine Shortall*. Boston: Gorham Press, 1918.

Sims, Anastatia. *The Power of Femininity in the New South: Women's Organizations and Politics in North Carolina, 1880–1930*. Columbia: University of South Carolina Press, 1997.

Singal, Daniel Joseph. *The War Within: From Victorian to Modernist Thought in the South, 1919–1945*. Chapel Hill: University of North Carolina Press, 1982.

Sloan, Wm. David, ed. *The Media in America: A History*. Northport, Ala.: Vision Press, 2002.

Sloan, Wm. David, and Laird B. Anderson. *Pulitzer Prize Editorials: America's Best Editorial Writing, 1917–1993*. Ames: Iowa State University Press, 1994.

Smith College Association for Christian Work. *Students' Hand-Book of Smith College, 1916–1917*. Northampton? N.p., 1916.

*Smith College Class Book*. N.p., 1914.

*Smith College Class Book*. Buffalo: Hausauer-Jones, 1915.

*Smith College Class Book*. Buffalo: Hausauer-Jones, 1917.

Smith, J. Douglas. *Managing White Supremacy: Race, Politics, and Citizenship in Jim Crow Virginia*. Chapel Hill: University of North Carolina Press, 2002.

Smith, Margaret Supplee, and Emily Herring Wilson. *North Carolina Women: Making History*. Chapel Hill: University of North Carolina Press, 1999.

Snider, William D. *Light on the Hill: A History of the University of North Carolina at Chapel Hill*. Chapel Hill: University of North Carolina Press, 1992.

Solomon, Barbara Miller. *In the Company of Educated Women: A History of Women and Higher Education in America*. New Haven: Yale University Press, 1985.

Sosna, Morton. *In Search of the Silent South: Southern Liberals and the Race Issue*. New York: Columbia University Press, 1977.

Special Staff of Writers. *History of Virginia*. Vol. 4. *Virginia Biography*. New York: American Historical Society, 1924.

Starr, Paul. *The Creation of the Media: Political Origins of Modern Communications*. New York: Basic Books, 2004.

Stem, Thad, Jr. *The Tar Heel Press*. Charlotte: Heritage Printers, 1973.

*St. Mary's Muse*. Raleigh: St. Mary's School, 1908–11.

Stoops, Martha. *The Heritage: The Education of Women at St. Mary's College, Raleigh, North Carolina, 1842–1982*. Raleigh: The College, 1984.

Story, Ronald, ed. *Five Colleges: Five Histories*. Amherst, Mass.: Five Colleges, and Historic Deerfield, 1992.

*Students' Handbook: Goucher College, 1913–1914*. Baltimore: Waverly Press, 1913.

*Students of the University of Virginia: A Semi-Centennial Catalogue with Brief Biographical Sketches*. Baltimore: Charles Harvey & Co., 1878.

Suggs, Henry Lewis, ed. *The Black Press in the South*. Westport, Conn.: Greenwood Press, 1984.

Sullivan, Mark. *Our Times: America at the Birth of the Twentieth Century*. Edited by Dan Rather. New York: Scribner, 1996.

Taylor, Peter. *The Old Forest and Other Stories.* New York: Picador Press, 1996.

Teachout, Terry. *The Skeptic: A Life of H. L. Mencken.* New York: HarperCollins, 2002.

Thomson, Lloyd, and Winfield Scott Downs, eds. *Who's Who in American Medicine, 1925.* New York: Who's Who Publications, 1925.

Tindall, George Brown. *A History of the South.* Edited by Wendell Holmes Stephenson and E. Merton Coulter. Vol. 10. *The Emergence of the New South, 1913–1945.* Baton Rouge: Louisiana State University Press and the Littlefield Fund for Southern History, University of Texas, 1967.

Tippett, Tom. *When Southern Labor Stirs.* New York: Jonathan Cape & Harrison Smith, 1931.

Torrey, E. Fuller, and Michael B. Knable. *Surviving Manic Depression: A Manual on Bipolar Disorder for Patients, Families, and Providers.* New York: Basic Books, 2002.

Turner, J. Kelly, and Jno. L. Bridgers Jr. *History of Edgecombe County, North Carolina.* Raleigh: Edwards & Broughton, 1920.

Tushnet, Mark V. *The NAACP's Legal Strategy against Segregated Education, 1925–1950.* Chapel Hill: University of North Carolina Press, 1987.

Tussman, Joseph, ed. *The Supreme Court on Racial Discrimination.* New York: Oxford University Press, 1963.

Tyler-McGraw, Marie. *At the Falls: Richmond, Virginia, and Its People.* Chapel Hill: University of North Carolina Press, 1994.

Van Voris, Jacqueline. *College: A Smith Mosaic.* Westfield, Mass.: Smith College, 1975.

Virginia Department of Mental Hygiene and Hospitals. *A Directory of Mental Hygiene and Psychiatric Facilities in the Commonwealth of Virginia and Historical Summary.* Richmond: Virginia Department of Mental Hygiene and Hospitals, 1951.

Wallenstein, Peter. *Cradle of America: Four Centuries of Virginia History.* Lawrence: University Press of Kansas, 2007.

Warren, Marion E., and Mame Warren. *Baltimore—When She Was What She Used to Be, 1850–1930.* Baltimore: Johns Hopkins University Press, 1983.

Weisbord, Vera Buch. *A Radical Life.* Bloomington: Indiana University Press, 1977.

Welsh, Lilian. *Reminiscences of Thirty Years in Baltimore.* Baltimore: Norman, Remington Co., 1925.

Wheeler, Marjorie Spruill. *New Women of the New South: The Leaders of the Woman Suffrage Movement in the Southern States.* New York: Oxford University Press, 1993.

White, Walter. *A Man Called White.* New York: Viking Press, 1948.

White, William A. *The Outlines of Psychiatry.* Washington, D.C.: Nervous and Mental Disease Publishing Co., 1932.

*Who's Who in the South.* Washington, D.C.: Mayflower Publishing Co., 1927.

Wilhoit, Francis M. *The Politics of Massive Resistance.* New York: George Braziller, 1973.

Wilkinson, J. Harvie, III. *Harry Byrd and the Changing Face of Virginia Politics, 1945–1966.* Charlottesville: University Press of Virginia, 1968.

Williams, Juan. *Thurgood Marshall: American Revolutionary.* New York: Times Books, 1998.

Williams, William F., ed. *Encyclopedia of Pseudoscience.* New York: Facts on File, 2000.

Wilson, Charles Reagan, and William Ferris, eds. *Encyclopedia of Southern Culture.* Chapel Hill: University of North Carolina Press, 1989.

Wilson, Louis R. *The University of North Carolina, 1900–1930: The Making of a Modern University.* Chapel Hill: University of North Carolina Press, 1957.

Woodward, C. Vann. *A History of the South.* Edited by Wendell Holmes Stephenson and E. Merton Coulter. Vol. 9. *Origins of the New South, 1877–1913.* Baton Rouge: Louisiana State University Press and the Littlefield Fund for Southern History, University of Texas, 1951.

———. *The Strange Career of Jim Crow.* New York: Oxford University Press, 2002.

Worcester, Elwood. *Life's Adventure: The Story of a Varied Career.* New York: Charles Scribner's Sons, 1932.

Workers of the Writers' Program of the Work Projects Administration in the State of Virginia, comp. *Virginia: A Guide to the Old Dominion.* Richmond: Virginia State Library and Archives, 1992.

## THESES AND HONORS ESSAYS

Bryan, Kay. "The History of Desegregation at the University of Virginia, 1950–1969." Honors thesis, University of Virginia, 1979.

Frye, Michael W. "The Loray Strike Viewed by Six North Carolina Newspapers." Master's thesis, University of North Carolina, 1972.

Green, Linda Lou. "Nell Battle Lewis: Crusading Columnist, 1921–1938." Master's thesis, East Carolina University, 1969.

Hood, Robin. "The Loray Mill Strike." Master's thesis, University of North Carolina, 1932.

Mitchell, Victoria L. "Nell Battle Lewis: From 'South-Saving' Reformer to Southern Reactionary." Honors essay, University of North Carolina, 1985.

Pearson, Susan. "Samarcand, Nell Battle Lewis, and the 1931 Arson Trial." Honors essay, University of North Carolina, 1989.

Sellars, Linda Williams. "South Saver: Nell Battle Lewis in the 1920s." Master's thesis, University of North Carolina, 1984.

Van Dyke, Jeffrey Alan. "Bedsheets and Broadsheets: Covering the Ku Klux Klan in North Carolina." Master's thesis, University of North Carolina, 1986.

## ARTICLES, BULLETINS, CONFERENCE PAPERS, AND RADIO TALKS

Abelson, Joan S., ed. "The First 100 Years: Goucher College 1885–1995." *Goucher Quarterly* 62, no. 4 (summer 1984): 1–48.

"Aderholt Murderers Convicted." *Southern Textile Bulletin,* 24 October 1929, 26.

"Alumnae Notes." *Smith Alumnae Quarterly* 9, no. 4 (July 1918): 391.

"Alumnae Notes." *Smith Alumnae Quarterly* 10, no. 4 (July 1919): 378.

"April 30—The Annual Debate." *St. Mary's Muse* 14, no. 8 (May 1910): 183–84.

Aydlett, A. Laurance. "The North Carolina State Board of Public Welfare." *North Carolina Historical Review* 24, no. 1 (January 1947): 1–33.

Bailey, Forrest. "Gastonia Goes to Trial." *New Republic*, 14 August 1929, 332–34.

"Baltimore." *Goucher Kalends* 24, no. 5 (March 1913): 151–54.

Barrett, Joseph E. "Psychiatric Facilities in Virginia and Some Neighboring States." *American Journal of Psychiatry*, no. 97 (March 1941): 1219–37.

Bassett, John Spencer. "Stirring Up the Fires of Racial Antipathy." *South Atlantic Quarterly* 2, no. 4 (1903): 297–305.

"The Battle Cry." *St. Mary's Muse* 15, no. 5 (December 1910–January 1911): 155–56.

Beal, Fred E. "I Was a Communist Martyr." *American Mercury* 42, no. 165 (September 1937): 32–45.

———. "Who Are the Gastonia Prisoners?" *Labor Defender*, September 1929, 171–72.

Blanshard, Paul. "Communism in Southern Cotton Mills." *Nation*, 24 April 1929, 500–501.

Boyle, Sarah Patton. "Southerners Will *Like* Integration." *Saturday Evening Post*, 19 February 1955, 25, 133–34.

"Building the I.L.D." *Labor Defender*, May 1929, 109.

Burns, Augustus M. III. "Graduate Education for Blacks in North Carolina, 1930–1951." *Journal of Southern History* 46, no. 2 (May 1980): 195–218.

Cahn, Susan. "Spirited Youth or Fiends Incarnate: The Samarcand Arson Case and Female Adolescence in the American South." *Journal of Women's History* 9, no. 4 (winter 1998): 152–80.

Carter, Hodding. "A Wave of Terror Threatens the South." *Look*, 22 March 1955, 32–36.

"'Cases' and Friendships." *Goucher Kalends* 24, no. 3 (January 1913): 102–5.

Cheshire, Joseph B. "Dr. Richard H. Lewis: An Intimate Sketch by a Life-Long Friend." *Carolina Churchman*, October 1926, 3–4.

"The Classification of Students." *Bulletin of Goucher College*, 3d ser., 1, no. 1 (October 1913): 89.

"Class Notes." *Goucher Kalends* 24, no. 1 (November 1912): 33–34.

Colton, Elizabeth Avery. "Standards of Southern Colleges for Women." *School Review* 20, no. 7 (September 1912): 458–75.

Covington, Kate. "Interviewing Nell Battle Lewis." *Meredith College Acorn* 27, no. 4 (May 1936): 16–17.

Dabney, Virginius. "Nearer and Nearer the Precipice." *Atlantic Monthly*, January 1943, 94–100.

Danby, Alfred, and Kathleen Sykes. "A Case of Chronic Mental Disease Associated with Ovarian Dysfunction." *Lancet*, no. 216 (1929): 129.

"Dean Graham's Picture of Ella May Wiggins." *Southern Textile Bulletin*, 10 April 1930, 22.

Dierenfield, Kathleen Murphy. "One 'Desegregated Heart': Sarah Patton Boyle and the Crusade for Civil Rights in Virginia." *Virginia Magazine of History and Biography* 104, no. 2 (spring 1996): 251–84.

Dorr, Gregory Michael. "Assuring America's Place in the Sun: Ivey Foreman Lewis and the Teaching of Eugenics at the University of Virginia, 1915–1953." *Journal of Southern History* 66, no. 2 (May 2000): 257–96.

Eastman, Max. "The Religion of Patriotism." *Masses* 9, no. 9 (July 1917): 8–12.

"Entrance Inquiries and Applications." *Bulletin of Goucher College*, 2d ser., 6, no. 2 (March 1912): 18–31.

"Gastonia, North Carolina: The South's City of Spindles: Three Radio Talks Made over Station, WBT, Charlotte, N.C., 14 May 1930.

"The German." *St. Mary's Muse* 15, no. 2 (October 1910): 56.

"The Graduation Exercises and Address." *St. Mary's Muse* 16, no. 1 (June 1911): 10–23.

"The Grind and the All-Round Girl." *Goucher Kalends* 24, no. 2 (December 1912): 60–63.

Hall, Jacquelyn Dowd. "Disorderly Women: Gender and Labor Militancy in the Appalachian South." *Journal of American History* 72, no. 2 (September 1986): 354–82.

Halperin, Edward C. "Frank Porter Graham, Isaac Hall Manning, and the Jewish Quota at the University of North Carolina Medical School." *North Carolina Historical Review* 67, no. 4 (October 1990): 385–410.

———. "The Jewish Problem in U.S. Medical Education, 1920–1955." *Journal of the History of Medicine and Allied Sciences* 56, no. 2 (April 2001): 140–67.

Hamilton, Samuel W. "The Psychiatric Resources of New York." *American Journal of Psychiatry*, no. 90 (March 1934): 1097–1128.

"Ideals." *Bulletin of Goucher College*, 2d ser., 5, no. 1 (January 1911): 15.

Jameison, G. R., and James H. Wall. "Mental Reactions at the Climacterium." *American Journal of Psychiatry*, no. 88 (March 1932): 895–909.

Jimison, Tom P. "Mill Hands and the Law." *Labor Defender*, July 1929, 138–39.

Johnson, Gerald W. "A Tilt with Southern Wind-Mills," *Virginia Quarterly Review* 1, no. 2 (July 1925): 184–92.

Johnson, Kate Burr, and Nell Battle Lewis. "A Decade of Social Progress in North Carolina." *Journal of Social Forces* 1, no. 4 (1 May 1923): 400–403.

Jones, Howard Mumford. "Social Notes on the South." *Virginia Quarterly Review* 11, no. 3 (July 1935): 451–57.

Korstad, Robert, and Nelson Lichtenstein. "Opportunities Found and Lost: Labor, Radicals, and the Early Civil Rights Movement." *Journal of American History* 75, no. 3 (December 1988): 786–811.

Larkin, Margaret. "Ella May's Songs." *Nation*, 9 October 1929, 382–83.

Larkin, Margaret. "The Story of Ella May." *New Masses*, November 1929, 3–5.

Leidholdt, Alex. "Virginius Dabney and Lenoir Chambers: Two Southern Newspaper Editors Face Virginia's Massive Resistance to Public School Integration." *American Journalism* 15, no. 4 (fall 1998): 35–68.

Lewis, George. "'Scientific Certainty': Wesley Critz George, Racial Science and Organised White Resistance in North Carolina, 1954–1962." *Journal of American Studies* 38, no. 2 (August 2004): 227–47.

Lewis, Nell Battle. "Anarchy vs. Communism in Gastonia." *Nation*, 25 September 1929, 321–22.

———. "Banjo Love Song." *Smith College Monthly* 22, no. 6 (March 1915): 343.

———. "Black Devil's Rock." *Smith College Monthly* 22, no. 7 (April 1915): 366–71.

———." Coin of the Realm." *Smith College Monthly* 23, no. 1 (October 1915): 13–18.

———. "North Carolina." *American Mercury* 8, no. 29 (May 1926): 36–43.

———. "The North Carolina Conference for Social Service." *Journal of Social Forces* 1, no. 3 (1 March 1923): 265–68.

———. "North Carolina at the Cross-Roads." *Virginia Quarterly Review* 6, no. 1 (January 1930): 37–47.

———. "Raleigh, Capital of a Neighborhood." *Reviewer* 5, no. 3 (July 1925): 63–70.

———. "Tar Heel Justice." *Nation*, 11 September 1929, 272–73.

———. "Translation of the 11th Ode of the 1st Book of Horace." *Smith College Monthly* 22, no. 7 (April 1915): 387–88.

———. "The University of North Carolina Gets Its Orders." *Nation*, 3 February 1926, 114–15.

———. "When Gabriel Blows." *Smith College Monthly* 24, no. 6 (April 1917): 299–301.

Lisby, Gregory C. "Julian Harris and the *Columbus Enquirer-Sun:* The Consequences of Winning the Pulitzer Prize." *Journalism Monographs*, no. 105 (April 1988): 1–30.

Lowell, Esther. "A Columnist with a Purpose." *Woman's Journal*," March 1929, 24–25.

Masters, Howard R. "Nervous, Mental and Endocrine Manifestations in Menopause." *Virginia Medical Monthly*, no. 50 (August 1923): 317–20.

McCarthy, Katherine. "Psychotherapy and Religion: The Emmanuel Movement." *Journal of Religion and Health* 23, no. 2 (summer 1984): 92–105.

McRae, Elizabeth Gillespie. "To Save a Home: Nell Battle Lewis and the Rise of Southern Conservatism, 1941–1956." *North Carolina Historical Review* 81, no. 3 (July 2004): 261–87.

McWhorter, Diane. "The Day Autherine Lucy Dared to Integrate the University of Alabama." *Journal of Blacks in Higher Education*, no. 32 (summer 2001): 100–101.

Mencken, H. L. "Under the Southern Moon." *Smart Set*, no. 72 (October 1923): 61–63.

Mitchell, Broadus. "Fleshpots in the South." *Virginia Quarterly Review* 3, no. 2 (April 1927): 161–76.

"Nell Battle Lewis." *Goucher Alumnae Quarterly* 35, no. 2 (winter 1957): 32.

"Nell Battle Lewis." *Saint Mary's School Bulletin* 28, no. 2A (March 1939): 6–7.

"New Officers." *St. Mary's Muse* 15, no. 2 (October 1910): 56–57.

Nickell, Joe. "Psychic Pets and Pet Psychics." *Skeptical Inquirer* 26, no. 6 (November–December 2002): 12–15, 18.

"Notes of the Faculty—The Old and the New." *St. Mary's Muse* 13, no. 1 (June–July 1908): 24–30.

Owens, John H. "Strike Vignettes." *Labor Defender*, May 1929, 101.

Pekor, Charles Jr. "An Adventure in Georgia." *American Mercury* 8, no. 32 (August 1926): 408–13.

Picott, J. Rupert. "Desegregation of Higher Education of Virginia." *Journal of Negro Education* 27, no. 3 (summer 1958): 324–31.

Ratchford, Benjamin Ulysses. "Toward Preliminary Social Analysis: II. Economic Aspects of the Gastonia Situation." *Social Forces* 8, no. 3 (March 1930): 359–67.

Reeve, Karl. "The Awakening South." *Labor Defender*, May 1929, 91.

———. "Gastonia Sees and Learns." *Labor Defender*, June 1929, 117.

Richardson, William H. "Plenty of Obstacles and Some Mistakes Could Not Keep John A.

Park from Becoming One of the South's Outstanding Publishers at Age Forty." *Southern Advertising and Publishing*, September 1926, 15, 18.

"The Right of Violence." *Southern Textile Bulletin*, 25 April 1929, 30–31.

Rollins, William, Jr. "A Gentleman's Game." *New Masses*, October 1929, 3–4.

"The Routine." *St. Mary's Muse* 16, no. 3 (November 1911): 79–80.

Scott, Anne Firor. "After Suffrage: Southern Women in the Twenties." *Journal of Southern History* 30, no. 1 (February 1964): 298–318.

Severinghaus, Elmer L. "The Relief of Menopause Symptoms by Estrogenic Preparations." *Journal of the American Medical Association*, no. 104 (February 1935): 624–28.

*Smith Alumnae Quarterly* 9, no. 4 (July 1918): 391.

*Smith Alumnae Quarterly* 10, no. 4 (July 1919): 378.

"Social Notes." *Goucher Kalends* 24, no. 1 (November 1912): 32–33.

"Social Notes." *Goucher Kalends* 24, no. 2 (December 1912): 72.

"Some Saint Mary's Alumnae of Note." *Saint Mary's School Bulletin* (June 1953): 39–43.

"St. Mary's Spirit." *St. Mary's Muse* 15, no. 3 (November 1910): 120.

Stolberg, Benjamin. "Madness in Marion." *Nation*, 23 October 1929, 462–64.

"Students." *Bulletin of Goucher College*, 2d ser., 6, no. 4 (October 1912): 5–47.

"This Firm Wanted the Facts—and Got Them!" *Southern Textile Bulletin*, 27 March 1930, 20–21.

Veler, Clement D., Sidney Thayer, and Edward A. Doisy. "The Preparation of the Crystalline Follicular Ovarian Hormone: Theelin." *Journal of Biological Chemistry* 87, no 2 (June 1930): 357–71.

Vorse, Mary Heaton. "Gastonia." *Harper's*, November 1929, 700–710.

Way, J. Howell. "Richard Henry Lewis, M.D., LL.D., F.A.P.H.A. (Hon.): An Appreciation." *Southern Medicine and Surgery* 88, no. 12 (December 1926): 781–85.

Weisbord, Vera Buch. "Gastonia, 1929: Strike at the Loray Mill." *Southern Culture* 1, nos. 3–4 (winter 1974): 185–203.

Werner, August A., and W. D. Collier. "The Effect of Theelin Injections on the Castrated Woman." *Journal of the American Medical Association* 100, no. 9 (March 1933): 633–40.

White, Walter. "Decline of Southern Liberals." *Negro Digest*, January 1943, 43–46.

Wilk, Rona M. "'What's a Crush?' A Study of Crushes and Romantic Friendships at Barnard College, 1900–1920." *Organization of American Historians Magazine of History* 18, no. 4 (July 2004): 20–22.

"With the Faculty—The Teachers Old and New." *St. Mary's Muse* 15, no. 1 (September 1910): 3.

## PUBLIC DOCUMENTS

*Acts and Joint Resolutions of the General Assembly of the State of Virginia*. Richmond: Division of Purchase and Printing, 1924 and 1926.

*Congressional Record*. 80th Cong., 1st sess., 1947, vol. 93, pt. 6.

*Congressional Record.* 81st Cong., 1st sess., 1949, vol. 95, pt. 3.

Federal Bureau of Investigation. *Menace of Communism, Statement of J. Edgar Hoover, Director, before the Committee on Un-American Activities, House of Representatives, March 26, 1947.* Washington, D.C.: U.S. Government Printing Office, 1947.

President's Committee on Civil Rights. *To Secure These Rights: The Report of the President's Committee on Civil Rights.* Washington, D.C.: U.S. Government Printing Office, 1947.

NEWSPAPERS

*Asheville* (N.C.) *Citizen,* 1929.

*Baltimore Evening Sun,* 1925, 1929, 1936.

*Belles of St. Mary's* (St. Mary's College), 1940.

*Birmingham News,* 1938.

*Birmingham News-Age Herald,* 1938.

*Carolina Israelite,* 1956.

*Cavalier Daily* (University of Virginia), 1950.

*Chapel Hill Weekly,* 1941, 1952, 1964.

*Charlotte News,* 1935.

*Charlotte Observer,* 1929.

*Charlottesville Daily Progress,* 1950, 1955.

*Chattanooga News-Free Press,* 1940.

*College Topics* (University of Virginia), 1923, 1924.

*Daily Worker,* 1929.

*Durham Morning Herald,* 1934, 1952.

*Durham Sunday Herald-Sun,* 1934.

*Elizabeth City* (N.C.) *Daily Advance,* 1931.

Federated Press (news service), 1929.

*Gastonia* (N.C.) *Daily Gazette,* 1929.

*Greensboro Daily News,* 1931.

*New York Evening World,* 1929.

*New York Herald Tribune,* 1929, 1933.

*New York Telegram,* 1929.

*New York Times,* 1913, 1916, 1917, 1924, 1926, 1929, 1933, 1936, 1938, 1941, 1942, 1946–49, 1954, 1956.

*New York World,* 1921, 1929.

*Norfolk Virginian-Pilot,* 1926.

*Northampton* (Mass.) *Daily Hampshire Gazette,* 1917.

*Oxford* (N.C.) *Public Ledger,* 1934, 1947.

*Raleigh News and Observer,* 1886, 1895, 1903–5, 1917, 1920–33, 1935–43, 1945, 1947, 1948, 1950–57, 1964.

*Raleigh State Chronicle,* October 1886, 1887.

*Raleigh Times*, 1948.
*Richmond News Leader*, 1923.
*Richmond Times-Dispatch*, 1923, 1935, 1964.
*Savannah Morning News*, 1947.
*Seattle Industrial Worker*, 1929.
*Smith College Weekly*, 1913–17.
*Springfield* (Mass.) *Daily Republican*, 1917.
*Wall Street Journal*, 1965.
*Washington Post*, 1934, 1938, 1946–49, 1956.

## COMPUTER SOURCES

"1948 Presidential Election Results" (cited 12 June 2007), www.uselectionatlas.org/RESULTS/national.php?f=0&year=1948.

Ayers, Edward L. "A Southern Chronicle: The *Virginia Quarterly Review* and the American South, 1925–2000" (cited 20 March 2006), www.vqronline.org/viewmedia.php/prmMID/8057.

"Gertrude Weil, 1879–1971" (cited 18 June 2007), www.jwa.org/exhibits/wov/weil/over.html.

"Hyperemesis Gravidarum" (cited 30 July 2007), www.rarediseases.org/

"Jesse Helms" (cited 6 July 2007), www.unctv.org/biocon/jhelms/timeline.html.

"Lady Wonder" (cited 1 September 2006), www.randi.org/encyclopedia/Lady%20Wonder.html.

"Living at Smith" (cited 27 September 2004), www.smith.edu/sao/reslife/houses/sessions.php.

"Pavilion Residents, 1895–1995" (cited 20 March 2006), www.virginia.edu/100yearslawn/html/pavilions.html.

# INDEX